Measuring Second Language Performance

APPLIED LINGUISTICS AND LANGUAGE STUDY

General Editor
Professor Christopher N. Candlin, Macquarie University

For a complete list of books in this series see pages vii and viii

Measuring Second Language Performance

T. F. McNAMARA

LONGMAN
LONDON AND NEW YORK

Addison Wesley Longman Limited,
Edinburgh Gate, Harlow,
Essex CM20 2JE, England
and Associated Companies throughout the world.

Published in the United States of America
by Addison Wesley Longman, New York

First published 1996

ISBN 0 582 089077 PPR

British Library Cataloguing-in-Publication Data
A catalogue record for this book is available from the British Library

Library of Congress Cataloging-in-Publication Data
McNamara, T. F. (Timothy Francis), 1949–
    Measuring second language performance
    / T.F. McNamara.
        p.   cm. — (Applied linguistics and language study)
    Includes bibliographical references (p.   ) and index.
    ISBN 0–582–08907–7
    1. Language and languages—Ability testing.   2. Language and
languages—Examinations.   I. Title.   II. Series.
P53.4.M36   1996
418'.0076—dc20   95–26148
                                                            CIP

Set by 8 in 10/12pt Ehrhardt
Produced through Longman Malaysia, TCP

For Daniel

APPLIED LINGUISTICS AND LANGUAGE STUDY

GENERAL EDITOR

PROFESSOR CHRISTOPHER N. CANDLIN

Macquarie University, Sydney

Contents

Author's Acknowledgements

This book has made a long slow progress to publication, and I would like to acknowledge the help of all those who contributed to the process. It began life as a research project for the Council on Overseas Professional Qualifications, Canberra, in which I was supported by the Project Officer, Dr Roslyn Kelleher. That project then turned into a PhD thesis, during which I was introduced to Rasch measurement by Dr Geoff Masters, then of the University of Melbourne and subsequently of the Australian Council of Educational Research. Dr Ray Adams of ACER has also been a patient instructor in Rasch measurement over the years. My PhD supervisor (and friend and mentor), Dr Terry Quinn, gave me excellent feedback and consistent encouragement at that time. In 1990 the Language Testing Research Centre (LTRC) (its current name) was established at the University of Melbourne as a research and development centre of the National Languages and Literacy Institute of Australia (NLLIA), with funding from the Commonwealth of Australia Department of Employment, Education and Training and the Victorian Education Foundation. The establishment of the NLLIA, and hence of the LTRC, was an achievement essentially of the founding Director of the NLLIA, Joe Lo Bianco, to whom I, like many others, owe an abiding debt of gratitude. The LTRC was a perfect environment in which to work on a project such as this, and I wish to acknowledge the role of the funding agencies which enabled its creation. I wish to express my gratitude to my colleagues in the LTRC: the Director, Alan Davies, Annie Brown, Cathie Elder, Tom Lumley, Joy McQueen, Kieran O'Loughlin, Gillian Wigglesworth, as well as Lis Grove, Kathryn Hill, Helen Lunt and all my other LTRC colleagues past and present. Tom Lumley was joint author of two papers which are drawn on extensively in Chapter 8; Joy McQueen's work is discussed in detail in Chapter 7; joint work with Tom Lumley and Brian Lynch (a colleague in the Applied Linguistics programme at Melbourne) is reported in Chapter 8. I am particularly grateful to Helen Lunt, who assisted in the preparation of the final version of the manuscript, including the bibliography, and to administrative support staff in the LTRC and the Department of Applied Linguistics and Language Studies at Melbourne, particularly Françoise Gelb, Fiona Watson, Gladys Cubberley, Vittoria Grossi and Luisa Caelli.

The book is also the fruit of my teaching, both in the Applied Linguistics programme at the University of Melbourne and on sabbatical leave in the Department of TESL/Applied Linguistics at UCLA in 1992. I am very grateful to Lyle Bachman of UCLA for creating the opportunity for me to come to Los Angeles, and for encouraging me to co-teach with him two courses on recent developments in measurement which resulted directly in the content of Chapters 5, 6, 7 and 9. Students at UCLA, particularly Sara Weigel, Jim Purpura and Don Weasenforth, provided valuable comments on parts of the manuscript. The argument about performance at the end of Chapter 3 evolved in the context of discussions with Sally Jacoby at UCLA. Comments on material used in teaching courses on language testing from students at Melbourne and elsewhere have also influenced the text considerably. At Melbourne, collaborative work with students working on MA theses (Jan Hamilton, Marilyn Lopes and Eileen Sheridan) developed into a joint publication (Hamilton *et al.*, 1993) which is drawn on extensively in Chapter 7.

As the material which had evolved in these different contexts slowly consolidated into the manuscript for the present book, Chris Candlin, editor of the series, provided sharp, timely and comprehensive comments on drafts of successive chapters, and gave generous encouragement and support.

Finally, on a personal level, I wish to acknowledge the support and encouragement of all those close friends and family members who helped me see this project through to its completion, particularly Marie-Thérèse Jensen, our son Daniel ('I think you can make it, Dad'), Lillian Nativ, Terry Quinn and Charles Drousiotou, John Rosin ('The book? Not *that* book?'), and my mother, Nell McNamara.

Material in this book has appeared in modified form elsewhere, as follows: material from Chapters 2 and 3 in McNamara, T.F. (1995) Modelling performance: opening Pandora's Box, in *Applied Linguistics* 16,2: 159–79; from Chapter 4 in McNamara (1990b); from Chapter 7 in Hamilton *et al.* (1993); from Chapter 8 in McNamara (1990a), Lumley and McNamara (1995) and McNamara and Lumley (1993); and from Chapter 9 in McNamara (1991) (also under the title 'The role of Item Response Theory in language test validation' in S. Anivan (ed.) (1991) *Current developments in langauge testing*. SEAMEO Regional Language Centre, Singapore pp. 165–84); from Chapters 7 and 9 in Brown, A., C. Elder, T. Lumley, T.F. McNamara and J. McQueen (1992) Mapping abilities and skill levels using Rasch techniques, *Melbourne Papers in Language* Testing 1,1: 34–66.

Readers who are interested in obtaining further information about the computer programs Quest and FACETS, referred to in the text, may obtain further information as follows:

Quest: Australian Council for Educational Research, 19 Prospect Hill Road, Camberwell, Melbourne, Victoria 3124, Australia. Tel: (+61 3) 9277 5555; fax: (+61 3) 9277 5500; e-mail: quest@acer.edu.au

FACETS: MESA Press, 5835 S. Kimbark Ave, Chicago, IL, USA 60637–1609. Tel: (312) 702 1596; fax: (312) 702 0248; e-mail: MESA@uchicago.edu

Publisher's Acknowledgements

The Publishers are grateful to the following for permission to reproduce copyright material:

Oxford University Press for our Figures 3.5 and 3.6 from *Fundamental considerations in language testing* by L.F. Bachman (1990) and our Figure 3.7 from *Language testing in practice: designing and developing useful language tests* by Bachman and Palmer (forthcoming) © by permission of Oxford University Press; UCLES for Tables 7.1 and 7.2; and Arnold Publishers Limited for Figure 4a and part of Table 2 (our Figure 5.6 and Table 8.7) from 'Exploring bias analysis as a tool for improving rater consistency in assessing oral interaction' by G. Wigglesworth (1993) *Language Testing* 10: 305–335, and for Table 1b (our Table 8.8) from 'Rater characteristics and rater bias: implications for training by T. Lumley and T.F. McNamara TF (1995) *Language Testing* 12: 54–71.

Whilst every effort has been made to trace the owners of copyright material, in a few cases this has proved impossible and we take this opportunity to offer our apologies to any copyright holders.

1 Introduction

1.1 The ascendancy of performance assessment

Language assessment is in a period of rapid change, in terms of both policy and research. In schools, performance assessment, where learners have to demonstrate practical command of skills acquired, is rapidly replacing more traditional test formats such as pencil-and-paper tests involving multiple-choice questions. The driving force behind these changes has been government policy, which increasingly is requiring performance-based assessment in all areas of education, language education being one of them (Baker, 1995). In adult and vocational education, a new drive for workforce flexibility and skill and the transferability of credentials, and a concern for accountability in educational expenditure, has led in many societies to pressure for demonstrable outcomes of learning in terms of concrete, practical and relevant skills. Again, this move has had major implications for language assessment, as language plays a crucial role in the workplace.

The demand for performance-based language assessment has served to renew interest in traditions of language assessment that have been well established in some areas of education and training for many years. There is in fact a long history of second language performance assessment (Spolsky, 1995). In the 1950s, in the heyday of the introduction of 'scientific' approaches to testing, with their focus on the careful assessment of knowledge of discrete points of language, a complementary need was felt outside education for practical testing of productive language skills, particularly speaking: this resulted in the introduction in the United States Government of the hugely influential Foreign Service Institute test of spoken skills in a number of foreign languages for personnel being considered for postings abroad. In the 1960s, the increase in the number of foreign students studying at British and North American universities meant that there was a need for widespread testing of relevant language skills, and the resulting test batteries contained a component of performance assessment. With the advent of the communicative movement in language teaching in the 1970s, performance assessment found a rationale in the theory of communicative competence. In a way, then, the field is well equipped to respond to the recent changes in public

1

educational policy and practice as it has a long history of relevant practice on which to draw.

1.2   Theories of performance

In fact, however, this practice and the theory underlying it are long overdue for critical examination, particularly as the educational and public policy stakes grow higher, and the consequences of the widespread introduction of performance assessment begin to be felt, not least by those being assessed, whose life chances in many cases are significantly at stake. One of the two principal aims of this book is to undertake a critical examination of the thinking behind the practice of performance assessment.

In Chapter 2 we introduce two main approaches to second language performance assessment: (1) the *work sample* approach, which has its origins in general and vocational education and in personnel selection, and has influenced both general purpose and specific purpose assessment in second languages; and (2) a more *cognitive* and distinctively linguistic approach, in which attention is focused less on the task, which may be relatively unrealistic in real-world terms, but on the qualities of execution in the performance, and/or the evidence it provides about the candidate's control of the underlying linguistic system. The chapter begins with a discussion of general issues in performance assessment – how it is to be defined, how validity is established, how test content is determined and the role of assessment criteria in determining what is being measured. In the second part of the chapter, examples of the two main approaches to second language performance assessment are discussed in detail. We trace the evolution of practice in second language performance assessment in North America and the UK in order to understand current thinking and the possibilities and difficulties of current practice. The last part of the chapter introduces a consideration of the way in which non-linguistic criteria figure in the assessment of second language performance, and the theoretical and practical issues that are associated with this. We introduce a distinction between a *strong* and a *weak* sense of the term *second language performance assessment*, depending on the extent to which assessment criteria reflect these non-linguistic aspects of task performance.

In Chapter 3 we examine how key writers in the history of performance assessment and communicative language testing have conceptualized what is involved in the display of language ability under performance conditions. We look in detail at the work of Dell Hymes on communicative competence, Michael Canale and Merrill Swain in applying that work to the assessment of communicative competence in second languages and Lyle Bachman and Adrian Palmer, whose model of second language communicative ability has evolved steadily over a period of 15 years. From this analysis a number of unresolved issues central to language performance assessment emerge. For example, the role of personality factors in performance, the relevance of real world skills when undertaking the simulated real-world tasks which often characterize performance assessment, the influence of aspects of the test setting other than those brought to it by the test taker – all of these issues have been poorly understood.

1.3   The new measurement

At the same time as the importance of performance assessment has been growing, our power to conduct empirical research on performance assessment has been enormously expanded by recent developments in the field of measurement, with the advent of new measurement approaches which are particularly suited to the investigation of performance assessment. Typically, performance assessment involves judgements of quality against some rating scale. This introduces new features of the assessment setting such as:

(1) the *raters* themselves, who will vary in the standards they use and the consistency of their application of those standards;
(2) the *rating procedures* they are required to implement.

The interaction of rater characteristics and the qualities of the rating scales they are using has a crucial influence on the ratings that are given, regardless of the quality of the performance. In order to have confidence in the rating procedures for which we may be responsible, or whose results we may be relying on, it is necessary to investigate and control for the effect of rater variation and scale characteristics. Similarly, task choice may have an influence on test outcome, and we need to understand the effect of task. In fact, the richness of the performance assessment setting (when compared with a pencil-and-paper test in multiple-choice format) brings with it enormous complexity and potential variability, which can easily jeopardize the fairness and the generalizability of conclusions we may reach about individual candidates. We need new measurement tools and approaches that can handle the questions we will want to ask of our performance assessment data.

The second principal aim of this book, then, is to introduce the reader to the most useful of the new measurement theories available to us, Rasch measurement (and, in particular, multi-faceted measurement), and to its potential for helping us to conduct the necessary research on performance assessment. The new measurement enables us to investigate those aspects (facets) of the performance setting (rater and task characteristics, for example) that are of concern to us.

The presentation will be based on the assumption that the reader has little prior knowledge of theories of measurement. It is assumed that readers of this book (language teacher/researchers, students of language education and applied linguistics, test developers and administrators, researchers on language testing, and research students whose work involves the measurement of language performance) need to understand the theory and techniques involved in research on performance assessment, but are likely to come from a background in applied linguistics and language education rather than in measurement. This situation is a familiar one in applied linguistics, which as an interdisciplinary pursuit draws on theory and practice from a wide range of fields, creating in the reader of applied linguistics research an ongoing need to master concepts and material from relevant but relatively unfamiliar fields. Often what is needed is mediation between the field of expertise to be learned (in this case, the new measurement as applied to language assessment) and the field of expertise central to the professional life of the student or researcher (applied linguistics, language education); the more technical the area to be drawn on, the more necessary such mediation is likely to be. Apart from some articles and relatively short sections of books (Henning, 1987a), no relatively complete but non-technical introduction to Rasch measurement for an applied linguistics audience has so far been available.

In order to thoroughly ground the new in the familiar and the practical, certain parts of the presentation will be in the context of a particular performance test development and research project, the Occupational English Test (OET), a performance-based test of ESL for health professionals. The stages in the development of this test, and the issues involved, are presented in Chapter 4, together with a detailed description of the test format and materials.

In Chapters 5 and 6 we present the basic theory and procedures of the new measurement, beginning in Chapter 5 with a discussion of the variability associated with raters and how this can be estimated and compensated for in the measurement process. A more thorough introduction to concepts and procedures is given in Chapter 6, using data from the reading sub-test of the OET.

In Chapter 7 we consider how candidate performance can be summarized and reported, and look at approaches to the development of rating and reporting scales. We give a critical analysis of some existing rating scales, particularly in relation to the supposed performance of native speakers on the assessment tasks. This critique is again long overdue, as practices that were developed in the 1950s – and inevitably show the influence of outdated ideas of language ability – have survived without serious examination. We examine and evaluate recent developments in the content-referenced reporting of candidate ability, which draws on mapping features in Rasch-based programs.

The way in which research using the new measurement can reveal the complex nature of language performance assessment is presented in Chapter 8. This chapter is important to the overall argument of the book, namely that naïve approaches to performance assessment prevent us from dealing with crucial questions of validity which can be exposed and in many cases dealt with using the potential of the new measurement.

The field of language testing has taken some time to accept the legitimacy of Rasch approaches, and language testers have shared the caution of some of their colleagues in other areas in education. It will be argued in Chapter 9 that these fears and reservations have no proper basis, and are essentially grounded in a misunderstanding of the concepts and models involved in Rasch methods. There are encouraging signs that Rasch measurement is being accepted as one of a range of possible tools in the field, and its controversial status may soon be a thing of the past. It is the author's hope that this book may contribute to an acceptance of the rationale and usefulness of Rasch techniques generally in the field of language testing, and particularly in performance assessment.

1.4 How to read the book

A word of advice may be appropriate on how to proceed. The chapters on the theory of performance assessment are self-contained, but are interrelated. Although they can be read in sequence, Chapter 2 may bear re-reading in the light of Chapter 3. The presentation in the part of the book dealing with the new measurement is cumulative and cyclical: you may therefore wish to proceed sequentially through the measurement chapters (5, 6, part of 7, and 9) but, for example, re-read Chapter 5 after you have read Chapter 6, and so on. Chapter 9 is the most technical chapter, and should be read after the others. Summaries at the beginnings and ends of chapters and of major sections should act as a guide if you wish to know the material to be dealt with before you begin reading it in detail.

2 Second language performance assessment

2.1 Introduction

The aim of this chapter is to introduce the idea of *performance assessment*, with particular reference to second language contexts.

The term *performance assessment* did not, of course, originate in applied linguistics; it has a long history and widespread current usage in other fields. A defining characteristic is that actual performances of relevant tasks are required of candidates, rather than more abstract demonstration of knowledge, often by means of pencil-and-paper tests. This tradition has been very important for second language performance assessment, and will be discussed in detail. However, performance assessment within second language contexts involves specific issues, largely because of the complex question (as we will see in the following chapter) of what communicative ability in a second language is understood to be. Performance assessment within second language contexts has meant something more, and more complex, than the application of techniques developed in non-language contexts.

Two traditions of second language performance assessment can thus be found:

(1) a simple application of the techniques of performance assessment developed in non-language contexts, which we will call the *work sample* approach; and

(2) a tradition that sees performance in a second language as a complex *cognitive* achievement, involving integration of a number of psycholinguistic processes.

In (2) assessment focuses on two issues: (a) the *quality of the execution* of the performance, rather as in music, ballet or gymnastics; and (b) what the performance reveals about the *underlying state of language knowledge* in the individual being assessed. This tradition tends to be more theory driven, or to be informed more by theory, although this is not always the case.

The first part of the chapter, therefore, will consider the nature of performance assessment in non-language (general and vocational education) contexts, and the way in which the validity of the interpretation of scores deriving from such assessments has traditionally been established. A number of important practical and theoretical questions are raised; these have direct relevance to language performance assessment, which has borrowed ideas and techniques from this broader educational field. We will look in detail at performance assessment in occupational contexts, an important model for second language performance assessment in ESP and EAP settings.

The second part of the chapter deals with performance assessment in *second language* contexts, beginning with examples from the 1960s and earlier, developed in response to practical needs in specific-purpose contexts, and drawing on the theory and methods of performance assessment in vocational education. Second language performance assessment received an enormous impetus with the formulation and spread of the notion of communicative competence in the late 1960s and early 1970s. A performance-based approach to communicative language testing for general-purpose contexts was initiated in response to the theoretical advances of Hymes (1967, 1972), first by Clark and Savignon in the United States and, subsequently, by Morrow and others in the United Kingdom. However, we will discover that the theoretical foundation of second language performance assessment in theories of communicative ability is in fact surprisingly weak, and that the language assessment field (with some notable exceptions) has shown a reluctance to face properly the theoretical basis and implications of its practices.

Specifically, in this chapter we will make the following claims:

1. The validity of second language performance assessments involves more than content- and criterion-related aspects of validity; the larger issue of construct validity has been insufficiently considered. In particular, empirical evidence in support of the claims concerning the validity of second language performance tests has in general been lacking.
2. There are two main influences on the practice of performance assessment in a second language; each raises different aspects of validity.
3. The first of these represents a straightforward application in second language contexts of approaches developed in personnel selection and vocational education contexts. The complex issues of validity arising in these contexts are thus relevant to second language performance assessment. Here the emphasis is on content-related and criterion-related aspects of validity.
4. The second influence is distinctively linguistic and cognitive, deriving from conceptualizations of language ability and their manifestation in

instances of actual communication. Here the emphasis is on the theoretical rationales (and accompanying empirical evidence) supporting
the construct validity of tests. However, as we shall see in Chapter 3, a
critical evaluation of the positions taken by leading figures in language
performance assessment reveals considerable ambiguity, even confusion, in relation to these issues.

5. The distinction between these two sources of ideas and influence on
   language performance testing and the relationship between them have
   not been widely discussed, and this has led to a lack of clarity and
   coherence in the arguments advanced in favour of a performance-based
   approach to second language assessment.

6. Second language performance assessment is distinguished from performance assessment in other contexts because of the simultaneous
   role of language as a medium or vehicle of performance, and as a
   potential target of assessment itself.

7. We can distinguish a *strong* and a *weak* sense of the term *second language performance assessment*. This is necessary for carrying out appropriate investigations into the validity of such assessments.

8. In general, research on the validity of language performance tests
   requires reference to a model of the relationship between language
   ability, skills in performance and actual instances of communication;
   that is, it is inevitably situated in the conceptual universe to be outlined in Chapter 3. It must also be empirical, that is, data-driven.

The need to base language performance testing on a broad theory of language abilities, other abilities involved in language use, and their manifestation in actual communication is not widely accepted, despite
repeated calls (Upshur, 1979; Stevenson, 1985; Bachman, 1990) for a
proper theoretical basis for practice. A heavily operational approach
seems to be a particular feature of occupationally related language performance tests. This phenomenon is commented upon by Wesche (1992:
104) as follows:

> Relatively little has been published about performance-based
> approaches in the second language testing professional literature –
> presumably because most of the work has involved test development
> for practical purposes outside the traditional academic network. ...
> While good practice can and should contribute to better theoretical
> insights, the links are unfortunately often not made.

One aim of this chapter will be to move beyond the practical orientation
of much of the literature on language performance assessment to examine
its conceptual basis. What theory is it based on? What is its relationship

to performance tests in other areas? What is the role of language in relation to non-language factors in a second language performance test?

2.2   General issues in performance assessment

2.2.1   Introduction

In this section, basic concepts and practices in performance assessment in the fields of *education* (both general and vocational) and *personnel selection* will be introduced. This is relevant because second language performance assessment has drawn extensively on the theory and practice of performance assessment in each of these fields. As we shall see, the tradition of performance assessment in education and personnel selection has been heavily practical in its orientation and has focused its attention largely on issues of content and predictive validity.

2.2.2   Performance test as test method

What is distinctive about a performance test? The usual answer to this question is given in operational terms: performance assessment is essentially a methodological issue. Typically, the *performance process* (the nature of the performance task) is considered to be the distinctive feature of performance assessment.[1] Figure 2.1, adapted from Kenyon (1992), provides a schematic representation of the features of a typical second language performance test in comparison with a traditional pencil-and-paper language test.

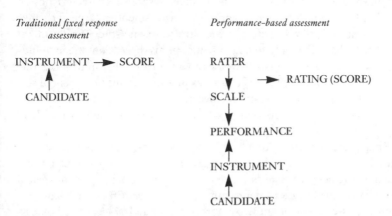

FIGURE 2.1   The characteristics of performed assessment

The *format* of a performance-based assessment is distinguished from the traditional assessment by the presence of two factors: a *performance* by the candidate which is observed and judged using an agreed *judging process*. The performance is frequently elicited by a test instrument, although this is not necessarily the case (for example, when the performance is part of the normal working cycle of the testee, who is assessed on site; cf. the discussion of *direct assessment* and *work sample* techniques, below).

Cronbach (1971: 26) defines a 'test' in general as 'a systematic procedure for observing a person's behavior and describing it with the aid of a numerical scale or category system'. Slater (1980: 3) observes in relation to Cronbach's definition:

> The big variable in this definition is how the term 'behavior' is operationalized; doing so prescribes the characteristics of the stimulus eliciting the behavior, the type of response called for, and the conditions under which the behavior is displayed. Operationalizing behavior in these three respects is a heuristic technique for distinguishing between performance tests and other kinds of tests.

Slater (1980) gives clear and helpful examples of the differences between performance and non-performance tests, and the new considerations that performance tests introduce. Under 'stimulus characteristics of tests', Slater considers the assessment of a student in an emergency medical technician training course, and contrasts pencil-and-paper, multiple-choice format assessments of knowledge of proper procedures in the case of an accidental poisoning, with a simulation involving a near-hysterical parent demanding information to help a child who has swallowed an unknown quantity of medication. Under 'response characteristics of tests', Slater contrasts pencil-and-paper assessment and performance assessment on a pilot's course: in the latter case, the student pilot might be given a chance actually to land a plane. In his discussion of 'surrounding conditions', he contrasts two assessments of a teacher in training: one teacher is observed with a difficult class in a tough inner-city school setting and does not manage to achieve the aims of the lesson, whereas another achieves the aims effortlessly with a class in a suburban school located near a university.[2]

Fitzpatrick and Morrison (1971: 238) offer a general definition of *performance test* as 'one in which some criterion situation is simulated to a much greater degree than is represented by the usual paper-and-pencil test'.[3] Performance assessments can cover *processes* (in second language contexts, assessment of speaking, for example) and *products* (e.g. assessment of writing samples). (Fitzpatrick and Morrison (1971: 238) explain that the term *performance assessment* is shorthand for the fuller 'perfor-mance and product evaluation'.)

Definitions of performance tests distinguish between *test* and *criterion*,[4] so that performance tests are defined in terms of simulation of the criterion. (In the discussion that follows, and elsewhere in the book, we will use the term *work sample* tests to refer to performance assessments where simulation of the criterion in the test materials and procedures is a feature of the test.) On the one hand, performance tests are characterized by the relationship of test task to reality: the relationship is close, 'direct'; the tasks are 'authentic'. On the other hand, test and reality are to be distinguished, and thus the relationship between them is a matter of interest. Fitzpatrick and Morrison consider two aspects of this relation-ship: (1) the degree of reality of the simulation and (2) the relevance of the performance in the simulation to performance in the criterion (non-test) situation. Real life thus has a double role in performance assessment: ✗ as a touchstone for the quality of the simulation, and as the realm of the criterion behaviour to which the test performance is relevant.

As far as the first of these is concerned, Fitzpatrick and Morrison argue that the *representativeness* of the simulation comprises two aspects (1971: 240):

> *comprehensiveness*, or the range of different aspects of the situation that are simulated, and *fidelity*, the degree to which each aspect approxi-mates a fair representation of that aspect in the criterion situation. [Emphasis in original.]

This raises the important general question of the exact degree to which the criterion situation must be simulated before the assessment becomes a performance test. Fitzpatrick and Morrison (1971: 240) go on to explain that realism is a relative matter:

> There is no absolute distinction between performance tests and other classes of tests – the performance test is one that is *relatively* realistic. Since performance tests tend to involve special problems and to require decisions and procedures not usually required for conventional tests, it is useful to distinguish the performance test from other classes of test ... [Emphasis in original.]

Haertel (1992: 984) agrees, and contrasts narrower and broader defini-tions of *performance test*, the latter including

> ... any test in which the stimuli presented or the response elicited emulate some aspects of the nontest settings ... [Some] performance measurements are based on performances or products elicited solely

for the purpose of evaluation. In writing assessments, examinees generally respond to assigned prompts, and their writing serves no other purpose than demonstrating their proficiency ... In tasks designed exclusively for assessment purposes, duplicating all the features of naturally occurring tasks may be unnecessary, as well as difficult or costly. Tasks used for performance measurement are often simpler in many respects than the corresponding tasks in natural settings.

But this question of simplification and dilution of the requirements of the criterion situation raises further questions than where to draw the line on what one will categorize as a performance assessment. The inferences that can be drawn from performance on such tasks in terms of ability to perform in the real world become an issue. Empirical evidence will be required. This will be considered further below.

Another aspect of the fidelity of simulation is whether performance tests should also simulate the standards by which performances in the non-test situation are normally judged (Wiggins, 1989). The role of criteria in performance assessments will be discussed further below, in a consideration of the validity of such tests. This issue has important implications for language performance assessment in particular, where judgements against real-world standards are not common, and raise difficult issues (Brown, 1995; Elder, 1993b).

There is a tendency in some approaches to performance assessment to conflate the assessment task and the criterion (Davies, 1992: 9). For example, consider the following comment of Linn *et al.* (1991: 15):

> Such measures are frequently referred to as 'authentic' assessments ... because they involve the performance of tasks that are valued in their own right. In contrast, paper-and-pencil, multiple-choice tests derive their value primarily as indicators or correlates of other valued performances.

There is an ambiguity here: is the performance of these tasks in the test situation 'valued in its own right',[5] or are the tasks in the real world valued in their own right? If the former, there appears again to be a conflating of assessment task and criterion; even in performance tests the performance is surely an indicator or correlate (consider the term *simulation*, which suggest this is indeed the case) of 'other valued performances' in the non-test situation. It depends partly on the context of assessment, and what performances are considered to be direct, authentic and the like. Linn *et al.* (1991: 15) include 'open-ended problems, essays, hands-on science problems, computer simulations of real-world problems, and portfolios of student work'. These tasks are valued in their own right in the educational context, including the non-test situation, but still bear an indirect relationship to 'valued performances' in the real world outside the school. Wiggins (1989: 704) in a way obscures this issue by appearing to claim that school-based performances and real-world performances are identical:

> Authentic assessments replicate the challenges and standards of performance that typically face writers, business people, scientists, community leaders, designers, or historians. These include writing essays and reports, conducting individual and group research, designing proposals and mock-ups, assembling portfolios, and so on.

He includes an ACTFL (American Council on the Teaching of Foreign Languages) interview-based foreign language performance assessment (ACTFL, 1986) as an example of an authentic test; yet Wesche (1992: 106) says that 'oral interviews ... would not be classified as true performance tests' because they are not direct simulations of real-world roles and tasks. Yet the Oral Proficiency Interview (OPI) (Clark and Clifford, 1988) is usually taken to be an example of a performance test. The issue raised here is whether one adopts a broad or narrow definition of performance tests, as discussed above. Additionally, the question may be one of product and process. The OPI can claim to involve certain psycholinguistic processing aspects of authentic communicative interaction (cf. discussion in Chapter 3) although from other points of view (linguistic, pragmatic, social) it may be unrepresentative (Perrett, 1990; van Lier, 1989).

2.2.3 Performance assessment in occupational settings

Many of the ideas and techniques central to performance assessment in general educational settings overlap with those used in the field of occupational training and personnel selection (Ryans and Frederiksen, 1951). However, the latter field has had an explicit and direct influence on second language testing in occupational contexts since the 1970s. Reference to the practice of performance assessment in personnel measurement is frequent in the work of Jones (1977, 1979, 1985), Wesche (1985, 1987, 1992) and others. Jones (1979) adopts the distinction in personnel measurement between *performance* tests and *knowledge* or pencil-and-paper tests. The former are useful according to Jones (1979: 51) 'if the ability to demonstrate proficiency in the task cannot be measured by a pencil-and-paper test, e.g., for typing, bricklaying, hairdressing or playing the violin'.

Jones's recommendation of the extension of this type of test to language testing is in the context of the growth of ESP at the time, particularly occupation-related ESP (Jones, 1979: 51):

There is an increasing demand for language tests to provide predictive information about how well a candidate will perform in a given situation ... it is impossible for a language test to predict task-oriented proficiency unless it includes or approximates actual samples of the tasks.

Jones discusses a number of work-related contexts in which second language performance tests would seem to be warranted: teaching; working as a steward or stewardess on an airline; and, following van Naerssen (1978), the certification of foreign medical graduates (FMGs) to work in the United States.

Jones (1985), following Slater (1980), discusses three main types of performance test: *direct assessment*; *work sample methods*; and *simulation techniques*.

In *direct assessment*, observation takes place directly in the workplace. An example would be where someone is given provisional admission to the work setting, and is appraised over a probationary period; for example, a teacher whose first language is not English may wish to work as a teacher in an English-speaking country; the teacher may be registered on the basis of the overseas qualifications, but confirmation in the new local setting may depend on performance on the job during an initial period. This is similar to the proposal made by Coleman (1980: 39) for a 'Communicative proficiency test for dentists from overseas'. However, as Jones points out (1985: 18), 'Language behavior is very complex, and it would be necessary to make observations over a relatively long period of time before one could be satisfied that an adequate sample had been obtained.' Often, too, the aim of the assessment is to screen or select, in which case provisional admission to the workplace (or place of study in the case of a student) is unlikely to be an option.

In *work sample methods*, assessment again takes place in the workplace, but the tasks set are controlled to achieve standardization of assessment. For example, an overseas-trained teacher might take a university-based bridging course in the new cultural context and be assessed on the basis of performance in particular lessons on practical teaching rounds. Performance-based assessment procedures to assess the English language communication skills of overseas-trained teachers of science and mathematics in Australian secondary school settings have been developed by Elder (1993b); assessment of language takes place as part of the normal process of assessment of teaching skills on teaching rounds.

Simulation techniques are distinguished by the fact that the tasks involve a degree of abstraction from workplace reality. Performance on the task is then used to predict performance on similar real-world tasks.

Simulation techniques are widely used in the pre-clinical training of health professionals (cf. discussion in Chapter 3). In the case of overseas-trained teachers, assessment might be carried out in micro-teaching sessions with small classes of volunteer students, or with peers who take the roles of class members. Or abstraction may be taken a stage further, so that the candidate is asked to imagine a classroom setting and carry out specific tasks that are typical of the domain. (Elder, 1994, takes this approach in the development of teacher proficiency tests for Italian as a foreign language in primary school settings.) Clearly, extrapolation from such procedures to the real-world context will be an issue in this approach, and will need to be supported by the usual variety of types of evidence, including empirical evidence. This question of the relationship of test to criterion has been raised above.

Jones (1985: 19) describes this third approach (simulation) as 'the most feasible for language testing', and specifically mentions role playing as the best known simulation technique in such settings.[6] He reminds us (1985: 21) that

> Even though I have mentioned only oral language testing, performance tests can exist for the other modalities as well ... Indeed, there are numerous situations requiring various combinations of language skills. It is important that all these skills be tested in a way that reflects the real tasks associated with the situations.

Note that in their three-part characterization, Slater and Jones distinguish 'work sample methods' from 'simulation techniques'. The term *work sample tests* is used more inclusively in this book, and refers to assessments using either approach.

Although we have distinguished occupationally related measurement contexts from general educational ones in the above discussion, there is a good deal of overlap in the practices and terminology used in each case. Indeed, occupational training represents an educational context, and in that case it is not possible to differentiate the two fields. The teaching and testing of typing skills represents a case in point. We will notice a good deal of commonality between these approaches when we consider their application in both general-purpose and specific-purpose second language performance assessment.

2.3 Establishing validity in performance testing

In the discussion above, we have already touched on a number of aspects of the validity of performance assessments. The main issue is *how* and *how well* we can generalize from the test performance to the criterion behaviour. *How* involves decisions of test *design*; *how well* is an empirical matter which can be investigated on the basis of *data* from trial or operational administrations of the test, supplemented if appropriate with additional data, for example, on the *predictive* power of the test. Weir (1988a) contrasts validity issues at the *a priori* test design stage with the empirical validation of the construct validity of a test *a posteriori* – that is, once the test has become operational.

2.3.1   Validity considerations in test design

Validity considerations at the test *design* stage in performance testing centre on (1) the question of sampling from the criterion situation (the *content validity* of the test) and (2) the development of *rating criteria*.

2.3.1.1   Content validity

Jones (1979: 52), following Ryans and Frederiksen (1951: 483–93), recommends the following three stages in the development of a language performance assessment procedure of the work sample type:

1. Make a job analysis.
2. Select tasks to represent the job.
3. Develop a rating form.

The first two stages represent the process of domain definition and domain sampling. The selection of test content needs to be principled, based on careful characterization of the criterion domain, and adequate sampling. An extended example of how this was done in the design of a performance-based ESP test for health professionals, the Occupational English Test (McNamara, 1990a), is presented in Chapter 4.

   The approach to test design in which the test is based on samples or simulations of real-world tasks implies a view of the performance as the *target* of assessment, in the words of Messick (1994). Such an approach raises issues of replicability and generalizability (Messick, 1994). One aspect of this issue is how we might generalize across different relevant task types, as not all of them may be able to be included in a test. Linn, Baker and Dunbar (1991: 19) summarize results from studies which showed a high degree of task dependency in performance and argue that 'the limited degree of generalizability across tasks needs to be taken into account in the design of an assessment program'.

   The issue here is that of representativeness of sample; but there is more to validity than representativeness of test content – a point made by

Fitzpatrick and Morrison (1971: 240), who caution against the conclusion that 'high representativeness of simulation and high test validity are synonymous'. Linn, Baker and Dunbar (1991: 16) also caution us in the same vein: 'Simply because the [direct, performance-based] measures are derived from actual performance or relatively high-fidelity simulations of performance, it is too often assumed that they are more valid than multiple-choice tests.' Content validity is a necessary but not sufficient condition for the validity of performance tests of the work sample type. Messick (1989: 17) states the point with great force:

> In a fundamental sense so-called content validity does not count as validity at all, although ... considerations of content relevance and representativeness clearly do and should influence the nature of score inferences supported by other evidence ... Some test specialists contend that what a test is measuring is operationally defined by specifying the universe of item content and the item-selection process. But as we shall see, determining what a test is measuring always requires recourse to other forms of evidence.

Tests based on domain sampling represent what Messick (1994) terms a *task-centred* approach to performance assessment (as distinguished from *competency-* or *construct-centred* approaches, based on a theory of ability). Such tests, no matter what their attention to content validity, still require us to address the fundamental problem in test validation, that is, the question of justifying inferences from test performance. Messick (1989. 13) describes validity as 'an integrated evaluative judgement of the degree to which empirical evidence and theoretical rationales support the adequacy and appropriateness of inferences and actions based on test scores'. He uses the term *construct validation* as an overarching term to refer to all aspects of this enterprise.[7] Haertel (1992: 987), following Messick, reminds us that validation is necessary in both task-centred and construct-centred approaches:

> Construct validity embraces all the evidential basis of test interpretation, including content- and criterion-related lines of validity evidence. It is relevant to performance measurement even if the intended test interpretations do not appear to involve psychological constructs. Test interpretations must be qualified to the extent that the test fails to sample some parts of the performance domain it is supposed to represent (construct underrepresentation) or depends on knowledge or skills from outside of that domain (construct-irrelevant variance).

That is, construct validation, whether the test is explicitly based on a 'psychological construct' or not, remains a requirement of any test development process.

2.3.1.2   Content and construct validity in EAP testing

As an example of how these issues arise in the context of debate about language performance tests, an example will be given from discussion of British EAP tests developed in the late 1970s and 1980s. The work sample tradition became particularly important in ESP testing, including EAP testing, from the late 1970s and was accompanied by a strong, one might say almost exclusive, focus on content validity.[8] Weir (1988a: 17) comments on the overlap between content and construct validity in relation to the British ELTS test, used throughout the 1980s in the selection of overseas students for study at British universities:

> Because we lack an adequate theory of language in use, *a priori* attempts to determine the construct validity of proficiency tests involve us in matters which relate more evidently to content validity. We need to talk of the communicative construct in descriptive terms, and as a result, we become involved in questions of content relevance and content coverage. Thus for Kelly (1978: 8) content validity seemed an 'almost completely overlapping concept' with construct validity, and for Moller (1982: 68): '... the distinction between construct and content validity in language testing is not always very marked, particularly for tests of general language proficiency.'

Davies (1984a: 52), discussing his experience with the validation of three tests in EAP contexts in Britain, reports that 'the conclusion arrived at after this experience with proficiency tests and with validation is that what matter above all are construct and content validity'. The yoking of construct and content validity here is significant. He goes on:

> What this suggests is that [the] first stage [of test construction] ('plan the content and general layout of the test ... decide the type of test item') is the crucial stage ... The best safeguard against an unsatisfactory test is a professional job analysis at the outset.

Notice that the term *job analysis* is used above by Jones, drawing on the occupationally related performance test tradition. If there were any doubt, the term is glossed for us by Davies, quoting Anstey (1966: 24):

> Job analysis can be carried out by an occupational psychologist in intimate cooperation with people with expert knowledge of the job. The psychologist should visit people at work on the job and preferably try it for himself for as long as he can spare before he starts forming any conclusions.

Oddly, in the context of EAP tests, Davies seems to equate 'the job' with language teaching, rather than being a foreign student in an English-medium university:

> The language tester takes the place in Anstey's proposal of the occupational psychologist; furthermore, it is unlikely that the second part of the proposal ('The psychologist should visit … ') will be required, since the language tester will have previous experience of language teaching.

Henning (1988), in a discussion of the validity of these British EAP tests, cautions against an exclusive preoccupation with *a priori* aspects of validity and calls for the empirical validation of the tests on the basis of operational test data.

2.3.1.3 Criteria

At the design stage, decisions also have to be made about *how* performances will be judged. An important aspect of this is the determination of relevant criteria against which judgements are made. These criteria often make implicit reference to a psychological construct or constructs, which then emerge as the object of measurement. Thus, even though work sample tests in general performance assessment typically do not make explicit reference to a theory of the underlying knowledge and ability displayed in performance, a theoretical position is implicit in the criteria by which raters are to make their judgements.

Despite the importance of this process, writers on performance assessment in general educational and vocational contexts deal with the issue of construct definition in rating criteria mostly in passing, if at all. For example, Slater (1980: 13) considers this issue only as part of a discussion of reliability. He makes the point that rating scales with clearly defined levels of achievement can enhance reliability of judge-mediated ratings:

> Rather than using such global scale anchors as superior, average, good, and so on, behaviorally anchored rating scales define scale points with unambiguous descriptions of observable behavior. *By providing a clear definition of the trait being rated* and a more objective frame of reference for judging individuals on that trait, behaviorally anchored rating scales limit raters' tendencies to subconsciously bias scores. [Emphasis added.]

Linn *et al.* (1991: 19) do not directly include as one of their criteria for assessing the validity of performance assessments a consideration of the explicitness and coherence of the elaboration of the criteria for judging a performance. Instead, they acknowledge indirectly the way in which aspects of the construct being measured in the performance are reflected in performance criteria:

> One of the promises of performance-based assessments is that they will place greater emphasis on problem solving, comprehension, critical thinking, reasoning, and metacognitive processes. These are worthwhile goals, but they will require that criteria for judging all forms of assessment include attention to the processes that students are required to exercise ...
>
> Whatever the nature of an assessment ... we should include among the criteria an analysis of the cognitive complexity of the tasks and the nature of the responses that they engender.

Siegel (1986: 132) includes 'Develop standardized test situations and scoring forms' as one of 14 stages in the construction of a performance test, but gives it no particular status. The scoring form he uses as an illustration involves a precise list of criterial behaviours for the process being observed, implying even in this very practical context a view of the relative importance of different aspects of the performance; in other words, an implicit theory of the performance.

In contrast, Stiggins (1987: 36–7), in a practical guide to teachers, stresses the importance of the statement of performance criteria:

> C. List performance criteria. *No other single specification will contribute more to the quality of your performance assessment than this one.* Before the assessment is conducted, you must state the performance criteria, in other words, the dimensions of examinee performance (observable behaviors or attributes of products) you will consider in rating....
>
> Performance criteria should reflect those important skills that are the focus of instruction. Definitions spell out what we, as the evaluators, mean by each particular criterion. [Emphasis in original.]

The issue of rating criteria and their relation to validity will be discussed in the context of rating and reporting scales for achievement on language performance tests in Chapter 7, below.

2.3.2   Validation issues in operational tests

The main validation research will be carried out in the field trials that precede the operational introduction of a test, or on operational versions of the test. As we have seen, Messick (1989) stresses that empirical evidence is as important as a theoretical rationale in establishing the validity of tests. Throughout the latter part of this book, we will be introducing in detail techniques for carrying out such studies, and a number of validation studies of language performance assessments will be considered in detail. Two particular aspects of the validity of performance tests which can only be investigated once a test has become operational will be considered in this section. The first of these, predictive validity, is sometimes seen as having a special significance for establishing the validity of performance tests. We prefer to see evidence of predictive validity as only one kind of validation evidence relevant to performance tests.

2.3.2.1   Predictive validity

Predictive validity is the extent to which the predictions we would make on the basis of test performance about subsequent performance in the criterion situation are likely to be borne out. Slater (1980: 18) describes a famous study by Bray and Greenleaf (Bray and Grant, 1966; Bray, Campbell and Grant, 1974) in which junior management level employees in an American corporation were assessed via a battery of performance-based measures over three days and predictions made about their likely career prospects in the firm. Eight years later the participants still in the company were reassessed and the predictions found to be strikingly accurate. This study is, however, the exception rather than the rule, according to Borow (1980), who claims that the predictive validity of many commonly used performance measures has not been investigated empirically. Similar complaints have been made about the predictive validity of language proficiency measures based on the Oral Proficiency Interview, despite promises by the advocates of such measures to remedy the situation, promises which remain largely unfulfilled. Follow-up studies of this kind can be notoriously difficult to conduct where the performance assessment is used for gate-keeping (selection and exclusion), for example in the admission of international students to universities in Britain or the US. In such cases, the study of the relationship of test scores to subsequent performance has to be conducted with a truncated sample, because the subsequent success or otherwise of those failing to achieve the score required for admission cannot be examined. Furthermore, the role of language as a factor in success in an academic environment is necessarily limited. In a predictive validation study of the ELTS test (Criper and Davies, 1988), language proficiency as measured by ELTS was found to account for no more than about 10 per cent of the observed variance in outcome measures (success in chosen course of study, etc.). Surveys of the predictive validity of EAP tests (Light *et al.*

1987; Graham, 1987) have generally reported similar findings. More recently, Elder (1993a) has again found a similar result in a small-scale study of the predictive validity of the IELTS test used with overseas-trained teachers completing a one-year bridging course prior to re-entry to their profession in Australia.

Predictive validity is usually and often necessarily investigated after the test has become operational, which is perhaps another reason why so few studies are done; the pressure is off the test developers and their sponsors, so to speak.

2.3.2.2   Consequential validity

Performance assessment is generally held by its advocates to be a progressive form of assessment (Wiggins, 1989; Shohamy, 1993), particularly in terms of its impact on the educational contexts in which it is practised. The responsibility of test developers for considering the impact of the tests they develop has been strongly advocated by Messick (1989) in his discussion of what he terms *consequential validity*, and by Frederiksen and Collins (1989), who have introduced the idea of the *systemic validity* of tests, that is, their effect on the educational system in which they feature. The argument is that because of the greater closeness of performance assessments to real-world tasks (their 'directness' or 'transparency' in the terms of Frederiksen and Collins, 1989), class time spent on preparation of students for performance on the assessment tasks is thus preparation for the real-world tasks which they are simulating. This is in contrast to test formats which bear only an *indirect* relationship to the target performance, for example multiple-choice items which act only as indirect indicators of the skills involved. These latter test formats are thought to encourage negative consequences in educational terms when teachers and students focus their efforts on preparing for the test rather than on the target performances themselves.

However, as Linn *et al.* (1991), Messick (1994) and Haertel (1992) point out, these beneficial consequences cannot be assumed, they must be demonstrated; there is a need for an evidential basis for the consequential validity claimed for performance assessments. Linn *et al.* (1991: 17) stress that

> High priority needs to be given to the collection of evidence about the intended and unintended effects of assessments on the ways teachers and students spend their time and think about the goals of education. It cannot be assumed that a more 'authentic' assessment will result in classroom activities that are more conducive to learning.

2.3.2.3   Washback

Aspects of the consequential validity of language tests have been recognized under the heading 'washback' (or 'backwash'). The term is used to refer to the impact of tests on the teaching programme that leads up to them. This is particularly relevant for public tests which are established not primarily as part of a curriculum but which nevertheless become the focus of teaching programmes which may be organized around them (TOEFL preparation courses are an important example). It has been claimed that communicative, performance-based tests would have beneficial washback on the teaching that led up to them (cf. Wesche, 1987), as the teaching would focus on preparing students for the representative communicative tasks in the tests, and thus indirectly for the real-world communicative tasks beyond the test. The assumed negative washback of non-performance-based tests was held to be an unfortunate constraint on curriculum reform. Despite the assertion of these claims (e.g. Hughes, 1989), and some anecdotal evidence to support them (for example, cf. McNamara (1989b) on the beneficial effects of the reform of the Occupational English Test: see Chapter 4), little empirical evidence has been brought to support these claims. Recently, evidence of the complexity of these effects has begun to appear. Wall and Alderson (1993) investigated what was assumed to be the beneficial washback effect of the introduction of more communicative language assessment procedures to the secondary English curriculum in Sri Lanka, and found that the assumptions needed to be radically revised; the effect of the changes was complex and not always positive. Currently, an ongoing study (Alderson and Hamp-Lyons, in preparation) is investigating the washback effect of TOEFL on classroom practice in TOEFL preparation courses. Analysis of the data so far suggests that here too effects are much more complex than typically claimed by opponents of the TOEFL. While teaching to the TOEFL seriously affects teachers' materials it has less obvious and less consistent effects on their methodology. To date, washback studies in second language contexts have focused solely on the effects on classroom teaching and learning, and thus represent only one aspect of Messick's 'consequential validity'. The broader impact of language tests in terms of the entire curriculum, the teaching materials, and the life chances of test candidates, not to mention the effect on other interested stakeholders, has hardly been studied, although it seems that the TOEFL study mentioned above may be extended to include this broader range of considerations. If so, this will be an entirely welcome development, given the crucial social functions of language tests.

2.4   Performance assessment in second language contexts

2.4.1   Overview

In this part of the chapter we will give a critical account of the development of performance testing in second language contexts. Two broad traditions will be identified. Of particular importance in the discussion will be the extent to which, and the ways in which, second language performance testing has recognized and made reference to models of communicative knowledge and ability (to be discussed in Chapter 3), and to models of the communicative setting itself, as the basis for empirical validation of inferences based on test scores.

The structure of this part of the chapter is as follows. First, the evolution of the practice of language performance assessment and its relation to theory is traced, starting with work predating the influence of the theory of communicative competence. In this section, we will consider the nature of the performance tests proposed by Carroll (1961 [1972]) and Davies (1968) for selecting foreign students for university study in the USA and the UK, respectively. The advent of the era of communicative language testing in the early 1970s represented a major shift in favour of performance-based methods in general-purpose language assessment. Influential and representative work in the United States (Clark, 1972), building directly on the tradition of the FSI (Foreign Service Institute) test (Clark and Clifford, 1988) and Savignon, 1972) and the United Kingdom (e.g. Morrow, 1977, 1979) is considered in some detail, in order to clarify the complex issues of validity involved in the (distinctively different) approaches of these writers. The role of sociolinguistic theory is also examined. These initial responses to the problem of communicative testing helped define the main traditions of language performance assessment for the next two decades, and an understanding of the work of these earlier writers is thus important for understanding the nature of current practice.

In the final part of the chapter, we return to the question of criteria and the implications for the theoretical rationale (and construct validity) of language performance assessment. We contrast 'real world' and language proficiency-related criteria, and use this contrast as the basis for a distinction between a *strong* and a *weak* sense of the term *second language performance test*. Various performance-based tests are considered in the light of this distinction.

2.4.2   Traditions of second language performance assessment

Performance testing in second language contexts is not new; in the current era, it has been a consistent strand within second language testing for the last 40 years. Language performance tests developed in response to two main needs:

(1) the practical need to develop selection procedures involving, for example, the selection of foreign students for study at English-medium universities, or personnel selection for particular occupa-tions requiring communicative skill in a second language; and
(2) the need to bring testing into line with developments in language teaching which had resulted from the advent of theories of communicative competence.

These responses have constituted two rather separate traditions of second language performance assessment, although there is considerable blurring of the lines. The first tradition we will call the *work sample* tradition, as it derives largely from the work sample approach to general performance assessment, discussed in the previous section. We saw there that, in this approach, the performance is the *target* of assessment (Messick, 1994). In many ways this tradition represents a simple application of the principles and practices outlined in the first part of this chapter; the issues concerning validity raised there are equally relevant to the specific context of second language testing. As we saw above, this approach is clearly illustrated in language testing for specific occupational and academic purposes, but it has also had an important influence on general-purpose performance testing (see the discussion of Clark, 1972, below). The work sample tradition tends to be resolutely pragmatic and atheoretical, although careful specification of the sociolinguistic context of use, a feature of recent examples of this tradition, owes much to Hymes's work on sociolinguistic competence (Hymes, 1967, 1972). Considered from a theoretical point of view, this tradition can be characterized as behaviour-based and sociolinguistic in orientation.

The second tradition is cognitive and psycholinguistic, focusing less on the verisimilitude of performances and more on what they reveal about underlying ability and knowledge. In the words of Messick (1994), the performance is the *vehicle* of assessment; the performance task itself is of less interest than what the performance reveals; the underlying knowledge and ability is the actual target of assessment. This tradition has its origins in precommunicative testing, in the work of Lado (1961) on pencil-and-paper tests, who attempted to specify clearly, within a structuralist framework, the language knowledge that tests were trying to capture. In the 1970s, it continued in the work of Oller (see discussion in Chapter 3 below), as well as in testing with a more communicative orientation (see Savignon, 1972, for an early example; this will be discussed below). This second tradition represents the most common approach to general-purpose performance assessment.

In both approaches, the *empirical* validity of the inferences drawn about candidates must be established, as we discussed in the first part of the chapter. In order for this to be done there is a need for explicitness about the rationale for these inferences: this takes us into the issues to be discussed in Chapter 3. We shall also need technical skills, for example, of the kind to be introduced in subsequent chapters in this book.

In some ways, compared to other kinds of performance assessment, *language* performance assessment is particularly complex. For example, we may distinguish at least three common uses of the term *performance* in work in this field, each relevant to an understanding of practice:

(1) as a term in a theory of second language ability and use, as in Chomsky's *competence* and *performance*, or the discussion of the term *performance* in the work of Hymes (1972) and Canale and Swain (1980) (cf. Chapter 3);

(2) implying *skilled execution*, as in a musical or theatrical performance, or of some athletic or gymnastic skill; here the emphasis is on display, for an audience, and the demonstration of level of underlying skill; and

(3) *performances of real-world tasks*, as in work sample tests, where the test involves direct simulation of real-world roles and tasks.

Although some writers (e.g. Wesche, 1992) have suggested restricting the term *performance tests* to tests of the third type, broader definitions are possible, as we have seen, and this book adopts such a broader view. In this broader sense, second language performance tests are characterized by a relatively simple performance requirement, that is, that assessment will take place when the candidate is engaged 'in an act of communication' (see discussion of Savignon, 1972, below). Such tests will draw on the second and third senses of *performance*, above. Proficiency assessment in the ACTFL tradition (ACTFL, 1986) is an example of this kind of assessment. However, second language performance tests have been progressively influenced by changing theories of *performance* in the first sense, albeit somewhat intermittently and in a rather incoherent way, for 25 years at least. Their validity will depend crucially on an understanding of factors involved in language performance, as we will argue in Chapter 3.

2.4.3   Precommunicative traditions of language performance
assessment: Carroll and Davies

Early and influential applications of principles of performance assessment to second language contexts happened as result of a response to
practical needs for selection in contexts where practical rather than theoretical command of the language was required. In fact, two decades of
performance testing in second languages predated the formulation of the
theory of communicative competence (Hymes, 1967, 1972) which had the
potential to provide a more adequate theoretical justification. This early
work did not challenge the then current theories of the nature of language or language use, which at the time were structuralist and atomistic,
but was rather grafted pragmatically onto such approaches. Two examples of this will be given here, in the work of J.B. Carroll in the United
States and Alan Davies in the UK, both within the context of testing
English for academic purposes.

In a seminal discussion of the testing of the English language
proficiency of foreign students wishing to study in the US, Carroll (1961
[1972]) recommended a significant performance component in language
testing for this purpose. In a famous passage, Carroll (1961 [1972: 318])
recommends what he calls an ' "integrative" approach' to complement
what he calls the ' "discrete structure point" approach' common at the
time:

> The work of Lado and other language testing specialists has correctly
> pointed to the desirability of testing for very specific items of
> language knowledge and skill judiciously sampled from the usually
> enormous pool of possible items. This makes for highly reliable and
> valid testing.
>
> I do not think, however, that language testing (or the specification of
> language proficiency) is complete without the use of ... an approach
> requiring an integrated, facile performance on the part of the exam-
> inee.... I recommend tests in which there is less attention paid to
> specific structure points or lexicon than to the total communicative
> effect of an utterance.[9]

The fact that Carroll's concern for 'integrative' testing came in the context of EAP testing is significant. In this context, assessment could not be
based on what was known of courses that students had followed prior to
the test (a feature of the Lado approach), as this information was not
available. In any case, this was irrelevant as the purpose of the test was
selection for a future activity (university study) based on a screening for
adequate language skills. In such a context, too, the test is independent of

the first language of the candidates (Lado's work had emphasized the basis of test content in contrastive analysis); the point is, according to Carroll (1961 [1972: 319]), to determine 'how well the examinee is functioning in the target language, regardless of what his native language happens to be'.

✳   From the early 1960s, then, test *purpose* began to determine the form of tests as much as any linguistic theory of the knowledge or skills being tested. When test purpose required performance, then test formats should reflect this. This forward-looking view required two features of a language proficiency test: test content should be independent of what was known of the candidate's first language or learning history; and it required performance on tasks in which different aspects of language knowledge or skill were integrated. The exact nature of these performances was not specified.

The distinction between achievement and proficiency tests implicit in Carroll's work was made explicit by Davies (1968: 6–7; 1977: 45–6). For Davies (1977: 46), a proficiency test is (1) concerned with *control* and (2) future-oriented or predictive. Unlike a proficiency test, an achievement test

> cannot make predictions as to pupils' future performance.... Proficiency in a language implies adequate control over language skills for an extralinguistic purpose ... we can think of a proficiency test as assessing adequacy of control in a second language for studying other things through the medium of that language.

The reference to studying is significant here; it is presumably offered only as an example of a context in which a proficiency test may be used, but it was the definitive context in the period in which Carroll and Davies were writing.

Davies's distinction between achievement and proficiency tests did not, however, necessarily mean that proficiency tests would *only* measure the communicative aspects of proficiency; or that tests would even contain a performance component. In this sense, Davies is less explicit on this latter requirement than Carroll, although his notion of *control* (cf. discussion in Chapter 3) strongly suggests skilled execution in performance. Such a notion suggests that a test of grammatical competence alone would be inadequate as a test of proficiency.[10] The defining feature of a test of language proficiency, then, is that the learner be required to demonstrate not only knowledge of language but skill in the use of that knowledge in settings which are in some degree communicative. Such a test may require a demonstration of knowledge, but it will also demand demonstration of skill in performance: it will, as Shohamy

(1983: 528) puts it, 'require the test taker to apply ... knowledge [about the language] by actually using the language in [communicative] situations'.

Concern for the *predictive* validity of proficiency tests inevitably led in time to a greater specification of the predictive target or criterion, that is, the context in which subsequent performance was to be predicted. This specification was facilitated by the emphasis on sociolinguistic contexts of use which became a feature of a certain strand of communicative teaching and testing. The developments are foreshadowed in further remarks by Carroll (1961 [1972: 319]):

> An ideal English language proficiency test should make it possible to dif-
> ferentiate, to the greatest possible extent, levels of performance in those
> dimensions of performance which are relevant to the kinds of situations
> in which the examinees will find themselves after being selected on the
> basis of the test. The validity of the test can be established not solely on
> the basis of whether it appears to involve a good sample of the English
> language but more on the basis of whether it predicts success in the
> learning tasks and social situations to which the examinees will be
> exposed. I have attempted to suggest what might be the relevant dimen-
> sions of test performance, although I have not attempted to link them
> with collegiate learning and social situations – that is a task for college
> foreign student advisers and others who are familiar with the matrix of
> foreign student experiences.

In this passage, we see the link between proficiency testing in the context of foreign student selection and subsequent developments in communicative language testing, in particular ESP tests for foreign students. The new theories of communicative competence enabled a specification of the 'relevant dimensions of test performance', and the reference to establishing the 'matrix of foreign student experiences' prefigures the content validity approach of Weir (1983a, 1983b, 1988b), who carried out a thorough identification and categorization of the contexts of language use facing foreign students in British universities.[11]

In summary, two themes are of interest. First, it is clear that the new proficiency tests recommended by Carroll and Davies were types of performance test. Their focus was on prediction of performance in a specific real-world context (coping with the role of being a foreign student in an English speaking university setting). Secondly, the phrase 'integrated, facile performance' suggests another reason for conceptualizing language behaviour in performance terms. That is the common-sense notion (but one that was elusive in the strict psychometric-structuralist period, for example as exemplified in the work of Lado) that using language is a skilled performance involving the integration of many subskills, both linguistic and non-linguistic.

Although, as Bachman (1990: 301) has noted, a proper theoretical foundation on which performance could be characterized was 'well beyond both the goals and capability of linguistic theory of that time', by the end of the 1960s such a theory appeared likely in the notion of communicative competence (Hymes, 1967). The implications of this notion for language testing were quickly appreciated by Spolsky (1968), Cooper (1968), Jakobovits (1969) and Brière (1971).[12] But the first elaborated responses, with practical suggestions, are in Clark (1972) and Savignon (1972). Their proposals are important because they, in effect, initiated two alternative and in some ways complementary traditions of what soon became known as 'communicative language testing' in general-purpose settings. These traditions have survived in discussions of issues and advice to practitioners for over 20 years now, and represent the mainstream of current second language performance assessment theory and practice.

2.4.4   Clark: performance testing, situational specificity and general proficiency

Clark (1972) represents an early response to the advent of the notion of communicative competence. In fact, despite the promise of the title, *Foreign language testing: theory and practice*, his approach is relatively atheoretical and practical in focus; there is no explicit reference to Hymes, whose ideas are referred to second hand in fleeting citations of 'Brière (1971), Cooper (1968) and Spolsky (1968)'. A much more important source for the test is in fact the well-established tradition of oral proficiency interview testing represented by the Foreign Service Institute (FSI) test (Clark and Clifford, 1988). This test was a response to the practical requirements of personnel recruitment within the American government for officials who were to be placed in posts abroad requiring an active command of the local language. It appeared in the 1950s at the height of the psychometric-structuralist period in language testing (Spolsky, 1978), whose assumptions it continued to reflect in some ways, for example in its focus on accuracy in grammar, pronunciation and lexical choice. It certainly presented no explicit challenge to then-current theories.

What is interesting about Clark's approach in the context of this chapter is its sources in the theory and practice of performance assessment as outlined in the first part of this chapter. The testing of what Clark (1972: 119) calls 'communicative proficiency' was to be performance testing in the work sample tradition. He discusses the issue of content validity as follows (1972: 120), in terms clearly borrowed from the standard language of general performance testing:

> What appear to be needed are *work-sample* tests of communicative proficiency in which the student's performance is evaluated not on the basis of extent of vocabulary, accuracy of morphology and syntax, excellence of pronunciation, and so forth, but rather in terms of the adequacy with which the student can communicate in specified language-use situations. [Emphasis added.]

Although the gap between test and criterion is acknowledged (Clark, 1972: 124) ('... the social and psychological aspects of the interview are necessarily quite different from those present in the real-life situations represented'), and the extent and significance of such differences would appear to raise issues of empirical validation, Clark (1972: 125) appears to want to limit the type of research which he considers appropriate:

> There will always be the possibility of a discrepancy between student performance on the test and his performance in the real-life situations which the test is intended to represent. The magnitude of this discrepancy cannot be determined using experimental or statistical means, but can only be estimated through close observational and logical comparison of the 'real-life' and 'test' situations.

In a subsequent paper, Clark (1975) again uses the terminology of performance testing, but appears to be adopting a stronger position. He is in favour of exact specification of tasks in terms of *language* as well as content; and now confidently speaks of replicating reality in the test's 'setting and operation', despite his earlier caution on this point. He states (Clark, 1975: 11):

> A major requirement of direct proficiency tests is that they must provide a very close facsimile or 'work sample' of the real-life language situations in question, with respect to both the setting and operation of the tests and the linguistic areas and content which they embody.

This commitment to specificity inevitably raises issues both of describability and of generalizability, as well as the relationship of linguistic to more task-oriented assessment criteria. It seems that Clark comes close to arguing that there is no such thing as a general-purpose performance test; there are only specific-purpose performance tests, as in his view a direct test must be situation-based. Ingram (1981: 113), whose Australian Second Language Proficiency Ratings (ASLPR) derives directly from

Clark, recognizes the potential difficulties of an approach where content and construct validity involve specification of the relevant dimensions of 'specified language use situations': 'Clearly, the notion of language register and situational variation poses serious difficulties for a scale such as the ASLPR which, basically, seeks to describe the development of general proficiency.'

Clark (1972: 128) recognizes that the conceptual basis of oral proficiency assessment is not (or not only) the procedure for eliciting evidence of the student's proficiency, the interview itself, but the performance criteria in the rating scales against which that performance is judged. That is, the test's view of language and language proficiency is encoded in the wording of the rating scales. His position is to reiterate the necessity for adopting a task-centred ('operational') rather than a construct–centred approach (1972: 126):

> A temptation in the development and use of a communication–defined scoring system, and one which the FSI technique does not avoid completely, is to intermingle statements about desired *linguistic* abilities with the operational statements of communicative competence ... The mixing of communicative and linguistic criteria in a single system or rating scheme serves only to obscure the distinction between the two types of measurement and decrease the validity of the test as a direct measure of communicative proficiency. [Emphasis in original.][13]

But various aspects of the performance, other than a simple demonstration of mastery of the criterion behaviour, as in a simple work sample approach, are canvassed, immediately involving us in consideration of *ability for use*, in Hymes's terms (see Chapter 3). For example, in a discussion of the types of criteria to be used in evaluating performance, qualities of execution and non–cognitive dimensions of underlying performance skills appear to be recognized (and conflated), in addition to questions of adherence to the sociolinguistic norms of the situation:

> In addition to specifying the types of language use situations to be included in the test, the test developers would have to consider the degree of emphasis which is placed in these situations on the smoothness, accuracy and overall naturalness of the student's performance.... Sociological and psychological aspects of a particular communicative situation have a strong bearing on the 'acceptability' of the communication ... the scoring system adopted would have to take this into account.

Despite his awareness of some of the complexity of a performance–based approach, Clark (1972: 126–7) appears to be somewhat complacent about the validity of the direct tests he espouses: 'Scoring procedures based directly and exclusively on an appraisal of the student's communicative ability may be considered highly valid.' The cautions against such assumptions and claims given by writers in discussions of general performance assessment have been presented in the first part of this chapter.

2.4.5   Savignon: assessment 'in an act of communication'

The title of Savignon (1972) is *Communicative competence: an experiment in foreign language teaching*, but it contains no reference to Hymes's framework[14]. Instead, it refers briefly to the papers by Spolsky (1968) and Jakobovits (1969), and bases its approach on their discussion of the distinction between linguistic and communicative competence. Savignon basically adopts a simple (but one must say powerful) interpretation of this distinction in the language assessment context: she insists that language skills should be assessed 'in an act of communication'. This is a crucial idea. She criticizes traditional discrete-point tests of language proficiency (1972: 11–12):

> The trend in recent years has been to rely heavily on evaluations of the elements of language – pronunciation, syntax, and lexicon – made *apart from an act of communication.* ... [Such tests] may be said to measure *linguistic competence* while actual use of the language for communication requires *communicative competence.* ... What often passes for an evaluation of communicative competence is, in fact, an inaccurate reflection of the student's ability to function in an authentic communicative context ... [Emphasis in original.]

What is central in this approach is *instances of use* or *actual performance* (this sense of the term *performance* is discussed in Chapter 3). That is, performance testing in this approach depends on a requirement about the conditions under which language will be assessed, no more (or less) than that. It does not appeal to an explicit theory of the components of knowledge required for such conditions, although that would subsequently be added by those taking a more thoroughly sociolinguistic perspective (especially Shohamy, 1983); nor, least of all, does it propose or consider an appropriate model of performance, of the role of underlying skills and abilities in performance. Thus, despite its apparent ultimate basis in Hymes's powerful theory, it remains only superficially theoretical.

In fact, Savignon's detailed proposals contain a rich model of communication in the way in which tasks and assessment criteria are specified, but it remains quite inexplicit. Savignon has four tests of communicative competence in her study:

(1) discussion with a native speaker;
(2) seeking information from a native speaker;
(3) talking on a topic;
(4) description.

The criteria for evaluating the performances on each of these four tests respectively are

(1)   (a) effort to communicate and
            (b) amount of communication;
(2)   (a) comprehensibility and suitability of the introduction;
            (b) naturalness and poise;
            (c) comprehension by the native speaker;
            (d) comprehensibility and suitability of the conclusion and
            (e) amount of information elicited;
(3) and (4): (a) fluency;
            (b) comprehension by a native speaker listener and
            (c) amount of information conveyed.

Savignon appears to be including several different types of criteria. Some of Savignon's proposed criteria focus on aspects of the skill required to meet the condition of being assessed in an *instance of use*, best exemplified in the criterion of *fluency*. Here, a performance is understood in a sense similar to the idea of a musical performance or of a performance in the theatre, where it is the *execution* which is of interest (cf. the discussion of the different senses of the term performance introduced earlier in this chapter). A second group focuses on the *linguistic resources* necessary for the success of the communication: in particular, mastery of the pronunci- ation (phonology and suprasegmentals) required for comprehensibility, and the lexical (and to a lesser extent, syntactic) resources involved in successful completion of the third and fourth tasks. Thirdly, we have aspects of the personality or interpersonal skills of the speaker – poise, naturalness, and possibly tact (the ambiguity is in the term *suitability*) – as well as motivation ('effort to communicate'). Fourthly, there are crite- ria to do with outcomes: how much information was exchanged? The first three types of criteria have to do with the *antecedents* of the performance and the *process* of the performance; the last set of criteria has to do with the *product* of the performance (cf. the reminder from Fitzpatrick and Morrison (1971), quoted above, that the term *performance assessment* is shorthand for 'performance and product evaluation'.) Clearly, a lot is involved in this switch to performance-based assessment, but it is mostly inexplicit.

Sociolinguistic awareness, a feature of later approaches to communica- tive assessment, is only weakly present in Savignon's proposals. Savignon refers to specific communicative contexts, but does not include any dimension of sociolinguistic variability in her proposals for assessment. Rather, she seems to be implying that an evaluation of a person's capacity to perform as part of 'an act of communication' can be generalized from any act of communication to any other, for example those listed in the following remarks (Savignon, 1972: 8):

> Communicative competence may be defined as the ability to function in a truly communicative setting – that is, in a dynamic exchange in which linguistic competence must adapt itself to the total informational input, both linguistic and paralinguistic, of one or more interlocutors. How successful would an individual be, for example, in getting directions to the nearest pharmacy? How accurate an account could he give of an accident to which he had just been witness? Could he make introductions at a dinner party?

Despite her concern for real-world contexts of use, Savignon's approach rests on a notion of general proficiency which is guaranteed by a general performance requirement, that is, that assessment will take place as part of 'an act of communication'. We can thus characterize Savignon's position as general (i.e. relatively unspecific as to contexts of use), rich (in that her assessment criteria are complex, and include implicit reference to underlying abilities in performance) and undertheorized.

Savignon's performance requirement – like Carroll's, simple on the surface – is a little like the tip of an iceberg; it has very substantial and not always recognized implications. Earlier in this chapter we considered the examples given by Slater (1980) of how characteristics of the stimulus, the response and the surrounding conditions are definitional of performance assessment (the examples were assessments in which candidates had to deal with a hysterical patient, land a plane, teach a class). What is striking in each of these cases is the range of complex psychological and interpersonal variables introduced; in other words, it is no light matter to introduce a performance requirement. The influence of such variables on performance seems rarely to have been systematically thought through in the second language performance assessment literature – a point which will be developed in the next chapter. We will return to this theme below.

2.4.6 Performance testing in the communicative paradigm: British approaches

In the United Kingdom, the influence of the notion of communicative competence was widely felt throughout the 1970s. Work in curriculum design by Wilkins (1973) and Munby (1978) had an important influence on those working in language testing, particularly Morrow (1977, 1979) and B.J. Carroll (1977, 1978). Wilkins's contribution to the work of the Council of Europe helped define what became known as the notional/functional syllabus. Morrow was based with Wilkins at Reading; the title of his manifesto (Morrow, 1977) is *Techniques of Evaluation for a Notional Syllabus*. Munby (1978) worked for the British Council in the field of English for Specific Purposes syllabus design. Carroll, a colleague of Munby's in the British Council, had overall responsibility for the development of the British Council's new test of English for Academic Purposes, the ELTS test (Carroll, 1980).

Munby (1978) is a significant influence on the work of the British developers of communicative tests, for two reasons.

First, he proposed detailed if rather unwieldy methods for determining the effect of sociolinguistic context on language use in occupational and academic settings. These techniques of *needs analysis* were developed to assist in syllabus design, but also provided a means of arriving at the test content specification of a performance test. As performance testing in the work sample tradition requires careful content specification, Munby's application of sociolinguistic theory to the definition of communicative context and the communicative task was obviously highly relevant and was adopted by Carroll (1980). In fact, the feasibility of Munby's elaborate mechanism for developing a 'communication needs profile' had been widely questioned on its appearance (cf. Davies, 1981; Mead, 1982); and the application of this technique in the development of the ELTS test was very much an armchair one, as was soon noted (cf. Alderson and Hughes, 1981). However, it was an important milestone in the development of sociolinguistically sensitive performance tests. Munby and Carroll established an approach which survived in spirit in the work of Weir (1983a, 1983b) who used more empirically based techniques in the design of another British EAP test, the Test of English for Educational Purposes (TEEP).

Secondly, Munby's attempts to specify *dimensions of performance* through his taxonomy of *enabling skills* had an enormous influence on the design of language tests. These were a set of subskills deemed to be involved in performances involving the receptive skills of listening and reading, and, as they were accessed to varying degrees in any listening or reading task, provided a basis for generalizing across tasks, which, as we have seen more than once, is a fundamental issue in performance assessment. Although Morrow (1979: 152) acknowledges the importance of Munby's sociolinguistically based needs analysis apparatus, his main debt to Munby is in fact for the notion of performance-related enabling skills, which Morrow adopted and which has been influential ever since (Lumley, 1993). Morrow's programme was realized in examinations for the Royal Society of Arts Communicative Tests of English as a Foreign Language (Morrow, 1983).

More explicitly than that of Savignon or Clark, the work of Carroll and Morrow appeals to work in linguistic theory in support of its approach. Yet it is still theoretically weak. Although Morrow acknowledges the influence of the new work in sociolinguistics, his discussion of the issues it raises is rather sketchy. Particularly important in Morrow's work, as in the work of the Americans, is the link between communicative testing and *performance*, which is seen as its fundamental characteristic. For example, Morrow (1979: 150) states:

> More emphasis needs to be placed in a communicative context on the notion of behaviour. A test of communication must take as its starting point the measurement of what the candidate can actually achieve through language.

Morrow (1979: 149) called this his 'performance criterion', that is

> the candidate's ability to actually use the language, to translate the competence (or lack of it) which he is demonstrating into actual performance 'in ordinary situations', i.e. actually using the language to read, write, speak or listen in ways and contexts which correspond to real life.

On the one hand, Morrow distinguishes conceptually between communicative tests – tests which relate to an explicit theory of communicative competence – and performance tests as usually understood (Morrow, 1979: 150–1):

> We can expect a test of communicative ability to have the following characteristics:
> 1. It will be criterion-referenced against the operational performance of a set of authentic language tasks. In other words it will set out to show whether or not (or how well) the candidate can perform a set of specified activities....
> Asking the question, 'What can this candidate do?' clearly implies a performance-based test. The idea that performance (rather than competence) is a legitimate area of concern for tests ... poses a number of problems, chiefly in terms of extrapolation and assessment [reliability] ...
> Given these problems, the question arises as to whether communicative testing does necessarily involve performance tests.

But he concludes (1979: 152) that 'performance tests ... are of most value in a communicative context'. Thus, despite his more explicit appeal to the notion of communicative competence, Morrow remains close to the performance-based tradition of Clark.

2.4.7   Pragmatic vs theory-related second language performance assessment

As we have seen, second language performance tests owe much to the tradition of general performance testing, to which they sometimes explicitly refer in the discussion of their rationale, and in their focus on real-world tasks. They have also been influenced (if only notionally) by the developments in models of language ability, particularly the work of Hymes. Hymes introduced the notion of sociolinguistic appropriateness, in which the relationship between the context of situation and the aspects of language competence required to operate within such contexts is described. More crucially, Hymes proposed a general model of language knowledge and language performance, including the abilities that underlie actual instances of communication; in so doing he built (or appeared to build) on the distinction between *competence* and *performance* originally proposed by Chomsky but in fact substantially reinterpreted and elaborated it. The influence of these developments in sociolinguistics has sometimes been programmatic, in that they have tended to focus attention generally on language use in context, and so have pushed assessment in the direction of task-based performance tests in general: we have traced this in the work of Savignon, Clark and Morrow. In other cases, a more systematic attempt has been made to incorporate more sociolinguistically exact specifications of the nature of communicative tasks facing the candidate in the target use situation, for example in the work of Brendan Carroll and others on the ELTS test, and by Shohamy (1983) and Weir (1988b). In general, 'communicative' language tests have tended to be performance based, although there has been considerable ambivalence over the relevance or value of a theory of performance such as that available in the model of Hymes. This is of course ironic, as Hymes's introduction of the notion of communicative competence is arguably the single most important influence on performance based communicative tests. The most significant expression of this ambivalence is in the definition of communicative performance in Canale and Swain (1980: 6), to be discussed further in Chapter 3:

the actual demonstration of this knowledge [i.e. knowledge in the domains comprising 'communicative competence' in their definition] in *real* second language situations and for *authentic* communication purposes. [Emphasis in original.]

where there is a dual focus, the one practical, the other theoretical, without the necessary integration.

2.5 The question of criteria: non-linguistic factors in performance on language performance tests

2.5.1 The place of non-linguistic factors in assessment criteria

In concluding this chapter, we will return to an issue which will be central to the discussion in Chapter 3; that is, the relation of linguistic to non-linguistic factors in performance on language performance tests. This issue has long been recognized (Carroll, 1954, 1968; Clark, 1972; Upshur, 1979; Wesche, 1992) but somehow the impact of this realization has remained muted. In a discussion of the issue, Wesche (1992: 105) emphasizes the necessity for recognition of the role of non-linguistic factors in performance, and places confidence in predictive validity studies:[15]

> The distinguishing feature of performance tests, then, is that they tap both second language ability and the ability to fulfill the nonlinguistic requirements of given tasks ...
>
> How can a language testing approach be justified in which nonlinguistic factors are deliberately introduced? The rationale is essentially that nonlinguistic factors are present in any language performance, and that it is therefore important to understand their role and channel their influence. ...
>
> Instead of an ultimately vain effort to develop context-neutral, universally fair language tests, proponents of performance testing seek to improve predictive validity for specific situations.

Jones is perhaps clearest about the role of non-linguistic factors and their implications for performance-based language tests (1985: 20):

> With regard to second language performance testing it must be kept in mind that language is only one of several factors being evaluated. The overall criterion is the successful completion of a task in which the use of language is essential. A performance test is more than a basic proficiency test of communicative competence in that it is related to some kind of performance task. It is entirely possible for some examinees to compensate for low language proficiency by astuteness in other areas. For example, certain personality traits can assist examinees in scoring

high on interpersonal tasks, even though their proficiency in the language may be substandard. On the other hand, examinees who demonstrate high general language proficiency may not score well on a performance because of deficiencies in other areas.

Jones (1979: 54–5) discusses his own performance on a performance test for a job as a State Department German-speaking escort interpreter (which he failed; Jones is a professor of German):

> I thought the test was a good simulation of the potential task, and that the examiners learned exactly what they needed to know. I have no idea of what kind of scoring procedure they used, but I assume that they looked for certain cues having to do not only with language proficiency but also general knowledge, personality, and overall presence.

Jones's analysis implies a possible distinction between two kinds of language performance test, differing according to the weight accorded to real-world criteria in assessing performance.

To illustrate the issue, we will consider an Australian ESP test, the Occupational English Test (OET) (McNamara, 1990a), a work sample language performance test for health professionals, which is described in detail in Chapter 4. Briefly, the content of this test is derived from a series of job analyses for each of the professions involved, and simulates a number of job-related performance tasks. However, when it comes to establishing criteria for judging the performance, it cannot meet Jones's requirement of a performance test that non-linguistic factors also be included in the evaluation criteria, which are restricted on the whole to aspects of the *language* performance. There are a number of issues involved.

First, there is a legal problem. The government body responsible for the OET is required by law to assess the English language proficiency of overseas-trained health professionals, but is not permitted to make assessments of their professional competence. This is left in the hands of separate assessment panels for each of the professions concerned, who use a variety of methods to make their assessment, usually a combination of pencil-and-paper tests and performance tests in clinical settings.

Secondly, there is an issue of social equity involved. It is unreasonable to require performances from non-native-speakers which are not required of native speakers. The OET is task-based, so that candidates in the speaking sub-test perform simulated tasks of persuasion, reassurance and the like in the context of simulated interactions with patients or their relatives. How should such interactions be evaluated? In the performance assessments of clinical communication skills as part of the education of *native speaking* medical undergraduates, similar types of simulated interactions are evaluated in terms of their overall outcomes in real-world terms: was the patient reassured/persuaded/helped to express his or her needs, etc.?[16] Native speakers tend not to do very well on such tasks; in fact, the very reason they are now being trained is that, as patients know, communication with health professionals can be very difficult: the deficiencies of doctors as communicators are proverbial. With the increase in medico-legal litigation, the profession has decided to do something about the problem. It would be unreasonable to demand behaviour of overseas graduates which is not (yet) typical of their native English-speaking Australian colleagues.

Thirdly, there is the issue of whether all of the factors Jones would like to include are ever likely to be operationalizable. We will return in Chapter 3, to this question of feasibility and the necessity for defining the 'limits of testability' (Candlin, 1986).

Elsewhere, performance tests for overseas-trained medical graduates have appeared to come closer to Jones's ideal. For example, the assessment of oral language skills is integrated with the assessment of clinical competence in a British part-equivalent of the OET (Occupational English Test), the PLAB test (formerly the TRAB test) for doctors (cf. Alderson *et al.*, 1986: 35, A12–A15). In this test, the Oral Examination is conducted by two medical examiners; it is simultaneously a test of clinical judgement and of proficiency in spoken English. The language assessments are reported separately, but are made by the medical examiners, not by language specialists, on a 5-point numerical scale. Regrettably, the validity and reliability of this interesting procedure have not been addressed in published reports, but informal comments suggest that the test is problematic. As mentioned above, as part of a larger research project on dentist–patient communication (Candlin *et al.*, 1980a, 1980b) in the context of the assessment of overseas dentists in Britain, Coleman (1980: 39) made a related proposal for integration of clinical and language assessment, but again significantly it was not adopted, being seen as too complex and costly by the profession.

Overall, one must be modest about any claims one may wish to make that tests such as the Occupational English Test provide information on 'the ability of candidates to communicate effectively in the workplace' (Recommendation 3 of the report which led to the test being commissioned: cf. Alderson *et al.*, 1986: 3), although this was the requirement of the brief for the test's development (cf. Chapter 4).

In the field of EAP testing, too, there is some ambiguity about whether tests such as the ELTS test or the OTESL (Wesche, 1987), which are proposed as models of performance tests by Wesche (1987, 1992), are or indeed should be performance tests in the full sense in which Jones intended. This is not an easy question to settle, and there is scope for empirical research on the issue. Two sources of evidence are available at the present time. One, to be presented in detail in Chapter 7, investigates the performance of native speakers with varying levels of post-secondary education on IELTS reading and writing tasks and finds that performance is closely related to educational level. Moreover, the criteria used in judging performance in the writing task explicitly include factors other than simple language proficiency. This would lead one to conclude that such tests are indeed performance tests in Jones's sense; but this has implications for equity which have not been recognized (see discussion in Chapter 7). On the other hand, the simulation of real-world tasks in such tests is superficial. For example, in the real world, students with low language proficiency may adopt strategies (for example, reading in advance some of the material related to the lecture topic, taping lectures, seeking explanations from friends, copying others' notes, seeking translations, etc.) which will enable them to successfully perform the task superficially simulated in the language test. In apparent confirmation of this point, we have evidence from the validation study of the ELTS test (Criper and Davies, 1988) on the predictive validity of the test. In line with studies of other language proficiency tests in academic contexts, the study concluded that ELTS scores accounted for about 10 per cent of the variance in the academic outcomes of the students in the study. The authors comment (Criper and Davies, 1988: 63):

> This figure is low in that it indicates that language level at the beginning of a period of study is not a good predictor of final success. However, it accords with the results of previous studies of other language tests.

They comment subsequently (Criper and Davies, 1988: 113):

> Language plays a role but not a dominant role in academic success once the minimum threshold of adequate proficiency has been reached. Thereafter it is individual non-linguistic characteristics, both cognitive and affective, that determine success.

Criper and Davies's data seem to imply that ELTS is something short of being a performance test in Jones's sense.

2.5.2   Strong and weak language performance tests

In the light of the discussion so far, it may be helpful to make a distinction between a *strong* and a *weak* sense of the term *second language performance test*. This dichotomy is a conceptual one, and is presented as a way of clarifying issues in actual tests; pure examples of either type will be difficult to find.

The distinction is proposed in terms of the *criteria* used in assessing performance on the tasks set. In second language performance tests in the *strong* sense, tasks will represent real-world tasks, and performance will primarily be judged on real-world criteria, that is, the fulfilment of the task set. Aspects of language ability as such may or may not be assessed at all; if they are, criteria reflecting language ability will only be part of a larger set of criteria used in assessing performance, and will have primarily a diagnostic function. Such a test thus involves a second language as the *medium* of the performance; performance of the *task* itself is the *target* of assessment (Messick, 1994). Adequate second language proficiency is a necessary but not a sufficient condition for success on the performance task. Jones proposes language performance tests of this type (non-linguistic factors will also be taken into account in assessing performance). For example, in the case of a task requiring the candidate to persuade or reassure, performances will be assessed against real-world criteria (am I persuaded? do I feel reassured?), and non-linguistic contextual factors such as the personality and sympathetic qualities of the person doing the persuading or reassuring will play an explicit role in the candidate's chances of success. In such a test, there will be a full and explicit integration of language knowledge and ability for use, in Hymes's terms (see Chapter 3 for a discussion of these terms).

It should be clear that this type of test is not strictly a language test at all. Where is it to be found? Well, in a sense real life-tasks in the real world demonstrate such an integration, and it will be helpful to our understanding of what our tests are (and what they are not) to investigate naturalized assessment practices in everyday and in professional life.[17] Moreover, this kind of test cannot be simulated, because the material and psychological context is missing. To take the example given above, it is not possible to simulate seriously the task of persuading or reassuring in a language test (despite the fact that simulations of such tasks are frequently set), because the interlocutor does not in reality need persuading or reassuring, and the conditions under which he or she would be persuaded or reassured in reality – which are likely to be extremely complex and variable, involving all manner of motivational and attitudinal factors – cannot possibly be simulated in a test. The best one can achieve is a kind of guessing on the part of the rater: 'If I were in a position of needing to be reassured or persuaded, would I in general terms find this reassuring or persuasive?' Similarly, the candidate will lack a motivational context in which to attempt the task, other than success on the language test; and this latter motivational context will almost certainly elicit a rather different kind of behaviour.

The closest one can get is not in performance tests which involve simulation, but in the more direct types of assessment (Slater, 1980; Jones, 1985) discussed earlier in this chapter: *direct assessment* (continuous observation over extended periods of time) and *work sample methods* (in the more restricted sense of on-the-job or on-site observation at agreed times; cf. Elder, 1993). The feasibility of such tests is a major problem, as, apart from the time and expense and the necessity of admitting candidates on a probationary basis to the very sites for which the testing procedure is intended to act as a form of gate-keeping, we return again to the question of sampling, and the effect on performance of knowledge of the fact that one is being observed; we have an assessment equivalent of the sociolinguistic problem of the Observer's Paradox (Labov, 1970).

In second language performance tests in the *weak* sense, the focus is on *language performance*. Tasks may resemble or simulate real-world tasks, or be artificial in other ways (for example, the oral proficiency interview). The candidate is required to perform on a task which may represent tasks he or she may subsequently face in the real world; however, the capacity to perform the *task* is not actually the focus of assessment. Rather, the purpose of the assessment is to elicit a language sample so that second language proficiency, and perhaps additionally qualities of the execution of the performance, may be assessed. Assessment criteria will reflect these concerns, and even such general criteria as *Overall task fulfilment* will generally be interpreted in language-related terms.[18] Most general-purpose performance-based proficiency tests are of this type, including tests such as the ASLPR and the ETS/ACTFL Oral Proficiency Interview. Confusingly, even most occupationally related language performance tests are of this type, as for example the Occupational English Test, for the reasons given above. In this context, the tasks chosen for the display of proficiency are likely to be selected for their face validity and assumed positive 'washback effect'. Because of the concern for face validity, such performance tests will in a superficial way performance tests in the strong sense, but this will only be a 'face' resemblance. Performance tests in the weak sense seem to have had such convincing face validity that they have managed to convince language testers themselves that they were more than tests of language proficiency.

This dichotomy in fact represents the ends of a conceptual continuum. Given that most language performance tests are *weak* in this sense, such tests may still be distinguished as relatively stronger or weaker, and even different parts of a single test may be distinguished in this way. For example, we have seen that tests of English for Academic Purposes such as the IELTS test and OTESL have some kind of intermediate status in relation to the proposed distinction. The point is to get test developers to be clearer about what they are requiring of test takers and raters, and to think through the consequences of such requirements. As far as research on performance testing goes, the distinction may help the researcher to take more adequate account of the interactional and psychological characteristics of the test situation, to be discussed in the following chapter, in investigating empirically the validity of language performance tests.

2.6 Conclusion

In this chapter, we have outlined traditions of performance assessment within general and vocational education in order to understand better the theory and practice of second language performance assessment. We have seen that language performance assessment has drawn heavily on non-language fields in both specific purpose (occupation-related) testing and for general-purpose tests which make use of the practice of work sample assessment. However, we have also seen that a focus on the medium of the performance – language – as manifested under conditions of performance (as part of an act of communication) is characteristic of much second language performance assessment. An ambiguity in focus, reflected in lack of clarity about the choice of criteria for assessment, particularly where tests involve simulation of real-world tasks, is typical of much practice. This lack of clarity will be less surprising when we see the way in which the field has avoided confronting the difficulties associated with the whole notion of performance, to be considered in the following chapter. The discussion in the present chapter has concluded with a proposal for a broad categorization of language performance tests as relatively strong or weak according to whether the assessment criteria reflect real-world evaluative criteria, or focus more narrowly on dimensions of language performance. In either case, the role of non-linguistic and interactional factors, either acknowledged as explicitly relevant, or assumed (wrongly) to be irrelevant, needs to be investigated in the empirical validation of inferences from test scores. Examples of research attempting to do this are given in Chapters 7 and 8.

In Chapter 4, an extended example is given of the development of a work sample type of occupationally related language performance test, the Occupational English Test. This is done to illustrate the sequence of steps required in the development of language performance tests of this common type, to establish a context for research on the test discussed elsewhere in the book, and to raise questions about the nature of the simulation involved in such tests. But before we move on to this example, it is time for a detailed analysis of the notion of performance in theories of language ability.

Notes

1. Sometimes the *judging* process (the *assessment* component of performance assessment) is seen to be criterial. For example, Stiggins (1987: 33) states that:

   > Achievement can be, and often is, measured by means of observation and professional judgment. This form of measurement is called performance assessment.

   In similar vein, Berk (1986: ix) offers the following 'operational definition': 'Performance assessment is the process of gathering data by systematic observation for making decisions about an individual'. But Cronbach (1971: 26) had defined a 'test' in general as 'a systematic procedure for observing a person's behavior and describing it with the aid of a numerical scale or category system', so it seems that the process of judging cannot after all be the distinguishing feature.

2. We shall consider later in this chapter the parallels to the above kinds of testing situations in the case of language performance tests, which have a 'performance requirement' that knowledge and use of language be assessed under performance conditions. It is clear that a range of emotional and contextual variables will become relevant in such assessments, and this raises fundamental issues of validity.

3. By this definition, performance assessment has a long history in educational measurement, as Linn, Baker and Dunbar (1991: 15) point out. They quote Lindquist (1951: 154): '... the most important consideration is that the test requires the examinee to do the *same* things, *however complex*, that he is required to do in the criterion situations' [emphasis in Lindquist's original]. (Of course the tradition of performance assessment is very old: the ancient Olympic Games is an example.)

4. In testing, the technical term *criterion* has two meanings: (1) performances in the *non-test* situation; (2) an aspect on which a performance is to be judged, e.g. *fluency, appropriateness*. We are using it in its first sense here. The aim of the test is to use judgements of performance in the *test* situation in order to predict accurately a person's ability to handle performances in the *non-test* situation, the criterion. For example, in a driving test, the criterion is all the relevant driving behaviour of the test-taker subsequent to successful performance on the test.

5. This position is reflected in the following comment by Haertel (1992: 984):

   > The term *performance test* is often reserved for assessments that involve sampling and quantifying some observable behavior or product of behavior valued in itself, outside of the test setting. Writing samples may be used to assess writing ability; an object created in a machine shop may be evaluated to assess skill in using power tools; a teacher's classroom performance may be observed and rated to assess teaching proficiency.

6. In fact, Jones does not consider the feasibility and representativeness of role play to be a problematic issue; for a context in which the difficulties are clearly set out, cf. the work of Elder (1994) referred to above.

7. Notice that the term construct is being used by Messick in two rather different senses here: (1) construct validity as an overarching term; (2) a psychological construct or

explicit theoretical rationale on which it is proposed that inferences from test scores be based.

8. In this it was influenced by the work of Munby (1978) on the content of ESP syllabuses; Munby's approach was adopted by Carroll (1980) in his work on EAP testing. These developments are discussed in detail later in this chapter.

9. Notice that Carroll is here not rejecting the existing tradition of testing separate items of grammar and lexis, but is saying that it should be complemented. This point about complementarity has not always been understood, as Carroll (1986: 124) has pointed out:

> It may have been thought by some that I was criticizing or opposing the discrete-point approach. That is not the case at all ...
>
> The discrete-point approach, if the 'points' are adequately sampled, is often a good way to measure the language competence on which language performance is based, but it needs to be supplemented by measures of integrative performance.

10. For example, the Test of English as a Foreign Language (TOEFL) is a discrete-point test used in the selection of overseas students for American universities, but it does not contain the kinds of performance component recommended by Carroll. However, it is mentioned by Davies (1977: 46) among other tests as an example of a proficiency test (as distinct from an achievement test), because of its context of prediction and selection. The current TOEFL test has been widely criticized on communicative grounds (Stansfield, 1986). TOEFL is currently the subject of major revision to address these criticisms (Buck, 1994; Ross, 1994).

11. Less direct means for determining relevant content have also been used, for example by consulting experts, as in the development of IELTS (Alderson, 1988).

12. Another early contribution is in a paper by Spolsky (1973), originally given as a paper at a conference in 1968.

13. This attempt to separate the 'linguistic' from the 'communicative' is characteristic of the time.

14. Nor to the interesting and relevant work going on in Europe, particularly Britain, at the time: cf papers prepared for the Council of Europe (e.g. Wilkins, 1973) and the Conference on Communicative Language Teaching held at the University of Lancaster in 1972.

15. Problems associated with predictive validity studies have been discussed earlier in this chapter.

16. These assessments are discussed further in Chapter 3. Another aspect of the assessments is that candidates may be rewarded for keeping silent (to let the 'patient' speak), a rather unlikely feature of a test of second language proficiency.

17. Jacoby (1995) is an example of such a study; she investigates how assessment feedback is given by physicists working in a team in the course of rehearsals for conference presentations they are about to make.

18. Empirical evidence in support of this view is given in Chapter 8.

3 Modelling performance: opening Pandora's Box

3.1 Introduction

What is the role of performance in a theory of second language ability? In this chapter we argue the case for a better understanding of the nature of performance and the role of underlying performance capacities in second language performance assessment contexts. However, basing language performance testing on a broad theory of the capacities involved in language use presents a number of knotty theoretical problems, on which test developers have often turned their backs.

Despite the scepticism and pragmatism of many practitioners, several important writers *have* attempted to state clearly how they see the role of performance within a model of second language communicative ability. The most influential discussions to date have been in the work of (1) Canale and Swain (published in 1980, and later revised) and (2) Bachman and Palmer, who have continued to develop their model of language ability over a period of fifteen years. It will be shown in this chapter that these and other influential discussions of the nature of second language communicative ability can be summarized in terms of three basic dimensions:

(1) what they have to say about the factors constituting *knowledge* of a language;
(2) what they have to say about the underlying factors (*not* specific to language) which form part of an individual's ability to perform communicative tasks involving language; these underlying factors Hymes (1972) termed *ability for use*;
(3) the way in which they see actual real-time *instances of language use* in the light of the preceding dimensions.

Typically, for example, inferences about the first (and second) dimension can be made on the basis of observation of selected instances of performance. These inferences ultimately rest on an understanding of how language *knowledge* interacts with the other non-linguistic factors constituting *ability for use*.

There is a need to be explicit about the role of each of these dimensions; to ignore any one of them is to risk falling into practical difficulty and, at worst, incoherence. In this chapter we will describe and evaluate successive attempts to develop models of what is involved in a performance in a language performance test, paying particular attention to those of Canale and Swain on the one hand and Bachman and Palmer on the other. The discussion of second language ability in these models is rather general and abstract, and increasingly elaborate as our thinking about the factors involved in any language performance deepens. Given this, some may question their usefulness. In fact, there has been a resistance to the need for explicit models of the capacity involved in second language performance tests: one reason for this lies in the practical origins of performance testing, traced in the previous chapter. Performance testing, it seemed, could get along very nicely without the assistance of appropriate linguistic theory.

This chapter will claim that this atheoretical approach in fact provides an inadequate basis for practice, and attempt to demonstrate why an understanding of the issues raised in models of language performance is crucial for development of and coherent research on the validity of language performance tests. As stated in the previous chapter, Messick (1989: 13) describes validity as 'an integrated evaluative judgement of the degree to which empirical evidence and theoretical rationales support the adequacy and appropriateness of inferences and actions based on test scores'. Models such as those examined in this chapter help us to articulate the 'theoretical rationale' for such inferences: they permit the necessary clarity, specificity and explicitness in stating the grounds for inferences about candidates' abilities made on the basis of test performance, thereby also facilitating the empirical investigation of the validity of these inferences. Of course, any such model is a map, not a prescription; it is still up to us as test *developers* to determine which aspects of any model we wish to incorporate in our assessment procedure, which aspects we can choose not to include, and the implications of our decisions for the inferences that may be made from the scores that will result. In addition, for those who are carrying out *research* on the validity of language performance assessment or who simply need to read and understand it, the completeness, adequacy and coherence of such models is crucial; they are the framework within which such research is carried out.

The structure of this chapter is as follows:

1. We begin by considering why, if at all, we need an abstract understanding of second language performance. Five arguments are advanced for the necessity of developing such an understanding.

2. This is followed by a ground-clearing exercise, in which an analysis is provided of various uses of the terms *competence, performance, knowledge* and *control* in the works of some influential earlier writers on the nature of language proficiency, who thus provided the framework within which Canale and Swain and Bachman and Palmer operated. A fundamental distinction proposed by Hymes (1967) between language *knowledge* and *ability for use* is introduced and discussed. (Hymes proposed this distinction in the context of a discussion of communicative competence in a *first* language.) The approach taken is critical and analytical, drawing attention to parallels and contradictions in the way that the terms have been understood, and offering a framework for making sense of the evolving and continuing debate on their meaning.

3. The way in which Hymes's model of communicative competence was reinterpreted in a *second* language context in the models of Canale and Swain and Bachman and Palmer is considered. These models are discussed and evaluated in some detail.

4. We look further at the way in which performance has been understood in the tradition of proficiency testing through the Oral Proficiency Interview (OPI) (Clark and Clifford, 1988).

5. The chapter concludes with a discussion of the dimensions of an adequate model of second language performance. In this section, we consider the issue raised by the interaction of language-specific knowledge and more general cognitive and other psychological factors in any performance in a second language.

3.2 Do we need a model of abilities in performance?

Why, if at all, do we need a discussion of abstract models? In answer to this question, a number of arguments in favour of such models may be advanced.

3.2.1 The need for greater clarity

The existing discussion of key terms in this area is seriously confused. There is a pressing need for definitional clarity, as the construct validity of performance-based language proficiency tests which claim to reflect the notion of communicative competence is by no means clear, despite the often-claimed 'directness' of such tests (Clark, 1975; cf. the discussion in Bachman, 1990, chs 7 and 8). According to Lantolf and Frawley

(1988: 186), 'A review of the recent literature on proficiency and communicative competence demonstrates quite clearly that there is nothing even approaching a reasonable and unified theory of proficiency.'

The distinction (if any) between the terms *proficiency* and *communicative competence* is a case in point: it is a matter for strong disagreement. For example, according to Savignon (1983: 246), 'Language proficiency *is* communicative competence and should be defined and evaluated as such' [emphasis in original].[1] Ingram (1981: 124), on the other hand, states that the Australian Second Language Proficiency Ratings (ASLPR) oral proficiency interview and scale are 'essentially concerned with language proficiency and not with communicative competence'. Moreover, the ASLPR is derived directly from the American FSI scale, itself described by Savignon (1983: 245) as 'one of the first tests to attempt to evaluate communicative competence'.

Other instances of statements, claims and definitions which can only result in confusion for the reader are not hard to find. For example, according to Richards (1985: 4), 'Language proficiency is hence not a global factor.' But according to Alderson *et al.* (1987: iv), 'Proficiency is a global construct.'

An attempt is needed to resolve some of these apparent contradictions.

3.2.2 The problem of generalization

As we saw in the previous chapter, the practical problem in performance assessment is the generalization from one observed instance of behaviour to other unobserved instances. To recapitulate briefly the argument presented there: the threat to the validity of such generalizations has been pointed out by numerous writers on performance assessment (Fitzpatrick and Morrison, 1971; Linn *et al.* 1991; Messick, 1994). One approach to the problem has been to adopt a sociolinguistic framework for the specification of the dimensions of the communicative task; that is, to view the question as reducible to one of content validity (cf. Weir, 1988a; Kelly, 1978; Moller, 1982). But Messick (1989: 17) explicitly rejects this view: 'In a fundamental sense so-called content validity does not count as validity at all.'

Even a writer such as Morrow (1979: 150–1), who advocates a severely practical approach and is sceptical of theory, recognizes the problem of what he calls 'extrapolation' in performance testing. His solution is to espouse the notion of 'enabling skills' proposed by Munby (1978). Morrow (1979: 152–3) comments on the function and status of these enabling skills in the following way:

The status of these enabling skills *vis-à-vis* competence : performance is interesting. They may be identified by an analysis of performance in operational terms, and thus they are clearly, ultimately performance-based. But at the same time, their application extends far beyond any one instance of performance and in this creativity they reflect an aspect of what is generally understood by competence. In this way they offer a possible approach to the problem of extrapolation.

This notion of enabling skills has been important in the design of language tests, particularly tests of reading, as well as of instructional materials: for a discussion of this, and a critique of the assumptions behind such an approach, see Lumley (1993).

3.2.3   Implicit vs explicit models

Even practical approaches which try to eschew theory imply a theoretical position. As noted in the previous chapter, this is often to be found in the *criteria* for assessment, which embody an implicit view of the construct being assessed. Such criteria spell out the relative importance to be attributed to different aspects of the performance; in other words, they contain an implicit theory of performance. We discussed two examples of this in Chapter 2: the rich model of communication, including of underlying abilities in performance, implicit in the tasks and criteria for assessment proposed by Savignon (1972); and the approach to criteria in the work of Clark, who refers to 'the ... performance criteria on which the test is conceptually based' (1972: 128).

3.2.4   The role of non-linguistic factors and the performance of native speakers

As we saw in the previous chapter, we need to understand the role of non-linguistic factors in performance, and their effect on inferences we may make about candidates' proficiency. J.B. Carroll (1954: 38) formulated the issue as early as 1954, in a discussion of performance on an oral task (talking on a topic for two or three minutes) in a first and in a second language:

> If we ask a group of examinees to discourse on a given theme in their *native* language, wide variation in performance will be noted.... There is a good likelihood, I think, that performance in a foreign language will reflect speaking ability in the native language. [Emphasis in original.]

Carroll himself was one of the first to develop some of the implications of Chomsky's competence/performance distinction for work in language assessment, including foreign language testing, and was clearly aware (Carroll, 1968: 50–1) of the issue of the role in second language performance contexts of non-linguistic variables which are not *specific* to such contexts:

> *The actual manifestation of linguistic competence ... in behavior may be called linguistic performance, and is affected by a large number of non-linguistic variables....* The single most important problem confronted by the language tester is that he cannot test competence in any direct sense; he can measure it only through manifestations of it in performance. Inevitably, therefore, there is the danger that non-linguistic variables in performance will mask the manifestations of competence. [Emphasis in original.]

Upshur (1979) was another to recognize and articulate the need for a model of abilities underlying performance, and the complexity of the issues involved. Of particular interest is his discussion of the role of non-linguistic factors in performance on second language performance tests. He discusses a hypothetical test of two non-native speakers of English, whose task it is to woo an American teenager. One is successful; the other fails. There is no difference in the candidates' language proficiency; it is just that the successful suitor encouraged and allowed the girl to talk. Is this the kind of sensitivity we should be measuring in a second language performance assessment, if we are to take tasks and task outcomes seriously? Wesche (1992: 105) similarly acknowledges the relevance of non-linguistic factors, when she raises the important issue of real-world criteria for judging performances:

> The criteria used to evaluate examinee performance likewise aim to approximate the way the performance would be judged in the actual target circumstances, including adequate fulfillment of the task. The distinguishing feature of performance tests, then, is that they tap both second language ability and the ability to fulfill the nonlinguistic requirements of given tasks.

If these non-linguistic variables are not specific to the second language performance situation, then we cannot assume that native speakers will perform better than non-native speakers in the tasks on our tests, as native and non-native speakers may not easily be distinguished in terms of the non-linguistic performance capacities that are involved in the tasks. A recent study (Hamilton *et al.*, 1993; see Chapter 7 below) has investigated the performance of native speakers on the IELTS test, and has shown that performance is systematically related to general cognitive skills as reflected in educational level. The assumptions about native speaker performance in the rating scale descriptors in this and related tests are not only factually wrong but are conceptually problematic. Issues of fairness about pass standards are raised by this overlap between native and non-native speaker performance on such tests.

3.2.5   Theory is needed to inform a research agenda

We need a theory of the role of non-language-specific cognitive and affective variables in language performance settings in order to make sense of research on performance testing and to provide a general framework in which to formulate explicit hypotheses about the relationship between candidate and rater behaviour and test scores. Examples are research on such issues as the effect of gender variables in oral interviews (Porter, 1991), the effect of differing pairings and groupings in task-based oral tests involving more than one candidate at a time (Iwashita, 1993), and raters' differing perceptions of the relevance of non-language skills (cf. Brown, 1995, on the difference between industry-based and education-based raters in the test of Japanese for tour guides, to be discussed in Chapter 8, or Elder, 1993b, on ratings of the classroom proficiency of foreign-trained teachers of maths and science by maths-background and ESL-background raters).

3.3   What is a theory of performance?

The most influential general discussion of language performance in applied linguistics is to be found in Hymes's theory of communicative competence (Hymes, 1967, 1972).[2] Features of this theory relevant to the discussion in this chapter are represented in tabular form in Figure 3.1.

Most relevant in this context is Hymes's distinction between, on the one hand, actual instances of language use in real time (as, for example,

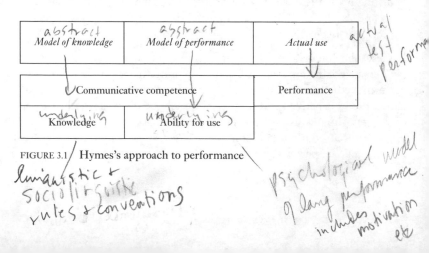

FIGURE 3.1 / Hymes's approach to performance

in actual test performance) and, on the other, abstract models of the underlying knowledge and capacities involved in language use. The importance of a distinction of this general kind – between actual use and underlying models – is a development of Chomsky's (1965: 4) competence/performance distinction[3]:

> We thus make a fundamental distinction between *competence* (the speaker–hearer's knowledge of his language) and *performance* (the actual use of language in concrete situations): [Emphasis in original.]

Hymes (1972) early on pointed out that there is an ambiguity in Chomsky's use of the term *performance*. Hymes (1972: 280) distinguishes two uses of the term:

1. (underlying) competence v. (actual) performance;
2. (underlying) grammatical competence v. (underlying) models/rules of performance.

Hymes distinguishes between *performance models* – ability as potential – and *actual use*, instances of the realization of this potential – 'actual performance' (Chomsky, 1965: 3). For Hymes, *ability for use* refers (Hornberger, 1989: 226) to 'the individual's potential to realize a possible, feasible and appropriate speech act, not to the realization itself'. Hymes (1989: 247) confirms that this is what he intended; *ability for use* is something 'underlying', a 'state'. The term *performance* is therefore reserved by Hymes for 'actual use and actual events' (1972: 283).[4]

The partial overlap between Hymes's distinctions and those proposed by Chomsky can easily lead to confusion, and so it is worth clearing up some terminology here. Further to the basic distinction between *competence* and *performance*, Chomsky (1980: 59) introduces a distinction between *grammatical competence* and *pragmatic competence*:

> I assume that it is possible in principle to have full grammatical competence and no pragmatic competence, hence no ability to use a language appropriately, though its syntax and semantics are intact.[5]

Figure 3.2 presents a tabular summary of distinctions made by Chomsky which are related to those made by Hymes.

Chomsky's focus of interest was of course in knowledge of language, not the capacities underlying performance. In contrast, *communicative competence* for Hymes encompasses *both* aspects of *knowledge* (now extended to include, in particular, sociolinguistic knowledge) and aspects of *performance*, or what Hymes terms *ability for use*.[6] That is, two areas of abstract modelling are proposed: *both* a *sociolinguistic* model of language knowledge *and* a broadly *psychological* model of language

Model of knowledge	Model of performance	Actual use
competence	performance	
grammatical competence	pragmatic competence	actual performance

FIGURE 3.2   Chomsky's approach to performance

performance, all subsumed under a single term, *communicative competence*.

The scope of *ability for use* is broad, and includes a range of cognitive and non-cognitive factors, none of them exclusive to language performance. Hymes (1972: 283) includes *motivation*:

> The specification of *ability for use* as part of competence allows for the role of noncognitive factors, such as motivation, as partly determining competence [emphasis in original]

as well as a range of other factors (explicated in detail by Goffman, 1967):

> ... capacities in interaction such as courage, gameness, gallantry, composure, presence of mind, dignity, stage confidence....

Of course such a list is not exhaustive, nor will it be possible to specify all such factors individually. The point rather is that some scope for consideration of such factors must be included in any adequate model.

An example may help. Native speakers are not all equally communicatively competent, as Hymes pointed out. Two educated native speakers may differ in their ability to tell jokes, for instance. What characterizes such a difference between them? It may still be partly a question of command of linguistic knowledge: jokes typically require the teller to imitate speakers of different registers or varieties – characters who are old, young, of a particular gender, or ethnic, national or professional background. Thus, command of speech styles or accents becomes important. But the joke teller possesses other characteristics which will determine the character and the quality of any particular instance of joke telling: a sense of timing, memory for the joke, an awareness of audience, confidence, an appreciation of the beauty of the joke (a sense of humour!), etc. There are also other factors to do with one's personality or identity as a person who tells jokes, and the social value of this in particular contexts.

In order then to properly understand a single instance of performance, and thus to distinguish between performances, as in performance assessment, Hymes is surely right to insist on a rich characterization of the performance capacities involved.

The distinctions proposed by Hymes are reflected in the discussions of other writers, who often (rather confusingly) use different terms for the same concepts. The terminological proliferation to be outlined in the following paragraphs is likely to cause confusion, and readers are encouraged to refer to Figure 3.3 as they read. This figure summarizes the key relation of the distinctions made by each writer in turn to those made by Hymes; essentially, these writers are reinforcing and restating Hymes's distinctions in different terms; cumulatively, they offer confirmation of the power of his distinctions. The reader should not dwell too much on the terminology; the main point is the way in which other writers have confirmed Hymes's basic insights.

Davies (1989) points out the need to distinguish two aspects of communicative competence, as Hymes does: knowledge *that* (Hymes's *knowledge*) from knowledge *how* (Hymes's *ability for use*). Davies (following Hymes) restricts the term *knowledge* to the former, but uses the terms *proficiency* or *control* to refer to the latter.[7] Davies's rephrasing of Hymes's basic distinction in terms of a frequently made distinction in philosophy[8] is helpful, although we may feel that the recommended terminology may in the end only lead to confusion, particularly the suggested restriction of the use of the term *proficiency*. Taylor (1988) has also examined and criticized Hymes's model. He has proposed relabelling the elements in Hymes's scheme – in terms of the distinctions in Figure 3.1, substituting the terms *competence* for *knowledge*, and *proficiency* for *ability for use* – but does not otherwise significantly develop Hymes's discussion; in fact the terminological quibbling is probably unhelpful in the end.

Hymes also points out that psycholinguistic performance models are models of aspects of his *ability for use*, hence part of *communicative competence*. An example of such a model, addressing the mental processing of language, is that of the psycholinguists Bialystok and Sharwood-Smith (1985); their work is typical of the strand of research in the area of second language acquisition which attempts to understand how language processing occurs in the course of language use. These authors substitute the terms *ability* and/or *proficiency* for Hymes's overarching term *communicative competence*, and propose a distinction within this between what they call *knowledge* and *control*, this latter term representing a psycholinguistic performance model of the kind just discussed. We can thus

Writer	Model of knowledge	Model of performance	Actual use
Hymes	communicative competence		performance
	knowledge	ability for use	
Davies	knowledge *that*	knowledge *how*	
	(knowledge)	(proficiency/control)	
Taylor	competence	proficiency	performance
Bialystok & Sharwood-Smith	ability/proficiency		
	(knowledge)	(control)	
Widdowson	communicative competence	communicative capacity	
	rules	procedures	

(handwritten annotations: "Knowledge of rules"; "ling & socioling Knowledge"; "procedural"; "ways of going about the task of making sense in particular contexts")

FIGURE 3.3   Variations on a theme: models of knowledge and performance

see that what they mean by *control* is one aspect of what Hymes terms *ability for use*.

The most important and helpful sustained engagement with Hymes's work is to be found in the writings of Widdowson (1983, 1984, 1989). This will be considered again below in the context of a discussion of the work of Canale and Swain (1980) and Canale (1983a, 1983b). It will be sufficient to say here that Widdowson again acknowledges and reinforces the usefulness of Hymes's distinction between *knowledge* and *ability for use*; but again, possibly less helpfully, he suggests changes in the use of familiar terms. He distinguishes (Widdowson, 1979) *rules* (knowledge of linguistic and sociolinguistics conventions – Hymes's *knowledge*) from *procedures* in the interpretation and creation of discourse coherence (ways of going about the task of making sense in particular contexts – an aspect of Hymes's *ability for use*), and thus distinguishes procedural or *communicative capacity*, which underpins the latter, from *communicative competence*, which he wishes to restrict to knowledge of rules.

The point of the analysis presented in this section has not been simply to catalogue a (potentially confusing) set of proliferating distinctions. Two main points have been established so far in the discussion.

First, Hymes introduced a distinction between language *knowledge* and *ability for use* of language which proves useful for understanding subsequent discussions of language performance tests. Language *knowledge* is relatively straightforward, and in the next section we will see that somewhat of a consensus has emerged about what aspects of this knowledge (of grammatical and other formal linguistic rules, sociolinguistic rules, etc.) it is appropriate to consider. *Ability for use*, on the other hand, is more difficult to grasp, because we need to consider here a range of underlying language-relevant but not language-exclusive cognitive and affective factors (including general reasoning powers, emotional states and personality factors) which are involved in performance of communicative tasks. Because these factors are not exclusive to the domain of language use they are not the preserve of language specialists; that have therefore been less often discussed in the language field and, consequently, their role in communication is less clearly understood.

Secondly, the distinction between *knowledge* and *ability for use* does not overlap neatly with the meaning of the terms *competence* and *performance* as introduced by Chomsky – terms which have greatly influenced discussion in applied linguistics of models of language knowledge and use. The main point is that we need to distinguish between *actual instances* of language use (in real time), what we might call *(actual) performance*, and the *potential* for that performance which is available to the speaker: this underlying potential is what Hymes calls *ability for use*. Making this distinction between potential for performance and actual instances of use is helpful when it comes to understanding discussions of communicative language testing, performance-based language tests, the approach to testing known as the Proficiency Movement, and the like.

3.4   Influential models of second language performance

We have looked briefly at Hymes's model of performance in his theory of communicative competence. In the next part of this chapter we will consider the two most important adaptations of Hymes's *first* language framework[9] for *second* language testing: the work of Canale and Swain and, more recently, that of Bachman and Palmer (Figure 3.4). The notion of *ability for use*, the model of underlying capacities in performance, has proved an area of difficulty in both cases. The discussion will focus on two aspects of the work of these writers:

(1) the different ways in which these sets of authors have accounted for the area covered by *ability for use* – that is, their models of performance-related non-language capacities;

(2) the relative coherence (or otherwise) of these accounts.

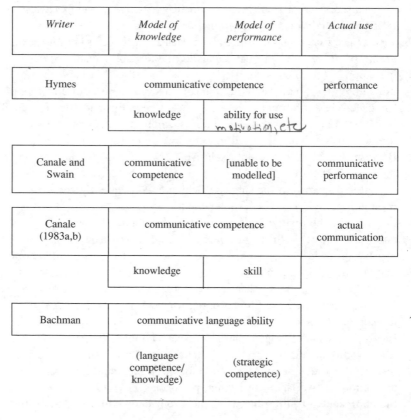

Writer	Model of knowledge	Model of performance	Actual use
Hymes	communicative competence		performance
	knowledge	ability for use	
Canale and Swain	communicative competence	[unable to be modelled]	communicative performance
Canale (1983a,b)	communicative competence		actual communication
	knowledge	skill	
Bachman	communicative language ability		
	(language competence/ knowledge)	(strategic competence)	

FIGURE 3.4   Major models of second language performance, and their relationship to Hymes's original distinctions

3.4.1 Canale and Swain

Although, as Spolsky (1989a: 151) has reminded us, the implications of Hymes's work for *second* language testing were quickly realized by Cooper (1968), Jakobovits (1969) and Brière (1971), it was not until over a decade later that a full discussion in the context of second language testing appeared, in the work of Canale and Swain (1980) (subsequently refined in Canale 1983a, 1983b). The model they proposed[10] dominated the field for a decade. Its most influential feature was its treatment of the domains of language knowledge as including, in addition to *grammatical* competence, *sociolinguistic* competence (following Hymes), *strategic* competence and (subsequently) *discourse* competence. The discussion in this chapter will perhaps ungenerously focus on the inconsistencies and contradictions resulting from the position taken in their model on the question of *ability for use*, that is, the way it deals with performance.

We consider what Canale and Swain have to say about *knowledge* of language, then about *ability for use*, and finally how they see the relation between actual *instances of use* and underlying knowledge and ability.

On the question of *knowledge* of language, Canale and Swain see it as consisting of linguistic, social and general cognitive aspects:

* *grammatical competence*
* *sociolinguistic competence*
* *strategic competence.*

Grammatical competence includes (Canale and Swain, 1980: 29) 'knowledge of lexical items and of rules of morphology, syntax, sentence-grammar semantics, and phonology'.

Sociolinguistic competence includes knowledge of sociocultural rules of use.

Strategic competence refers to the possession of ' "coping" strategies' (Canale and Swain, 1980: 31) in actual performance in the face of inadequacies in any of the other areas of competence.

Together, these three sub-competencies make up what Canale and Swain call *communicative competence*, thereby using the term in a fundamentally different way from Hymes, as it is restricted to language *knowledge*, solely. Canale and Swain (1980: 7) deliberately exclude *ability for use* from their model of communicative competence. This means that the model lacks a notion of potential for use or underlying skill. They are quite clear about this: they argue that while performance may demonstrate such factors as volition, motivation, etc., they 'doubt that there is any theory of human action that can adequately explicate *ability for use*' (1980: 7); and hence, as it cannot be modelled, it cannot be included in their framework. *Ability for use* is a Pandora's Box which they firmly refuse to open. They are also concerned that native speakers would appear not to display equal *ability for use*, and they object to the notion on grounds of social justice, quoting the debate about Bernstein's early work.

Instead, they view *ability for use* as simply part of what they call *communicative performance*, which they define (Canale and Swain, 1980: 6) as

> *the realization of these competencies* [i.e. the components of communicative competence proposed in their model] *and their interaction in the actual production and comprehension of utterances*

and subsequently (1980: 6) as

> *the actual demonstration of this knowledge* [i.e. of each of the four spheres of communicative competence in their definition] in *real* second language situations and for *authentic* communication purposes. [Emphasis in original.]

But it seems clear from this that *communicative performance* in fact refers only to *actual use*; it is behaviour, simply.

To summarize: Canale and Swain follow Hymes in seeing language *knowledge* as including knowledge of sociocultural rules of use (following Hymes), and also introduce a notion of *strategic competence* (to be discussed further below); they refuse to address the area of *ability for use* beyond saying that it is impossibly complex; and they see *instances of use*, which they call *communicative performance*, as 'demonstrating' or 'realizing' the aspects of knowledge they have proposed.

But there are problems with their position. First, it turns out that they do include aspects of *ability for use* in their discussion after all, although they do not acknowledge this. The difficulty is revealed in their discussion of *strategic competence*, which as we have seen refers to the possession of '"coping" strategies' (Canale and Swain, 1980: 31) in actual performance in the face of inadequacies in any of the other areas of competence. It is hard to see that what is involved here is knowledge rather than ability or skill; surely 'coping' is an aspect of performance, involving general reasoning or problem-solving capacities, as well as imaginativeness, and also possibly personality factors – preparedness to take risks, versatility, adaptability – Goffman's 'capacities in interaction'. Bachman (1990) recognizes the problem here. In his model, to be discussed below, he recognizes the importance of *strategic competence* in performance but does not see it as an aspect of language *knowledge*.

Another problematic feature of the Canale and Swain model is acknowledged by Canale (1983a: 12):

The question of *how* these components interact with one another (or with other factors involved in actual communication) has been largely ignored here; that is, this theoretical framework is not a model of communicative competence, where model implies some specification of the manner and order in which the components interact and in which the various competencies are normally acquired. [Emphasis in original.]

The interaction of the components is again relegated to the area of *communicative performance* (Canale and Swain, 1980: 6).

The discussion of this term (the definition is given above) itself reveals an important issue. The first thing to note is that the stress on 'actual' performance is in line with the generally accepted notion, first developed in the 1970s, that a test of communicative competence will require performance-based assessment. Secondly, the comment is relevant to the discussion of the two traditions in language performance assessment in the previous chapter. In the first, known as the 'work sample' tradition, instances of use are valued in their own right, as representing relevant real-world tasks, reflecting relevant situations and purposes; the object of assessment is to establish whether and how well a candidate can cope with the tasks set. In the second tradition, instances of use are seen as revealing underlying psychological constructs – for example, language knowledge or language-relevant performance skills. If we examine Canale and Swain's remarks on communicative performance carefully, then we see an unacknowledged, potentially uneasy compounding of both traditions. On the one hand, the references to '*real* second language situations and for *authentic* communication purposes' clearly derive from the tradition of 'work sample' performance testing and echo the language of Clark (1972). However, there is something else: the performance also has the function of revealing underlying knowledge of language in the domains specified in Canale and Swain's model. That is, there is now explicit and detailed reference to a theory of broad areas of language knowledge, in addition to a content specification in terms of situational needs. However, as we have seen, there is a refusal in this model to consider a theory of underlying skills or abilities in performance.

By way of confirmation of this interpretation, it seems in fact that Swain and Canale could not agree on the role of such a theory, as is evident from a comparison of the original 1980 jointly authored paper with a later paper written by Canale alone (Canale, 1983a). In this later paper, a model of underlying abilities in performance is called for, thus reversing the position taken in the 1980 paper. Canale prefers the term *actual communication* to the previous term *performance*, because of the possibility that the term will be understood only in the sense introduced by Chomsky (1965). Canale (1983a: 6) distinguishes *actual communication* and the knowledge and skills underlying it in the following way:

> Both knowledge and skill underlie actual communication in a systematic and necessary way, and are thus included in communicative competence.... This view is not only consistent with the distinction between communicative competence and actual communication but depends crucially on it; in particular, this notion of skill – how well one can perform knowledge in actual situations – requires a distinction between underlying capacities (competence) and their manifestation in concrete situations (actual communication).

Canale thus aligns himself far more closely with the position of Hymes than in the previous jointly authored paper, and is altering the scope of the term *communicative competence*; he is now using it in precisely the way Hymes used it, as covering both *knowledge* AND *ability for use*. He is also clear about the necessity of modelling other factors in performance (1983a: 6):

> It is assumed that this theory of communicative competence interacts in as yet unspecified ways with other systems of knowledge and skill (e.g. world knowledge) as well as with a theory of human action (dealing with such factors as volition and personality).

Swain (personal communication) comments on the Canale (1983a) paper as follows:

> Michael [Canale] and I disagreed on this point [i.e. the question of performance] – I was much more 'performance oriented' but Michael wanted to maintain the performance/competence distinction ... What you see in the Richards and Schmidt book [i.e. Canale (1983a)] is Michael's view.

Despite Canale's recognition of the need for a theory of performance, other aspects of his position as outlined in two papers written about the same time (Canale 1983a, 1983b) remain inconsistent. In these papers, Canale introduces a fourth aspect of language knowledge, *discourse competence*, which concerns (Canale, 1983a: 9)

> mastery of how to combine grammatical forms and meanings to achieve a unified spoken or written text in different genres.... Unity of a text is achieved through *cohesion* in form and *coherence* in meaning. [Emphasis in original.]

Cohesion clearly involves linguistic knowledge, of the sort set out in Halliday and Hasan (1976). However, it is not clear that the ability to perceive and create coherence in discourse is a matter of knowledge entirely. Canale (1983a: 9) appeals to Widdowson's work to explicate the notion of coherence. However, as we have seen, Widdowson has distinguished *rules* from *procedures* in the interpretation and creation of discourse coherence (see, for example, Widdowson, 1979: ch. 10); he also distinguishes procedural or communicative *capacity*, which cannot be reduced to a knowledge of rules, from *communicative competence* in his sense (Widdowson, 1983, 1984). For example (Widdowson, 1984: 238):

> Actual communication involves the use of interpretative procedures to associate particular instances of behaviour with familiar schemata and to modify them where necessary by using a knowledge of syntax and semantics as a resource. These procedures, then, exploit and extend knowledge of language at the level of communicative schema, communicative competence, and at the level of system rules, linguistic competence. It is ability to engage or activate this knowledge for actual behavioural outcomes by means of these interpretative procedures that I refer to as communicative *capacity*. It is this which mediates between knowledge and behaviour and which is exercised in the discourse process. [Emphasis in original.]

Widdowson here actually uses the term *ability* to refer to what is involved in the use of the procedures, and distinguishes *knowledge* both from the procedures themselves and the ability involved in their use.

Further, Canale (1983b: 339) extends the scope of *strategic competence* to include the ability 'to enhance the rhetorical effect of utterances'. More generally, he sees *strategic competence* as operating in relation to each of *grammatical competence, sociolinguistic competence* and *discourse competence* (Canale, 1983a: 11):

> Of course such strategies need not be limited to resolving grammatical problems: actual communication will also require learners to handle problems of a sociolinguistic nature ... and of a discourse nature (e.g. how to achieve coherence in a text when unsure of cohesion devices).

As before, what is involved here is not so much knowledge as ability or skill. The example of *strategic competence* in relation to discourse seems to be precisely what Widdowson had in mind in his notion of the 'exercise of communicative capacity'.

Critics of the Canale and Swain model (cf. Candlin, 1986; Shohamy, 1988; Hornberger, 1989; Spolsky, 1985, 1989a) have taken up some of the points raised so far. For example, in the context of his discussion of tests of functional proficiency, Spolsky (1985) regrets Canale and Swain's exclusion of performance from their model of communicative competence.[11]

Shohamy (1988: 167) also comments on the need for investigation of the interaction of the components of communicative competence:

> Current approaches to second language testing view language in a communicative context. In order to describe the communicative oral trait, one needs to identify its main components and their internal relationship. A review of the literature, however, makes clear that the available communicative models mostly *list* their components without examining their relationship. [Emphasis in original.]

This point is in fact recognized by Canale (1983a: 12), as we have seen. Of particular interest is the relationship of grammatical competence to other aspects of communicative competence, and research on this issue is reported in Chapter 8.

In summary, the model of Canale and Swain (1980) attempts to eschew models of performance, though it fails to hold to this position itself. Canale subsequently modified his position to admit of such a model, but maintains and extends the inconsistencies in the earlier model in relation to *knowledge* and *ability for use*. Some of these problems are recognized and corrected by Bachman, although not all, as we shall now see.

3.4.2   Bachman (1990)

The model of Canale and Swain has been the basis for an elaboration by Bachman and Palmer (1982, 1984), Bachman (1988) and most importantly Bachman (1990), which contains the fullest treatment of the topic. Bachman (1990) proposes a model of *Communicative Language Ability* in which he distinguishes three components:

- Language competence
- Strategic competence
- Psychophysiological mechanisms/skills.

The conceptual structure of Communicative Language Ability is shown in Figure 3.5 (Bachman, 1990: 85) and Figure 3.6 (Bachman, 1990: 87).

Bachman's 1990 model looks dauntingly complex at first sight, but it is easier to understand if we see it as a refinement and elaboration of Canale and Swain's work, rather than an altogether new departure. Bachman has something new to say about *knowledge* of language: he proposes a reorganization and some degree of recategorization of the components of this

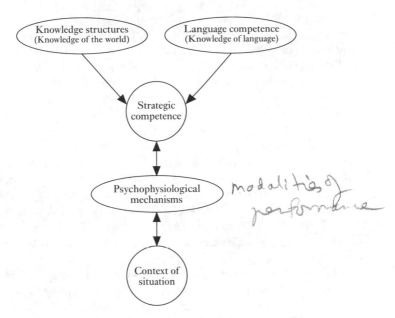

FIGURE 3.5   Components of communicative language ability in communicative language use (Bachman, 1990: 85)

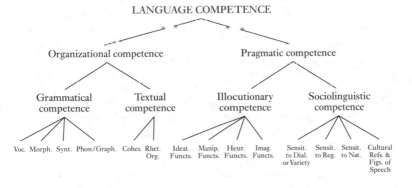

FIGURE 3.6   Components of language competence (Bachman, 1990: 87)

knowledge. This is useful, but does not constitute a major change. More importantly, Bachman begins to discuss, explicitly, aspects of the area Hymes called *ability for use*, in his treatment of an expanded *strategic competence*: this corrects the inconsistency in Canale and Swain's model, noted above. But Bachman does not go as far as Canale (1983a, 1983b), and the model contains inconsistencies of its own.

The model covers three basic areas: *knowledge* of language, here termed *language competence*; some cognitive aspects of *ability for use*, here termed *strategic competence*; and a discussion of modalities of performance (rather grandly titled *psychophysiological mechanisms*[12]).

First, what does the Bachman model say about *knowledge* of language?

Language competence (glossed (Bachman, 1990: 105) as 'control of the rules of usage and use') is seen as consisting of two main aspects: *organizational* and *pragmatic competence*.

Organizational competence includes the knowledge involved in creating or recognizing grammatically correct utterances and comprehending their propositional content (*grammatical competence*), and in organizing them to form texts (*textual competence*).

Pragmatic competence includes knowledge of the pragmatic conventions for performing felicitous language functions (*illocutionary competence*) and knowledge of sociolinguistic rules of appropriateness (*sociolinguistic competence*).

Bachman's reorganization of the components of language knowledge is on the basis of the results of empirical studies attempting to validate the constructs proposed in the Canale and Swain model (Bachman and Palmer, 1982; Allen *et al.*, 1983). Bachman and Palmer (1982), using data from adult speakers of English as a second language, found that what later came to be called *grammatical* and *textual* competence clustered together in the results of a confirmatory factor analysis, and were distinct from *sociolinguistic* competence. Allen *et al.* (1983) compared data from grade 6 children in a French immersion programme with data from a smaller group of grade 6 native speakers of French, and found that (1983: 50)

> the grammatical trait is clearly different from the discourse trait, though the position of the sociolinguistic trait is less clear ...
>
> [The results provide] some strong validation at least for the model's distinction between grammatical and discourse competence.

Bachman's reorganization and relabelling of some of the components of the Canale and Swain model involves some risk of confusion for readers. However, Bachman's is a more coherent model and deals with some of the inconsistencies noted in the discussion of Canale and Swain above. One important new aspect is in the way discourse capacity (still loosely defined) is handled.

First, Canale's unsatisfactory *Discourse competence* is broken up, and the elements (*cohesion* and *coherence*) redistributed. Cohesion goes to *textual competence*, part of *organizational competence* (the other part being *grammatical competence*, the two together representing 'those abilities involved in controlling the formal structure of language'). Coherence is itself divided between *illocutionary competence* and *strategic competence.* Secondly, the area covered by Canale and Swain's term *strategic competence* is reconceptualized, as we shall now see: it is recognized as being more properly part of *ability for use*, not *knowledge.*

The significant feature of Bachman's model, from the point of view of the present discussion, is that Bachman, unlike Canale and Swain, is prepared to open the Pandora's Box of *ability for use* – or at least to open it a crack. *Communicative language ability* does include a limited model of underlying capacities in performance, corresponding to at least the cognitive aspects of *ability for use.* In the model, Bachman separates knowledge of and about language (*language competence*) from more general cognitive skills involved in language use, which he calls *strategic competence.*[13]

Strategic competence is not part of *language competence.* It involves ability in assessing and planning as part of determining and executing the most effective means of achieving a communicative goal. *Strategic competence* is defined (Bachman, 1990: 106) as 'a general ability, which enables an individual to make the most effective use of available abilities in carrying out a given task'.[14]

Bachman's *strategic competence* is more appropriately understood as ability, capability or capacity than an area of knowledge. Bachman (1990: 102) defines it in this way:

> communication involves a dynamic interchange between context and discourse, so that communicative language use is not characterized simply by the production or interpretation of texts, but by the relationship that obtains between a text and the context in which it occurs. The interpretation of discourse, in other words, requires the ability to utilize available language competencies to assess the context for relevant information and then match this information to information in the discourse. It is the function of strategic competence to match the new information to be processed with relevant information that is available (including presuppositional and real world knowledge) and map this onto the maximally efficient use of existing language abilities.

Strategic competence is seen as differentiating the performance of native speakers as well as of non-native speakers.[15] In certain kinds of language test (e.g. those involving tasks requiring negotiation) (Bachman, 1990: 105) 'it may well be that performance is affected more by *strategic competence* than by the specific language ability the test was originally intended to measure'.[16]

Strategic competence is here seen as a potential source of difficulty in the interpretation of test scores if its role in the test-taking situation is unrecognized and it remains simply an unknown quantity in any particular assessment context. The problem is, as Bachman argues (1990: 106), that 'some types of language test tasks seem to involve strategic competence to a greater degree than do others'.

Elsewhere (Bachman and Savignon, 1986: 384) the implications of this fact for the interpretation of test scores are considered:

> we are usually interested in interpreting a language test score as an indicator of an individual's *language* ability, rather than as an indicator of his or her ability to take tests of a particular type. ...
>
> The interpretation of test scores is particularly problematic when the distinction between ability and method is not clear, as is generally the case in tests where modalities (expressive/interpretive, oral/visual) of ability and method match (of which the oral interview is an example). [Emphasis in original.]

The construct validity of 'direct' tests is thus not as transparent as some might like to think. This issue is discussed with great clarity in Bachman (1990: chs 7 and 8).

Strategic competence then seems to include cognitive factors other than language ability; it is not clear to what extent it includes the type of affective or volitional factors included by Hymes in his model. Volitional factors at least do seem to be included; language users (1990: 105) 'differ in their willingness to exploit what they [know] and their flexibility in doing so'.

Two further observations may be made of the Bachman model. First, it recognizes the issue of the interaction of the components of communicative competence (1990: 81): ' ... it attempts to characterize the processes by which the various components interact with each other and with the context in which language use occurs'. *Strategic competence* is the means by which this is handled in the model.

Secondly, despite the inclusion in the model of the abilities covered under *strategic competence*, Bachman still seems to have failed to take satisfactory account of Widdowson's notion of interpretative capacity as expressed above. It was argued in relation to the discussion of Canale (1983a) that *discourse competence* is not a question of knowledge alone. The same point is true of Bachman's *illocutionary competence* (1990: 94):

> Illocutionary competence enables us to use language to express a wide range of functions, and to interpret the illocutionary force of utterances or discourse.

If *illocutionary competence* were taken to include only the routinized realizations of language functions referred to by Widdowson in his term 'communicative schemata', then we could see *illocutionary competence* as a form of knowledge. However, Bachman also uses it to refer to cases involving (1990: 91)

> a sentence type whose form is not generally associated with the given illocutionary act, and whose interpretation depends very heavily on the circumstances under which the act is performed.

The successful interpretation of such utterances involves Widdowson's *communicative capacity*, which, as we have argued above, does not involve rule use but procedural activity. There is clear overlap between *illocutionary competence* and *strategic competence*: consider the following (1990: 102), presented in the discussion of *strategic competence*, but clearly directly relevant to the issue raised in the quotation above:

> The interpretation of discourse, in other words, requires the ability to utilize available language competencies to assess the context for relevant information and then to match this information to information in the discourse.

Bachman's notion of *illocutionary competence*, then, involves some of the same difficulties as Canale's notion of *discourse competence*.

Despite this, Bachman's model is more adequate than that of Canale and Swain (1980): as in the later work of Michael Canale, a start has been made on acknowledging the role of aspects of *ability for use* in performance, although in Bachman (1990) these are restricted mainly to general cognitive factors. Nonetheless, the separation of *strategic competence* from *language competence* is an important step. The model helps to clarify our conceptualization of language performance in test settings, and thus enables better investigation of the claims of tests to be assessing communicative language ability. No model can remove the problem of test validation, either conceptually or empirically; but it can provide a framework within which this may be done. To repeat a point made at the beginning of the chapter: Messick (1989: 13) describes validity as 'an integrated evaluative judgement of the degree to which empirical evidence and theoretical rationales support the adequacy and appropriateness of inferences and actions based on test scores'. A model such as Bachman's helps us to articulate the 'theoretical rationale' for such inferences: it helps us develop the necessary clarity, specificity and explicitness in stating the grounds for inferences about candidates' abilities made on the basis of test performance, thereby also facilitating the empirical investigation of such claims. It is disappointing that Bachman

(1990), a major work, has been so little reviewed and discussed in the main journals in our field, although it is having a significant influence on major practical testing projects in the US, the UK and Australia. One response to Bachman's work has come from Spolsky, who comments (1989a: 147) that although Bachman's model, like Canale and Swain's, is complex, it is not complex enough:

> I am forced to conclude, then, that the model of communicative competence proposed by Canale and Swain is oversimplified, as is the somewhat different three-component model described by Bachman (1988).

Spolsky in turn offers a 'preference model' of language proficiency, 'drawing on communicative competence' (1989a: 145), although it is as yet not entirely clear what this would mean in detail. Spolsky seems to be pointing out the inevitability of the influence of current conceptual developments in linguistics and cognitive science on future models of second language knowledge and use, but the precise form of the resulting models remains a subject for speculation at this stage.[17]

3.4.3   Bachman and Palmer: an amended model

More recently, Bachman and Palmer (in press) have made significant revisions of their framework, to include for the first time an explicit modelling of the role of affective factors in language use; that is, the role of non-cognitive factors underlying performance is explicitly addressed. We will now briefly outline some of the issues raised in this work.

The changes are of three main kinds (Figure 3.7). An affective component has been added; and *Strategic competence* has been reconceptualized as a set of *Metacognitive strategies*. In addition, there has been some re-labelling, so that, for example, the former *Knowledge structures* is now *Topical knowledge*.

As before we will consider the new model from the point of view of what it has to stay about language *knowledge*, and about *ability for use*. There are minor changes in the former area, more substantial changes in the latter.[18]

In terms of *knowledge* of language, the changes are mainly nominal. Within the category of *Pragmatic knowledge*, the earlier *illocutionary competence* has been relabelled *Functional knowledge*, but is otherwise unchanged.

In terms of *ability for use*, the changes are more significant for our discussion. The overall model has been given a new component, called *affective schemata* (sometimes *affect*); these are glossed as 'the affective or

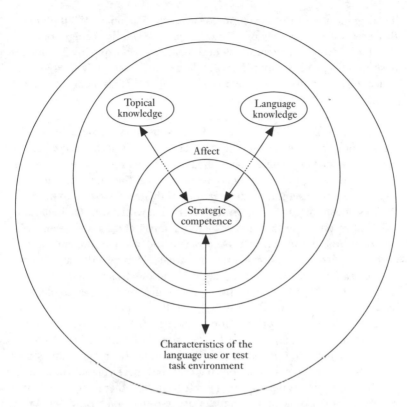

FIGURE 3.7   Language use and language test performance (Bachman and Palmer, in press)

emotional correlates of topical knowledge', which in turn are character-ized as 'knowledge structures in long-term memory'. The justification for the inclusion of *affective schemata* in the model of language ability is argued in the following terms:

> These affective schemata are the means by which language users assess the characteristics of the language use task and its environment in terms of past emotional experiences in similar contexts. The affective schemata, in combination with the characteristics of the particular task, determine, to a large extent, the language user's affective response to the task, and can both facilitate and limit the flexibility with which he responds in a given context. The affective responses of language users will thus determine not only whether they even attempt to use language in a given situation, but also how flexible they are in adapting their language use to variations in the environment.

The significance of this development from the Bachman (1990) model is that progressively, aspects of Hymes's *ability for use* are being modelled. For the first time, an attempt has been made to deal explicitly in a model of second language communicative ability with the aspect of *ability for use* which relates to affective or volitional factors.[19] This is an important advance.

In fact, however, Bachman and Palmer, having confidently lifted the lid on Pandora's Box, shut it again. Their subsequent discussion of the significance of the inclusion of the affective domain in language perfor-mance is restricted to some advice about how to 'bias for the best' (Swain, 1984) in the design of test procedures; that is, in the words of Bachman and Palmer, 'to design the characteristics of the test task so as to promote feelings of comfort and safety in test takers that will in turn facilitate flex-ibility of response on their part'. Here Bachman and Palmer seem to be restricting the discussion of the impact of the affective domain on test performance to the desire to improve what Henning (1987a: 96) calls *response validity* (cf. Henning *et al.*, 1985, and the discussion of this issue in Chapter 9). Moreover, the advice they do give on the need to consider test taker characteristics[20] in the test task design only partly recognizes the complications and opportunities presented as a result. We should not underestimate the complexity of the practical decisions arising. Bachman and Palmer point out, for example, that emotionally charged topics may inhibit some students from displaying their best performance (one might object that this is not necessarily the case). On the other hand, 'emotional responses can also facilitate language use', so that some candidates may do well on a face-to-face oral interview because it gives outlet to their confident social and interactional skills. They recommend attention to the interviewer's manner with those test takers who are uncomfortable with oral interviews. (The necessary research is only just beginning to be carried out (e.g. Morton and Wigglesworth, 1994) and the practical implications are not yet clear.) On the other hand, they argue that deci-sions about choice of test method (for example in favour of face-to-face formats in assessments of oral interaction) which may have been made on the grounds of faithfulness to the target language use situation should not be reversed because of concerns about the variability of learners' affective reactions to particular test formats; this implies that in certain cirum-stances the variable of the candidate's affective response to the task forms part of appropriate test content (that is should be included in the test), and in other circumstances the test task should be designed to avoid the effect of this on test scores. It is not clear on what basis in principle these kinds of circumstances can be distinguished; presumably the affective domain is in principle equally relevant in all language performance.

To return to our discussion of the broader dimensions of the new model proposed by Bachman and Palmer: within *ability for use* two kinds of broad aspects are now being conceptualized: cognitive and non-cognitive. Cognitively, we now have *topical knowledge* (*knowledge structures, knowledge of the world* in the 1990 version) and *affective schemata*. Both of these are cognitive structures (essentially memories) and in this respect resemble *language knowledge*, i.e. they contain the fruits of previous experience of the world and of language use; they are as it were repositories which are drawn upon as a resource in a communicative situation. The other broad aspect of *ability for use* is a process dimension, *strategic competence*, consisting of areas of *metacognitive strategy* use.[21]

We will not attempt to discuss all aspects of how metacognitive strategies are dealt with in the latest work. Briefly, three such strategies are recognized: *Goal-setting, assessment* and *planning*. Each of these strategies is seen as interacting with each of the components of the model (*language knowledge, topical knowledge* and *affective schemata*). The picture of cognitive activity is thus relatively complex, although the discussion is extremely brief. As an example, we will consider how the metacognitive strategy of *assessment* is seen as interacting with *affective schemata* (*assessment* is glossed as 'taking stock of what is needed, what one has to work with, and how well one has done'.) In general, 'assessment ... takes into consideration the individual's affective responses, which function as a global "filter" in the application of assessment strategies'. (We might note here the echoes of the well-known 'affective filter' proposed by Krashen, 1982.) In one part of the assessment process, assessment takes into account 'the individual's available affective schemata for coping with the demands of the task'. In assessment subsequent to the performance, 'affective schemata are involved in determining the extent to which failure was due to inadequate effort, to the difficulty of the task, or because there were random sources of interference.'

This account strikes the reader as being extremely preliminary; obviously, such strategic use touches on major topics in psychology, social psychology and pragmatics, and in a fuller discussion reference to the literature in those areas would be helpful and appropriate. A further point, to be returned to below, is that the view of communication involved is strangely one-sided; a view of communicative performance as interactive and co-constructed would be more appropriate.

Nevertheless, the current revision to the 1990 model represents a potentially far-reaching development. Volitional and affective dimensions of *ability for use* are at last being explored; the difficulties Bachman and Palmer experience in doing so may appear to justify Canale and Swain's initial scepticism about the feasibility of this endeavour. But as we have seen, failure to address the issue at all leads to contradiction and incoherence; and we need some account of these matters as a necessary framework for validation research.

As an illustration of the way in which these issues and problems can arise in a popular procedure for performance assessment, we will consider the way in which performance is understood in one of the most prominent kinds of language performance test, the oral proficiency interview.

3.5   The Proficiency Movement: 'proficiency' versus 'communicative competence'

Lowe (1988) provides a history of the 'Proficiency Movement' (Omaggio, 1983), which had its origins in an approach (first developed in the 1950s) to the testing of ability in spoken communication in a variety of foreign languages among employees in US government agencies, including the Foreign Service Institute (FSI), the Peace Corps, the CIA and others (Clark and Clifford, 1988). The approach spread to the measurement of achievement in foreign languages in university settings in the early 1980s through the efforts of the American Council on the Teaching of Foreign Languages (ACTFL, 1986), under whose auspices it became a full-scale curriculum and assessment movement. The best-known feature of the assessment procedure associated with the Proficiency Movement is the Oral Proficiency Interview (OPI) and associated rating scale for determining the level of the candidate's performance; the ACTFL scale derives from the original FSI scale, although there are differences between the two.[22]

The practical stance of the Proficiency Movement, which essentially rejects the position taken in this chapter on the need for an explicit theory of performance in performance assessment, is asserted as an advantage by its proponents: the Proficiency Guidelines (ACTFL, 1986) 'are experientially, rather than theoretically based' (Omaggio, 1983: 331). But, according to Bachman (1988: 160), the fact that the ACTFL Oral Proficiency Interview (OPI) 'is based on procedures that have been developed over years of practice and about which a good deal of experience has accumulated ... in no way constitutes direct evidence for the validity of the test'.

Bachman and other critics have repeatedly questioned the validity of the OPI (for example, Lantolf and Frawley, 1985; Bachman and Savignon, 1986; Shohamy, 1990). As the debate between advocates and

critics of the proficiency movement in the American context is well docu-
mented, we will consider the issues as they arise in relation to the
Australian Second Language Proficiency Ratings (ASLPR) (Ingram,
1984), an Australian proficiency scale and interview procedure derived
directly from the American models.

First, what do the Proficiency Movement and its proficiency scales say
about *knowledge of language*? Lowe (1988: 12) offers the following definition of proficiency:

> Proficiency equals achievement (functions, content, accuracy) plus
> functional evidence of internalized strategies for creativity expressed
> in a single global rating of general language ability over a wide range of
> functions and topics at any given level.

The scope of this definition has been criticized by Bachman and
Savignon (1986) and Bachman (1988). At issue have been the weight
given to sociolinguistic and discourse–related knowledge on the one
hand, and accuracy on the other. Lowe (1988: 14–15) suggests that
Bachman's model of Communicative Language Ability (CLA) and the
approach of the Proficiency Movement 'may prove incompatible. The
position of accuracy within CLA remains unclear.' On the other hand,
Bachman and Savignon (1986: 381), in comparing the two models or
approaches, stress commonalities:

> Discussions of language proficiency [within the Proficiency Move-
> ment] explicitly include components of language use other than gram-
> mar.... We are struck more by similarities than differences [in the two
> approaches]. Indeed, we find substantive differences only in the rela-
> tive importance accorded to the different components, rather than in
> the components themselves.

They suggest that the Proficiency Movement adopt a definition of proficiency 'that includes (at least) grammatical, discourse, and sociolinguistic
competence'.

On the question of performance, the Proficiency Movement is in a
curious position. Central to the idea of proficiency testing in this
approach is the requirement of actual performance: performance is criterial for this kind of testing. In 'direct' tests such as the ASLPR the components of knowledge are to be measured *in actual performance*.

However, the ASLPR and related approaches do not include a model
of factors underlying performance – a model of performance, in our
terms; in fact, like Canale and Swain, they wish to deliberately exclude
ability for use as a component in their understanding of proficiency. We

thus have the contradictory position of, on the one hand, a performance requirement (a focus on actual *instances of use*) but, on the other, a principled exclusion of underlying general performance capacities in evaluations of test performance. This is expressed in a curious way by Ingram in the distinction he consistently draws between *proficiency* and *communicative competence*: the ASLPR oral proficiency interview and scale are 'essentially concerned with language proficiency and not with communicative competence' (Ingram, 1981: 124).

Quoting Sollenberger (1978), Ingram seems to be equating *language proficiency* with 'the technical ability to use a foreign language without noticeable accent or grammatical errors'. The same implication is present in the further quote from Sollenberger (1978: 8):

> On the other hand I know people who butcher the language, whose accents are atrocious and whose vocabularies are limited. For those reasons we give them a low proficiency rating. Yet, for some reason, some of them are effective communicators.

Clearly, for Ingram and Sollenberger, *proficiency* relates to *knowledge* rather than *ability for use*, where factors which may compensate for gaps in the speaker's command of formal resources are usually located. This interpretation is supported by the following remarks (Ingram, 1981: 124):

> Granted that language is used by people with different personalities, with different levels of intelligence and education, and with different experiences, it is unlikely that any discrete measure of communicative competence can realistically be achieved.

It seems that Ingram recognizes that performance will be determined in part by a range of factors to do with personality, intelligence and education, and so on: *ability for use*, in short. Ingram, like Canale and Swain, wishes to somehow exclude this. But it cannot, of course, be excluded. Ingram recognizes that the difficulty may extend to the interactional aspect of the interview, where the sociocultural identity and resulting socioculturally determined behaviour of the interviewer come into play (Ingram, 1981: 122):

> It should be remembered that the interview is measuring the learner's performance in the second language and culture, and hence it is language proficiency and not communicative competence that is at issue, and some compromise in sociocultural matters may be needed to allow the learner to perform to the full extent of his ability....

The 'compromise' is that, for example, a candidate should not be expected to have to cope with an interviewer who has been perceived by the candidate (on the basis of a lack of relevant sociocultural knowledge) as being 'distant' or 'off-hand'. Apart from the fact that it is not clear how this could be controlled operationally, the recommendation to exclude sociocultural competence from the assessment is odd, given that the argument for its *inclusion* by Hymes is universally accepted, and regarded as one of his most significant contributions.

Ingram's position seems to be something like this: the task of an assessor is to make an assessment of abstract underlying *knowledge* of language (*proficiency*) on the basis of performance, while not getting distracted by the 'irrelevant' factors (including questions of sociocultural competence) that a performance requirement can introduce. Even if we accept Ingram's position at face value, the desire for a separation of underlying proficiency and contextual factors in the assessment setting is programmatic at best, merely a desideratum: it is a statement of the *intended* validity of the test. But by assuming this process is unproblematic, it provides no basis for investigating threats to the validity of rater judgements, and providing empirical evidence for their validity. It *assumes* the validity of the procedure rather than being committed to demonstrating it, as Messick (1989: 13) requires. Ingram (1984: 5) devotes a single sentence to the construct validity of the ASLPR: 'The process described above by which the ASLPR was developed has, hopefully, ensured these forms of validity [i.e. construct and content validity].' Hopefully indeed: the 'process' has been described on a single page (Ingram, 1984: 1–2), and contains no theoretical discussion. Ingram's belief in the automatic validity of his procedure amounts to no more than a broad claim about its face validity; the apparent naïveté of this position stifles investigation into the hard questions about fairness and validity that need to asked about this and kindred procedures. Of course Ingram is not alone in this complacency, which is an unfortunate characteristic of much practice in performance-based assessment, including criterion-referenced assessment, competency-based assessment and the like.

It may be helpful to compare the essential features of Ingram's model of language proficiency with those of Hymes and Canale and Swain, in order to note the main similarities and differences (Figure 3.8).

3.6   A note on the theory of performance in Oller's 'pragmatic tests'

It is necessary to say a word about the place of John Oller in this discussion of the nature of performance in second language tests. Oller (1979) advocated types of performance test (*pragmatic tests*) which focused not so

Writer	Model of knowledge	Model of performance	Actual use
Hymes	communicative competence		performance
	knowledge	ability for use	

Writer	Model of knowledge	Model of performance	Actual use
Canale and Swain	communicative competence	[unable to be modelled]	communicative performance

Writer	Model of knowledge	Model of performance	Actual use
Ingram	communicative competence		performance
	language proficiency		

FIGURE 3.8   'Proficiency' and its relation to performance

much on replicating tasks candidates might face in the world as on tasks which demanded of candidates the same processing of language (understood in psycholinguistic terms) as is required in any real-world second language performance. Thus, tests requiring performances on relatively artificial tasks such as filling in gaps in a cloze passage or taking dictation were held to be as valid as performance tests involving more 'authentic' tasks which more obviously simulated real-world activities.

Oller developed an explicit theory of performance in these pragmatic (i.e. communicative) tests. Oller's 'pragmatic expectancy grammar' (Oller, 1979: 16) represents the first serious attempt to discuss the nature of performance in second language testing contexts (thus predating Canale and Swain):

> The object of interest is language as it is used for communicative purposes ... The notion of *expectancy* is introduced as a key to understanding the nature of psychologically real processes that underlie language use.

The 'processes that underlie language use' clearly reflect Hymes's concept of *ability for use*, defined, as we have seen earlier, as '*(underlying) models/rules of performance*'. There are two aspects of Oller's view of performance: Oller refers to them (1979: 33) as '*pragmatic naturalness criteria*' for valid pragmatic tests:

First, they must cause the learner to process ... temporal sequences of elements in the language that conform to normal contextual constraints (linguistic and extralinguistic); second, they must require the learner to understand the pragmatic interrelationship of linguistic contexts and extralinguistic contexts.

The first requirement is of naturalness of real-time processing; it represents *both* a performance requirement (an *instance of use*) *and* a (relatively inexplicit) psycholinguistic processing model (cf. the comments made above on other psycholinguistic processing models, such as that of Bialystok and Sharwood-Smith (1985)). The second requirement is of the integration of linguistic and extralinguistic or real-world knowledge; different aspects of cognitive organization are involved.[23]

The relevance of this model to the 'work sample' tradition of performance testing (see previous chapter) is suggested by Wesche (1985), who draws on Oller to characterize the nature of performance in such tests. Wesche sees 'work sample' tests as a subcategory of pragmatic tests, in that they involve sociolinguistically precise specifications of the 'extralinguistic contexts' relevant to the test use context.

3.7 Communicative competence in first and second languages

A theme of this chapter has been the difficulty with which Hymes's rich understanding of communicative competence, developed in a first language context, has been incorporated into thinking about the ability to communicate in a second language. But why should communicative competence be understood differently for first and second languages? – not that Hymes himself intended any such distinction. Work settings in which first and second language learners share the same communicative tasks present *prima facie* cases for the appropriateness of a single model of communicative competence for first and second language speakers. The same issue arises in educational settings. The justification for distinct forms of assessment for native and non-native speakers in certain contexts – for example, on exiting from secondary education – is a matter of debate (cf. Davies, 1984b). And why should the role-specific communicative competence of prospective undergraduates be a matter of concern for second language speakers, but not for first language speakers? (cf. discussion of Hamilton *et al.* (1993) in Chapter 7). As workforces and classrooms become more and more linguistically diverse, the distinction between first and second communicative ability becomes harder and harder to maintain.

In this section, we will give an example of competing conceptions of communicative ability in the workplace and their impact on assessment. The example is from the training and assessment of native-speaking medical students in communication skills; such assessment is a routine part of medical education in medical schools in some countries. The assessment of clinical communication skills in courses for native speaker medical students is conducted within a performance assessment paradigm. Performance assessment in the area of clinical skills is discussed by Maatsch and Gordon (1978) and by Stiggins (1981), among others. Apart from the practical relevance of this practice to the development of second language performance tests in the same area, there are a number of further reasons for considering such tests. This assessment can be compared with the way in which the communicative ability of foreign medical graduates is assessed in an ESP performance test (see Chapter 4). The question arises of the desirability or otherwise of distinguishing between the competence requirements of first and second language speakers (of English, in this case) in the clinical setting, and the implications this has for assessment criteria and assessment practices. This is clearly an issue in the case of non-native speaking health professionals wishing to live and work in the same settings and under the same conditions as their native-speaking-counterparts, for example immigrant health professionals. There will not necessarily be any concession made to the fact that overseas-trained staff are working in the medium of a second language.

The discussion will focus on the notion of an adequate performance, and how this might be assessed. This issue became apparent in discussions with medical educators responsible for performance tests in undergraduate medical training.

As part of the process of development of the Occupational English Test, an ESP performance test for health professionals (McNamara, 1990b; see Chapter 4 below), discussions were held with doctors and behavioural scientists responsible for the communication skills training of medical undergraduates at the University of Newcastle, New South Wales. At Monash University, Melbourne, a role play-based performance test of communication skills as part of the fourth-year medical course was also observed. These medical schools were chosen for their innovative work in medical education, particularly in the amount and type of attention they paid to the development of communication skills in clinical contexts.

For example, in the Monash examination, the candidate (a medical student) took the role of doctor, the examiner the role of patient. It was striking how little language was actually used by the candidate; approximately 90 per cent of the time, the 'patient' was talking, and candidates were scored more highly the more successful they were in eliciting language from the 'patient'. Candidates were actually penalized if they spoke too much. Secondly, some candidates did poorly in the examination because of non-linguistic factors such as personality traits. One rather shy male candidate had to counsel an embarrassed soon-to-be-married 'patient' who was anxious about his ability to 'perform' sexually, and in particular about the size of his penis. The candidate simply could not cope with his own embarrassment and inexperience, and was ineffective in communicating with the 'patient' as a result. The points observed here are precisely those raised by Upshur (1979), mentioned at the beginning of this chapter, on the role of silence as encouragement to your interlocutor to speak in the accomplishment of some communicative tasks.

Rating scales used in performance tests at Newcastle raise similar issues. Candidates are rated on their handling of specific content areas, such as investigation of obstacles in the patient's social background to his or her compliance with the doctor's instructions or advice. Ratings are also given for candidates' general empathy with the patient, together with their attitudes and sensitivity, as well as the way these are expressed paralinguistically through 'body language' and the like. Certain assessment categories focus on language, but they only serve to underline how unlike language proficiency tests these performance tests are. For example, candidates are assessed in terms of whether they ask 'single' or 'multiple' questions (single questions being awarded higher marks as they are claimed to be more readily processed and remembered by the patient). The issues raised by the assessment scales were sharply focused for the author by a comment from a behavioural scientist at Newcastle: 'Oh, so you're not interested in communication, only language.' This comment was challenging in view of the claims to a communicative orientation of current language testing practice.

Another non-linguistic factor in clinical communication situations is the role of professional knowledge and competence. This emerged in discussions with clinical educators working with foreign medical graduates in bridging retraining programmes in a Melbourne hospital. It involved the question of what constituted an acceptable procedure for taking a case history and an acceptable case presentation. In the latter case, the person presenting the case is required to take a case history, read relevant clinical records and research as necessary the differential diagnosis of the patient's condition (the most likely diagnosis and competing alternative diagnoses). This is then presented formally to professional colleagues, who will then discuss the case as a group to arrive at a consensus on diagnosis and (further) treatment. The frequent long-windedness of the presentations of overseas graduates was commented upon, and taken to be an indication of lack of diagnostic skill. The point was made that the skilful and rapid organization of the presentation of a case and the taking of a history are crucially related to the question of the diagnosis. A shrewd diagnostic hunch will lead to the history being taken more efficiently and more confident and economical presentation of the case to colleagues. Discourse organization is thus a function of professional knowledge as well as linguistic skill: in Bachman and Palmer's terms, both *knowledge schemata* and *language knowledge* are involved. It is not a question of purely linguistic skill alone, which might be separately assessable; components of *knowledge* and *ability for use* are integrated in the organization of the discourse.

This example suggests the urgency of the need to clarify the object of assessment in second language performance tests. Even in general proficiency contexts, more is going on than meets the eye. Research in related areas has much to offer us. In an interview situation, for example, models from communication studies and behavioural science have long since recognized how non-cognitive factors deeply influence the evolution of the discourse and the interpretation by the participants of what is going on. The issues raised here relate to the distinction proposed in Chapter 2 between a strong and a weak sense of the term *second language performance test*.

As we saw in the discussion earlier in this chapter, the incorporation of affective and other non-linguistic variables in a model of second language communicative ability is recognized by several authors as potentially problematic (and cf. the discussion at the end of the previous chapter); we get such a rich picture of the assessment situation that it may be difficult to draw inferences confidently from it, as it contains too many variables. Widdowson (1989: 134–5) has pointed out the difficulty in general terms:

> As soon as you talk about competence as *ability*, or what people can actually *do* with their language, you get into all kinds of difficulty … The relationship between knowledge and ability is problematic for empirical work in the description of learner and user language. It is problematic too, of course, in language pedagogy. [Emphasis in original.]

And, it may be added, in language assessment. For example, it is not clear that we have yet a comprehensive understanding of the factors that are relevant to consider as underlying *ability for use*. We have seen that Goffman (1967) only begins to list the factors that may be relevant: '… capacities in interaction such as courage, gameness, gallantry, composure, presence of mind, dignity, stage confidence …'.

A further problem is the role of native speaker competence as a model.[24] Briefly, Widdowson (1989: 135) expresses the difficulty as follows: 'Whose ability and in what circumstances do we ... call *competence* and provide as a reference for learners?' Native speaker performance is inherently variable, as has often been pointed out (cf., for example, Alderson, 1980; Bachman, 1990; Davies, 1991; and see Chapter 7).

3.8   The dimensions of an adequate model

It seems then that one cannot escape the inclusion of a range of under-lying capacities in a model of communicative competence in a second language: yet the result is unmanageable. We are back (in Yeats's phrase) 'where all the ladders start'. However, too often, efforts are made to dispose of the difficulties by simply defining them out of existence. In this category we must place the views of Savignon (1983: 246), quoted earlier: 'Language proficiency *is* communicative competence, and should be defined and evaluated as such' [emphasis in original], and of Ingram (1981, 1984), discussed above.

Perhaps what is needed is a three-pronged attack.

First, we need a model that is rich enough for us to conceptualize any issue we might think is potentially relevant to understanding second language performance; there should be no limit in principle to the dimensions of such a model. We should attempt to develop as rich and as complete a model as possible within the necessary limits of parsimony and clarity. All current discussions, as we have seen, are problematic.

A weakness of current models is that they focus too much on the individual candidate rather than the candidate in interaction. Given the interactional nature of performance assessment (Figure 3.9),[25] we should be looking more to those in our field who are studying talk in interaction. It is clear that the models discussed in this chapter are loosely psychological in orientation, focusing on knowledge, and incorporating social interaction in a static way, via knowledge dimensions deriving from work in sociolinguistics. Strategic competence addresses questions of interaction from a cognitive viewpoint, and that of only one of the participants (the candidate). The idea of performance as involving social interaction has thus so far featured only weakly in the work of theorists of second language performance. In fact the study of language and interaction continues to flourish (cf. Jacoby and Ochs (1995) on recent work on 'co-construction') although it is all too rarely cited by researchers in language testing, and almost not at all by those proposing general theories of

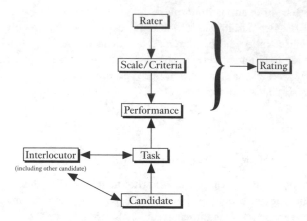

FIGURE 3.9   'Proficiency' and its relation to performance

performance in language performance tests; this situation must change. The study of interaction within the traditions of ethnography (Schieffelin and Ochs, 1986; Ochs, 1988; Duranti, 1988; Duranti and Goodwin, 1992), ethnomethodology (e.g. Garfinkel, 1967; Heritage, 1984) and conversation analysis (Sacks *et al.*, 1974; Schegloff *et al.*, 1977) richly deserve our attention.

Secondly, we need a research agenda to investigate the significance for measurement of variables that our models may tell us are likely to be important. Referring again to Figure 3.9, in the case of a speaking test, for example, the candidate may be required to interact with an interlocutor, who may be another candidate, a trained native speaker, or a highly proficient non-native speaker. The age, sex, educational level, proficiency/native speaker status and personal qualities of the interlocutor relative to the same qualities in the candidate are all likely to be significant in influencing the candidate's performance. The interlocutor may or may not be the person who judges the performance; often, this may be done subsequently, from an audiotape or videotape, although it may also be done 'live'. There may well be a choice of task or test materials available. The extent of potential variability introduced by these interactions between candidate and other individuals (including, of course, the judge) and non-human features of the test setting (materials, location, time, etc.) is enormous. Understanding the effect of these variables on the pattern of test scores is a major research enterprise. The application within performance assessment contexts of new measurement tools such as multi-faceted Rasch measurement (Linacre, 1989b; McNamara and Adams, 1991/1994; Lumley and McNamara, 1995; McNamara and Lumley,

1993) (this tool is one of the main subjects of the present text) and Generalizability Theory (Brennan, 1983; Bachman, 1990; Bachman *et al.*, 1995; Lynch and McNamara, 1994; McNamara and Lynch, in press) has proved revealing of the extent and effects of such variability. New insights are also coming from discourse analytic and conversation analytic techniques (Lazaraton, 1991, 1994; Filipi, 1994; Shohamy, 1994; O'Loughlin, 1995; Young, 1994). But the variables themselves must first be modelled, and an adequate model of factors in the candidate must thus include non-linguistic factors, including both cognitive and non-cognitive.

Finally, we need to determine what it is appropriate and possible to assess in a given test situation. This will raise both ideological (what position are we taking, and why?) and administrative issues (how feasible or practical is this assessment proposal?). In other words we are forced into deciding precisely what it is that we are testing, and what it is that we are not. Candlin (1986: 53) makes a useful distinction between models of communicative competence on the one hand, and what he calls the 'limits of testability' of such models on the other:

> The answers [to the problems discussed in Candlin's paper] lie elsewhere than in testing. They depend on improving the quality of our description of communicative competence, and then on making educational and administrative judgments on where the boundaries of communicative competence are to be drawn. Once we have made our particular peace between these two forces, we can tackle what must be the second order problem, namely the design and validation procedures we advocate as appropriate.

3.9 Conclusion

This chapter has shown the extent to which writers in the field have experienced problems in conceptualizing the performance dimension of language performance tests. These writers have, with one or two notable exceptions, shied away from articulating, or simply underestimated, the implications for the validity of language performance tests of the requirement that language ability is to be assessed under performance conditions, that is, as part of an act of communication. In fact there is a tradition of seeing language performance tests as being of self-evident validity (cf. the discussion of Ingram (1981, 1984) above, who reduces the matter to an issue of face validity), and of occupying an essentially practical domain in which the role of theoretical models of language ability and the skills underlying performance of language tasks are of doubtful relevance. This is nicely illustrated in the disagreement between Merrill Swain and Michael Canale, discussed earlier. Progress in understanding the nature of second language performance testing and conducting the necessary research on its validity requires a commitment to rigorous analysis of what is involved in a language performance test. Only in such a context can empirical validation of scores from such assessments be carried out.

Canale and Swain quite justly saw Hymes's notion of *ability for use* as a Pandora's Box; they were perhaps right to 'doubt that there is any theory of human action that can adequately explicate *ability for use*' (1980: 7). The problem for performance assessment however is that Pandora's Box just won't stay closed. We will have to try to unpack its contents and sort them out. The search for an adequate conceptualization of second language performance is not easy, but the need to broaden the discussion of the issues involved is pressing.

Notes

1. Admittedly this was a remark in a forum on TOEFL and perhaps should be accepted as rather an oversimplification of Savignon's position. Her approach to the testing of language proficiency was discussed in detail in Chapter 2.
2. Hymes's work itself derives from the work of Jakobson (1960), and reformulates distinctions proposed by Chomsky that can be traced back to de Saussure's distinction between *langue* and *parole*. In this sense it is a particular response to the discourse of the time, and its concession to Chomsky's distinction is in contrast to the more radical position of Halliday (1978), who rejected the necessity for any such distinction altogether. As the influence of Hallidayan thought on language testing practice is not strongly developed as yet, and is itself inadequate as a framework for understanding performance assessment (see note 4 below), it is convenient in terms of understanding the development of thinking about what is being measured in language tests to accept Hymes's distinction, as we will see that the most influential writers on language testing have worked within this framework. The framework thus offers a useful way of organizing our discussion of the literature of the past twenty-five years on the nature of language ability and the role of performance within it.
3. Cf. discussion in note 2, above.
4. Halliday (1978) is less interested in what he calls the *intraindividual* orientation of Chomsky and Hymes, and is more interested in an *interindividual* (i.e. social and contextual) one. He is thus not interested in the cognitive organization of the individual speaker-hearer, but in the organization of language as a shared resource for meaning. Nevertheless, a distinction between potential ('meaning potential', the 'semantic system' of the language) and actual realization in instances of use ('text') is crucial to his theory. In this he is closer to Hymes than to Chomsky; although he rejects the knowledge/performance distinction in favour of a view of 'knowledge in performance', he implicitly accepts the distinction between the two senses of *performance* pointed out by Hymes. Halliday's influence on language assessment is beginning to be felt (cf. Matthiessen *et al.*, 1992; Macken and Slade, 1993). An inadequate conceptualization of the psychological dimension of performance, and of the perception/reception of the performance by the rater, lead to an implicit endorsement of the sufficiency of appro-

priate and explicit assessment criteria in this work (in common with many who advocate criterion-referenced assessment); the problem with such positions in general
should become clear from the discussion in Chapters 2 and 5.

5. Widdowson (1989: 130) points out that Chomsky's *pragmatic competence* refers to ability
   only, whereas the corresponding aspects of Hymes's *communicative competence* (*feasibility*, *appropriateness*, *performance*) refer to both knowledge and ability.
6. Although the major influence of Hymes has seemed to be his incorporation of sociolinguistic knowledge into the framework of communicative competence, in fact the more
   radical challenge for performance assessment is contained in the notion *ability for use*.
   Communicative language testing has been influenced by both of these aspects, but the
   latter has the greater significance for performance testing, and the issues have been less
   well articulated.
7. 'The ambiguity in communicative competence is just this, that it confuses knowledge
   and control, or, in other words, knowledge and proficiency' (Davies, 1989: 162). One
   might feel that the word 'confuses' is a little unfair here. The term *control* appears to
   suggest practised skill, mastery, ability to deploy a resource, and is clearly a psycholinguistic matter, an aspect of Hymes's category of *ability for use*.
8. Davies is applying a famous distinction made by Ryle (1949).
9. Hymes did not restrict the framework to first language contexts, but it originated in a
   concern for them.
10. and its subsequent modification (cf. Canale, 1983a, 1983b).
11. Spolsky (1985: 183) would prefer a performance or processing model, models which in
    his view embody a statement about the nature of 'the form of storage of knowledge, i.e.
    of a grammar, which is what a competence model is'. That is, performance models
    imply competence models, but not vice versa. He recommends basing further work on
    a preference or connectionist model, a performance grammar, but states (1989a: 150)
    that its realization 'will surely take years of work'.
12. *Psychophysiological Mechanisms* represent the channel (auditory, visual) and mode
    (receptive, productive) involved in language use. They are a rather elaborate way of
    including the language macroskills in the model.
13. The use of the term 'competence' here is potentially misleading. Elsewhere, Bachman
    uses this term synonymously with 'knowledge': '... it [the model] recognizes that ability
    to use language communicatively involves both knowledge of or competence in the lan-
    guage, and the capacity for implementing, or using this competence' (Bachman, 1990:
    81). This equation of *competence* with *knowledge* is a continuation of the usage proposed
    by Canale and Swain, but not consistent with that of Hymes. This is potentially con-
    fusing; Bachman has subsequently changed his terminology again (see below).
14. Despite the use of the same term, Bachman's view represents a fundamental reconcep-
    tualization of Canale and Swain's notion of *strategic competence*.
15. This contrasts with Canale and Swain's concerns on this point.
16. There is an ambiguity in the phrase 'specific language ability'. If Communicative
    Language Ability includes *strategic competence*, then presumably there should be no
    opposition between 'the language ability the test [is] ... intended to measure' and *strate-
    gic competence*. Bachman perhaps means 'specific areas of language competence'.
17. Spolsky's own rather elaborate attempt is presented in Spolsky (1989b).
18. One other rather large change from the previous work is that the unwieldy
    Psychophysiological Mechanisms has been dropped.
19. As we noted earlier, this had already been foreshadowed in Bachman (1990), where it
    was pointed out in the discussion of *strategic competence* (1990: 105) that language users
    'differ in their willingness to exploit what they [know] and their flexibility in doing so'.
20. The discussion in Bachman and Palmer on this point relates to a tradition of research
    on test takers' affective reactions (Shohamy, 1982; Zeidner and Bensoussan, 1988;
    Brown, 1993 *inter alia*), and also to the work of Douglas and Selinker (1985) on dis-
    course domains.

21. Notice that in retaining the term *strategic competence*, Bachman and Palmer have still not cleared up the confusion created by Bachman's earlier inconsistent use of the term 'competence', discussed above. Elsewhere in the new model, however, the term *competence* has been replaced with *knowledge*. Thus we have terms such as *language knowledge*, *organizational knowledge* and *pragmatic knowledge* in the new model; this accords well with the categorization of these aspects of the model in the discussion in this chapter so far. This aspect of Bachman and Palmer's current usage is based on the sensible grounds that the term 'knowledge' is more widely used in the psychological and cognitive science literature, and the term 'competence' has, as we have seen, been associated with some ambiguity in discussions in our field (Bachman, personal communication).

22. The FSI scale defines levels from 0 (no ability to communicate effectively or understand the language) to 5 (ability equivalent to that of a well-educated native-speaking user of the language); there are eleven levels of proficiency in all. The ACTFL scale has more distinctions at the lower level, to cater for the expected proficiency levels of graduating students at university, but groups achievement equivalent to level 3 and up on the FSI scale into a single level ('Superior'); it has nine levels in all.

23. In Bachman and Palmer's terms (see above), there is an interaction between *knowledge schemata* and *language knowledge*, mediated by *metacognitive strategies*.

24. This will be the subject of extensive discussion in Chapter 7.

25. This is an elaborated version of a schematic representation first presented by Dorry Kenyon at the Language Testing Research Colloquium in Vancouver in 1992; cf. Figure 2.1 in Chapter 2 above.

4 Designing a performance test: the Occupational English Test

4.1 Introduction

In this chapter, the stages of the development of an occupationally related performance test of the work sample type[1] will be outlined, through an extended example, the development of the Occupational English Test (OET), a test of ESL for health professionals. As further research involving this test is discussed in subsequent chapters, it is appropriate to provide some detailed background on the OET at this stage. As was pointed out in Chapter 2, the establishment of appropriate test content is of particular concern in work sample tests, and the test development process will illustrate how this was attempted in this case. More substantially, however, the discussion in the last two chapters has raised a number of complex questions about the nature of performance in performance assessment, and about the validity of the work sample approach to language performance testing, and these will be considered in the context of this presentation.

4.2 Stages in the development of a performance test

In this section, a brief overview will be given of the stages of the development of a language performance test of the work sample type. Some of the stages (trialling of test materials for example) are not peculiar to performance tests, being necessary in the development of tests of any type, and so will not be given any particular emphasis. More attention will be paid to stages specific to performance tests, particularly those involving the selection of test content and format. The treatment here is necessarily brief and programmatic; the feasibility of these procedures in terms of logistics and resources, and the issues of validity surrounding test development decisions, will have to be evaluated in any particular development context. Following this overview a 'worked example' (the development of the OET) will be given, in which the issues arising there concerning practicality on the one hand and validity on the other will be considered, as an example of the inevitably problematic nature of test development in practice.

4.2.1   Test rationale

It is useful to articulate the reasons for the introduction of the test, as these will constrain the test specifications in basic ways. Tests are motivated by their educational, social and political contexts.[2] As a preliminary to investigating the domain to be covered by the test, and then creating test specifications, it will be helpful to establish for the particular test development project,

> *who* wants to know *what* about *whom*, for what *purpose*?[3]

4.2.1.1   WHO *wants to know?*

The audience for test results will have an influence on test design, including test content (an aspect of face validity) and the way test performance is reported (an administrative problem of clear communication between those responsible for the test and those depending on the information it can provide). Performance tests are often used for screening or selection purposes. In educational contexts, English for Academic Purposes tests such as IELTS, OTESL (Wesche, 1987) and TEEP (Weir, 1988b) provide evidence on test takers' ability to function in academic contexts, information which is relevant to those responsible for selection of students. Professionally related tests such as the OET form part of the screening mechanisms controlling entry or re-entry to the workplace. The needs of those ultimately responsible for this screening function are important in test design and in test-reporting procedures. The sophistication and complexity of the information provided on test candidates will vary according to the expertise of those required to interpret test results, and the support available to them in interpreting the results. Performance tests may also provide information to teachers, in which case a different kind and level of information will be appropriate. Alderson (1991) usefully discusses the wording of rating scales in the light of the need to communicate with different audiences, including those who will be using the information provided by the test in decision making.

4.2.1.2   WHAT *do they want to know about?*

Following from the point made above, the focus of interest of the test users such as admissions officers who are not teachers, may be rather different from that of language teachers, who may have specialized professional interests in, say, mastery of formal aspects of the language system. The former are more likely to be interested in real-world outcomes rather than in mastery of the language system in its own right. In any case, the role of language knowledge in performance is extremely complex, as we saw in Chapter 3. In performance testing, the specification of relevant aspects of language knowledge will often be subsumed within the specification of the kinds of communicative tasks that test takers will face in the world beyond the test. In answering the question of what test users want to know about the candidates, then, the scope of the test is specified in broad terms: e.g. can the test takers cope with the communicative demands of participating in first-year undergraduate studies towards a science degree at an English-medium university?

4.2.1.3   About WHOM is information required?

A profile of the test-taker population will constrain the test specifications in important ways, particularly for specific-purpose performance tests. We need to know such things as

1. What background of relevant knowledge and experience do test takers have? What background knowledge and experience may be assumed in the selection of test materials and tasks?
2. What is the range of abilities likely to be present in the test-taker population? Is the test narrowly or broadly focused in the ability range it is targeting?
3. Within the whole test-taker population, is there a particular level of ability that is of greatest interest? For example, in competency tests for employment purposes where a threshold level of competence is required, distinctions between those who are competent, very competent and extremely competent are not relevant; the test will need to focus its attention on those on the borderline of competence, and ensure that its judgements are fair and meaningful at that point, rather than across the whole range of test takers. This situation is true of the OET and of other screening tests.

4.2.1.4   For WHAT purpose is information about the language abilities of test takers being sought?

As we have seen, language tests often have important gate-keeping functions, that is, they permit or restrict access to opportunities for further education (as in EAP tests such as OTESL or IELTS), employment (as in the OET, or the Japanese Language Test for Tour Guides (Brown, 1995)) or immigration (the Australian government **access:** test for intending immigrants: cf. Chapter 5). When a high-stakes decision is based on the information reported from the test, corresponding care needs to be taken (which will necessarily entail appropriate expense) to ensure that we are in a position to justify or defend the inferences about the candidate's ability to cope in the target use situation which are drawn from his or her performance on the test. This process of language test validation is complex, and it is important to try wherever possible to reduce the load that the test bears for decision-making, by using multiple sources of evidence (test and non-test) about the abilities in question – reports from teachers, reports from workplace supervisors, portfolios of student work, etc. Often language tests form part of a general educational reporting process and the stakes are not so high for any particular test, in which case the requirements of validation are not so onerous. These considerations are not unique to performance tests – the Test of English as a Foreign Language (TOEFL) bears identical responsibilities, and is not a performance test, but performance tests make specific claims about their validity in these contexts.

4.2.2   Resources/constraints

There will usually be a fairly strict budget for test development and test operation. Unfortunately performance testing is costly, as the training of raters and the time taken to carry out ratings, usually repeated to ensure fairness, necessarily involve considerable expense. It may be that while a performance-based approach is desirable, it is unaffordable in a particular context. The test and the test development need to be practical in terms of time, financial resources, personnel resources, and administrative load.

4.2.3   Content selection

In work sample tests, an attempt is made to sample test content from the communicative tasks facing the candidate in the target language use situation. The design of the test will therefore involve research on the communicative demands of the target setting. This research is likely to have four components, as follows.[4]

1. *Consultation with expert informants.* People responsible for professional education and training for the workplace are likely to have a more explicitly articulated view of the nature of the workplace and its demands than those engaged in the work less reflectively. Such expertise constitutes a resource for the test designer in the process of task specification. Others such as work supervisors may also serve as informants. Interviews with these informants may help at the stage of an initial orientation to the workplace, particularly if it is relatively unfamiliar to the researcher. Informants may help in establishing a preliminary inventory of tasks, to

be examined critically at stage 3 of the process (observation and job analysis). They may also be a useful sounding board as the researcher more clearly formulates his or her understanding in the course of the investigation. The views of such informants should not of course simply be accepted at face value, but considered in the light of evidence from other sources. Expert informants may also be involved in the subsequent preparation and validation of test materials (see below).

2. *Literature search.* It is necessary to establish what research has already been carried out on the communicative demands of the target setting. For example, relevant to EAP test design, a body of research exists on the communicative tasks facing students at universities in the UK (Weir, 1983a, 1983b, 1988b; Emmett, 1985) and in North America (Powers, 1986). In job-specific assessment, less may be known.

3. *Job analysis and workplace observation.* This stage involves categorization of communicative tasks in the workplace (or other target language use situation) based on observation, interviews, questionnaires/surveys, and other methods. The complexity of this stage has often been underestimated, and the range of techniques used rather limited (Mawer, 1991). Morgan (1994) for example argues convincingly that the assessment of the role of literacy tasks in the workplace in accordance with recent Australian government policy has been naïve and misguided, as it has been conducted by ESL teachers with little understanding of the culture of industry and with inadequate training in methods of data collection in such settings. She suggests a range of techniques that might be used.

4. *Collection and examination of texts (spoken and written) from the workplace.* As part of the empirical investigation in (3) above, texts may be collected and examined for complexity, length, discourse organization and other linguistic features. Material from these texts may appear in the test itself, although the inauthenticity of the conditions of production and reception of texts in the testing situation compromises the authenticity of such texts as representative of workplace communication tasks. This will be discussed further below.

4.2.4 Development of specifications (including scoring procedures) and writing of materials

A decision must be made about broad test method. A choice will usually be made from the possible approaches discussed by Slater (1980) and Jones (1985) (see Chapter 2):

1. extensive observation of the candidate's performance in the workplace or target language use situation (*direct assessment*);
2. selective observation of the same (*work sample* methods as defined in a narrow sense); or
3. simulation techniques.

The further one moves away from direct observation within the workplace setting, the more problematic the tasks become as representative of the workplace. Compromises will inevitably have to be made, and the nature of the compromises and the implications for test validity acknowledged and dealt with (see discussion in Chapter 2). Other methods that fall within Haertel's (1992) broader definition of performance test (cf. the discussion in Chapter 2) may also be included. In addition, decisions will be made as to whether the demonstration of the response to the test material in comprehension-based tests will simulate real-world responses, or be more artificially constrained, as in the case of multiple-choice questions.

Test specifications (Davidson and Lynch, 1993; Lynch and Davidson, 1994) are required. These are a set of detailed procedures for writers of successive versions of the test to follow; these procedures will cover the test content and the test format in detail – the characteristics of texts, the format of items or tasks, the exact rubrics (instructions to candidates), with examples.

Test specifications will also establish scoring standards and procedures, including the development of appropriate assessment criteria (rating scales), the selection, training and (re-)accreditation of raters, and decisions about the reporting of results with the end user in mind.

The test specifications are followed and revised in the course of preparation of trial test materials. This preparation may involve expert informants (see 4.2.3 above) in writing and/or vetting the materials.

The development of test specifications is not a simple and mechanical procedure, but involves the test developer in facing a number of complex issues of test validity. This point will be illustrated in the discussion of the development of the OET, below.

4.2.5   Trials of pilot version

A pilot version of the test instrument or procedure must be developed, and properly trialled on an appropriately representative population (this may be difficult in the case of a highly specific test, that is, one where the test population is small, if test security is not to be compromised). The number of trial subjects should be such as to make possible the necessary data analysis. Procedures should be adopted to incorporate feedback from trial subjects (Cohen, 1984; Brown, 1993; Hill, 1995).

4.2.6   Selection and training of raters

As performance assessment typically involves judgement, the selection and preparation of raters is important. The justification for and effect of rater training is in fact a complex issue, which will be discussed in detail in Chapters 5 and 8. Performances from the test trials are used in such training.

4.2.7   Data analysis of trial data

In addition to determining the qualities of the test, as a basis for revision of test content and procedure, the data may also be used for research (cf. Chapter 8) and for standard setting (4.2.9 below).

4.2.8   Revision of test materials and specifications.

This will be done in the light of the information available from the trial test takers (4.2.5) and the data analysis (4.2.7).

4.2.9   Standard setting

The determination of minimum acceptable performance standards on workplace communicative tasks will usually involve eliciting the opinions of expert informants on the quality of a series of particular performances. An example of how this may be carried out is given below.

4.2.10   Implementation and monitoring under operational conditions

Information should be sought on the test's properties under normal conditions of operation; for example, the performance of raters needs to be carefully monitored, and test reliability under operational conditions established. Empirical validation of the test should proceed; an example of an aspect of this is provided in Chapter 8.

4.3   An example: the case of the Occupational English Test (OET)

In this section, we will consider how certain aspects of the above process of test design and development were carried out in the case of the

Occupational English Test (OET), an Australian government test of ESL for health professionals. Particular attention will be paid to the process of content selection and validation, as this is distinctive of performance tests of this type.

4.3.1   Test background

As part of its annual intake of immigrants and refugees, some hundreds of overseas-trained health professionals are currently entering Australia each year as permanent residents. The majority of these are medical practitioners, but a number of other health professional groups (nurses, dentists, physiotherapists, occupational therapists, speech pathologists, veterinary surgeons and several others) are also represented. The process of registration for practice in Australia typically involves the following three steps after an initial verification of documentation:

1. The Occupational English Test, an English language proficiency test taken by each of the professions involved; its development and administration are in the hands of the National Languages and Literacy Institute of Australia (NLLIA) on behalf of the National Office for Overseas Skills Recognition.
2. Profession-specific pencil-and-paper tests of professional clinical knowledge, developed by the relevant professional examining body, for example the Australian Medical Council.
3. Performance-based tests of clinical competence, again conducted by the relevant professional examining bodies.

The first two stages may be completed before entry to Australia, and official policy encourages this, although in fact only a small percentage of those seeking registration do so (for example, approximately 10 per cent of candidates for the OET sit outside Australia). Passage through the three stages may take some considerable time – a period of up to two years is quite common.

Prior to 1987, the OET was a test of general English proficiency, and was attracting increasing criticism from test takers and test users in terms of its validity and reliability. In response to this, a series of consultancies was initiated on reform of the test. The report on the first of these, which was carried out by a team at Lancaster University in the United Kingdom, recommended the creation of a test which would 'assess the ability of candidates to communicate effectively in the workplace' (Alderson *et al.* 1986: 3). A series of further consultancies (McNamara 1987, 1988a, 1989a) attempted to operationalize this recommendation by establishing the format of the new test and developing and trialling materials for it.

Steps 2 and 3 for registration are demanding for those health profession-als whose clinical experience is restricted to contexts rather different from Australia, a country with a technically sophisticated health care system, where diseases are linked to the lifestyle of a relatively affluent industrial and post-industrial society. This is true for a majority of candidates, who most frequently come from countries in Eastern Europe, the Middle East, the Indian sub-continent and South-East Asia. In order to have a chance of success on these practical, clinically based tests, reflecting roughly the standard of final year medical training in Australia, candidates must have some access to experience of clinical practice in Australia. A limited num-ber of places on hospital-based bridging programmes is available.

Thus, it was recognized that an important function of the reformed Occupational English Test would be to serve as a screening for entry to a setting providing supervised clinical familiarization. Experience of the clin-ical setting, no matter how informally or in however limited a way, is indis-pensable for success in the clinical examinations. Institutions who conduct such programmes felt that a screening of candidates' ability to cope lin-guistically with bridging programmes was a necessary function of the test.

4.3.2   Resources/constraints

As indicated above, the OET was initially under-resourced, but eventu-ally the Australian government responded to repeated protests about its unsatisfactory status, initiated consultancies on its reform and has since borne the cost of the routine development of appropriate test materials (two or three new forms per year) and test administration. As a relatively specialized performance test, the OET is expensive to operate, but its function is important politically and socially; as a result, resources have been available for a performance testing approach involving specialization of materials for different health professions. Administratively, there is a preference for separate reporting of sub scores in each of the macroskills. The main constraint on the test is the legal one discussed above in Section 2.5 of Chapter 2, namely that the testing of English language *communication* skills must be entirely separate from the testing of clinical aspects of professional competence carried out by assessment panels specific to the health professions concerned. The implications of this constraint were discussed in that chapter, and the contrast with the equivalent test in the UK, the PLAB test, noted.

4.3.3   Content selection

We saw in Chapter 2 that in work sample tests, content selection has been seen as crucial. We also saw that there is a debate on the status of content selection in relation to test validity. Messick (1989: 17) takes the position that 'in a fundamental sense so-called content validity does not count as validity at all'. This position has not been reflected in thinking in language testing, where, as we saw in Chapter 2, there has been a great emphasis on content validation, particularly in the important British tradition of EAP testing. Davies (1984a), for example, sees the stage in which the content and the general layout of the test are planned and the type of test item is decided on as the crucial stage in the development of such tests.

The establishment of content validity, according to Davies (1977: 62), involves the following:

> An assessment must be made of just what the learners whose proficiency is to be tested need to do with the language, what varieties they must employ and in what situations they must use those varieties. This is an arduous task, and one based largely on guesswork, but it can be intelligent guesswork and it is essential for constructing a proficiency test.

A number of procedures were employed to guide the 'guesswork' in the case of the OET: these included *interviews* with those involved in the professional education and training of both overseas trained and locally-trained health professionals, the administration of a *questionnaire* to those with direct experience of the relevant workplace roles, *direct observation* of the workplace, and *analysis* of available characterizations (both within and outside applied linguistics) of key communication tasks.

4.3.3.1   Consultation with expert informants

Relevant expertise was to be found among three groups of informants:

(1) those responsible for professional education in clinical settings in each of the professions concerned; of particular help were those who had had direct experience of clinical supervision of overseas-trained health professionals;

(2) overseas-trained graduates with some experience of bridging programmes in clinical settings in Australia;

(3) ESL teachers contributing to such programmes (such teachers observe interactions between the graduates and hospital staff and patients in the clinical setting, and base assistance on what they observe to be the communicative difficulties experienced).

In the first part of this data-gathering stage, the views of those concerned with the education of doctors were sought, as doctors are the largest group taking the test.[5] Interviews were conducted, some observation of the workplace was conducted, and a tentative list of relevant workplace communicative tasks was drawn up; this was then discussed with the informants in group (1) and some of the informants in group (2) above. A questionnaire was then developed which attempted, following Weir (1983b), to identify those communication tasks facing graduates in clinical bridging programmes which were perceived to be most *frequent*, and those which were seen to be most *complex* or *difficult* (see also Candlin, Leather and Bruton, 1974).

The questionnaire was administered in three areas of Australia to 42 overseas medical graduates who had current or recent experience of the hospital setting in Australia in an observer or trainee role. The graduates were asked to estimate the *frequency* of contact with various other personnel in a variety of channels (face-to-face, telephone, reading/writing). A 5-point scale was used to measure frequency, with 0 representing 'no contact' and 5 representing 'very frequent contact'. Table 4.1 gives details of the 20 commonest communication tasks, based on an analysis of 42 completed questionnaires.

The results show that the main communication tasks facing overseas-trained doctors in the hospital setting involved mainly oral communication skills. The ten most frequent communication tasks were oral: the most frequent task was face-to-face communication with patients, the next four ranks being taken up by face-to-face communication tasks involving hospital personnel

The graduates were also asked to gauge the relative *complexity* or *difficulty* of specific communication tasks for doctors with limited English skills, using a scale from 0 'not difficult' to 5 'extremely complex or difficult'. Table 4.2 gives details of the results obtained.

Several tasks relating to aspects of oral communication with *patients* were seen as complex tasks; one aspect of oral communication with other doctors was also singled out (*case presentation*). Interestingly, other aspects of inter-professional oral communication did not seem to present great difficulties (*understanding colleagues' language on ward rounds* and *understanding case discussions*), despite their perceived frequency, perhaps because of the greater degree of shared knowledge in the case of communication among health professionals compared with doctor–patient communication.

Writing tasks were less frequent, and perceived to be of moderate difficulty.

4.3.3.2   Literature search

The extensive literature on medical communication from a number of perspectives was examined and evaluated for its relevance to the characterization of the consultation. An issue emerged from the contrasting perspectives of this extensive research. On the one hand, there were studies which characterized the consultation as an event, with stages, organized temporally and sequentially. On the other, several other broad traditions of research examined the processes in which the participants were engaged, for example from the points of view of social psychology, conversation analysis or detailed discourse analysis.[6] A decision had to be made about what in this literature should inform the process of establishing the content specifications. As it was obviously easier to specify stages of the consultation, some of which could in a rather obvious (and perhaps superficial) sense be simulated in the task design, rather than attempt to specify the replication of communicative processes (which were themselves often only revealed by extensive analytical effort), a decision was made to specify test content at the macro rather than the micro level. The limited available resources, particularly in terms of time, were a further constraint. But the implications of this decision in terms of test validity are problematic. On the other hand, it was not clear whether it was possible to simulate process under test conditions; as we noted above, authenticity of process is a major problem in performance assessment in the work sample tradition (more on this below).

TABLE 4.1   Perceived frequency of communication tasks
(doctors, hospital setting, $n = 42$)

Rank	Mean frequency	Channel	Person(s)
1	4.24	Face-to-face	Patient
2	4.07	Face-to-face	Registrar/resident
3	3.76	Face-to-face	Other foreign graduate
4	3.40	Face-to-face	Consultant
5	3.10	Face-to-face	Nursing staff
6	3.00	Face-to-face	Medical student
7	2.45	Telephone	Telephonist
8	2.30	Telephone	Other foreign graduate
9	2.26	Face-to-face	Receptionist/secretary
10	2.15	Telephone	Registrar/resident
11	2.13	Reading/writing	Registrar/resident
12	2.00	Telephone	Receptionist/secretary
13	1.93	Face-to-face	Radiologist
14	1.75	Telephone	Nurse
15	1.68	Reading/writing	Radiologist
16	1.60	Face-to-face	Hospital administration
16	1.60	Face-to-face	Patient's relative
18	1.58	Reading/writing	G.P.
19	1.53	Reading/writing	Nurse
20	1.48	Reading/writing	Consultant

Scale: 0 (no contact); 5 (very frequent contact)

TABLE 4.2   Perceived complexity or difficulty of communication tasks (doctors, hospital setting, $n = 42$)

Rank	Mean complexity	Nature of task
1	3.14	Understanding colloquial language from patients
2	2.63	Understanding local cultural references in order to make judgements about patients' lifestyles
2	2.63	Case presentation
4	2.33	Explaining medical ideas in easy language for patients
5	2.21	Taking a case history
6	2.10	Asking patients questions
6	2.10	Writing letters/reports
8	2.05	Speaking on the telephone
9	2.02	Reading handwritten notes/letters, etc.
10	1.88	Clarifying symptoms
11	1.83	Taking part in a group tutorial
11	1.83	Dealing with patients' families
13	1.75	Socializing with other staff
14	1.52	Getting cooperation from patients
15	1.51	Dealing with administration
16	1.40	Dealing with other non-professional hospital staff
17	1.36	Understanding colleagues' language on ward rounds
18	1.33	Getting cooperation from nurses
19	1.30	Dealing with outside personnel
20	1.24	Understanding case discussions

Scale: 0 (not difficult); 5 (extremely complex or difficult)

Of the studies carried out by discourse analysts, the most helpful in defining the stages of the consultation were those by Coulthard and Ashby (1975) and Skopek (1979); the work of Candlin *et al.* (1974) was also particularly useful. Most important of all were studies of the medical consultation conducted from within the medical profession itself, particularly the study by Byrne and Long (1976) of the structure of some 2500 medical interviews conducted by general practitioners.

4.3.3.3   Direct observation of the workplace and job analysis

In the light of the questionnaire results, and the obvious importance of the consultation, time was spent observing workplace communication in all of the professions served by the test. Throughout, an attempt was made to establish commonalities among the professions as the basis for test task design.

The centrality of *talk* in the work of each of the professions was readily established. Observation confirmed that the consultation (known by several names across the various professions) was common to all. The purpose of the consultation is *assessment* of the patient; physiotherapists and occupational therapists, for example, are expected to make a detailed assessment of the patient before any treatment is given. This assessment is independent of any that might be available from other health professionals involved in the care of the patient, although records of these other assessments also form an important part of the final assessment by each professional.

Consultations between professionals and their patients or clients were observed to contain the following elements[7] which were common to all the professions, although not all of them might be present in every consultation:

1. Assessment of the patient ('subjective assessment') including history taking.
2. Physical examination.
3. Explanation to patient of diagnosis and prognosis and course of treatment.
4. Treatment.
5. Patient/client/relative education and counselling.

Such commonalities provided the basis for a common format for assessment of *speaking* and *listening* skills (see below).[8]

Frequent and important *reading* tasks fell under two headings: keeping up with the professional literature; and reading case notes. As for *writing*, the letter of referral was found to be common to all the professions. When responsibility for care of a patient or client is handed over to another health professional (usually within the same profession, although not always) a short letter may be written summarizing the main facts of the case and the stage treatment has reached, and making a suggestion for further assessment or treatment. Where necessary, the writer bases the information in the letter on records such as case history notes, letters from other professionals concerned in the case, and other documents in the medical record of the patient. Of course, the above characterization of this writing task is an idealization; in fact letters may be written without reference to notes, often at the time of the referring consultation, and the letter itself may be a proforma note. Nevertheless, informants by and large supported the inclusion of a more elaborate and formal version of this writing task in the test, perhaps as much guided by views of appropriate test content and format as by fidelity to the reality of practice.

4.3.3.4   Collection and examination of texts from the workplace

Numerous audiotaped recordings were made, including of case confer-ences and ward rounds; videotapes of authentic doctor–patient consulta-tions were also available. Examples of written texts were collected or copied. These materials were considered in the light of possible test for-mats. For example, it had been hoped that a recording of a case conference might be used as the basis for part of the listening test, but the question of confidentiality arose, and it was decided to re-record the case conference from a transcription, using actors. The results proved unconvincing, because of the lack of familiarity of actors in using transcripts of actual spoken interaction (involving overlap, incomplete utterances, etc.) as the script from which they were to work.

4.3.4   Development of specifications

As always with specific-purpose performance tests, compromises had to be made about the degree to which it was practicable to tailor materials for particular professions.[9] It was decided to have single sub-tests of Listening and Reading while providing profession-specific content within a common format for the Speaking and Writing sub-tests.

The broad specifications for the test were thus as follows:[10]

Speaking   Profession-specific content within a common format. 15 min-utes. Role play-based interaction:[11] candidate in own professional role, interlocutor in role of patient (client) or relative of patient (client). Two role plays, plus short (unassessed) interview. Assessment in six catego-ries, using rating scale format scoring grid of the semantic differential type.

Writing   Profession-specific content within a common format. 40 min-utes. Letter of referral (12–15 lines) based on case notes or extracts from medical records. Assessment in five categories, using rating scale format scoring grid of the semantic differential type.

Listening   Common to all professions. 50 minutes. Short answer ques-tion format. Two texts:
(a)   talk on a professionally relevant subject;
(b)   consultation between a general practitioner and a patient.

Reading   Common to all professions. 40 minutes. Multiple-choice ques-tion (MCQ) format.[12] Articles from professional journals.[13]

4.3.4.1   Development of a scoring system

A procedure used in the original FSI speaking test (Wilds, 1975) was used as the basis for the development of a set of scoring categories for the Speaking sub-test (cf. Appendix 4A), and subsequently for the Writing sub-test (cf. Appendix 4B).

For *speaking*, raters assess the performance on each role play on six dimensions separately, and mark their ratings on scales presented in a type of semantic differential format, with anchor terms at either end. In addition, raters are given guidance as to the interpretation of different score points along the scale, described in terms of how they relate to the minimum level of proficiency required of a participant in a clinically based bridging programme.

The assessment categories are defined communicatively. For example, where the original FSI scoring system had categories for *Accent*, *Grammar* and *Vocabulary*, these were redefined as *Intelligibility* and *Resources of grammar and expression*. The communicative categories of *Fluency* and *Comprehension* (of interlocutor's input) were retained, and another (*Appropriateness*) introduced. An overall impression category, *Overall communicative effectiveness*, was introduced, and weighted more heavily: scores in this category are added to the average of the scores in the other five categories to achieve the final total score. Raters are asked to make provisional assessments after each role play, and at the end of the interaction to record a final definitive assessment.

For *writing* there are five assessment categories, as follows: *Overall task fulfilment* (weighted in the same way as the equivalent overall category in the speaking test); *Appropriateness of language*; *Comprehension of stimulus*; *Control of linguistic features (grammar and cohesion)*; and *Control of linguistic features (spelling, punctuation)*.

4.3.5   Writing and trialling of pilot versions of test materials

The development of materials for the Speaking and Writing sub-tests involved securing the cooperation of expert informants. Informants were identified within each of the professions involved in the test. These were usually educators within the profession. For the Speaking sub-test materials, each was asked to identify topics commonly occurring in consultations which could form the basis of role play materials. The topics should not involve or appear to involve anything other than basic professional knowledge, as this was to be assessed exclusively in the subsequent pencil-and-paper and clinical tests. Nor should the materials involve too complex a task for the interlocutor, who would obviously not have any medical expertise, and could not be expected to invent plausible symptoms, for example. Ideas for role play situations were subsequently written up as role play cards, and shown again to the informant for further comment.[14] A second informant from within the profession was then shown the role cards and asked to comment.. A final revised version of the role cards was subsequently prepared for trialling (cf. Figure 4.1 for sample materials).

A similar process took place for the *writing* materials, except that this time the informants were commissioned to write the case notes acting as the stimulus for the letter of referral, and a typical letter that might result, to be used as a reference point by the raters. Again, the materials were shown to another informant for comment prior to final revision. Sample materials can be found in Figure 4.2.

Reading test materials were drawn from suitable professional journals, as well as more general sources. Topics were chosen so as to be accessible to the range of professionals taking the test; multiple-choice questions were then written.

For the first part of the Listening sub-test, speakers familiar with the task of conducting professional upgrading seminars for health professionals were sought. A studio recording of a talk on a suitable topic was made and transcribed, then edited, and test questions written. A solution to the problem of producing authentic listening material without breaking confidentiality was found for the consultation. It was discovered that a 'simulated patient' service was available, supplying actors who had learned the symptoms of an actual patient with a particular condition and who would then 'present' as the patient in a simulated consultation. (This service is used in the training of health professionals in communication skills in interaction with patients.) Actors from the service were hired and paired with medical practitioners who were instructed to take medical histories from them in the usual way. The interaction, which was unscripted, achieved remarkable authenticity as the medical practitioners said that they found the actors and the whole simulation credible and natural and were then able to fall naturally into the familiar role of history taker.

The setting of an appropriate listening task proved more problematic, however. The test format requires candidates to take case history notes as they listen. At first, candidates were allowed freedom over the form of these notes, which were marked for content. However, the absence in the candidate's response of a detail of the history that was deemed relevant and was required in the marking scheme was felt to be ambiguous. It was not clear whether it signified that the detail had not been heard or understood, or that it had not been judged worth noting by the candidate. In fact, expert informants explained that in reality note-taking in case

FIGURE 4.1   Sample materials – speaking sub-test (physiotherapists)

CANDIDATE'S CARD

Setting: Hospital clinic.

Patient: An elderly person who is recovering from a stroke (CVA). The patient is making slow progress in learning to walk again.

Task: Talk to the patient about the following pieces of equipment
- a wheelchair
- a walking frame
- a walking stick.

Explain the advantages and disadvantages of each one.

You would like the patient to be as independent in his or her movements as possible. You feel the frame is not appropriate.

You want the patient to have a stick. You do not want the patient to have a wheelchair at this stage.

ROLE PLAYER'S CARD

Setting: Hospital clinic.

Patient: You are an elderly person who is recovering from a stroke. You feel you are making painfully slow progress, and don't really expect to be able to walk again.

You feel you should be allowed to have a wheelchair.

Task: Ask the physiotherapist when you will be given a wheelchair.

Insist on your need for this equipment. Explain that you feel that the painful exercises you are doing at the moment are pointless, and that you are pessimistic about your chances of making real progress.

Be difficult!

FIGURE 4.2   Sample materials – writing sub-test

OCCUPATIONAL ENGLISH TEST – WRITING TEST (MEDICAL PRACTITIONERS)

Time allowed: 40 minutes

Mrs Lyons is a patient in your general practice. Read the case notes below and complete the writing task that follows.

CASE NOTES   *Mrs Harriet Lyons*, 84-year old woman.

14/5/88

PH: • Osteoarthritis ® hip → THR 1985.
      • Hypertension $\times$ 20 yrs.

	• Type II diabetes × 15 yrs.
	• Recurrent UTIs.
	• Dementia × 10 yrs.
Medications:	• Daonil 5 mg bd.
	• Aldomet 500 mg bd.
	• Indocid 25 mg tds.

Brought in by daughter, with whom she lives.
Increasingly difficult to cope with her.
  • Urinary incontinence for last week. Dysuria?
  • Abdominal pain.
  • No fevers/sweats/loin pain.
  • More confused than usual. Refusing to eat.
  • No vomiting, diarrhoea.

O/E:	Afebrile. Confused.
	Mild suprapubic tenderness.
	Urine: protein +++ RBC +++ glucose $\frac{1}{2}$ %.

Assessment:	Worsening mental state 2° to UTI.
	As MSU impossible to obtain,
	℞ with Amoxil 500 mg tds × 7 days.

21/5/88	No more incontinence. Confusion improved.
12/6/88	Found wandering in the street by neighbours. Becoming increasingly vague. No other specific symptoms. Daughter very tearful. Reassured.
4/7/88	Found lying next to bed by daughter. Tripped over rug on way to toilet. Incontinent. Behaviour becoming more difficult lately; emotional outbursts, refusing to cooperate. Unsteady gait recently.

O/E:	Confused.
	BP 140/75 lying 110/60 standing.
	Bruise on ® hip. Movements good.
	No other injuries noted.

Assessment:	Postural hypertension 2° to Aldomet.
For:	↓ to 250 mg bd.
21/7/88	Gait has improved, but mental state continuing to be a problem. Daughter feels that she 'just can't cope any more' without outside help. Thinks that 'a nursing home might be best for everyone' and requests specialist opinion.
For:	Refer to Dr Chalming (geriatrician) re improved medical management and/or placement.

WRITING TASK

Using the information in the case notes, write a letter of referral to Dr Chalming. The main part of the letter should be 12–15 lines long. Do not use note form in the letter; expand the case notes where relevant into full sentences.

---

histories varies considerably from practitioner to practitioner: some take detailed notes, others almost none. In any case, note–taking will be organized around diagnostic considerations; if the diagnosis is clear then a brief note may suffice. But in order to get a *scorable* listening performance, note–taking had to be constrained in a potentially quite inauthentic way: candidates were instructed that notes were required under specific content headings.

The integration of expert professional knowledge and observable language behaviour in this instance, raised as an issue towards the end of Chapter 3, goes to the heart of the difficulty of the work sample tradition of performance testing. Authentic performances cannot easily be replicated in the test setting; writing on this subject in the language-testing literature often appear rather complacent on this point. As we said at the end of Chapter 2, appearances have often disguised deeper issues of validity.

4.3.6   Subsequent stages in test trialling and implementation

Prior to the introduction of each new form of the OET, materials are trialled and revised in the light of data analysis. As the issues raised here are not peculiar to performance assessments, they will not be described in detail; full information is available in McNamara (1990b). Operationally, the OET has been the subject of considerable ongoing research, much of which is reported in Chapter 8. The remainder of this chapter will be devoted to describing briefly the process of rater selection and training, and the process of standard setting, as each of these is characteristic of performance tests and involves important issues for the reliability and validity of such procedures.

4.3.6.1   Rater training and selection

Raters with appropriate qualifications and experience (teaching and specialist TESOL qualifications and experience of teaching advanced ESP classes) were chosen for training. For each of the Speaking and Writing sub-tests, raters were introduced to the rating forms, and asked to rate independently a number of sample performances chosen to illustrate different levels of performance, particularly those at or near the cut-score in the test. After each performance had been rated by the entire group, each individual rater was asked to reveal what rating he or she had given for that performance, and the ratings were entered into a table of ratings that was displayed to the whole group. It became immediately obvious each time who was 'out of line', and in cases of marked discrepancy each individual rater was called upon to defend his or her rating. This led to discussion and clarification of the criteria for scores in each category. This process was repeated for the entire set of selected performances. Clear movement in the direction of greater agreement was observed. Raters were then asked to take home a further set of performances, and to rate them within a few days, independently. These ratings were scrutinized by the trainer, and any rater failing to meet preset levels of consistency of rating or who showed marked relative harshness or severity was excluded from the cohort to be employed. This sanction of excluding raters must be available for raters to take rater training seriously.

4.3.6.2   Standard setting

There is considerable controversy over suitable methods of standard setting in performance assessment, and an example will be given here to indicate what is possible in a very difficult area. Ten senior doctors involved in the clinical supervision and/or clinical examination of overseas-trained graduates were asked to rate a set of 20 performances on the speaking subtest (performances from rater training sessions were included, as the levels of these performances were well known). Their ratings were compared with those of a group of trained raters. The doctors did not use the full rating grid, but were asked to judge to what extent the test candidate, on the basis of that performance, would be capable of surviving in a clinically based bridging course. This level, as agreed by the medical experts, was then set as the pass level on the test. High levels of agreement were found among the doctors, and between the doctors and the ESL-trained raters, appearing to confirm that the comparison of passing levels was meaningful. This study is reported in full in Lumley, Lynch and McNamara (1994) and discussed in some detail in Chapter 8.

4.4   Conclusion

In this chapter, the stages in the development of work sample performance tests have been outlined, and the carrying out of such a development project has been described in some detail. The example chosen, the Occupational English Test (OET), is the context in which some of the research reported in subsequent chapters has been conducted, and it is useful for the reader to have a clear idea of its structure and purpose. The account shows some of the difficulties encountered at the practical level in the development of a work sample test, and the kinds of decisions that are forced on the test developer, together with their implications for the validity of the resulting test. More importantly, the detail of the stage of content specification raises issues about the validity of this and other work sample tests on a number of grounds, including the difficulty of simulating authentic communicative process under test conditions, and the inseparability within authentic performance of professional knowledge and language behaviour. These issues were raised in more general terms in Chapters 2 and 3. As was stated there, work sample tests such'as the OET are strong on face validity, but any claim that the OET fulfils its brief of a test of 'the ability of candidates to communicate effectively in the workplace' (Alderson *et al.*, 1986: 3) must be interpreted with caution. This is not to say that the OET is a bad test; in fact it is a carefully constructed test and one that is administered in an entirely professional way. Rather, it illustrates the real difficulty of language performance testing in work-related contexts.

As stated earlier, the OET is a test which has been the subject of considerable research. Before going on to report that research in the latter part of this book, it is necessary to turn to a set of recently developed research techniques of great practical usefulness in investigating the validity of aspects of performance tests. As this research very often focuses on the behaviour of raters, it is in the context of raters and ratings that we will now introduce the measurement theory, multi-faceted Rasch measurement, on which these technical advances are based.

Appendix 4A   Scoring Grid – Speaking sub-test

Candidate's name: *Assessment mode*: Tape/Live
Name of assessor: *Date assessment made*:

YOU WILL HAVE TO MAKE TWO PROVISIONAL ASSESSMENTS AND A FINAL ASSESSMENT. ONLY THE FINAL ASSESSMENT WILL COUNT IN DETERMINING THE CANDIDATE'S SCORE.

Interview

This is *not* assessed. It is to allow the candidate to get used to the interlocutor, and to establish the candidate as a professional person in the eyes of the interlocutor.

First role play

At the end of the first role play, pause to enter the first of two *provisional* assessments using the following scales. Use a cross to mark which of the six points on each scale best locates the candidate's performance in that category. (In these provisional assessments, you may prefer to indicate a range on each scale rather than a single point on it, but in the final definitive assessment below, a single point on each scale must be decided upon.)

The first category (*Overall communicative effectiveness*) carries more weight than the others in the computation of results.

Each scale is meant to indicate a range from native or near-native skill to elementary competence in that category.

The middle of the scale (marked with a double line) indicates the minimum competence with which a candidate could cope with a bridging programme in a clinical setting, involving interaction with patients/clients, clinical teachers and colleagues. Scores *in* the middle range (that is, immediately either side of this dividing line) indicate performances just above or just below this minimum level of competence. Scores *either side* of this middle range indicate scores well above or below this minimum level. Scores at the *end* of the scale indicate native or near-native skill/elementary competence in the respective categories.

Overall communicative effectiveness
Near-native flexibility & range _|_|_||_|_|_ Limited

Intelligibility
Intelligible _|_|_||_|_|_ Unintelligible

Fluency
Even _|_|_||_|_|_ Uneven

Comprehension
Complete _|_|_||_|_|_ Incomplete

Appropriateness of language
Appropriate _|_|_||_|_|_ Inappropriate

Resources of grammar and expression
Rich, flexible _|_|_||_|_|_ Limited

Second role play

At the end of the second role play, make the second *provisional* assessment using the scale below. Base this assessment as far as possible on the evidence from the second role play only.

Overall communicative effectiveness
Near-native flexibility & range   _|_|_||_|_|_   Limited

Intelligibility
Intelligible   _|_|_||_|_|_   Unintelligible

Fluency
Even   _|_|_||_|_|_   Uneven

Comprehension
Complete   _|_|_||_|_|_   Incomplete

Appropriateness of language
Appropriate   _|_|_||_|_|_   Inappropriate

Resources of grammar and expression
Rich, flexible   _|_|_||_|_|_   Limited

Now, enter the FINAL DEFINITIVE ASSESSMENT using the scales below. You should base this final assessment on your overall judgement of both role plays. Remember, here you must mark a single cross *on* one of the lines on each scale. Do not indicate a range of points or place a cross intermediate between points; you must commit yourself to one of the six points.

Overall communicative effectiveness
Near-native flexibility & range   _|_|_||_|_|_   Limited

Intelligibility
Intelligible   _|_|_||_|_|_   Unintelligible

Fluency
Even   _|_|_||_|_|_   Uneven

Comprehension
Complete   _|_|_||_|_|_   Incomplete

Appropriateness of language
Appropriate   _|_|_||_|_|_   Inappropriate

Resources of grammar and expression
Rich, flexible   _|_|_||_|_|_   Limited

Appendix 4B   Scoring Grid – Writing sub-test

Candidate's name: *Assessor*:

Use a cross to mark which of the six points on each scale best locates the candidate's performance in that category. Do not indicate a range of points or place a cross intermediate between points; you must commit yourself to one of the six points.

The first category (*Overall task fulfilment*) carries more weight than the others in the computation of results from the scoring grid.

Each scale is meant to indicate a range from native or near-native skill to elementary competence in that category.

The middle of the scale (marked with a double line) indicates the minimum competence required to carry out professional writing tasks in conditions under supervision, for example on a clinically-based bridging programme. Scores in the middle range (that is, immediately either side of this dividing line) indicate performances just above or just below this minimum level of competence. Scores either side of this middle range indicate performances well above or below this minimum level. Scores at the ends of the scale indicate native or near-native skill/elementary competence in the respective categories.

Overall task fulfilment
              Completely satisfactory   _|_|_||_|_|_   Unsatisfactory

Appropriateness of language
              Appropriate   _|_|_||_|_|_   Inappropriate

Comprehension of stimulus
              Complete   _|_|_||_|_|_   Incomplete

Control of linguistic features (grammar and cohesion)
              Complete   _|_|_||_|_|_   Incomplete

Control of presentation features (spelling, punctuation)
              Complete   _|_|_||_|_|_   Incomplete

Notes

1. As pointed out in Chapter 2, the term *work sample* is used in this book in a broad sense and includes tests which involve simulation of any kind.
2. A full understanding of the significance of these contextual factors is beyond the scope of this book; their impact can be evaluated in part in investigations of the consequential validity of tests (Messick, 1989; see discussion in Chapter 2). The placing of all language testing within the framework of a critical applied linguistics (Pennycook, 1990) is overdue; cf. the discussion in Shohamy (1993).

3. Cf. Quinn and McNamara (1987).

4. A minimum of detail will be provided in the description of each of these components, as the extended example on the OET in the following section will illustrate more clearly what is intended.

5. The resources of time and money available meant that the time spent on the work of doctors could not be repeated for each of the professions concerned. This is one among many examples of the practical difficulty of dealing with disparate work settings in a single test. Of course, even for doctors, work settings will differ enormously, and assumptions about prototypicality had to be made.

6. Further details are available in McNamara (1990b), ch. 4.

7. Corresponding broadly to the stages identified by Byrne and Long (1976: see above) in consultations involving GPs.

8. Note that some of these elements (for example no. 5) are quite complex in terms of their generic structure (Martin, 1984; Swales, 1990; Paltridge, 1994); this brings us back to the problem of working at the macrolevel in characterizing the consultation as a basis for decisions about test content.

9. Leaving aside the question of potential diversity *within* professions.

10. Detailed specifications can usefully follow the format suggested in Davidson and Lynch (1993) and Lynch and Davidson (1994).

11. Role plays (cf. Burton's proposals in Candlin *et al.*, 1980b) allowed simulation of components 3 and 5 of the consultation, and aspects of 1, listed in Section 4.3.3.3 above.

12. The MCQ format itself represents a reading task which simulates the reading task facing the health professionals in the MCQ format tests of clinical competence subsequent to the OET. Some informants recommended the incorporation of MCQ format in the OET Reading sub-test as it was not clear if people who were doing poorly on the clinical MCQ exam were experiencing problems handling the MCQ format or clinical knowledge problems.

13. The Writing sub-test incorporates a substantial reading task, that of comprehending medical records, usually maintained in note form and containing standard abbreviations. Such records form the stimulus for the writing task where they provide the medical content to be included in the letter of referral.

14. In the development of subsequent versions of the test, the writing up was done by the informant and checked by the test developer and another expert informant.

5 Raters and ratings: introduction to multi-faceted measurement

5.1 Introduction

Performance assessment necessarily involves subjective judgements. This is appropriate: evaluation of any complex human performance can hardly be done automatically.[1] Judgements that are worthwhile will inevitably be complex and involve acts of interpretation on the part of the rater, and thus be subject to disagreement. This has long been recognized, and various methods have been proposed for identifying and quantifying the extent of disagreement between raters, and for reducing it to what are felt to be acceptable levels, usually by careful rater training and monitoring of ratings. Recently, a quite different approach to the issues involved has become available, which has the potential to improve our capacity to produce fair measures of the ability of test candidates in performance assessment settings.

Consider the following situation. Two candidates, Michael and Paula, are being assessed on a writing task on a test of English for Academic Purposes. The task involves writing a description of a simple technical procedure using information provided in a diagram showing in visual form the stages of the procedure. The written scripts are then rated. How can fairness of assessment be supported? Best practice traditionally would involve the following measures:

(1) the use of carefully worded descriptions of performance at each possible score level; so if it is believed that nine levels of achievement on the task can be distinguished, each of these will be defined carefully, and examples provided of scripts illustrating the characteristics of a performance at this level;
(2) the use of raters who have been trained carefully in the use of the rating procedure, and who have demonstrated a required level of agreement with other raters in moderation sessions;
(3) the practice of rating each script more than once, and the adoption of procedures for dealing with disagreement, such as averaging ratings, getting a further rating, or bringing the raters together to reach agreement.

Too often, of course, not all (or perhaps not even any) of these measures are taken, usually on grounds of economy. It is sometimes believed that clear definition of the criterion levels of achievement, supported by exemplar performances, together with careful rater training, make the involvement of more than a single rater unnecessary or even disruptive (for example, in the case of a live oral interview). Sometimes single ratings are permitted, with some looser control on the consistency of rater standards, for example by random double marking of a proportion of scripts. In these cases, even with proper rater training, substantial differences between raters will persist, with important (and unintended) possible consequences for the candidate. As we will show in this chapter, rater differences are reduced by training but do persist. As a result, raw scores (the original ratings given by the judge) are no reliable guide to candidate ability. In fact, as we shall see, numerous sources of variability in the performance setting may influence the likely outcome for a candidate, with possibly serious consequences. This chapter explores these issues in detail, and presents a new measurement procedure which has the potential to illuminate these issues very clearly, and to allow us to control the rating process better than we have been able to do in the past.

It is clear that raw scores may be an unreliable guide to ability. In another part of the test, imagine that Michael and Paula had to give a short talk on a topic chosen from a list provided. Imagine that Michael's performance is judged by a rater who, it turns out, is quite hard to impress (a 'hawk'); she gives him 5 on the 9-point rating scale used in the assessment. Paula's performance on the other hand is judged by a rater who is known to be generous (a 'dove'), and she also gets a score of 6. It also happens that Michael's chosen topic was unexpectedly difficult; candidates who chose it tended not to do well. Paula's topic was relatively easy, by comparison. So we have the situation as set out in Table 5.1.

Using the information in the raw scores, it looks as if Paula is more able. But interpreting the scores in the light of the information we have about the judges, and about the tasks, we might conclude that Michael's performance on this task is evidence of as great or even greater ability, because he faced a tough judge on a difficult task. The raw scores in other words are misleading. This leads us to a number of questions: *What* are

TABLE 5.1   How raw scores can disguise differences in ability in performance assessment settings

Candidate	Rater	Topic	Rating	Ability
Michael	'Hawk'	Tough	5	(Higher)
Paula	'Dove'	Easy	6	(Lower)

the characteristics of raters and task, and other relevant aspects of the assessment setting, and how can we determine them? Once these characteristics have been established, *how* can we take account of them when we form our picture of the ability of the candidate?

Answers to these questions can now be given in terms of the concepts and procedures of *multi-faceted measurement*,[2] a new theory and method of measurement relevant to performance assessment situations such as the above. The role of these important advances in measurement theory and practice is

(1) to illuminate the nature and extent of long-recognized rater and other effects in performance assessment settings;
(2) to enable us to carry out new kinds of research in these settings;
(3) in appropriate administrative contexts (that is, where what is at stake in the assessment warrants it, and where resources are adequate) to compensate for rater effects and the effect of a range of other variables in reporting candidate performance.

As with many advances, existing practice is thus not simply superseded but is clarified and improved.

In this chapter we will first consider the effect of the presence of the rater in the assessment process in performance assessment. We will then consider what other possible sources of influence (that is, apart from the ability of the candidate and the characteristics of the rater) there may be on patterns of test scores, and conceptualize the performance assessment setting in terms of *facets*, or aspects, of the setting. We will then show that particular interactions of these facets may determine the likelihood of particular test scores. We will distinguish between raw *scores* and what they may indicate of underlying ability in candidates, which may be estimated in rather more objective terms, known technically as *measures*. We will then introduce the possibility of a technology that can compensate for aspects of the test situation which vary from candidate to candidate: this technology is known as *multi-faceted measurement*. The potential of this exciting and powerful new technology will be sketched here, and some of its bases explained. We shall also consider the way in which multi-faceted measurement is executed by a readily available computer program known as FACETS (Linacre and Wright, 1992).

In the following chapter we will look in more detail at some of the basic concepts and tools of the measurement theory underlying multi-faceted measurement, and, later in the book, discuss how it has been used for research on language performance assessment and consider the debates that have arisen around it. In this chapter we will simply want to argue the case for using this powerful new tool in the context of performance assessment. The argument throughout this book is that the widespread introduction of performance assessment should properly be accompanied at the level of research and (where appropriate) administration by an understanding of the new technology of multi-faceted measurement.

5.2   The rater factor

As we saw in Chapter 2, we may contrast two types of assessment procedure; one involving a rater, the other not. The first of these is typical of performance-based assessment. In fact, so central is it to this type of assessment that Stiggins (1987: 33) makes the role of the rater rather than the activity of the person being rated the basis for his definition of *performance assessment*:

> Achievement can be, and often is, measured by observation and professional judgment. This form of measurement is called performance assessment.

Let us return to the contrast between traditional fixed response assessment and performance assessment presented in Chapter 2, and consider in more detail the schematic representation introduced there of the differences between the two approaches (adapted from Kenyon, 1992). The illustration in Chapter 2 is reproduced here, as Figure 5.1.

In traditional fixed response assessment, the score is derived directly from the instrument, which (for each item) offers the candidate a number of options or choices, only one of which is correct. Possible responses from candidates are constrained and anticipated in the form of the

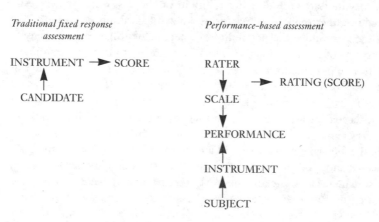

FIGURE 5.1   Characteristics of performance assessment

instrument itself; the scoring task is simply to count responses of a particular type, which are easily and unambiguously indicated by a checked box, a circled number, or something similar.

The focus of analysis of test data in fixed response assessment is twofold, each part being based on the interaction between the candidate and the test instrument. Candidates' responses are used as evidence of the abilities of the candidates and the quality of the instrument. Analysis of the responses can tell us about the adequacy of the items (item facility, item discrimination) and the instrument as a whole (overall reliability). In addition to these traditional analyses, new measurement approaches are available to analyse the adequacy of the items and instruments for the purposes intended (details of these new approaches will be presented in Chapter 6).

In performance-based assessment, on the other hand, the instrument elicits a performance or behaviour other than simple indication of choice (such assessment is often termed *constructed response* assessment). This performance or behaviour is then judged or rated, by means of a scale or other kind of scoring schedule. This introduces a new type of interaction, that between the rater and the scale; this interaction mediates the scoring of the performance. The rater–scale interaction resembles the subject–instrument interaction in that the rater–scale interaction is like a 'test' of the raters (and the scale) in the way that the subject–instrument interaction is a test of the subjects (and of the instrument). Just as we have always sought information on the instrument and the subject, so we should seek information on the scale and the raters; this is possible in multi-faceted Rasch measurement. Our estimates of subjects' abilities can then incorporate and compensate for what we discover about the raters and their interpretation of the rating scale. The same is true by extension of other aspects of the assessment context which may have an influence on the ratings given.

5.3 The nature and extent of variability in performance assessment

How extensive is the variability associated with aspects of the assessment setting, such as rater and task factors? Take, for example, the assessment of writing.[3] We can identify at least three main sources of variability in the scores obtained when candidates are assessed on writing they have produced. Not all candidates will get the same scores, for a number of reasons. First, the relative ability of the candidates will differ, and unless the test involves a simple task within the competence of all candidates (or a difficult one beyond their competence), this variation in ability will be reflected in the scores. Secondly, there may be variability associated with the task: if there is a choice of task, then candidates may gain different scores depending on which task they have chosen (cf. detailed discussion of research on this point in Huot, 1990: 240–6). Thirdly, there is variability associated with the raters, so that if a candidate had had a different rater, he or she might have gained a different score for the same performance.

The question then is, how much variation from these latter two sources can we expect? Linacre (1989b) provides an excellent discussion of variation associated with raters, pointing out that it has long been recognized (for at least a century!) that this is extensive, accounting for between one- and two-thirds of the variability in a set of scores, that is, as much as differences in ability among candidates. For example, Huot (1990: 250–1) summarizes a study by Diederich *et al.* (1961), who

> analyzed 300 papers on two topics written by freshmen at four Northeastern colleges. These 300 papers were scored on a 9-point scale by 53 readers ... Ninety-four percent of the papers received at least 7 grades, and no paper received less than five separate scores.

As far as variability associated with task demands is concerned, Linn *et al.* (1991: 19) report as follows: 'Generalizability studies of direct writing assessments that manipulate tasks ... indicate that the variance component for the sampling of tasks tends to be greater than that for the sampling of raters.'

In short, variability associated with both raters and tasks is extensive and is a fact of life that must be dealt with if we are to derive stable and fair estimates of how well learners can manage relevant tasks. In order to deal with this issue, however, we need to understand more about the sources of variability. The relevant characteristics of judges are of particular interest: what is it about judges and what they do in the rating situation that is associated with this instability in scoring? In the next section, we will examine the nature of rater characteristics.

5.3.1   Nature of variability among judges

Traditional theory conceptualized rater characteristics in terms of the difference between an idealized judge (the 'perfect' examiner) and actual judges ('ordinary' examiners); this difference was essentially seen as something to be regretted; the 'shortcomings' of ordinary examiners were the problem. Differences between judges could be understood in terms of overall *severity* (or leniency) on the one hand, and randomness (*error*) on the other. Linacre (1989b: 15) argues on the basis of earlier studies that the extent of error was as great as the extent of the differences in severity, and more problematic (because it was harder to eliminate or compensate for; equating the mean scores given by judges is a fairly simple matter).

One way of dealing with error is to see if it can be further broken down to reveal sub-patterns in the behaviour of raters which may be systematic in some way, that is, predictable, and thus able to be compensated for. Put more technically, we can attempt to decompose the error term into different sources of variance. In fact it turns out that judges typically do vary in predictable and consistent ways, a number of which have been identified, and will be discussed below. It is possible to model (and thus compensate for) all of these ways in which judges differ systematically from each other. We are then left with *random error*, defined by Linacre (1989b: 17) as 'the part of each rating which cannot be accounted for in any systematic way'.

Let us consider in more detail some of the important ways in which raters may differ from one another.[4]

1. Two raters may simply differ in their overall leniency.
2. Raters may display particular patterns of harshness or leniency in relation to only one group of candidates, not others, or in relation to particular tasks, not others. That is, there may be an *interaction* involving a rater and some other aspect of the rating situation. Leniency or harshness may not always work in the same direction for all items, or all things being rated. For example, raters in a speaking task may be asked to assess *intelligibility*, *fluency* and *accuracy*; raters may differ from one another in the way they rate any one of these aspects. A rater who overall is fairly lenient may be harsher than other raters when assessing, say, *intelligibility*. It has frequently been found that raters judge aspects of performance concerned with control of the formal resources of the language, particularly grammatical structure, more severely than they rate other aspects of the performance (McNamara, 1990a: 59–60; this study is discussed in detail in Chapter 8). In general, a rater may be consistently lenient on one item, consistently severe on another; this is a kind of *rater–item* interaction. Or raters may have a tendency to over- or underrate a candidate or class of candidates; this is an instance of a *rater–candidate* interaction.
3. Raters may differ from each other in the way they interpret the rating scale they are using. The problem arises because rating scales usually involve discrete rating categories: permissible ratings in the range of 1–6 are quite typical. Imagine a situation where a candidate of given ability falls roughly at the intersection of two of these rating

categories; not quite a '3', let us say, but better than most candidates who fall into the category '2'. The rater is forced into an 'either/or' judgement at this point: is the candidate a '3' or not? One rater may consistently score such candidates with a rating of '3', another not. At another point on the ability continuum, the tendency of such judges may be reversed, so that the previously more lenient rater may be harsher at this point on the scale, and vice versa.[5]

We can envisage this in the following way: imagine that candidate ability occupies a continuum. Raters may carve this up in different ways. Compare the way two raters interpret the relationship of the rating scale to this continuum:

1	2		3		4		5	6
1		2	3	4			5	6

Remember that both raters will be working with apparently the same rating scale, graphically displayed as having equal intervals, as follows:

1	2	3	4	5	6

But the appearance of equal intervals here is deceptive; such scales rarely have equal intervals in practice, that is, in the way the available rating categories are interpreted by raters. Moreover, it can be easily shown that raters in their actual interpretation of the scale do not behave in identical ways.

Another way of thinking about these differences between the raters is that, from the point of view of candidates, it will take differing increases in the ability required to have a given chance of achieving a particular score. The task of moving up to each successively higher level is like the distance between adjacent steps in a staircase, where such distances are non-equivalent, as in Figure 5.2.

These differences between raters may lead us to think in terms of rater types (McNamara and Adams, 1991/1994). Raters may differ systematically in the use they make of the range of scores available on a rating scale, for example by avoiding scores at the ends of the scale (this characteristic is known as *central tendency*). Others may avoid scores in the middle of the scale, tending to see differences between candidates more starkly and hedging their bets less.

4. Finally, and rather more obviously, raters may differ in terms of their consistency (or inconsistency); that is, the extent of the random error associated with their ratings. The patterns of scores allocated by a rater may not bear a consistent relationship to those allocated to the same candidates by other raters; they will be sometimes harsher, sometimes more lenient, even allowing for the normal variability in

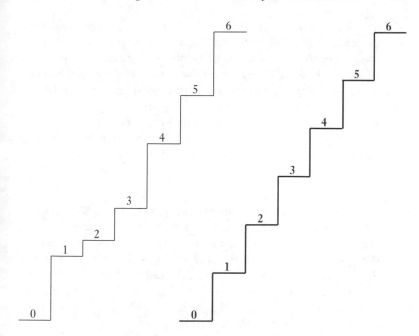

Left: actual step structure for a given rater (steps of unequal 'height')
Right: (**bold**) apparent step structure of rating scale (steps of equal 'height')

FIGURE 5.2   Apparent and actual step structure for 0–6 rating scale

these matters. It makes it hard to say exactly what sort of rater this is, other than that he or she is somewhat erratic; it thus becomes difficult to model the rater's characteristics, and thus to build in some compensation for them. Lack of consistency of this kind is not something that even the most sophisticated technology can do much about, and such raters, once identified, may need to be retrained or, failing this, excluded from the rating process.

5.3.2   Attempts to deal with differences between judges

Of course it would be simpler if judges differed less, and in particular random error is potentially a serious problem. Attempts are usually made to reduce the variability of judges' behaviour by means discussed at the beginning of this chapter. One of these is rater training, in which raters are introduced to the assessment criteria and asked to rate a series of carefully selected performances, usually illustrating a range of abilities and characteristic issues arising in the assessment. Ratings are carried out independently, and raters are shown the extent to which they are in line with other raters and thus achieving a common interpretation of the rating criteria. The rating session is usually followed by additional follow-up ratings, and on the basis of these an estimate is made of the reliability and consistency of the rater's judgements, in order to determine whether the rater can participate satisfactorily in the rating process.

Recently, however, the nature and effect of the rater-training process is being reconceptualized. Surprisingly, the effectiveness of rater training has been little studied. Recent research (McIntyre, 1993; Weigle, 1994; Shohamy *et al.*, 1992) has examined its effects, and has demonstrated the following:

1. Rater training is successful in making raters more self-consistent. That is, the main effect of training is to reduce the random error in rater judgements. This is essential if an orderly process of measurement is to be conducted. Weigle (1994) shows that reliable candidate ability measures are unlikely to be achieved from untrained raters, even when attempts are made to adjust for rater characteristics using multi-faceted measurement techniques, because of the large randomness associated with the ratings of such raters.
2. Rater training can reduce but by no means eliminate the extent of rater variability in terms of overall severity. In particular, extreme differences are reduced – outliers in terms of harshness or leniency are brought into line – but significant and substantial differences between raters persist. Lunz and Stahl (1990) argue that judges employ unique perceptions which are not easily altered by training. This stable finding will be discussed further in this chapter and particularly in Chapter 8, when output from analyses of rater behaviour using multi-faceted Rasch measurement is considered. This being the case, attempts to deal adequately with differences in rater severity through rater training are bound to be only partially successful, in which case compensation for rater characteristics needs to be built into the rating process.

In any case, is perfect agreement even desirable? Constable and Andrich (1984) raise this as an issue:

> It is usually required to have two or more raters who are trained to agree on independent ratings of the same performance. It is suggested that such a requirement may produce a paradox of attenuation associated with item analysis, in which too high a correlation between items, while enhancing reliability, decreases validity.

In the Japanese director Kurosawa's classic film *Rashomon*, the accounts of four witnesses to a dramatic incident are presented; they are profoundly different. Where does the truth lie? Each of the accounts is plausible, each deceptive, all frustratingly at odds with each other, but also, paradoxically, mutually illuminating. The same may be said (more trivially!) of assessments of human performance: in a matter of some complexity, no one judgement may be said to be definitive, although there is likely to be a considerable area of overlap between judgements. These differences and similarities need to be taken into account in determining the best estimate of a candidate's ability. (In multi-faceted measurement, the truth is held to lie somewhere in the middle.)

To sum up: raters display certain characteristics in their participation in the rating process, and these characteristics are a source of potentially considerable variability in the ratings of a performance. Traditional methods have tried to eliminate 'undesirable' rater characteristics through processes of training and accreditation. While rater training is essential for creating the conditions for an orderly measurement process based on ratings by making raters more self-consistent, there is a limit to how far this process can be successful, or whether the elimination of differences is indeed desirable! A different approach is to accept that the most appropriate aim of rater training is to make raters internally consistent so as to make statistical modelling of their characteristics possible, but beyond this to accept variability in stable rater characteristics as a fact of life, which must be compensated for in some way, either through multiple marking and averaging of scores, or using the more sophisticated techniques of multi-faceted analysis, to be presented below. The modelling of rater characteristics made possible by multi-faceted measurement may be done for two purposes. From a *practical* point of view, the estimation of the candidate's ability can take into account the characteristics of rater (or task) so discovered, to produce estimates of candidate ability that are comparable, i.e. that can be generalized across raters and across tasks. From a *research* point of view, a number of questions can be addressed. In what ways do raters differ? Can we identify distinct rater types? Are these rater characteristics amenable to modification by a training process, and if so, how much? What amount of training is required? Do raters display consistent characteristics over time? If a rater's characteristics are successfully modified by training, are these changes stable over time, or does the rater revert to old habits? How often do raters need to be retrained?

5.3.3 Other facets of the assessment setting

We have so far discussed the effect of rater and task variability on score outcomes. These are but two aspects of the performance setting. For example, in a performance assessment of speaking where the candidate is in direct face-to-face interaction with the assessor, a number of other factors may come into play. Particular raters may react in different ways to candidates of particular language backgrounds. Or there may be a gender effect: the gender of the candidate and rater may be an influence on scores (this influence need not, of course, be recognized by either party). Or it may be the time of day: if the rater is fresh, or the candidate is performing early in the morning, this may influence the likelihood of a certain kind of score. It may be that the physical setting has an influence: a well-organized, comfortable examination centre may improve your chances of a particular score. In some tests of speaking, the candidate interacts not with a rater but with an interlocutor who makes no rating; the interaction is audiotaped and the performance is rated from audiotape at some central location after the examination. Sometimes, the stimulus for speaking is not a live interaction but is presented to the candidate on tape, in a language laboratory. All of these aspects of the assessment setting may influence the likelihood of a particular pattern of scores.

Each of these aspects of the setting can be called a *facet*, and information on the effect of any of these facets, or any combination of them, can be sought. Once this information is available, it can then be incorporated automatically into our estimates of the ability of the candidate; in other words, this *measure* of the candidate's ability results from an automatic adjustment of the candidate's raw score to take account of what is known about the influence of these facets. Exactly what kind of adjustment or allowance should be made, and how it is made, are problems addressed by multi-faceted measurement theory. A computer program known as FACETS (Linacre and Wright, 1992) allows this information to be analysed and the appropriate adjustments or allowances to be made automatically. The main features of this analysis will now briefly be introduced; the conceptual groundwork for understanding this in more depth will be presented in the following chapter, and in Chapter 9. You may wish to read what follows at this point and then return to it after you have read more of the theoretical and conceptual background.

5.3.4   How important is it to model facets of the assessment setting in determining candidates' abilities?

The extent of the variability in ratings has been outlined above. We have shown that training can improve raters' self-consistency, but leaves other, systematic variability largely intact. How important is it then to compensate candidates' ratings to allow for the effect of the facets we have investigated on the ratings? Research on the extent of the differences in rater severity surviving rater training is discussed in detail in Chapter 8.

Briefly, typical differences in rater severity following training may affect a candidate's chances of getting a given rating (say, the rating needed for entry to some desired work or academic setting) by as much as 40 per cent. This is clearly an important matter in many contexts. Thus, from a practical point of view a knowledge of the techniques and procedures of multi-faceted measurement is worth while; this is to say nothing of the outstanding research potential of this new measurement tool. Two further examples will demonstrate the extent of rater differences.

Figure 5.3 (from Linacre, 1993) is based on data from a test of writing skills collected by George Engelhart of Emory University, Atlanta, Georgia. It shows part of a raw score/ability measure plot for candidates from this test. The vertical axis represents the raw, unadjusted scores of candidates taking the writing test: scores lay in the range 40 to 50. The horizontal axis shows the ability estimates (known technically as *measures*, to distinguish them from the raw scores) for the same candidates once the raw scores have been adjusted to allow for rater characteristics. It can be seen that the relationship between scores and measures is rather weak. For example, candidates with raw scores of 41 and 47 are estimated as having the *same* underlying ability; candidates with ability measures of 2 and 4 on a scale ranging from 1 to 4.5[6] (that is, very large differences in underlying ability) got the same raw score.

Figure 5.4 (from Stahl and Lunz, 1993) shows a clearer pattern of relationship of grades (raw scores) to measures, once the effect of two facets (judge severity and task difficulty) has been factored in. But the relationship is still far from linear; that is, grades 50 points apart can result in the same ability estimate; abilities two scale units apart on a 6-point scale represent the same raw score.

5.4   Multi-faceted measurement

In this section, we will illustrate in an introductory way how multi-faceted measurement provides us with information on the influence of rater and task characteristics on ability estimates in performance assessment settings. We will do this in the context of data analysis from trials of the Speaking module (McNamara *et al.*, 1993) of a larger ESL testing project, the **access:** test, developed for the Australian government in 1993 for use with intending immigrants to Australia. A fuller treatment of the concepts and procedures involved will be presented in the next two chapters.

The **access:** test[7] is used to give information about English language proficiency to assist in decisions about the processing of applicants for

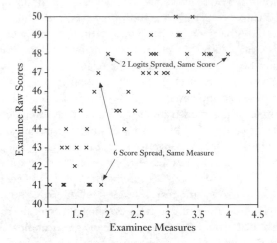

FIGURE 5.3   Measure/Rating plot (detail), Georgia Spring 1990 Writing Data (Linacre, 1993)

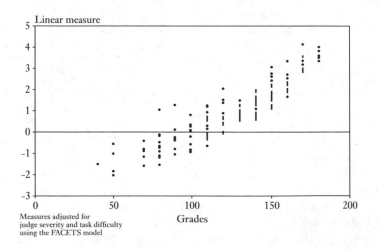

FIGURE 5.4   Plot of grades to linear measure (Stahl and Lunz, 1993)

immigration to Australia. The test involves an assessment of the four macroskills, and is administered in a number of different centres internationally, all outside Australia. The Speaking module is offered in two formats, depending on facilities available at the test administration venue. In format A, the 'live' version, the candidate is involved in a series of extended response oral interactions (narrative, role play, description, explanation, etc.) with a trained interviewer. The interviewer does not carry out an assessment (the guaranteeing of local rater quality is logistically impossible); instead, the interaction is recorded on audiotape and sent to an assessment centre in Australia, where it is rated at least twice by trained raters. In format B, the 'tape-based' version, candidates are engaged in tasks whose form and content are for the most part replicas of those in the live version, except that the stimulus is presented on audiotape (usually in a language laboratory) and the candidates record their responses directly onto audiotapes. These are also sent back to Australia for rating. Assessment of language skills has always formed part of the selection procedure for certain categories of intending immigrants to Australia, but it has been done informally on the spot, by immigration personnel without appropriate training in language assessment; the new test was designed to formalize and professionalize the procedure. It is in fact used for only a tiny fraction of intending immigrants, those in certain discretional categories; most immigrants are not tested for proficiency in English.

As part of the trialling of versions of the test, 83 subjects took the live version of the Speaking module and their performances were each separately rated by each of four trained raters. The test materials took the form of a number of discrete oral tasks (for example, descriptions and commentary on visual stimulus materials, narrative from picture stimulus, role plays, instruction-giving based on interpretation of material in diagrammatic display, extended interview). Performance on each task was rated on each of two or more aspects of the performance considered appropriate for the particular task: for example, *fluency, resources of grammar, appropriateness, vocabulary*, and so on. *Overall impression* ratings were also given. In all, four separate ratings of each candidate were given on each of 23 aspect/task combinations (referred to henceforth as *items*).

In the subsequent analysis, three facets of the assessment setting (*candidates, items* and *raters*) were investigated.[8]

For each *candidate*, there are performances on several items, and assessments by each of the four raters. We thus have multiple sources of information about the ability of candidates.

For each item, we have attempts by many candidates, whose performances on other items are known. We have judgements on each of these attempts by raters whose patterns of ratings on other items, and on the same item with other candidates, are known.

For each rater, we have ratings on many items and on many candidates; we have multiple other ratings from other raters on the same items and the same candidates.

The trial data available for analysis can be envisaged as a matrix of information, as set out as in Table 5.2. Essentially, multi-faceted measurement evaluates the significance of each cell in the matrix in the light of the information in the rest of the matrix. To the extent that the response in each cell is predictable in the light of the information in the rest of the matrix, and this predictability is found across the matrix, then consistent patterning of behaviour in relation to candidates, items and raters has been observed and the analysis has succeeded in modelling these consistencies. Essentially the analysis proceeds by seeking out any such consistent patterning in the data, and providing summaries of the extent to which this search renders individual ratings predictable.

Let us consider this in a little more detail. Each rating can be seen as a function of the interaction of three facets or factors: the *ability* of the *candidate*; the *difficulty* of the *item*; and the *characteristics* of the *rater*. Moreover, we can think of the contents of each cell not in isolation, but in the light of the rest of the data matrix. That is, for each combination of candidate, item and rater we have information in the rest of the matrix relevant to the likelihood of any individual rating. For example, we know quite a lot about the *characteristics* of the *rater* from all the other ratings he/she has given – both on other items with this same candidate, and, more importantly, on this and other items with other candidates. Similarly, we know quite a lot about the *ability* of the *candidate* from his or her performance on other items, on which we have information from the performance of other candidates; and we also have judgements of the candidate's ability from other raters. Finally, we know a lot about the *difficulty* of the *item* concerned by the performance of other candidates on the item; and we know about the ability of those candidates from their performance on other items of varying difficulty. We are thus in a position to predict the likely score for that combination of candidate, item and rater, and to evaluate the accurancy of our prediction. More technically, we can attempt to model the data in the data matrix – to make it predictable. To the extent that this is possible, the data fit the model we are using; to the extent that it is difficult to do this for individual items, candidates or raters, this will also become clear; we have identified data–model mismatch or misfit. The model in this case is known as a multi-faceted Rasch model. Rasch models will be discussed in detail in Chapter 6, and more technically in Chapter 9. The model states that the

TABLE 5.2   Data matrix

	Item														
	1				2				3				...	23	
Cand	Rater				Rater				Rater				...	Rater	
	A	B	C	D	A	B	C	D	A	B	C	D	...	A	B	C	D
1	2	3	3	3	3	3	2	4	4	3	3	4	...	3	1	1	2
2	4	5	5	5	5	5	4	4	6	5	6	6	...	5	4	3	4
3	1	2	2	1	2	3	2	3	3	2	2	3	...	2	1	3	2
.																
.																
.																
83	6	4	4	5	6	5	5	5	6	5	4	4	...	4	6	6	5

likelihood of a particular rating on an item from a particular rater for a particular candidate can be predicted mathematically from the ability of the candidate, the difficulty of the item and the severity of the rater.

Although the data in this example involve multiple ratings of every performance by each rater, the data requirements of multi-faceted Rasch analysis are in fact more flexible than this would suggest (Linacre, 1989a). The analysis can tolerate missing data,[9] provided that there is proper linking between elements of each facet in the matrix (that is, that somewhere in the matrix there are multiple ratings of each element of each facet). This flexibility can be exploited in a careful rating design, to minimize the amount of double rating required. McNamara and Adams (1991/1994) have shown the effect on estimates of a progressive reduction in information in the matrix. Basically, useful estimates can still be derived from a 'holey' data matrix, although the more information available to the analysis the better these estimates will be (that is, the closer to the best estimate, defined as the estimate derived from an analysis of the complete data matrix).

To the extent that the data in the matrix are found to conform to the Rasch model, it is possible to bring all the facets together into a single relationship, expressed in terms of the effect they are likely to have on a candidate's chance of success. That is, we can say precisely what sort of challenge the candidate was facing on that item with that rater, and are accordingly able to interpret the actual rating given. For example, let us go back to the illustrative situation set out at the beginning of this chapter: we are in a position to evaluate the significance of Michael getting a rating of 5 under the conditions he faced, rather than taking the rating at face value; and we can contrast this challenge with the lesser challenge facing Paula, and evaluate her raw score accordingly. We have moved beyond and (as it were) beneath raw scores to understand the effect of the conditions of assessment on the score levels achieved. In general, then, we can describe the ability of candidates in terms of the chance of their succeeding at a given level on an item, given what we have discovered about its difficulty and about the severity of the rater involved. Further, we can express the ability of the candidate as his or her precise chance of getting *any* given score level under *any* condition of assessment we have modelled.

Similarly, we can express the difficulty of items according to the likelihood of a candidate of given ability getting a given score (or better) from a rater of given severity on that item. Finally, we can express the severity of raters in terms of the chances of the rater awarding a given rating (or better) on a given item to a candidate of given ability. The facets can thus all be brought together in a single frame of reference. The relationship of the facets can be mapped, as in the map of facets for the analysis of data from an early trial of material for the **access**: test shown in Figure 5.5.[10] (The nature and function of mapping in output from such analyses is discussed in more detail in Chapter 7.)

Figure 5.5 displays visually the relative abilities of candidates, the relative toughness of raters and the relative difficulty of items on average in terms of the scale of probability developed in the analysis. We are given information in terms of this scale of the chances of success of candidates and the degree of challenge presented by particular raters and particular items. There are four columns in Figure 5.5: one for the scale of measurement used, and one for each of the facets *candidate*, *rater* and *item*. Individual candidates, raters and items are located at a certain point on the scale in column 1 (this acts as a 'ruler' to enable us to locate the ability of individual candidates, the severity of individual raters and the toughness of individual items). The measurement scale is used to report estimates of probabilities of candidate responses under the various conditions of measurement (ability, difficulty, rater severity) which have been entered into the analysis: the probabilities are expressed in units called 'logits' (pronounced 'LOH-jits'; stress on the first syllable). This unit is likely to be unfamiliar, even daunting, to many readers, but is a simple transformation of more familiar ways of expressing probability such as odds or percentage chance. (We will explain in more detail in the next chapter the nature of measures on the logit scale, and the relationship between such measures and more conventional expressions of probability.) For the moment, let us observe that the average item difficulty in terms of this scale is conveniently set at zero, so that items with negative signs are easier than average, and those with positive signs are tougher

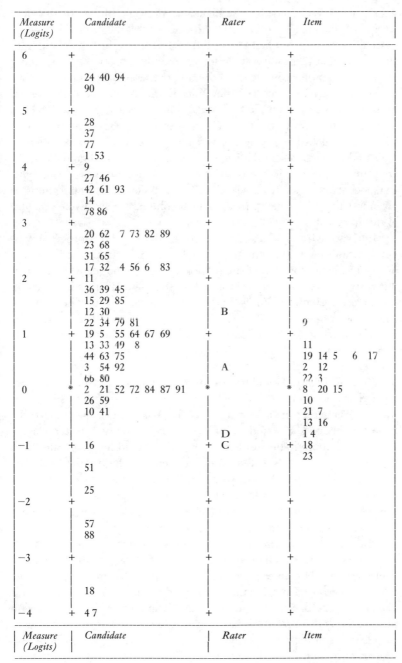

FIGURE 5.5   Facet map for **access:** test data

than average. With persons, the higher on the scale, the more able; and with raters the higher on the scale, the tougher.

Candidates are identified by their ID numbers in the second column. We can see that there was a wide spread of ability; many different ability levels were identified. In the third column, the severity of each of the four raters is given. We can see that they indeed differ in their relative severity, by as much as 2 units on the logit scale; this converts to a reduction of as much as 40 per cent in a candidate's chances of achieving a given rating if he or she happened on the most severe rater instead of the most lenient.[11] This finding has serious practical implications, but should not be considered unusual; in fact it is typical of almost all assessments of this type. Evidence in support of this view, and a discussion of its implications, is given in Chapter 8. Finally, in the fourth column, we are given a picture of the average difficulty of particular items.

Multi-faceted analysis executed through the FACETS program provides, in addition to the summary map (Figure 5.5), detailed information in separate tables for each of the individual facets (candidate ability, item difficulty and rater severity). Table 5.3 illustrates the kind of information provided on candidates (only part of the information provided by the analysis is presented here, for the first 15 and the last 10 candidates, for the sake of economy). Candidates are identified in column 1, and in column 2 an estimate of their ability provided, again in logits. Remember that zero on the logit scale represents the challenge presented by an item of average difficulty. A candidate who had a 50 per cent chance of achieving a given rating on this item would be well matched with this item – it would be targeting his or her ability well. Accordingly, the ability estimate for this person would be expressed by convention as zero logits. People with ability estimates higher than this would have a greater than 50 per cent chance of succeeding on the item; the higher the logit estimate, the higher their chances would be (logits are an exact expression of this chance; we will see in the next chapter how to make a simple conversion between logits and percentage chances). Candidates with estimates below zero would find the item in question more challenging.

Estimates of underlying ability are subject to error, of course, as they are extrapolations from the data available. Accordingly, an estimate of the likely *error* involved in each estimate is also provided in column 3. The size of this error term will naturally depend on how much information is available in the data matrix as a whole. If candidates are measured on many tasks, and are rated by many raters, then the errors associated with the estimates of their abilities will be relatively small. Information is also provided (column 4) on the extent to which the model was a good basis for estimating the observed scores for each candidate across all the items

TABLE 5.3 Report on measures of candidates' abilities, **access**: test (part)

Candidate	Ability Estimate	Error	Fit	
			(Infit mean square)	(Standardized infit)
1	4.18	0.18	1.2	1
2	−0.06	0.16	0.8	−1
3	0.43	0.16	0.6	−2
4	2.24	0.17	0.9	0
5	0.99	0.16	1.1	0
6	2.12	0.17	1.6*	3*
7	2.70	0.17	0.8	−1
8	0.72	0.16	0.7	−2
9	3.93	0.18	1.3	2
10	−0.32	0.16	0.9	0
11	2.07	0.17	1.2	1
12	1.45	0.17	0.9	0
13	0.72	0.16	1.2	0
14	3.41	0.17	1.0	0
15	1.64	0.17	0.9	0
.	.	.	.	.
.	.	.	.	.
.	.	.	.	.
85	1.56	0.17	1.0	0
86	3.23	0.17	0.9	0
87	−0.09	0.16	2.2*	5*
88	−2.69	0.16	0.9	0
89	2.79	0.17	1.0	0
90	5.41	0.20	0.9	0
91	−0.09	0.16	0.9	0
92	0.43	0.16	0.9	0
93	3.65	0.17	1.0	0
94	5.62	0.21	0.9	0
Candidate	Ability Estimate	Error	Fit	
			(Infit mean square)	(Standardized infit)
Mean (n = 83)	1.57	0.17	1.0	−0.1
SD	1.96	0.01	0.3	1.7

Reliability (reliable difference in ability of candidates) 0.99

* = unsatisfactory fit (misfit)

on the test. This is expressed in terms of the degree of match, or *fit*, between the expectations of the model and the actual data for that candidate on each item. The notion of fit is likely to be relatively unfamiliar, and is explained in detail in the next chapter. For the moment, it is enough to say that there are various ways of expressing this fit quantitatively; two measures of fit (*infit mean square* and *standardized infit*) are reported here. These technical terms will also be explained in the next chapter. Where the index of fit is unsatisfactory for a particular candidate (this has been indicated with asterisks in Table 5.3; the criteria for assessing fit are presented in Chapter 6), we have a warning that an orderly measurement process was not achieved for this candidate, and that inferences based on test scores may not be easily supported. This has important implications for our understanding of the fairness of the assessment process for such candidates, and action will have to be taken.

Finally, at the bottom of the table, we have summaries of the various estimates provided: the mean and standard deviation of the ability estimates, error, and fit. In addition, the extent to which the test defines different levels of ability – the capacity of the test to distinguish between candidates – is provided in a summary of the information on candidates, in the form of a

TABLE 5.4   Report on estimates of item difficulties, **access:** test

Candidate	Ability Estimate	Error	Fit (Infit mean square)	Fit (Standardized infit)
1	−0.81	0.09	1.0	0
2	0.46	0.09	0.8	−2
3	0.15	0.09	1.0	0
4	−0.79	0.09	0.8	−2
5	0.67	0.09	0.8	−2
6	0.52	0.09	0.8	−2
7	−0.45	0.09	1.0	0
8	−0.09	0.09	1.0	0
9	1.20	0.09	0.8	−2
10	−0.10	0.09	1.1	0
11	0.85	0.09	0.9	−1
12	0.42	0.09	1.9*	9*
13	−0.59	0.09	0.8	−2
14	0.56	0.09	1.0	0
15	−0.09	0.09	1.4	5*
16	−0.67	0.09	0.7	−3
17	0.63	0.09	0.7	−4
18	−0.91	0.09	0.9	−1
19	0.56	0.09	0.9	−1
20	−0.00	0.09	0.9	0
21	−0.38	0.09	1.3	3
22	0.11	0.09	0.9	0
23	−1.26	0.09	1.6*	6*

Candidate	Ability Estimate	Error	Fit (Infit mean square)	Fit (Standardized infit)
Mean (n = 23)	0.00	0.09	1.0	−0.1
SD	1.96	0.01	0.3	1.7

Reliability (reliable difference in difficulty of items) 0.98

* = unsatisfactory fit (misfit)

reliability index.[12] The index is on a scale of 0 to 1, with values close to 1 suggesting good reliability. It is important to note that this reliability is not the kind of reliability traditionally reported for performance assessments, which indicates the degree of agreement between raters. It is much more like the indices of reliability (such as Kuder-Richardson 21 or Cronbach's α) associated with tests with dichotomously scored (right/wrong) items, such as grammar tests, reading tests or vocabulary tests.

The information on estimated item difficulty (Table 5.4) is presented in a similar way. Items are identified (column 1), and an estimate given (column 2) of their underlying difficulty in terms of the likely challenge they present to candidates. As stated earlier, average item difficulty is set at zero logits, by convention. In other words, a person at an equivalent level of difficulty will find such an item presents a degree of challenge such that they have a 50 per cent chance of getting a given score on the item. Items with positive signs are more difficult, those with negative signs less difficult. Again, errors of these estimates are provided (column 3), together with indices of the degree of match between the model and the data, in the form of fit statistics (column 4). These are averages of the extent to which the actual scores of particular candidates are predicted by the model; we would expect some variation in this, and the extent of the variation is summarized across all candidates in the matrix for each item. Items which show greater than expected or lower than expected variation ('misfitting' or 'overfitting' items, respectively) are flagged for further inspection (these are marked with asterisks in the table; again, the issue of fit and the criteria for evaluating it are fully set out in the following chapter). An overall estimate is given at the bottom of the table of the extent to which items are at reliably different levels of difficulty, together with means and standard deviations for the figures in each column, as in Table 5.3.

Finally, we are provided with information on the characteristics (relative severity and consistency) of raters (Table 5.5). Raters are identified (column 1) and an estimate made of their severity (column 2), again in terms of the probability of achieving a given rating with that rater. Errors of these estimates are provided (column 3) , and the fit statistics as before (column 4), which in this case indicate the relative *consistency* in the judge's ratings. Lack of consistency (indicated by high fit values) is obviously a problem, and such raters would need to be retrained or possibly excluded from the rating process. (Rater B is on the borderline of concern here; interpretation of fit values will be discussed in the following chapter.[13]) If variation between predicted and observed values is less than the model predicts (indicated by unusually low fit values), it may mean that the judge is a good rater, or more likely that he or she is

TABLE 5.5   Report on estimates of rater severity, **access**: test

Rater	Severity Estimate	Error	Fit	
			(Infit mean square)	(Standardized infit)
A	0.41	0.04	1.0	0
B	1.40	0.04	1.2	5
C	−1.03	0.04	1.0	1
D	−0.77	0.04	0.8	−7
Mean (n = 23)	0.00	0.04	1.0	−0.2
SD	0.97	0.00	0.1	4.8

Reliability (reliable difference in severity of raters) 0.99

not using the whole available scale, and that caution has led him or her to avoid chances of error; in this case retraining may again be necessary. (Rater D is possibly of concern on this point.) At the bottom of the table a summary is provided of the extent to which differences between the estimated severity of raters are real differences – that is, are not accountable for in terms of the inevitable error of the estimates. This summary is provided in the form of a *reliability index*, a rather misleading term as it is *not* an indication of the extent of agreement between raters (the traditional meaning of reliability indices for raters) but the extent to which they really differ in their level of severity. High reliability indices in this table indicate real differences between raters, not in their overall ranking of candidates, but in the actual levels of scores assigned to them. Typically, these indices do tend to indicate substantial differences between raters, showing that one of the traditional aims of rater training (elimination of differences in severity) has not been achieved and is indeed unachievable (and possibly undesirable – see the extended discussion of this point earlier in the chapter, and empirical evidence on this whole topic in Chapter 8).[14]

5.4.1   Feasibility under operational conditions

It is worth commenting on the use of multi-faceted analysis under operational conditions. First, the design of the data collection is an important issue, as it is important to plan for some multiple rating of each element of each facet under each of the conditions of assessment of interest. Secondly, designs incorporating many facets will need large data sets to ensure stability of estimate of facets (see the cautionary message of de Jong and Stoyanova (1994) on data requirements). There is a need to limit the number of facets to be analysed in any single analysis, unless very large data sets are available. Thirdly, fresh analyses need to be conducted for each test administration; we cannot assume that rater characteristics will remain constant across administrations. Research to be reported in Chapter 8 (Lumley and McNamara, 1995) shows that this is not the case. Fourthly, it is possible to enlarge data sets by combining data from old and new analyses provided the data matrices have some overlap; this overlap is the basis for a procedure of linking across occasions known as *anchoring*, whereby the values of elements in a facet derived from one analysis are specified for the subsequent analysis, thus allowing comparability of output from the two analyses. Fifthly, sufficient time needs to be built in between test scoring and the reporting of results to allow the necessary analysis and transformation of raw scores into measures to take place, although with experience this can become an efficient process. In general, the routine use of multi-faceted analysis will be restricted to high-stakes test settings where resources and the necessary expertise are available; nevertheless, the cost and feasibility of multi-faceted measurement in these circumstances are similar to those where the traditional measures discussed at the beginning of the chapter are put into place. One disadvantage of multi-faceted measurement is that analysis requires relatively large data sets; an advantage however, as stated above, is that economies in the extent of multiple rating are possible because of the flexible data requirements of the analysis. Certainly, use of these procedures under operational test conditions has now become routine for a number of high-stakes language performance tests, and their feasibility has been amply demonstrated.

5.4.2   Bias analysis

So far we have considered the way in which multi-faceted measurement can characterize raters in terms of their overall behaviour, across all items and all candidates. Of course, it is possible, as we saw earlier, that raters may display particular patterns of harshness or leniency in relation to only one group of candidates, not others, or in relation to particular tasks, not others. That is, there may be an *interaction* involving a rater and some other aspect of the rating situation. The identification of these systematic sub-patterns of behaviour is achieved in multi-faceted Rasch measurement in so-called *bias analyses*.

As we have seen, multi-faceted analysis (in common with many statistical procedures) compares expected and observed values in a set of data. Differences between expected and observed values are known technically as *residuals*. Fit statistics (for raters, items, persons, and other facets) *summarize* for each rater, item, person, etc. the extent to which the differences between expected and observed values are within a normal range. The basic idea in bias analysis is to further analyse the residuals to see if any further sub-pattern emerges. For example, perhaps the differences are associated mainly with certain tasks or candidates for particular raters, or certain candidates on particular tasks, and so on. The study of bias is thus the study of *interaction* effects, e.g. systematic interaction between particular raters and particular candidates, or between particular raters and particular tasks/items, etc. There will still be some unexplained, random error left over at the end of this analysis; this represents unexplained random variation.

Table 5.6 shows the information provided in a bias analysis on the **access:** trial test data. Rater-by-item interactions were investigated, in order to provide feedback to each rater on unusual patterns of leniency or severity for each item.

Bias analysis works in the following way. Each rater-by-item combination is considered in turn (these are listed in columns 1 and 2). Columns 3–5 show us what we might expect in the pattern of scores for that particular combination, compared with what was actually found. The *overall* severity of each rater (across *all* items) has already been estimated; so has the *overall* difficulty of each item (across *all* raters). It is possible to use this information to predict the most likely score on each item from each rater *if the rater were rating that item in the way he or she rated the other items.* So, for example, in line 1 of Table 5.6, knowing the general severity of Rater A (cf. estimate in Table 5.5) and the difficulty of Item 1 (cf. estimate in Table 5.4), and knowing the estimated ability of each candidate (Table 5.3), we can predict the most likely rating (score) for each candidate with this rater on this item, based on his or her ability, the item difficulty and the rater severity. These individual scores are totalled across all candidates (n=83) to produce a total *expected* score from this rater on this item (359) (column 4). In fact, the *observed* total score for the 83 candidates was 374 (column 3); in other words, the candidates on the whole received higher scores than might have been expected. It seems, then, that this item elicited more lenient behaviour than usual on the part of the rater. The difference between the observed and expected score is on average 0.18 score points (considered over the 83 candidates) (column 5). In column 6, this difference is expressed as a measure on the logit scale: this tells us precisely how much less of a challenge was presented by this item with this rater than might have been expected, and the effect of this on the chances of success for candidates under those conditions.[15] We are also given an estimate of the likely error of this bias estimate (column 7).

TABLE 5.6   Bias calibration report, **access**: test, rater–item interactions (part)

Rater	Item	Observed score	Expected score	Obs–Exp average	Bias (logit)	Error	z-Score	Fit (Mean square)
A	1	374	359.0	0.18	−0.47	0.18	−2.6	1.0
B	1	315	324.4	−0.11	0.28	0.17	1.6	0.9
C	1	428	414.9	0.16	−0.47	0.19	−2.4	1.0
D	1	368	386.6	−0.22	0.63	0.18	3.5	0.9
A	2	325	316.7	0.10	−0.24	0.17	−1.4	0.5
B	2	282	282.2	−0.00	0.01	0.17	0.0	1.1
C	2	376	376.0	−0.00	0.00	0.18	0.0	0.9
D	2	340	348.0	−0.10	0.25	0.18	1.4	0.7
A	3	341	327.1	0.17	−0.41	0.17	−2.4	0.7
B	3	259	292.4	−0.40	1.00	0.17	5.8	0.9
C	3	399	385.8	0.16	−0.43	0.18	−2.4	1.0
D	3	364	357.7	0.08	−0.20	0.18	−1.1	1.0
A	4	371	358.2	0.15	−0.40	0.18	−2.2	0.6
B	4	316	323.6	−0.09	0.23	0.17	1.3	0.7
C	4	424	414.2	0.12	−0.35	0.19	−1.8	0.9
D	4	371	385.9	−0.18	0.51	0.18	2.8	0.7
A	5	319	309.4	0.12	−0.28	0.17	−1.6	0.7
B	5	285	275.2	0.12	−0.29	0.17	−1.7	0.8
C	5	356	369.2	−0.16	0.39	0.17	2.3	0.9
D	5	335	341.3	−0.08	0.20	0.18	1.1	0.7

But variability of rater behaviour from item to item is to be expected, of course. How can we evaluate whether this variability constitutes a statistically *significant* increase (or decrease) in challenge? Is the bias value greater than might have been expected by chance? The degree of departure from what might have been expected allowing for normal variation is expressed in terms of a summary statistic, the z-score (column 8).[16] Values outside the range of approximately +2 to –2 suggest significant bias. In the case of this particular rater–item interaction, the bias value is statistically significant ($z = -2.6$), suggesting that there is indeed a marked rater–item interaction for this item: the item is triggering a systematically more lenient behaviour than is normal for the rater in question.

Finally, in column 9, we learn how consistent this pattern of bias is across all the candidates involved on this item with this rater. Obviously, for a particular item, if the rater is sometimes *more* lenient, and at other times *less* lenient than expected, there is no *stable* pattern of bias in one or other direction, even though he or she may be more lenient on the whole on that item. As before, some variability is expected, and the fit statistic essentially summarizes whether this variability is as great as the model expects, or less, or more.

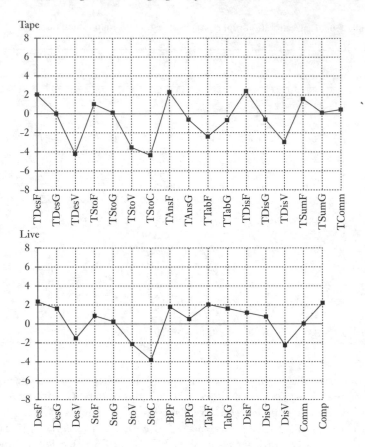

FIGURE 5.6   Judge performance report, **access:** test (from Wigglesworth, 1993: 326)

Information on the rater–item interaction in the form of bias z-scores can be plotted graphically for each rater. Stahl and Lunz (1992) use this graphic information as the basis for *judge performance reports*, whereby feedback is given to raters as part of rater training. Wigglesworth (1993) gives examples of such reports for raters in the **access:** test (cf. Figure 5.6, where the names of test items are listed on the horizontal axis and z-scores are plotted on the vertical axis; significant rater-by-item interactions (indicated by z-scores outside the range +2 to –2) are then readily noticeable).[17]

Bias analysis has significant potential for use in research on performance assessment.

As stated above, the existence of the two formats of the **access:** test Speaking module (*live* vs *tape-based*) raises questions about their equivalence or comparability. The live test appears to be an example of a direct test, while the tape-based format represents a semi-direct test; the equivalence of versions of tests in direct and semi-direct format has been raised as an issue previously by Stansfield (1991), Stansfield and Kenyon (1992) and Shohamy (1994).[18] The issue is important in practical terms, too, given the administrative convenience of a tape-based test.

As part of a study of the behaviour of raters assessing performances on the **access:** Speaking module, the performances of 94 trial subjects who each took both formats of the test were compared (McNamara *et al.*, 1993). In this analysis, test format was analysed as a facet, so that the effect of the test format over all raters, candidates and items could be estimated; it was found not to be large. However, was this true for all raters? A bias analysis was carried out for rater–test format interactions. The question addressed here was whether one or other of the formats triggered a consistent pattern of behaviour in some raters that was different from the general pattern of their behaviour overall. Table 5.7 shows part of the bias report.

It turns out that for some raters, there are very significant interactions with one or other test format. A particular test format – the tape stimulus, for example – may elicit a significantly harsher pattern of ratings, as with Rater A (observed scores are very much lower than expected scores, and the z score for this interaction is large and significant). But this pattern is not consistent across all raters: some, such as Rater D, show no such bias, while others, such as rater Q, show the exact reverse pattern –

TABLE 5.7 Bias calibration report, **access:** test, rater-test format interactions (part)

Rater	Format	Obs–Exp average	Bias (logit)	Error	z-Score	Fit (Mean square)
Q	Live	−0.40	0.94	0.09	11.0	1.1
R	Live	0.09	−0.23	0.10	−2.3	1.2
⋮	⋮	⋮	⋮	⋮	⋮	⋮
Q	Tape	0.45	−1.04	0.09	−11.5	0.9
R	Tape	−0.07	0.17	0.08	2.0	0.9
S	Tape	−0.12	0.27	0.08	3.3	0.9
⋮	⋮	⋮	⋮	⋮	⋮	⋮
T	Tape	0.07	−0.16	0.08	−1.9	0.7
A	Tape	−0.14	0.33	0.04	8.0	0.9
B	Tape	0.18	−0.42	0.04	−10.3	0.9
C	Tape	−0.04	0.10	0.04	2.3	0.9
D	Tape	0.02	−0.06	0.04	−1.3	0.8

that is, the tape-stimulus format elicits a significantly more lenient pattern of ratings. Practically speaking, the effects are quite small in terms of the average difference it makes to the raw score for most raters, except for Rater Q, who was on average half a score point (on a 6-point scale) more severe under the live condition.

5.5 Summary

In this chapter we have examined the nature and extent of variability in ratings associated with different aspects, or facets, of the performance assessment setting. We have argued that this variability is an important focus of research on performance assessment, and that although there are a number of traditional methods for controlling it, the impact of this variability is largely underestimated in practice. We have examined in broad terms the theory and procedures of multi-faceted Rasch measurement, and shown how, through multi-faceted analysis, raw scores from tests can be transformed so that reports of candidates' abilities can factor in the characteristics of raters, tasks, test format and so on that influence raw scores. We have also shown how bias analysis in multi-faceted measurement can reveal sub-patterns or interactions between different aspects of the assessment situation which have a systematic influence on scores. In particular, we have revealed systematic aspects of rater behaviour when confronted with particular candidates, particular tasks or particular test formats. These analyses are of great use in test development and administration – we have shown what a difference the use of transformed measures rather than raw scores can make in terms of fairness of measurement – and also in research on the many aspects of performance assessment settings.

We have chosen not to go into great detail on technical matters in this first chapter on Rasch measurement, as we have assumed little background in statistical or psychometric training in the reader. However, it is necessary to have a firmer grounding in the concepts and procedures of Rasch measurement if we are to make full use of its potential and, in particular, to be able to read and understand the information available in the output of computer programs that execute Rasch analyses. In the next two chapters we will explore the theory and practice of Rasch measurement in greater detail, always within language performance assessment contexts, as a prelude to discussing some of the research that is now being done in language testing using this new and powerful technology.

Notes

1. We are considering here direct evaluation of the performance rather than indirect measures of, for example, comprehension using objectively scored response formats. Automatic evaluation of aspects of pronunciation under performance conditions using sophisticated computerized equipment is now a possibility (Bernstein, 1994).
2. Also known as multi-faceted Rasch measurement; the general measurement approach on which it is based is called Rasch measurement after Georg Rasch, the Danish mathematician who developed it (cf. Chapter 9 for further background information).
3. Huot (1990) gives an excellent overview of the issues and factors involved here.
4. Linacre (1989b: 48-9, 51) uses the term *severity* to refer both to the overall severity of the rater and to interactions between raters, items and rating scale thresholds; McNamara and Adams (1991/1994: 3) suggest use of the term *rater characteristics* to cover both overall severity and interaction effects.
5. It may be argued that rater training can control for differences here, by getting raters to err on the side of caution: i.e. if they are in doubt, to go for the lower rating (as is the practice in ACTFL rater training). But differences between raters will still persist: raters will differ in their tendency to be 'in doubt' for any given case, and thus to apply the rule of giving the lower rating. Doubtful cases in other words do not belong to an objective category, but a subjectively perceived one.
6. The unit of measurement on the underlying ability scale, the logit, and its interpretation will be discussed in Chapter 6.
7. **access:** is a loose acronym for *Australian Assessment of Communicative English Skills*; it was initially developed in a nationwide project coordinated at the National Centre for English Language Teaching and Research at Macquarie University, and funded by the Australian Commonwealth Department of Immigration and Ethnic Affairs. The development of the speaking module of the test was the task of the National Languages and Literacy Institute of Australia Language Testing Research Centre at the University of Melbourne.
8. In other parts of the trialling, other facets were also built into the design and investigated; for example, for those trial candidates who took both forms of the test (live and tape-based), facets included which form they were taking, and in which order (first or second) the particular form had been taken. In principle, large numbers of facets can be investigated but this will have implications for the design and scope of data collection. Typically, three or four facets are chosen for investigation in any study; examples of studies investigating facets of the setting other than the classic candidate, item and rater are given in Chapter 8.
9. This is in contrast to the more rigid data requirements of analyses based on Generalizability Theory; cf. the discussion in Lynch and McNamara (1994) and McNamara and Lynch (in press).
10. The material in the figures and tables in the remainder of this chapter are extracted from output from multi-faceted analyses of **access:** trial test data using the program FACETS (Linacre and Wright, 1992). The actual tables from the FACETS program contain a great deal more detail; what is presented here is a selection of the information provided by the analysis, in the interests of clarity of presentation.
11. A table for converting logits into percentage chances of particular outcomes is given in Chapter 6.
12. In fact various reliability indices are provided in FACETS output; we are interested in the conceptual point here rather than the details of the output of a particular program.
13. As will be explained in the next chapter, mean square fit values are a more reliable guide than standardized fit values when a large number of data points (>400) is involved in the estimation. In this case, nearly 2000 observations were involved, which means that the standardized values will be inflated, and should be interpreted with caution.
14. Further information on raters is available; for example, if so requested in the analysis, we can obtain reports on how individual raters have interpreted the steps on the rating

scale; this is helpful for research purposes in summarizing the characteristics of particular raters (cf. McNamara and Adams, 1991/1994, for an extended treatment of this point). A note at the end of Chapter 9 explains some of the terminology used in these reports.

15. The negative sign of the bias logit value here corresponds to the fact that the rater was *less* severe than might have been expected; in other cases, where the rater is more severe than might have been expected, the sign will be positive.

16. The sign again corresponds to the sign of the bias logit (negative = more lenient than expected).

17. In a follow-up study, Lunt *et al.* (1994) failed to find any significant change in the pattern of ratings among raters who had been given feedback in this way, suggesting that the potential of the technique for rater training may not be as great as had been anticipated by Stahl and Lunz (1992) and Wigglesworth (1993).

18. The issue in relation to the **access:** test is the subject of ongoing research by O'Loughlin (cf. O'Loughlin, 1995).

6 Concepts and procedures in Rasch measurement

6.1 Introduction

In this chapter we will look in more detail at some of the basic concepts and tools of Rasch measurement, given its powerful role in helping us understand issues in performance assessment, as outlined in the previous chapter. There, we considered how facets of the rating situation, particularly the characteristics of the raters, can affect the candidate's chances of achieving a particular critical score, and argued that we need techniques to see beyond the raw score to form a measure of the candidate's ability undistorted by rater characteristics. In this chapter we will present the basic procedures of Rasch analysis in more detail, but in a way which should be reasonably clear and accessible for the non-expert. For the sake of simplicity we will begin with a relatively straightforward data set, involving *objectively* marked candidate responses to a discrete item test of the type frequently used in assessments of reading and listening. Although the data do not involve judge mediation, the concepts and procedures introduced form the basis for more complex analyses of data from judge-mediated assessments. These latter cases simply involve further facets than the basic ones of item difficulty and person ability – for example, the effect of rater characteristics. Multi-faceted Rasch analysis is more complex than the simpler Rasch analyses discussed here, but essentially not different in kind.

In order to illustrate the points to be made about Rasch analysis, we will consider a real set of data derived from the trialling of a 21-item reading test (the material is from the OET). The following notions will be introduced:

- the emergence of *patterning* and orderliness in the responses of the group of trial candidates to the set of test items;
- understanding the significance of an *individual* candidate's responses to the test items in the *context* of the responses of the other candidates;
- *modelling* the responses;
- the expression of patterning mathematically, in terms of *probabilities* of response;

• *lack of orderliness* in the responses of individual candidates, or in the responses of candidates to a particular item (that is, the question of *'fit'*).

A lot of the ideas and information to be found in the output from a Rasch analysis of test data, usually carried out using a computer program, are in fact detectable by careful examination of the raw data, as we shall see. We will start with the actual data, and introduce the output of a Rasch analysis of the data in the light of what we can observe directly. We will also draw parallels with more traditional analyses of item characteristics, such as item facility/difficulty and item discrimination, based directly on raw scores. It will be shown that raw scores continue to be the starting point for Rasch analysis, but that they are transformed in ways that make the final Rasch estimates of item difficulty and person ability more robust, mainly because they have factored in the particular and, necessarily, rather arbitrary characteristics of the trial group and the trial items on which these estimates are based. The concepts behind such methods of estimation will be introduced, though the actual mathematical techniques involved will not be discussed in any detail.[1]

6.1.1   Beyond raw scores

Why should the characteristics of the particular set of test items faced by a candidate represent a problem in determining measures of the candidate's ability? In determining the difficulty of items, why does the profile of abilities in the candidate group on which they are trialled matter? What is the problem with using raw scores?

The influence of test item characteristics on estimates of candidate abilities has always been recognized; it is a matter of common knowledge. People know that the degree of difficulty of the test is important in understanding the meaning of their achievement. The great American photographer Diane Arbus complained about her 'success' as a childhood artist in a school which had a policy of encouraging students. It bothered her that people always said how wonderful everything she did was. If it were this easy, then she couldn't see the point of doing it. A middling score on a difficult test is more impressive than a high score on an easy one. People are understandably concerned about the equivalence of various forms of a test – from one administration to the next, for example – for this reason. An elaborate set of techniques has been developed to check the equivalence of tests. However, test equating as it is called has proven to be very difficult, as the requirements for equivalent test forms are stringent and difficult to achieve. Test developers have resorted to *ad hoc* measures, such as keeping constant the percentage of candidates passing or achieving given grades. But this is unsatisfactory, as impressions of ability then become dependent on the ability levels of the cohort in which you are tested; if you happen to be tested among a relatively strong group, you will be seen to be less able than if you are tested in a relatively low ability group, and *vice versa*.

The difficulty of creating equivalent tests has also made the charting of the progress of learners or groups of learners difficult. It would be very ✕ helpful if candidate ability measures could be freed from dependence on particular test items, and if the relative difficulty of test items on different ✕ tests could be somehow established. The latter point is important in the development of *computer adaptive tests*, a new form of test, delivered by computer, in which the test consists of a bank of items. The particular items any individual candidate will encounter are chosen by the computer program in the light of the responses of the test taker to successive questions; the object is to match as exactly as possible the difficulty of the test item to the ability of the candidate, in the interests of efficiency and accuracy of estimate.[2]

6.1.2   Rasch measurement and traditional test theory

In the discussion that follows in this chapter contrasts will be drawn between Rasch measurement and the approach of traditional measurement theory (Classical Test Theory or True-Score Theory). Henning (1987a) provides a simple and clear summary for language testers of the procedures of traditional analysis. In general terms, a traditional analysis of test scores typically provides information on *item difficulty* and *item discrimination*, as well as giving global estimates of *overall test reliability*.

Item difficulty (or more correctly, *item facility*) in the case of a dichotomously scored item is presented in terms of the proportion (*p*) of candidates getting an item correct. The difficulty of items will thus inevitably depend on the ability of the group that is used in trialling the item.

Item discrimination is handled in terms of whether an item discriminates between those who do well on the test overall and those who do poorly on the test overall. In other words, we would require of an item of moderate difficulty that it be answered correctly by a substantially higher proportion of those scoring well on the test overall than of those scoring poorly overall. An item which is answered correctly by those whose overall score on the test is low but not answered correctly by those with overall high scores is considered to be an unsatisfactory item.

An important quality of a test in traditional analysis is its *overall reliability*, estimated in terms of a *reliability coefficient* such as KR-20 or Cronbach's alpha; this is a function or summary of the discrimination of individual items.[3]

Person ability in the traditional approach is represented by total scores on the test. However, ability is thus dependent on the difficulty of the test for the group; an easier or more difficult set of items would result in different total scores.

6.1.3   Generalizing from the particular: turning scores into measures

Rasch analysis takes the characteristics of the initial trial population into account in forming its estimates of features of items (item parameters) such as item difficulty. In this, Rasch is more complex and more sophisticated than traditional procedures for analysing test data, such as those mentioned above. In traditional analysis, the values for these indices directly reflect the abilities of the trial group (facility values represent the proportion of candidates in the trial group who got the item correct). These values are unstable because of the inevitable variability in trial groups; they are likely to be different, sometimes radically so, if the items are trialled on another group and a new analysis done. We need somehow to take account of the relative abilities of the trial group, so that we can get a picture of how difficult the items would be for other candidates than those represented in the trial group. Similarly, given that every test represents a particular selection of potential test items, ability estimates in traditional analysis are limited by the particular characteristics of the test items chosen – their difficulty, for example.

Rasch measurement theory offers attractive solutions to these practical problems of measurement. It enables estimates of candidate's underlying ability to be made by analysing the candidate's performance on a set of items, after allowance has been made for the difficulty of the items and how well they were matched to the candidate's ability level. Thus the ability estimates (known as *measures*) are not simply dependent on the items that were taken; we have avoided the trap of assuming that ability is transparently visible from raw scores. Similarly, the underlying difficulty of items can be estimated from the responses of a set of candidates, by taking into account the ability of the candidates and the degree to which there was a match between the ability of the trial group and the difficulty of the items. Central to this approach is the way in which candidate ability is related to item difficulty: this is done by estimating from the data the chances of a candidate of a given ability achieving a certain score on an item of given difficulty. The Rasch model proposes a simple mathematical relationship between ability and difficulty, and expresses this relationship as the probability of a certain response.

The difference between raw scores (counts of how many items a candidate got right) and item facility values (simple counts of how many candidates got an item right) on the one hand, and Rasch estimates of underlying ability and difficulty on the other, is similar to that between descriptive and inferential statistics. With descriptive statistics, a sample is taken and the characteristics of the sample are described, but no inferences are drawn about the characteristics of the population from which the sample is taken; no claim as to the representativeness of the sample is made. With inferential statistics, the characteristics of the sample are used to make estimates of the population from which it has been taken, with appropriate margins of error for these estimates. For example, if you wanted to estimate the degree of pollution of the water in San Francisco Bay, it would obviously be impractical to analyse all the water in the Bay. Instead, samples from a number of sites might be drawn, and analysed; the characteristics of the samples could then be described with descriptive statistics – the mean concentration of pollutants in repeated analyses, for example. These characteristics of the samples would then be used to draw inferences about the quality of the water in the Bay as a whole, with an estimate of the margin of error in these inferences; inferential statistics would be used in this process. We can compare traditional and Rasch analyses in the same way.

With traditional analysis, the characteristics of a particular group of test takers on a particular group of items, and the characteristics of those items for that particular group of test takers, are determined. But we have no way of knowing whether these characteristics of person ability and item difficulty would be maintained for the persons over different items and for the items if they were tried out on different subjects. Rasch analyses make generalizations from the performance of a particular sample of subjects on a particular sample of items to enable us to estimate the ability of candidates in relation to the entire universe of such items and the difficulty of the items for the entire population of prospective test takers.

This property of Rasch measurement has sometimes been misrepresented by unfortunate and misleading slogans such as 'person-free item estimates' and 'item-free ability estimates', which seem to run counter to common sense. Of course all estimates of item characteristics, including Rasch estimates, are based on responses of particular candidates to particular items, and will ultimately be limited by the quality of the data on which they are based. Small data sets and test items tried out on groups for whom they are ill matched will provide crude, scarcely usable estimates of underlying ability and difficulty; Rasch analyses provide no magic solutions to problems of poor or inadequate data.

The basic concepts of Rasch measurement may seem unfamiliar and difficult to grasp at first, but will become clearer in the context of an actual data analysis. In the remainder of this chapter, we will examine these concepts and procedures in some detail, and in relation to the analysis of a small trial data set from materials for the OET Reading sub-test.

6.2   Observing patterning in test data

Rasch measurement is an attempt to model the relationship between various facets of the test situation. Two facets common to all testing situations are the ability of the candidate and the difficulty of each of the particular tasks presented in the test items. The Rasch model in its basic version proposes that, where orderliness and patterning are found in test data, there will be a simple relationship between these two facets, such that the probability of a correct answer on an item is related to the difference between the ability of the candidate and the difficulty of the item.[4] The patterning that the model expects is understandable in a commonsense way: the more able the candidate, the higher his or her chance should be of getting the answer correct. Orderliness (and hence, predictability) in the data is often apparent simply by 'eyeballing' the data, provided we set them out in a way that enables us to see the kinds of relationship of interest. Let us take an example.

The data in Table 6.1 are from the trialling of a version of the Reading sub-test of the Occupational English Test.[5] There are 21 test items, seven on each of three passages. There were 27 trial subjects[6] (each identified by a number), a mixture of doctors and nurses, with one occupational therapist; all were non-native speakers of English, and were either recent immigrants to Australia (in the case of the nurses) or visitors to Australia on research scholarships (in the case of the doctors). The reading passages represented the kind of reading health professionals have to do to keep up with developments in their fields. The test items were in MCQ format, and the data matrix shows the actual choices given by candidates, with correct choices in italics. The items are presented in item order, the candidates in order of their identification number. Asterisks indicate missing data (the item was not attempted by the candidate). The row totals represent the candidates' raw scores on the test, ranging from 2 to 19; the column totals represent the number of correct responses to an item, and are the basis for calculating traditional item facility values.

TABLE 6.1   Data matrix of responses of 27 subjects to a 21-item ESP reading comprehension test for health professionals

Candidate ID #	Items 1–21 (1 2 3 4 5 6 7 8 9 10 11 12 13 14 15 16 17 18 19 20 21)	Total score
12	b a c a c c d c d * * * * * * * * * * * *	02
13	d a b d c b d c d c d c * * * * * * * * *	05
15	a d b a c a d d a a d c c d d c c c d a d	15
16	d a b b c d b d c c d b a d * * * * * * *	04
17	a d b d c b b d c a d d a d b c a * * * *	08
18	a a b a c b b d c b a c d d d a a c d a c	12
19	d d b d c d d c b a b c d d d c c c d a b	16
20	a a b a c a d b a a d * * * * * * * * * *	06
21	a a b b b d b a c c c * * * * * * * * * *	02
22	a c b a c d c d b a a c c d b a a c d d b	13
23	a c b d c b * d a b a c d b d a d c d a a	12
24	a d b d c a d d b a a c d d a a * c d a c	17
25	d c b d c a * d a d a d d a a c c c d a c	11
26	a d * a b a a d c d d d d a * * * * * * *	05
27	a a b d c d * d b a a c d d b b c c d a b	17
28	a a b d c a d d b a a c d a d b c c d a b	19
29	d a b d c a d d b a a c d d d a d c d a b	17
30	d c b b c b * b c a a c c a d a a c c a *	08
31	a c b d c d * d b a a c d d d a c c d a c	16
32	a d b d c a * d b b a c c d b a c c d a c	15
33	a d b d c a * d b a a c d d d d c c d a c	18
34	a d b d c a * d b a a d d d a b c c d a b	18
36	d a c b c b * d b a a d d a d a b * * * *	07
37	a a a a c d * b b d a d d a b a a b b c d	05
38	d a b d c d * d b a a a b d d a a c * d *	10
39	d a b d b d d d a d a c d d c b a b c b b	10
40	d a b a c a * c b a a d d d a c c c d a c	12
Item total correct	16 8 23 15 24 11 9 19 14 16 18 15 16 16 11 4 10 17 15 15 7	

The detail on particular choices of distractors available in the matrix is unnecessary for our purposes, although it would be required if we were to carry out an analysis of the effectiveness of distractors (cf. Henning, 1987a: 55). So let us simply represent the information in Table 6.1 in another way, replacing the underlined choices with '1' (representing correct choices) and all other choices with '0' (incorrect choices). The information available to us is now represented in Table 6.2.

It is difficult to detect any patterning in these data. However, if we make two simple reorganizations of the data matrix, one involving *candidates*, a second involving *items*, then obvious patterning begins to emerge, of the kind which is captured and summarized in Rasch analysis. The first reorganization involves arranging the responses of *candidates* not in

TABLE 6.2   OET data matrix, responses coded numerically

Candidate ID #	1	2	3	4	5	6	7	8	9	10	11	12	13	14	15	16	17	18	19	20	21	Total score
12	0	0	0	0	1	0	1	0	0	*	*	*	*	*	*	*	*	*	*	*	*	02
13	0	0	1	1	1	0	1	0	0	0	0	1	*	*	*	*	*	*	*	*	*	05
15	1	1	1	0	1	1	1	1	1	0	1	0	1	0	1	1	0	1	1	1	0	15
16	0	0	1	0	1	0	0	1	0	0	0	0	0	1	*	*	*	*	*	*	*	04
17	1	1	1	1	1	0	0	1	0	1	0	0	0	1	0	0	0	*	*	*	*	08
18	1	0	1	0	1	0	0	1	0	0	1	1	1	1	1	0	0	1	1	1	0	12
19	0	1	1	1	1	0	1	0	1	1	0	1	1	1	1	0	1	1	1	1	1	16
20	1	0	1	0	1	1	1	0	0	1	0	*	*	*	*	*	*	*	*	*	*	06
21	1	0	1	0	0	0	0	0	0	0	0	*	*	*	*	*	*	*	*	*	*	02
22	1	0	1	0	1	0	0	1	1	1	1	1	0	1	0	0	0	1	1	0	1	13
23	1	0	1	1	1	0	*	1	0	0	1	1	1	0	1	0	0	1	1	1	0	12
24	1	1	1	1	1	1	1	1	1	1	1	1	1	0	0	*	1	1	1	1	0	17
25	0	0	1	1	1	1	*	1	0	0	1	0	1	0	0	0	1	1	1	1	0	11
26	1	1	*	0	0	1	0	1	0	0	0	0	1	0	*	*	*	*	*	*	*	05
27	1	0	1	1	1	0	*	1	1	1	1	1	1	1	0	1	1	1	1	1	1	17
28	1	0	1	1	1	1	1	1	1	1	1	1	1	0	1	1	1	1	1	1	1	19
29	0	0	1	1	1	1	1	1	1	1	1	1	1	1	0	0	1	1	1	1	1	17
30	0	0	1	0	1	0	*	0	0	1	1	1	0	0	1	0	0	1	0	1	*	08
31	1	0	1	1	1	0	*	1	1	1	1	1	1	1	1	0	1	1	1	1	0	16
32	1	1	1	1	1	1	*	1	1	0	1	1	0	1	0	0	1	1	1	1	0	15
33	1	1	1	1	1	1	*	1	1	1	1	1	1	1	0	1	1	1	1	1	0	18
34	1	1	1	1	1	1	*	1	1	1	1	0	1	1	0	1	1	1	1	1	1	18
36	0	0	0	0	1	0	*	1	1	1	1	0	1	0	1	0	0	*	*	*	*	07
37	1	0	0	0	1	0	*	0	1	0	1	0	1	0	0	0	0	0	0	0	0	05
38	0	0	1	1	1	0	*	1	1	1	1	0	0	1	1	0	0	1	*	0	*	10
39	0	0	1	1	0	0	1	1	0	0	1	1	1	1	0	1	0	0	0	0	1	10
40	0	0	1	0	1	1	*	0	1	1	1	0	1	1	0	0	1	1	1	1	0	12
Item total correct	16	8	23	15	24	11	9	19	14	16	18	15	16	16	11	4	10	17	15	15	7	

ID order but in candidate total score order (shown in the right-hand column); thus the candidates with the lowest scores are found at the top of the matrix, those with highest scores at the bottom, and so on, as in Table 6.3.

The second reorganization involves arranging the *items* not in sequence order but in difficulty order, with the most difficult items to the left and the easiest to the right. (The line at the bottom of the page tells

TABLE 6.3   OET data matrix, with candidates in order of raw score total

Candidate ID #	1	2	3	4	5	6	7	8	9	10	11	12	13	14	15	16	17	18	19	20	21	Total score
12	0	0	0	0	1	0	1	0	0	*	*	*	*	*	*	*	*	*	*	*	*	02
21	1	0	1	0	0	0	0	0	0	0	0	*	*	*	*	*	*	*	*	*	*	02
16	0	0	1	0	1	0	0	1	0	0	0	0	0	1	*	*	*	*	*	*	*	04
13	0	0	1	1	1	0	1	0	0	0	0	1	*	*	*	*	*	*	*	*	*	05
26	1	1	*	0	0	1	0	1	0	0	0	0	1	0	*	*	*	*	*	*	*	05
37	1	0	0	0	1	0	*	0	1	0	1	0	1	0	0	0	0	0	0	0	0	05
20	1	0	1	0	1	1	1	0	0	1	0	*	*	*	*	*	*	*	*	*	*	06
36	0	0	0	0	1	0	*	1	1	1	1	0	1	0	1	0	0	*	*	*	*	07
17	1	1	1	1	1	0	0	1	0	1	0	0	0	1	0	0	0	*	*	*	*	08
30	0	0	1	0	1	0	*	0	0	1	1	1	0	0	1	0	0	1	0	1	*	08
38	0	0	1	1	1	0	*	1	1	1	1	0	0	1	1	0	0	1	*	0	*	10
39	0	0	1	1	0	0	1	1	0	0	1	1	1	1	0	1	0	0	0	0	1	10
25	0	0	1	1	1	1	*	1	0	0	1	0	1	0	0	0	1	1	1	1	0	11
18	1	0	1	0	1	0	0	1	0	0	1	1	1	1	1	0	0	1	1	1	0	12
23	1	0	1	1	1	0	*	1	0	0	1	1	1	0	1	0	0	1	1	1	0	12
40	0	0	1	0	1	1	*	0	1	1	1	0	1	1	0	0	1	1	1	1	0	12
22	1	0	1	0	1	0	0	1	1	1	1	1	0	1	0	0	0	1	1	0	1	13
15	1	1	1	0	1	1	1	1	0	1	0	1	0	1	1	0	1	1	1	1	0	15
32	1	1	1	1	1	1	*	1	1	0	1	1	0	1	0	0	1	1	1	1	0	15
19	0	1	1	1	1	0	1	0	1	1	0	1	1	1	1	0	1	1	1	1	1	16
31	1	0	1	1	1	0	*	1	1	1	1	1	1	1	1	0	1	1	1	1	0	16
24	1	1	1	1	1	1	1	1	1	1	1	1	1	1	0	0	*	1	1	1	0	17
27	1	0	1	1	1	0	*	1	1	1	1	1	1	1	0	1	1	1	1	1	1	17
29	0	0	1	1	1	1	1	1	1	1	1	1	1	1	0	0	1	1	1	1	1	17
33	1	1	1	1	1	1	*	1	1	1	1	1	1	1	1	0	1	1	1	1	0	18
34	1	1	1	1	1	1	*	1	1	1	0	1	1	0	1	1	1	1	1	1	1	18
28	1	0	1	1	1	1	1	1	1	1	1	1	1	0	1	1	1	1	1	1	1	19
Item total score	16	8	23	15	24	11	9	19	14	16	18	15	16	16	11	4	10	17	15	15	7	

us how many people got each item right.) The resulting form of the data matrix is shown in Table 6.4, and it is the patterning in this table that will now be the focus of our discussion.

An obvious pattern now emerges in the data. That is, the matrix has an area in the lower right quadrant where 1s predominate; this represents

TABLE 6.4   OET data matrix, items in order of item raw score totals, candidates in order of raw score total

Candidate ID #	Items most difficult ·········· easiest																						Total score
	16	21	2	7	17	6	15	9	4	12	19	20	1	10	13	14	18	11	8	3	5	
12	*	*	0	1	*	0	*	0	0	*	*	*	0	*	*	*	*	*	0	0	1	02
21	*	*	0	0	*	0	*	0	0	*	*	*	1	0	*	*	*	0	0	1	0	02
16	*	*	0	0	*	0	*	0	0	0	*	*	0	0	0	1	*	0	1	1	1	04
13	*	*	0	1	*	0	*	0	1	1	*	*	0	0	*	*	*	0	0	1	1	05
26	*	*	1	0	*	1	*	0	0	0	*	*	1	0	1	0	*	0	1	*	0	05
37	0	0	0	*	0	0	0	1	0	0	0	0	1	0	1	0	0	1	0	0	1	05
20	*	*	0	1	*	1	*	0	0	*	*	*	1	1	*	*	*	0	0	1	1	06
36	0	*	0	*	0	0	1	1	0	0	*	*	0	1	1	0	*	1	1	0	1	07
17	0	*	1	0	0	0	0	0	1	0	*	*	1	1	0	1	*	0	1	1	1	08
30	0	*	0	*	0	0	1	0	0	1	0	1	0	1	0	0	1	1	0	1	1	08
38	0	*	0	*	0	0	1	1	1	0	*	0	0	1	0	1	1	1	1	1	1	10
39	1	1	0	1	0	0	0	0	1	1	0	0	0	0	1	1	0	1	1	1	0	10
25	0	0	0	*	1	1	0	0	1	0	1	1	0	0	1	0	1	1	1	1	1	11
18	0	0	0	0	0	0	1	0	0	1	1	1	1	0	1	1	1	1	1	1	1	12
23	0	0	0	*	0	0	1	0	1	1	1	1	0	1	0	1	1	1	1	1	1	12
40	0	0	0	*	1	1	0	1	0	0	1	1	0	1	1	1	1	0	1	1		12
22	0	1	0	0	0	0	0	1	0	1	1	0	1	1	0	1	1	1	1	1	1	13
15	0	0	1	1	1	1	1	0	0	1	1	1	1	1	0	1	1	0	1	1	1	15
32	0	0	1	*	1	1	0	1	1	1	1	1	0	0	1	1	1	1	1	1	1	15
19	0	1	1	1	1	0	1	1	1	1	1	1	0	1	1	1	0	0	1	1	1	16
31	0	0	0	*	1	0	1	1	1	1	1	1	1	1	1	1	1	1	1	1	1	16
24	0	0	1	1	*	1	0	1	1	1	1	1	1	1	1	1	1	1	1	1	1	17
27	1	1	0	*	1	0	0	1	1	1	1	1	1	1	1	1	1	1	1	1	1	17
29	0	1	0	1	0	1	1	1	1	1	1	0	1	1	1	1	1	1	1	1	1	17
33	0	0	1	*	1	1	1	1	1	1	1	1	1	1	1	1	1	1	1	1	1	18
34	1	1	1	*	1	1	0	1	1	0	1	1	1	1	1	1	1	1	1	1	1	18
28	1	1	0	1	1	1	1	1	1	1	1	1	1	1	0	1	1	1	1	1	1	19
Item total score	4	7	8	9	10	11	11	14	15	15	15	15	16	16	16	16	17	18	19	23	24	

the area where the most able (the highest scoring) candidates are attempting the easiest questions. In the upper left quadrant, by contrast, 0s or no attempts predominate, and there are relatively few 1s; this represents data from the lowest scoring candidates on the most difficult questions. An intermediate zone running from lower left to top right shows a fairly mixed pattern of 0s and 1s; this represents the responses of candidates when they are responding to questions which are neither too easy nor too difficult for them; they have approximately a 50 per cent chance of getting a 0 or a 1 on such items, which can be seen as being in the difficulty range of challenge, but not of impossibility, for the candidate. It is possible to define the candidate's ability in terms of which items represent this kind of level of difficulty for them; that is, item difficulty can be used to define candidate ability.

6.2.1 Modelling the data

We are now in a position to understand some of the bases of Rasch analysis of a data matrix such as this. The analysis attempts to *model* the data matrix, that is, to summarize the observed patterning through a set of simple relations, expressed formally in mathematical terms. Before we introduce the Rasch model itself, a word on models in general is called for. Models are inevitably simplifications of reality (in this case, the reality being the data points in the matrix). The question with models is always, how economical are they? How successful are they in accounting for a set of observations (the data matrix)? How much of the data do they fail to account for – just the odd cell here and there, or whole sections of the matrix? In the latter case, is there something systematic about the responses which are not accounted for? In the case of this data, for example, are they the responses of a particular candidate to a number of items, or the responses of many candidates to a particular item? If there is a pattern in the exceptions, then this pattern too can be reported as an outcome of the modelling process. In modelling, a proposal is made about how to account for the observations (how to 'explain' them in terms of the model). The model is used to generate predictions about each observation. Any discrepancies between the predicted and the actual observations are noted and reported, and the success or otherwise of the attempt to model the data (called model–data fit) is evaluated. If most of the complexity can be accounted for by the model, then we have good fit and the model is a satisfactory way of accounting for, and hence summarizing, the data in simpler terms.

In the case of this test, we are interested in modelling the relationship between the ability of candidates and the difficulty of items, and seeing which candidates or items are associated with patterns of responses which cannot be satisfactorily described or summarized in terms of this model. In its simplest form (that used with right/wrong responses, as here), the Rasch model proposes that the observations in the data matrix such as this can be reduced to (predicted by) the following mathematically simple relation between the ability of the candidates and the difficulty of the items:

$$P = B_n - D_i$$

where P = a mathematical expression of the probability of a correct
     · response on an item,
    B_n = the ability (B)[7] of a particular person (n) and
    D_i = the difficulty (D)[8] of a particular item (i).[9]

In other words, the chances of a correct response are a function of the difference between the person's ability and the difficulty of the item, and nothing else.

We will now say a little more about each of the terms in this equation.

6.2.2   The probability of a given response

The basic means by which Rasch analysis extrapolates from a particular test data set to arrive at general estimates of person ability and item difficulty is to consider the *probabilities* of patterns of response in the data. This key idea in Rasch analysis, that of probabilities of response, is easy enough to understand in common sense terms. For example, consider the case of a dichotomously scored item, that is, one on which the responses may be 'correct' or 'incorrect'. If we know how an individual has performed on other items (we have some estimate of his or her ability), and if we know how other individuals have performed on the item in question (we have an estimate of how difficult the item is), then we are in a position to make an estimate of how likely it is that the individual will respond in a particular way – that is, to choose either the 'correct' or the 'incorrect' answer. If an item is easy, and the individual's ability is high, there will be a high likelihood of a correct response. On the other hand, if the item is difficult, and the individual's ability is low, it is unlikely that he or she will make a 'correct' response. Whether the actually observed response is as predicted (or is not) is then noted and reported; and so on for the whole data set. Note that as we are talking about expectancies, either outcome ('correct' or 'incorrect') is theoretically possible for each response to each item, but in proportions that will differ as a function of the estimated difficulty of the item and the estimated ability of the candidate. The analysis calculates the probability of either outcome on each item for candidates of given abilities. Furthermore, as this is not a deterministic model, it expects that some of the time the less likely of the two outcomes on a particular item will occur (see discussion of *fit*, below). Rasch models are probabilistic or *stochastic* models. Fisher (1992: 186) explains the latter term as follows:

> *Stochastic resonance occurs when faint and hard to detect signals are ampli-fied by additional input received from surrounding background noise, paradoxically making them more easily detected than if the background was free of noise. In astronomy, faint stars are more easily observed when the sky has a slight background glow than when it is black. ... Stochastic meas-urement models provide more useful and meaningful analysis of psychosocial data than deterministic models because stochastic models allow noise to amplify the signal instead of confusing it ... the unavoidable noise in the data contributes information essential to construct quantitative com-parisons.*

Item difficulty and person ability are jointly estimated in Rasch analysis, using a mathematical procedure known as maximum likelihood estima-tion. Put in relatively simple terms, this procedure aims to develop estimates of ability and item difficulty in terms of probabilities of expected responses to items by persons. The analysis begins with a provisional working hypothesis about the ability of persons (based on their total raw scores), and the difficulty of items (based on the number of people who got them right; that is, their facility values in traditional terms). It thus begins with working estimates of person ability and item difficulty which are seen as determining the probability of a person of the estimated abil-ity getting an item of the estimated level of difficulty right or wrong. Using the mathematical relationship between ability and difficulty pro-posed in the model, predictions are made as to the most likely outcome (right or wrong; that is, 1 or 0) for each cell in the matrix, given the abil-ity of the candidate overall and the difficulty of the item for candidates in general. The model thus generates a hypothesized (predicted) score set, and this is compared with the actual (observed) score set, to see how close the two are. If the discrepancy between the two is greater than a certain preset level of accuracy of prediction (usually a fairly stringent level: typ-ically, the total score for each individual candidates must be predicted to within half a score point of its actual value), then the estimated item diffi-culties are revised, and are used as the basis for a recalculation of the ability estimates. These in turn may be used to generate new item estim-ates; the new person ability and item difficulty estimates are used to generate a new predicted data matrix, which is compared with the observed data, the extent of discrepancy noted, and further adjustments made accordingly if the preset level of accuracy of prediction has not been met. The process is essentially recursive, in other words, until the required level of accuracy of prediction is met; at that point the calculations stop and the ability and difficulty estimates at that point are the ones finally reported.

It is worth mentioning one or two technical terms for what we have described here, as they appear in the programs used for this kind of analysis and feature in research and test development reports. The estimates of person ability are termed *measures*, to distinguish them from (raw) scores; the point being that measures are on an objective measurement scale, the scale constructed in the analysis. The estimation procedure is known as *calibration*. Each successive, recursive cycle of estimation is known as an *iteration*. When the required level of accuracy has been reached, the program is said to have *converged*, and the level of accuracy required is expressed in terms of *convergence criteria*.

To summarize the key features of the Rasch approach:

(1) it estimates ability by considering data from an individual in the context of data from the whole data matrix, that is, the responses of all candidates to all items;
(2) it *relates* person ability and item difficulty by estimating the likelihood of responses of particular persons to particular items;
(3) the difficulty of an item is expressed conventionally as the probability that a person of given ability will have a 50 per cent chance of getting the item right;
(4) similarly, a person's ability is defined as the probability of that person having a 50 per cent chance of getting an item of given difficulty right.

The person ability estimates (*measures*) are more stable than raw scores, as they have factored in the particular choice of items from which they were derived; that is, when data conform to the model, ability measurements go beyond the test instrument on which the abilities are measured. This means that we can securely predict the chances of a person succeeding on items *in addition* to those on which he or she has been tested, provided these items have been calibrated onto the same measurement scale. (Similarly, when data conform to the Rasch model, the estimates of item difficulty are not true only for the particular group on which the items are trialled; they constitute generalizations about the difficulty of the item across the whole population of subjects from which the trial group of subjects is drawn.) As we said earlier, the estimates are of course ultimately dependent on the quality of the data from which they are derived; the item difficulty estimates and person ability measures are *inferences* from the data, and will have a margin of error, which will be large or narrow according to the type and amount of data on which they are based. Each estimate in the output from Rasch analysis is accompanied by an error term. This means that we can be 95 per cent sure that the person's true ability or the true difficulty of an item will lie within the band or range represented by the relevant estimate plus or minus twice its estimated error.

Person ability measures for the candidates we have been considering are reported in Table 6.5.[10] The unit of measurement in which the measures are expressed is called the *logit* (mentioned briefly in Chapter 5), and as this is likely to be unfamiliar it will be discussed in some detail below. For the moment, let us say that ability measures expressed in this unit will be either positive or negative in sign; the higher the value, the more able the candidate; candidates with positive values will find items of average difficulty within their grasp, and some well within it; candidates with negative values will find such items a challenge, one that for some candidates is likely to prove overwhelming.

The table identifies the candidate in the column headed *ID*; reports the person's raw score total (*Raw score*) and the number of questions the person attempted (*Items attempted*); and reports the estimate of the candidate's ability measure in logits (*Estimate*) and the error associated with this measure (*Error*), together with the mean and standard deviation of the set of estimates.

Note that in this case the error terms are relatively large, because of the small data matrix; the analysis is cautious about inferring underlying measures on the basis of relatively poor data. (The larger the number of persons and/or items, the smaller will be the error; recommended *n* sizes for candidates are 100 or more, depending on the level of accuracy required, but estimates on smaller sample sizes may be useful for certain purposes if the size of the error term is not an imperative consideration.) Note also that the program has been instructed to treat any failure to attempt a question by a candidate as missing data rather than as evidence that the candidate could not have answered the question successfully; it would have been possible to code these no attempts as zeros in the data matrix, but they are indicated by asterisks and are thus considered missing data.

Item difficulties for the items in the trial are reported in Table 6.6. The item is identified in the column headed *Item name*; the columns headed *Correct* and *Attempted* refer to the number of persons getting the item right (*Correct*) and the number of persons attempting the item (*Attempted*) (from which we can derive the facility value of the item in traditional analysis); the estimate of the difficulty of the item is in the column headed *Difficulty*, and the error associated with this estimate is also given (*Error*). Note that there may be considerable transformation in the difficulty estimates from item raw score totals: for example, item 7 is seen as considerably

TABLE 6.5 Person ability measures, OET reading test trial data

Candidate ID	Raw score	Items attempted	Estimate	Error
12	2	9	−1.81	0.90
13	5	12	−0.59	0.65
15	15	21	1.13	0.54
16	4	14	−1.28	0.64
17	8	17	−0.08	0.54
18	12	21	0.34	0.50
19	16	21	1.44	0.57
20	6	11	0.02	0.67
21	2	11	−2.06	0.86
22	12	21	0.34	0.50
23	12	20	0.52	0.51
24	17	20	2.11	0.69
25	11	20	0.26	0.51
26	5	13	−0.60	0.61
27	17	20	2.17	0.69
28	19	21	2.75	0.80
29	17	21	1.79	0.62
30	8	19	−0.48	0.52
31	16	20	1.75	0.62
32	15	20	1.39	0.58
33	18	20	2.72	0.80
34	18	20	2.72	0.80
36	7	16	−0.21	0.56
37	5	20	−1.37	0.57
38	10	18	0.24	0.53
39	10	21	−0.14	0.49
40	12	20	0.52	0.51
Mean			0.50	
SD			1.38	

easier (see interpretation of logit values, below); this is because the number of correct responses as a proportion of attempted responses, not of possible responses, is related to the difficulty estimate. Note also that the mean of item difficulties is zero; the program sets this automatically (by convention the mean of item difficulties is anchored at zero[11]).

6.2.3 Expressing item difficulties and person abilities as probabilities of response: the logit

The expression of the probabilities or odds of a particular response is not in the normal popular fashion that is familiar from electoral prospects or betting (5 to 1, 1 in 5 and the like) or weather forecasting ('a 30 per cent chance of rain') but in a form that is more tractable mathematically: the odds are expressed as a logarithm ('log' for short) of the naturally occurring constant e.[12] We thus speak of the 'log odds' of a response, rather than the odds of the response, and the units on the measurement scale constructed in this way are called 'log odds units' or logits (pronounced 'LOH–jits'; stress on the first syllable). The logit scale has the advantage that it is an interval scale – that is, it can tell us not only that one item is more difficult than another, but also how much more difficult it is. The interval nature of the ability measurements means that growth in ability over time can be plotted on the scale; this has attractive implications for the evaluation of the effectiveness of teaching.

The logit scale is likely to be an unfamiliar measurement scale; as with any measurement scale it may take some time for a person to get a 'feel' for it, just as if you move to a culture with a relatively unfamiliar measurement scale for, say, distance or weight it may take some time to become accustomed to what a kilometre is, or a mile, or a pound or a ‚kilo. By convention, the average difficulty of items in a test is set at zero logits. Items of above-average difficulty will thus be positive in sign, those of

TABLE 6.6 Item difficulties, OET reading test trial data

Item name	Correct	Attempted	Difficulty	Error
Item 1	16	27	−0.02	0.46
Item 2	8	27	1.62	0.49
Item 3	23	26	−2.03	0.67
Item 4	15	27	0.18	0.46
Item 5	24	27	−2.10	0.66
Item 6	11	27	0.98	0.46
Item 7	9	15	−0.34	0.62
Item 8	19	27	−0.65	0.49
Item 9	14	27	0.38	0.45
Item 10	16	26	−0.05	0.47
Item 11	18	26	−0.47	0.48
Item 12	15	24	0.04	0.48
Item 13	16	23	−0.29	0.51
Item 14	16	23	−0.29	0.51
Item 15	11	21	0.79	0.50
Item 16	4	21	2.66	0.61
Item 17	10	20	0.84	0.51
Item 18	17	19	−1.47	0.80
Item 19	15	18	−0.85	0.69
Item 20	15	19	−0.56	0.62
Item 21	7	17	1.62	0.55
Mean			0.00	
SD			1.17	

below-average difficulty negative in sign. Ability estimates in turn are related to item difficulty estimates, so that a person of an ability expressed as 0 logits would have a 50 per cent chance of getting right an item of average difficulty. Candidates more able than that will have positive logit values; candidates less able than that will have negative logit values. Remember that ability estimates are a function of how able a person is (that is, his or her chances of success) in relation to *particular items*. If a person and an item are well matched, that is, they are at the same location on the logit scale, the person has a 50 per cent chance of success on it. If the difficulty of the item is 1 logit less than the person's ability level, the chances of success rise to approximately 75 per cent; if it is 2 logits less, the chances are closer to 90 per cent. On the other hand, if the item is 1 logit more difficult than the person's ability level, the chance of success falls to approximately 25 per cent, and to about 10 per cent in the case of a 2-logit gap. Table 6.7 (from Wright and Linacre, 1991: 79) provides information on the correspondence between expressions of probability in terms of logits and expressions of probability in more familiar terms.

6.2.4   Mapping abilities and difficulties

In the Rasch model, the same scale is used to express the measure of a person's ability and the difficulty of items, because these things are expressed in terms of each other; the logit scale is an expression of the

TABLE 6.7   Logit-to-probability conversion table (from Wright and Linacre, 1991)

Logit difference between ability measure and item calibration	Probability of success on a dichotomous item (%)	Logit difference between ability measure and item calibration	Probability of success on a dichotomous item (%)
5.0	99	−5.0	1
4.6	99	−4.6	1
4.0	98	−4.0	2
3.0	95	−3.0	5
2.2	90	−2.2	10
2.0	88	−2.0	12
1.4	80	−1.4	20
1.1	75	−1.1	25
1.0	73	−1.0	27
0.8	70	−0.8	30
0.5	62	−0.5	38
0.4	60	−0.4	40
0.2	55	−0.2	45
0.1	52	−0.1	48
0	50	−0	50

relationship between item difficulty and person ability. This means we can compare item difficulty and person ability for a particular group of test takers and test items, to see how well matched they are. The mapping of item difficulty and person ability on the same scale is one of the most useful properties of a Rasch analysis. For example, comparison of the range of ability of the group with the range of item difficulty enables us to see whether a test is too easy or too difficult for a particular group.
Mapping facilities available with most Rasch-based programs, to be discussed in detail in Chapter 7, allow a visual inspection of the matching up of the ability of a group and the difficulty of a test. Estimates of *person ability* and *item difficulty* are represented graphically in the form of an item–ability map. Such a map for the data in the matrix we have been considering is provided in Figure 6.1.

The map illustrates a continuum of ability and difficulty constructed by the analysis. On the left are the units of measurement on the scale (*logits*), extending in this case from −3 to +3 (a 6-unit range). The average item difficulty has been set at 0 logits. The ability of individual candidates is plotted on the scale; here the candidates are not identified by an ID number, but this would also be possible. On the right are the item numbers. The top of the scale represents greater item difficulty and greater candidate ability. Thus, the most difficult item was number 16; items 2 and 21 are significantly easier, and equivalent in difficulty; then there is a gap until we reach another cluster of items (6, 15 and 17) which define another level of difficulty.

The mapping of item difficulty and the ability of the group taking the test has several advantages, to be discussed in Chapter 7. For the moment, a simple and obvious advantage is that we can see how well matched the candidates and the items are. If the trial candidates are typical of the intended test population, then there is reasonable coverage of the ability range. Items have the greatest power to define the ability of candidates in the range of ability which matches the difficulty of the item; what is known technically as the *item information function* is greatest in this area.
Tests will differ in the extent to which all areas of the ability continuum need to be carefully defined. We may contrast the case of a test used to determine who is to be awarded a scholarship, in which discrimination will need to be greatest at the highest ability levels, from a test with a screening function, in which case information in the area around the decision point or threshold will be of greatest interest. Here the greatest number of items is found in the middle and just below the middle ability ranges, which is appropriate given the OET's function of establishing a threshold level of English rather than describing a number of different levels of English all the way along the ability continuum.

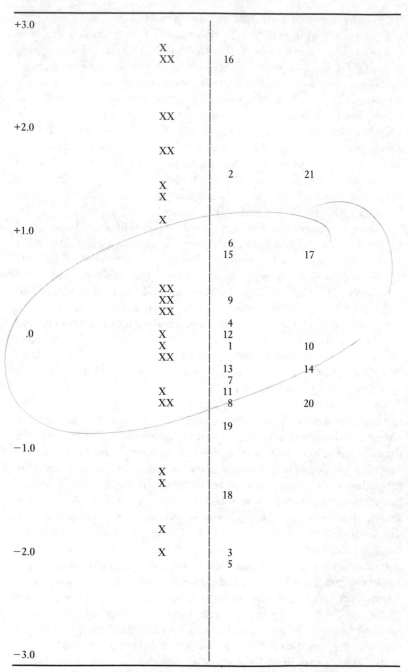

```
+3.0

             X
             XX          16



             XX
+2.0
             XX

                         2              21
             X
             X

             X
+1.0
                         6
                         15             17


             XX
             XX          9
             XX
                         4
  .0         X           12
             X           1              10
             XX
                         13             14
                         7
             X           11
             XX          8              20

                         19
−1.0

             X
             X
                         18


             X
−2.0         X           3
                         5




−3.0
```

FIGURE 6.1   Person ability and item difficulty map, OET reading test data

6.3   Lack of orderliness: the question of fit

In this section we will consider the extent to which the pattern of responses observed for individual items conforms to and reinforces the general pattern displayed in the matrix as a whole, or goes against it. We will consider three cases:

(1)   those in which the pattern for individual items, allowing for normal variability, fits the overall pattern (items showing appropriate 'fit');
(2)   those in which the pattern for individual items does not correspond with the overall pattern ('misfitting' items); and
(3)   those in which the general pattern of responses, which shows some 'noise' or unpredictability (cf. the discussion of stochastic models, above) is not observed, and the lack of variability means that an essentially deterministic pattern emerges for the items concerned ('overfitting' items).

Items drawn from our data matrix which demonstrate these three cases are reproduced in Table 6.8.

6.3.1   Items showing good 'fit'

Consider first the columns of responses in the matrix associated with item 6 (a relatively difficult item, answered correctly by 11 candidates), item 12 (moderate difficulty, answered correctly 15 times) and item 11 (relatively easy, answered correctly 18 times). For item 6, as we move down the column, initially (i.e. with the lowest scoring candidates overall) 0 is the most probable response; as candidates' total scores improve, so does the likelihood that they will score a 1, and we get a mixed pattern of success and failure on the item; finally, 1s predominate, suggesting that, for the highest scoring students, the probability of scoring a 1 is greater than that of scoring a 0 on this item. For item 12, the zone in which 1 is the most likely response begins higher up the column, that is, lower scoring candidates have a good chance of getting this item right; for item 11 this tendency is even more pronounced. In each case, the pattern of 0s and 1s is not perfectly predictable, that is, there are irregularities in the patterning. For item 12, for example, the second highest scoring candidate overall got the item wrong, thus breaking the solid sequence of 1s in that part of the ability range. In other words, it is probable but not absolutely certain that high-scoring candidates overall will get such an item right. Similarly with item 6: two candidates with relatively low scores overall in fact got this item right, so that there is not a perfect sequence of 0s for this item even in the lower ability range.

TABLE 6.8   Fitting, misfitting and overfitting patterns of responses to items

	Items					
6	12	11	15	1	19	
0	*	*	*	0	*	Least able candidates
0	*	0	*	1	*	
0	0	0	*	0	*	
0	1	0	*	0	*	
1	0	0	*	1	*	
0	0	1	0	1	0	
1	*	0	*	1	*	
0	0	1	1	0	*	
0	0	0	0	1	*	
0	1	1	1	0	0	
0	0	1	1	0	*	
0	1	1	0	0	0	
1	0	1	0	0	1	
0	1	1	1	1	1	
0	1	1	1	1	1	
1	0	1	0	0	1	
0	1	1	0	1	1	
1	1	0	1	1	1	
1	1	1	0	1	1	
0	1	0	1	0	1	
0	1	1	1	1	1	
1	1	1	0	1	1	
0	1	1	0	1	1	
1	1	1	1	0	1	
1	1	1	1	1	1	
1	0	1	0	1	1	
1	1	1	1	1	1	Most able candidates
Item total score						
11	15	18	11	16	15	

6.3.2   'Misfitting' items

We may contrast the orderliness of response to these three items with the lack of orderliness in responses to items 15 and 1. For item 15, answered correctly by 11 candidates, let us ignore the starred missed attempts, assuming that they provide us with no information. We see that there is a mixed pattern of success and failures all the way down the range of ability, as indicated by total overall scores; one's chances of success or failure on this item seem independent of ability. Of the six highest scoring candidates, three answered correctly, three incorrectly; the same pattern was true for the next six candidates; and again true for the next six candidates, who achieved modest scores on the test overall. For item 1, this random-ness is a little less pronounced – of the nine highest scoring candidates, seven answered the item correctly, but elsewhere this relation between total score and chances of success on this item is not preserved: for the nine lowest scoring candidates, five answered the item correctly, while for the remaining nine candidates (those scoring midway in the total score range), only four answered the item correctly.

In summary, items 15 and 1 elicited a pattern of responses which did not fit the general pattern or responses in the matrix, and can thus be classified as relatively *misfitting* items.

6.3.3 'Overfit'

Item 19 showed a different pattern again. In this case, again ignoring the starred 'no attempts', there is a deterministic rather than probabilistic relationship between total score and chances of success on the item: all those scoring below a certain point got the item wrong, whereas all those scoring above that point got the item correct. It seems as if this item is an 'all or nothing' item: at a certain point along the ability continuum, one's chances of a correct response to this item change from 0 to 100 per cent.

Such a deterministic pattern does not fit the expectations of the model, which expects a more complex pattern of responses. For example, it cal-culates the chances of an individual of a given ability getting an item of given difficulty correct. Let us say that there is a 70 per cent chance of such an individual getting such an item correct. We will therefore not be surprised if the individual in question does get the item correct. Similarly with the next item: let us say that the individual has a 75 per cent chance of getting it correct. We will thus not be surprised if the individual gets it correct. However, occasionally we shall expect that individuals with this level of ability will not get such items correct. While we would not expect this to happen for any particular item (because the balance of probability says that the individual will get a correct response), we expect it to hap-pen on a certain number of items – that is, we expect occasional violations of our expectations: 30 or 25 per cent of the time in the cases mentioned. Thus, we expect that occasionally an individual of lower ability will get a relatively difficult item correct, or an individual of higher ability will get a relatively easy item wrong. If these results occur less frequently than the probabilistic model anticipates, then this form of model-data misfit is identified through the fit statistics. In this case, the fit statistic will tend to have a negative value (significant overfit is conventionally defined as a value of t in excess of -2); this is sometimes, and erroneously in the opinion of many, termed 'overfitting'. In such cases, an explanation for the 'overfitting' is sought in terms of lack of independence of items in the test. This concept will be of particular significance in the analysis in Chapter 8 of performance on the Speaking and Writing sub-tests of the OET.

6.3.4   Measurement of fit: fit statistics

We have said above that Rasch analysis proceeds by comparing expected and observed responses by individual candidates to particular items, and successively refining the predictions until there is a sufficiently close match between the expected and observed data. Once the analysis is complete and best estimates of person abilities and item difficulties have been arrived at, the program is in a position to summarize for each person and each item the extent of fit between prediction and observation. In other words, the fit for each *row* (person) and each *column* (item) in the data matrix is calculated and reported as a single figure.

The extent to which responses show acceptable levels of fit, are 'misfitting', or are 'overfitting' can be summarized for each person and for each item, and reported as part of the output of the analysis. We are thus routinely provided with set of statistics known as *fit statistics* in Rasch analyses.

The *item* fit statistics from the OET data are set out in Table 6.9.

Confusingly, four statistics are produced for each item. There are two groups of two: *infit* and *outfit* statistics, each expressed in two alternative ways, as *mean square* or *t*. Briefly, the infit statistics (in bold type in Table 6.9) are the ones usually considered the most informative, as they focus on the degree of fit in the most typical observations in the matrix.[13]

In statistical analyses, discrepancies between predicted and observed data are known as *residuals*.[14] Item fit statistics in Rasch analyses provide summaries of the size and direction (sign) of the residuals for each item (the extent to which, in the data matrix, the column of cells representing individual candidate responses to that item was *not* predicted accurately). When an item is misfitting, the individual responses will be the opposite of predicted more than might have been expected (as we said above, Rasch models are probabilistic, not deterministic, so that some failure to predict individual cell values is expected). The pattern of residuals is transformed for the sake of ease of interpretation to produce two sets of fit statistics, *mean square* and *t*.

Mean square values (columns 2 and 3 in Table 6.9) have an expected value of 1; individual values will be above or below this according to whether the observed values show greater variation (resulting in values *greater* than 1) or less variation (resulting in values *less* than 1) than might normally be expected. How far away from the mean of 1 can we expect

TABLE 6.9   Item fit, OET reading sub-test data

Item name	Infit Mean Square	Outfit Mean Square	Infit t	Outfit t
Item 1	1.30	1.38	1.5	1.1
Item 2	1.15	1.15	0.6	0.5
Item 3	0.91	0.50	−0.1	−0.2
Item 4	0.85	0.68	−0.8	−1.0
Item 5	0.98	0.62	0.1	0.0
Item 6	1.04	0.93	0.2	−0.1
Item 7	1.12	0.97	0.5	0.1
Item 8	0.96	0.90	−0.1	−0.1
Item 9	0.85	0.79	−0.7	−0.6
Item 10	0.90	0.75	−0.5	−0.6
Item 11	1.05	1.00	0.3	0.1
Item 12	1.00	1.27	0.1	0.8
Item 13	1.21	1.08	0.9	0.3
Item 14	1.06	1.59	0.3	1.3
Item 15	1.45	1.57	1.9	1.8
Item 16	0.92	1.25	−0.2	0.6
Item 17	0.71	0.64	−1.4	−1.3
Item 18	0.71	0.36	−0.4	−0.4
Item 19	0.60	0.35	−1.0	−0.8
Item 20	0.79	0.53	−0.6	−0.7
Item 21	1.19	1.27	0.9	0.8
Mean	0.99	0.93	0.1	0.1
SD	0.21	0.37	0.8	0.8

such values to vary, given that they will of course vary, before statistically *significant* problems of fit are indicated? A useful rule of thumb is that values in the range of approximately 0.75 to 1.3 are acceptable,[15] and these values are built into the maps of item fit produced in some Rasch-based programs such as Quest (see Figure 6.2). Values greater than 1.3 show significant misfit – that is, lack of predictability; values below 0.75 show significant overfit.

Fit values expressed in terms of the *t*-distribution (columns 4 and 5 in Table 6.9) will vary around a mean of zero, and will be positive or negative according to whether the observed values show greater variation (resulting in *positive* value of *t*) or less variation (resulting in *negative* value of *t*) than might normally be expected. Values of *t* outside the range +2 to −2 are said to indicate significant departure from the expectations of the model. Values larger than +2 indicate significant misfit; values below −2 indicate significant overfit.

Items identified as having significant lack of fit by either the mean square statistic or the fit *t* statistic are termed *misfitting* items,[16] and can thus be examined and, if necessary, modified or deleted from the test instrument. We will consider the interpretation of fit in greater detail below.

Let us look at the *mean square* item fit values in Table 6.9. We find that items 1 and 15 show significant misfit, which corresponds to our analysis above. Note that the misfit is more pronounced for item 15 (mean square 1.45) than for item 1 (mean square 1.30), which corresponds to the extent of variability we observed in the raw data. The most overfitting item is item 19 (mean square 0.60), again for reasons which are confirmed by our observation of the data matrix.

A summary of information on item fit is represented graphically in Figure 6.2.

The vertical dotted lines in the map indicate the acceptable range of variability in the fit values for particular items; the asterisks indicate the fit values for each item. One item lies clearly to the *right* of these 'tram lines' (item 15), while another lies on the border of acceptability (item 1); these misfitting items are serious cause for concern, and would need to be examined carefully. Overfitting items lie to the left of the lines; the most pronounced of these is item 19. Fit maps such as these are extremely

```
Infit
Mean Square   0.63    0.71        0.83    1.00    1.20        1.40    1.60
             +        +           +       +       +           +

Item 1                            .       |                .*
Item 2                            .       |           *
Item 3                            .         *         |
Item 4                            .   *             |
Item 5                            .           *       |
Item 6                            .       |     *
Item 7                            .       |           *
Item 8                            .         *       |
Item 9                            .   *             |
Item 10                           .       *         |
Item 11                           .       |       *
Item 12                           .         *       |
Item 13                           .       |             *
Item 14                           .       |   *
Item 15                           .       |                  *
Item 16                           .         *       |
Item 17                      *    .                 |
Item 18                      *    .                 |
Item 19              *            .                 |
Item 20                           . *               |
Item 21                           .       |           *
```

FIGURE 6.2   Map of item fit, OET Reading sub-test trial data

useful as they allow us to see at a glance which items need inspection and possibly revision.

6.3.5   Interpreting item fit

Misfitting items can be interpreted as indicating one of two things.

First, they may signal poorly written items; in this sense the interpretation is similar to that of poorly discriminating items in traditional analysis.[17] Such items may need revision; perhaps the distractors are at fault.

Secondly, they may indicate that an item is perfectly good in itself, but that it does not form part of a set of items which together define a single measurement trait. Two or more measurement traits may have been confounded in the construction of the test, and in this case it does not make sense to simply add up the scores on the items on the test and report them as a single score; that would be like adding apples and oranges – the things being added are not alike. Instead, two separate scores should be reported, for groups of items that do 'fit' together.

Imagine you gave a group of people a test of general personal competence, consisting of the following tasks: (1) baking a cake, (2) running 100 metres, (3) solving some maths problems, (4) making a speech. It is unlikely that performance on one of the items could be predicted from performance on the others: they just do not go together as a set of items. Many items would be misfitting; it is not possible to measure 'personal competence' in a single test such as this. Misfitting items are simply those where an individual's performance on one item could not be predicted from the individual's performance on others. The item may be perfectly acceptable in itself; it just forms part of another set.[18]

An example from language testing is provided by O'Loughlin (1992),[19] who designed a comprehension-based writing task and scored the following as separate items: (1) *comprehension of the stimulus texts*, (2) *evaluation of argument*, (3) *overall task fulfilment*, (4) *arguments and evidence*, (5) *organization*, (6) *grammar and cohesion*, (7) *appropriateness* and (8) *spelling and punctuation*. When the items were analysed together, the fit map showed that items 1 (*comprehension of the stimulus texts*) and 2 (*evaluation of argument*) were misfitting. However, when these two items were analysed separately they showed good fit. The items associated directly with the writing task were then also analysed separately; this time it was found that they all fitted together with the exception of item 8 (*spelling and punctuation*). O'Loughlin therefore decided to report comprehension scores (items 1 and 2) separately from writing ability scores.

The question of overfitting items is rather different. These are redundant items; they give us no information that the other items do not give; the pattern of response to these items is too predictable from the overall pattern of response to other items. Worse, they may signal items which have a dependency on other items built into them; for example, if you can only get item 7 correct if you get item 6 correct, because understanding the point of item 7 depends on your having first understood the answer to item 6, then there will be too little variability in responses to item 7; the variability is constrained by the response to the previous item. Item 7 is not making an *independent* contribution to the measurement trait being measured by the test, and may therefore need to be revised or removed.

A case involving a more complex interpretation of the significance of overfit is provided in McNamara (1990a), in which the role of judgements of grammatical correctness in the assessment of spoken and written language is considered. This will be discussed in detail in Chapter 8.

6.3.6   Person fit

Unlike traditional analysis, Rasch analysis enables us to investigate the coherence of an individual's responses as part of a set of responses from a larger group of individuals, and allows us to ask: Can the ability of this individual be defined in the same terms as the ability of others in the group? Do these responses 'fit' the overall pattern?

We will return to the OET data matrix, and consider the response patterns of individual candidates; a selection of these are presented in Table 6.10.

Let us first look at the data from three candidates (38, 31 and 16) whose responses, each in its own way, are in general consistent with the overall pattern of responses observable in the matrix as a whole. Looking across the row of responses for Candidate 38, we see a pattern of 0s or no attempts (the hardest six items), then an intermediate zone of mixed

TABLE 6.10   Fitting and misfitting patterns responses of persons, OET data

Candidate ID #	Most difficult																Item					Easiest		Total score
16	*	*	0	0	*	0	*	0	0	0	*	*	0	0	0	1	*	0	1	1	1			04
26	*	*	1	0	*	1	*	0	0	0	*	*	1	0	1	0	*	0	1	*	0			05
38	0	*	0	*	0	0	1	1	1	0	*	0	0	1	0	1	1	1	1	1	1			10
39	1	1	0	1	0	0	0	0	1	1	0	0	0	0	1	1	0	1	1	1	0			10
31	0	0	0	*	1	0	1	1	1	1	1	1	1	1	1	1	1	1	1	1	1			16

success and failure (the next ten items) and then a string of successes (the last five items in the row, all relatively easy). Perhaps this zone of success stretches further, in fact, to include the eight easiest items, because only one of these is answered incorrectly; in this case the intermediate zone then consists of seven items. For Candidate 31 (the highest scoring of the three), the intermediate zone begins at a different point in the continuum of difficulty, and the zone of ease extends further. Candidate 16 (the lowest scoring of the three) finds all but the easiest three items relatively difficult, and the zone of failures or no attempts extends a good way along the continuum. The intermediate zone begins further to the right of the matrix (in relation to relatively easier items) than for the higher scoring candidates. Note that for this candidate there are *no* unexpected observations in the row of data, and this will lead us to expect that this will be signalled in the analysis (as 'overfit').

We can contrast the orderliness of the responses of these candidates to the absence of orderliness in the responses of Candidate 39. This candidate, who achieved a score in the middle range for this group, got the two most difficult items correct, and the easiest item wrong; there is an intermingling of success and failure right across the continuum of difficulty. We can see that this person's responses are not consistent with the general pattern, and are described as 'misfitting'. (This potentially ambiguous term and the danger of its misinterpretation are discussed below.) The responses of Candidate 26, a low-scoring candidate, are also puzzling as three of this candidate's five correct responses are among the more difficult items on the test.

The orderliness or otherwise of a candidate's responses are summarized for us in terms of person fit statistics, as with item fit statistics. The person fit statistics for the OET data are reproduced in Table 6.11.

As before, we are offered four fit statistics; the advice given above about item fit is appropriate here too (infit statistics are more informative in most cases). It is clear from the table, as we would predict from an inspection of the data matrix, that Candidates 26 and 39 are misfitting candidates. The interpretation of this misfit is complex. It is advisable to go back (as here) to the actual responses of the individual to see which ones are causing the disturbance in the pattern, and to consider an explanation in terms of failure of mastery of a particular area (diagnostic information which can be used to suggest a strategy of remedial teaching), failure of attention in the test-taking process, guessing, anxiety, poor test item construction and the like. For example, it is likely that guessing is an explanation for at least some of the surprisingly correct responses of Candidate 26. Individual learner maps (to be discussed in Chapter 7) can help identify diagnostic information readily. In general, a pattern of misfitting responses by an individual suggests that the individual's abilities are not being measured appropriately by this particular test instrument. Although a kind of shorthand term, 'misfitting individual', is sometimes used to describe this situation, it is important to stress that the direction of misfit is of the instrument to the person, not the person to the instrument! There is a certain danger that this technical term may`be taken (and mis-taken) metaphorically.

Person misfit is a major issue in test development. A test which produces significant levels of person misfit (greater than 2 per cent of candidates) suggests that it is unworkable as a measurement procedure for too many candidates, and will need revision to reduce this number. The ability to provide an analysis of person misfit is an advantage of

TABLE 6.11   Person fit, OET reading sub-test trial data

Candidate ID #	Infit Mean Square	Outfit Mean Square	Infit t	Outfit t
12	1.05	0.81	0.27	0.09
13	0.91	0.80	−0.27	−0.45
15	1.13	1.00	0.54	0.17
16	0.67	0.57	−1.01	−0.91
17	1.03	1.04	0.24	0.23
18	0.74	0.63	−1.40	−1.21
19	1.26	1.30	0.86	0.68
20	1.11	1.00	0.51	0.12
21	1.07	1.01	0.30	0.32
22	0.97	0.89	−0.11	−0.25
23	0.74	0.62	−1.27	−1.10
24	0.69	0.40	−0.63	−0.61
25	0.89	0.76	−0.49	−0.68
26	1.57	2.20	2.35	2.87
27	1.10	0.63	0.37	−0.18
28	1.21	1.31	0.54	0.63
29	0.83	0.65	−0.36	−0.35
30	0.95	0.85	−0.20	−0.30
31	0.56	0.35	−1.36	−1.01
32	0.99	0.86	0.07	−0.06
33	0.62	0.26	−0.61	−0.49
34	1.38	1.24	0.79	0.59
36	1.14	1.20	0.71	0.62
37	1.26	1.10	0.92	0.37
38	0.93	0.79	−0.31	−0.51
39	1.53	2.42	2.55	3.33
40	0.94	0.81	−0.23	−0.45
Mean	1.01	0.94	0.10	0.05
SD	0.26	0.48	0.95	1.03

Rasch analysis over traditional analysis, which focuses on item characteristics and lacks a ready means of determining person mismeasurement.

6.4   Summary

In this chapter, we have introduced a number of key concepts in Rasch analysis through examining the pattern of responses of a group of trial subjects on a performance-based ESP reading test. We have shown that a search for patterns in the data in order to make the responses (of individual candidates, and of candidates as a group to particular items) predictable is the basis of Rasch modelling. To the extent that the data are rendered predictable because they conform to the measurement model, we are in a position to infer that the relationship we have demonstrated between person ability and item difficulty for this particular group of subjects and items is likely to be true for these items with other subjects who are similar in language background, age and other relevant characteristics; and for these persons with other items of similar type. We are thus able to make powerful general statements about person ability and item difficulty which make possible extremely useful practical consequences, such as much simpler comparison of different test forms, the measurement of growth in ability over time, and the development of computer adaptive tests, among other things. We have shown that the degree of predictability of the pattern of responses for particular candidates and for particular items is also routinely reported in Rasch analyses by means of fit statistics. These form the basis for item revision, or for judgements about the suitability of the test for individual learners. In Chapter 5, and again in Chapters 8 and 9, we consider the extension of the simple Rasch model (which handles right–wrong data of the kind we have considered here) to the more important case for performance assessment contexts of ratings using a rating scale, and involving judges. We also review the application of Rasch measurement in recent testing research and test development.

Notes

1. The mathematics are set out clearly in Wright and Stone (1979). Simple calculations that can be done by hand are presented in Henning (1987a); these give a good feel for the mathematical calculations involved in Rasch analysis.
2. The initial responses of a test taker are used as the basis of provisional estimates of person ability, and a set of items corresponding to the likely range of that ability is selected for presentation to the candidate. Successive responses of the candidates to these items allow more precise estimates of the candidate's ability and a corresponding narrowing

of the range of difficulty of items, until an agreed level of precision of estimation is reached. This tailoring of a test to the test taker results in the possibility of test takers having to answer fewer items than in a usual test, as items outside the candidate's obvious ability range are not presented. The possibility of this testing presupposes the existence of a bank of items, all calibrated on a single ability–difficulty scale; items presented to candidates are selected by the computer from this bank.

3. Although the basic statistical tool in investigating reliability has been the correlation coefficient (Henning, 1987a: 107), analysis of variance techniques have been recommended in the calculation of overall reliability coefficients (Krzanowski and Woods, 1984; Woods *et al.*, 1986). In particular, Generalizability Theory is increasingly being advocated and adopted in the analysis of language test reliability (Bachman, 1990); this is an ANOVA-based technique which uses raw scores as its primary data.

4. The model will be presented and discussed in appropriate detail in Chapter 9.

5. Details of this test were given in Chapter 4.

6. This is too small a number to get very precise estimates, as we shall see (the errors in Tables 6.5 and 6.6 are rather large) but it is convenient for illustrative purposes here, as the complete data matrix is of manageable size for this presentation.

7. Ability is symbolized by the letter B in Rasch analyses. In earlier versions, Greek letters were used, so that ability was symbolized by *beta*. Confusingly, in other (two- and three-parameter) IRT models (see Chapter 9), ability is symbolized differently, by the letter *theta*.

8. Item difficulty is currently symbolized by the letter D in Rasch analysis, formerly *delta*; again rather confusingly it is symbolized by the letter *b* in two- and three-parameter IRT models.

9. Formal statements of Rasch models are discussed in Chapter 9, Appendix 9A.

10. Several of the tables in this chapter are based on output from the program Quest (Adams and Khoo, 1993); column headings have been changed in the interest of clarity.

11. Any measurement scale needs a zero point as a point of reference; this is often set arbitrarily according to convenience, as in expressions of height – human height is measured in terms of height above the ground (zero = ground level at the point at which the person is standing) but the height of naturally occurring geographical features is expressed in relation to a different reference point, sea level.

12. A logarithm is an *index* which has a *base*. The base can be any number, but the numbers 10 and 2 are frequently used as bases. The number 100 can be expressed as a logarithm of 10: using 10 as the base, 100 is the equivalent of 10^2. The index or logarithm is 2; so we can say that the logarithm of 100 is 2, or more correctly, the logarithm to the base 10 of 100 is 2. Traditionally, logarithms were expressed to the base 10 in the majority of cases, so the default or unmarked logarithm base was 10, and so 'to the base 10' could be omitted. Similarly, 4 is 2^2, so that the index is 2 and the base is 2; the logarithm of 4 to the base 2 is 2. In the same way, 8 is 2^3, so that the logarithm of 8 to the base 2 is 3. *e* is a naturally occurring constant; another, more familiar, naturally occurring constant is π (*pi*), which is the ratio of the circumference to the diameter of a circle. Logarithms to the base *e* are called natural logarithms, and the logarithm itself may be referred to as an exponent.

13. The outfit statistics include every single observation, even extremely unpredictable single observations; such single observations may have a disproportionate influence on the summary statistic for fit. The infit statistics do not include such extreme values, and hence provide a more sensitive picture of the fit in the set of observations of greatest interest. A comparison would be the attempt to include in a single photo two things which are rather far apart; the degree of detail on either will be limited. Deciding to focus on one or other region of interest in the photo will allow a finer grained representation of the object to be photographed. This practice of excluding single data points from the summary may seem odd at first sight, but on reflection gives us greater and more relevant information, not less.

14. When fitting a simple linear regression line, for example, the regression coefficients (the information needed to determine the slope and the origin of the line) enable us to

predict where observations will fall in the case of perfect model–data fit. Of course such perfect fit is rarely if ever observed, and so the distance of particular observations from the expected linear pattern is of interest, misfitting or outlying observations being of the greatest interest in many cases as they present the greatest challenge to the overall picture of the relationship between the two variables which the analysis is painting.

15. More accurately, for n sizes of 30 or more, the range is the mean $\pm$ twice the standard deviation of the mean square statistic, reported at the bottom of the table of fit values in the output. In this case, where the standard deviation is 0.21, the relevant range is 0.99 $\pm$ (2 $\times$ 0.21) = 0.57 − 1.41. The standard deviation is large in this case partly because of the small number of observations. The interpretation of fit values in this particular analysis is made a little more difficult because of the small amount of data available to the analysis, but it serves our purposes in explaining the basic issues in understanding fit.

16. Usually, the same items will be identified as acceptable or problematic in either analysis. Where differences occur, this is usually related to sample size. With small sample sizes, as here, the values tend to be a little less reliable; with very large sample sizes (say, over 400) then t-values will be inflated and may lie outside the acceptable range by chance, and will not necessarily indicate a significant problem of fit; the mean square statistic is safer as it is less sensitive to sample size.

17. The fact that item misfit captures similar information to item discrimination indices is not surprising, given that they both indicate patterns of response to particular items that are at odds with the pattern of responses of the same individuals to the other items in the test. This means that the question of the direct estimation of item discrimination, an issue over which there is great debate between proponents of one-parameter (Rasch) and two- (or three-)parameter Item Response Theory models (see Chapter 9), may not be such an important issue after all, as information about discrimination is available in fit statistics in analyses using a one-parameter Rasch model.

18. The extent to which responses to groups of items form a coherent set in this way can sometimes be predicted by an in-principle or *a priori* understanding of what we are trying to measure, sometimes not. This issues will be taken up further in Chapter 9.

19. This study is discussed in more detail in Chapter 9.

7 Mapping and reporting abilities and skill levels

7.1 Introduction

How and on what basis are the abilities of individuals reported in performance assessments? In this chapter, we will consider a number of issues raised by rating scales and other kinds of descriptive achievement scales. *Rating scales* (cf. Figure 7.1) are particularly significant in certain types of performance assessment, as they are used to guide the rating process, as well as being used for reporting.[1] Typically, in the development of such scales, criterion statements are developed to define a number of distinct levels of performance, usually between three and ten. Once the statements have been created, the performance of the individual is compared with the statements, and the one best describing the performance is selected as the descriptor. Other scales defining levels of achievement, to be discussed below, are not used in the rating process but have primarily a reporting or mapping function.

The question then arises: How are the descriptors themselves developed? Given the crucial role they play in performance assessments, one would expect that this subject would have been intensively researched and discussed. In fact, certainly in the field of language assessment, we find that this is not so; we are frequently simply presented with rating scales as products for consumption and are told too little of their provenance and of their rationale. In particular, we too frequently lack any account of empirical evidence for their validity.

Aspect of performance considered: Overall communicative effectiveness
1: elementary level of communicative effectiveness
2: clearly could not cope in a bridging programme in a clinical setting involving interactions with patients and colleagues
3: just below minimum competence needed to cope in a bridging programme in a clinical setting involving interactions with patients and colleagues
4: has minimum competence needed to cope in a bridging programme in a clinical setting involving interactions with patients and colleagues
5: could easily cope in a bridging programme in a clinical setting involving interactions with patients and colleagues
6: near-native communicative effectiveness

FIGURE 7.1   Rating scale, OET Speaking sub-test

In this chapter, therefore, we will consider research on the validity of rating and achievement scale descriptors. The chapter is in two parts. First, assumptions underlying the wording of descriptors in several widely used rating scales are questioned, through a series of studies of the performance of native speakers on an EAP test. It will be shown that idealization of native speaker performance is frequent in such scales, and that this has implications for the validity of the tests they are used to report, and for the fairness of gate-keeping decisions made on the basis of their use.

In the second part of the chapter we will consider the use of Rasch analysis to generate *maps* of how particular test tasks define levels of achievement, and the extent to which this feature of Rasch-based test analysis may enable use to develop empirically based descriptions of growth in aspects of language ability.

7.2   The wording of rating scale descriptors

In general, the creation of rating scales involves the development of descriptors for differing levels of performance. The descriptors can be defined on *a priori* grounds, deriving from theoretical notions of what the test is held to be measuring, or empirically, on the basis of an analysis of data from performances on test tasks. In the former case, descriptors fall into two broad categories, reflecting the underlying philosophies of the two main traditions in performance assessment discussed in Chapter 2. In the first of these, the context-oriented approach, the emphasis is on mastery of discrete, defined tasks in particular contexts. This is most clearly emphasized in competency-based language assessment (Brindley, 1989; Mawer, 1991; Quinn, 1993) and in criterion-referenced language assessment more generally (Brindley, 1989; Lynch and Davidson, 1994) where particular criterion behaviours are specified and 'checked off' as the candidate or student shows evidence of having mastered each. Given the importance of real-world performance contexts in performance testing, it is not surprising that statements of what candidates can do rather than what they know should be the focus of attention. In the second, more cognitive approach, underlying knowledge and skill in execution are the target of assessment, and reports are couched in terms of the level of knowledge or skill displayed by a candidate in performance.

Where levels of achievement are involved in relation to a single aspect of ability (e.g. pronunciation), a continuum of increasing proficiency is defined, allowing reporting to be done with reference to scales which chart the development of ability in performance. This, as Masters (1990:

57) points out, is central to the concept of criterion-referencing as it was introduced by Glaser (1963: 519) when he spoke of 'the behaviors which define each point along the continuum ranging from no proficiency at all to perfect performance'.

Even where discrete behaviours are defined, as in the mastery of tasks which have no *a priori*, in-principle relation to each other in terms of difficulty or complexity, an empirical analysis of the performance of candidates on the tasks may establish that they do in fact form a continuum of difficulty. This then forms the basis for reporting progress along that continuum, much in the way that rating scales do. This second, empirical, approach to describing achievement in developmental terms will be discussed further in the second part of the chapter.

The descriptors in rating scales can play a crucial role in assessment (see discussion above, and in Chapter 2) but all too often they have been the subject of very little careful evaluative scrutiny themselves. For example, in describing the top level of the scale, many rating scales make specific reference (explicitly or implicitly) to the assumed performance of native speakers; this practice dates from the earliest oral proficiency interview test, the Foreign Service Institute (FSI) Oral Proficiency Interview, where the highest level (5) is defined as follows (Clark and Clifford, 1988: 131): 'Native or Bilingual Proficiency: Speaking proficiency equivalent to that of an educated native speaker', and has survived (with some cosmetic modifications) in many related rating scales. The ASLPR defines its highest level in terms of the performance of native speakers in all four macroskills. For writing, the level is defined as follows (Ingram and Wylie, 1984: 22):

W:5   *NATIVE-LIKE PROFICIENCY*

Written proficiency equivalent to that of a native speaker of the same socio-cultural variety. The learner's written language in all its forms is fully accepted by such native speakers in all its features including formal accuracy, structural variation, word choice, idiom, colloquialisms, register appropriateness, discourse structure (including thought sequence and coherence), subtlety of meaning and cultural references. Deviations from educated native speaker forms, special register features, or stylistic conventions will only be those recognizable as native speaker variants.

Can perform as effectively as a native speaker in all writing tasks normally encountered and has native-like flexibility in mastering new ones.

But native speaker performance on the tasks used in assessments associated with such scales has never been seriously investigated. This evidence is crucial in establishing the validity of scales of this type. As will now be shown, empirical investigation can have disconcerting results for our understanding of what is being measured in performance tests which report achievement in terms of rating scales of this type. In the following section, data from native speaker performance on a test of reading and writing English for Academic Purposes (EAP) will be reported. The implications· of the findings for the construct validity of performance tests will be considered, with particular reference to the way in which scalar descriptions reflect such a construct. The implications of implicit or explicit reference to native speaker performance in such descriptors will be a particular focus of the discussion. Issues of equity will also be raised. The discussion will make reference to the distinction presented above, in Chapter 2, between a *strong* and a *weak* sense of the term *performance test*. In the present context, the point that emerges is the extent to which communicatively oriented performance-based EAP tests such as IELTS are simultaneously tests of language proficiency and other more general cognitive skills. To the extent that performance on the test involves factors other than straight second language proficiency, and these factors are included in the assessment, then we may expect there to be an overlap in the performance of native and non-native speakers; and the performance of native speakers will be highly variable, as we will demonstrate from the data.

7.3   The performance of native speakers on foreign language proficiency tests

(*The material in Sections 7.3–7.6 appeared first,·in modified format, in Hamilton et al. 1993*)

The performance of non-native speakers on language tests used for purposes of academic selection has long been an object of study. Studies can be divided into those involving non-communicative tests such as the TOEFL, and communicative EAP tests such as the TEEP (Weir, 1988a), ELTS (Alderson and Hughes, 1981; Weir, 1998b), IELTS (British Council/UCLES, 1989; British Council/UCLES/IDP, 1989) and others.

In the former category of tests, the performance of native speakers has been assumed to be relatively homogeneous, and at the top of the range of possible test scores, on the assumption that language proficiency is something that native speakers possess, and possess uniformly well; this distinguishes them from non-native speakers. A number of studies have concluded that TOEFL does discriminate between native and non-native speakers in this way (Angoff and Sharon, 1971; Clark, 1977; Johnson, 1977), although native speaker performance was less homogeneous, and relatively lower, in the sub-tests of reading comprehension and writing ability than in the other sub-tests (listening comprehension, English structure and vocabulary).

A more recent study in the same tradition is that of Oscarson (1986), who investigated the construct validity of a national test of English as a foreign language in Sweden by comparing the performance of Swedish upper secondary level students with a group of English subjects matched for age. Sub-tests of vocabulary, phrases, grammar, reading and listening comprehension were found overall to reveal significant differences between the two groups, but there were differences among the sub-tests. In particular, on the longer of two reading passages, the non-native speaker mean score in fact narrowly exceeded that of the native speakers. The native speaker mean for the whole test was relatively high (83.4 per cent), but by no means perfect. Oscarson argued nevertheless that the significant difference between the two groups in their results on the test overall was evidence of the construct validity of the test.

It is interesting that in both the TOEFL studies and in the Swedish study the argument for the distinctiveness of the performance of the two contrasting groups is weakest on the most communicative parts of the tests (those focusing on whole skills such as reading or listening).

EAP tests in the communicative tradition have been less certain about the competence of the native speaker as a reference point, both in the empirical validation of tests and in the wording of rating scales defining levels of performance on the tests. We can distinguish those who appear to be recommending and using the performance of native speakers as a reference point in test development and validation, those who caution about such an approach, and a number of fence sitters. A number of writers appear to favour reference to native speaker performance. Cziko (1983: 294) suggests the use of native speaker performance as a reference point in criterion-referenced assessment in general. In the specific context of EAP tests, Weir appears to have been a strong advocate of reference to the native speaker, both in his own development of the associated Examining Board's Test of English for Educational Purposes (TEEP), and in advice about the development of the IELTS test. For example, Weir (1988b) eliminated items in the reading comprehension sub-test of the TEEP test if native speakers found them difficult. Nevertheless the performance of native speakers was found not to be homogeneous: while there were clear differences between the performance of native and non-native speakers, the native speakers achieved scores ranging from 76 to 88 per cent for reading and from 65 to 88 per cent for writing, that is, less than perfect results. The TEEP itself uses an analytical assessment scale of six levels for *listening comprehension, accent, formal accuracy, referential adequacy, sociocultural appropriateness* and *fluency*. In each case, the top level is described in terms of the user displaying 'native speaker' competence (Emmett, 1985: 145–8).

On the other hand, empirical findings, mainly in the context of research outside EAP contexts, and involving semi-direct tests such as cloze, have led to the assumptions implicit in this position being questioned. Alderson (1980) found that although there were significant differences between the scores of native and non-native speakers on the cloze test, with the native speakers performing better, the difference was not very great and there was a considerable degree of overlap, with some non-native speaker scores exceeding those of native speakers. Nor did native speaker performance appear to be uniform. Alderson (1980: 75) concluded that

> attempts to use native speakers as a criterion for non-native speakers in ... such criterion referenced testing are misguided. Similarly perhaps proficiency tests should not be validated with native speakers on the assumption that native speakers will achieve perfect scores.

Oller and Conrad (1971) had similarly found variability in native speaker performance related to educational level, with significant overlap between advanced non-native speaker performance and that of some categories of native speakers. Bachman (1990) has also criticized the assumption of homogeneity in native speaker performance.

A number of scale developers, perhaps aware of these findings, have been ambivalent about referring to native speaker performance in scalar descriptions. Hughes (1989: 110), in advising the constructors of rating scales, points out that the use of a native speaker standard to judge non-native performance has come in for criticism. Nevertheless in his own EAP test for a Turkish University (Hughes, 1988) the native speaker is used as a reference point in defining performance levels (levels include *Educated Native Speaker Standard* and *Very Close to Native Speaker Standard*).

The test used in the studies to be reported below is the exemplar version of the reading and writing sub-tests of the IELTS test (British Council/UCLES 1989; British Council/UCLES/IDP 1989). This test, developed jointly by a British and Australian research team to replace the earlier British ELTS test, is a performance-based EAP test in which the reading and writing tasks simulate those encountered by students in university settings, either as graduates or undergraduates, and by students in more general training contexts. Until recently, four versions or modules of the reading and writing sub-tests were available, depending on the candidate's broad area of intended study; the current format has only a single module, following research by Clapham (1994) which found only weak evidence of a subject-specific effect in reading.

Weir (1988a) called for native speaker performance to be considered in the IELTS test development process, and to a limited extent this was done, using three groups of sixth form college students; the results of these trials are available in Clapham and Alderson (forthcoming), and will be discussed below. Further more extensive trials are currently under way. Evans (1990) produced some evidence that native speaker performance on the tests was far from uniform and far from perfect: her native speakers subjects ($n=16$) at a tertiary institute in Melbourne scored only in the middle range on the IELTS Exemplar Reading Test, at or just below the level required for entrance by foreign students to the institution concerned.

The supposed performance of native speakers is used directly and indirectly in the interpretation of the performance of non-native speakers on the tests. While the reporting scales (band scales) for IELTS do not refer explicitly to native speaker performance – avoiding doing so because of the cautions suggested by Alderson, Hughes and Bachman quoted above – the native speaker makes a covert but unmistakable reappearance in the highest Band Scale in the guise of the Expert User, defined as follows: 'has fully operational command of the language; appropriate, accurate and fluent with complete understanding' (British Council/UCLES/IDP, 1989: 14). It is clear, then, that the native speaker 'hovers' over IELTS;[2] and Alderson (personal communication) has stated that the FSI and other rating scales were examined and consulted carefully in the drawing up of the IELTS band descriptors. Reference to native speaker performance is also made in the IELTS reading test specification document for item writers (British Council/UCLES, 1989: 3), which says that native speakers in the first term of their study should be able to complete the tasks in this test successfully.

In what follows, native speaker performance on the IELTS exemplar test is reported in a series of related studies, two on the reading sub-test, one on the writing sub-test. The performance of educated native speakers of varying levels of post-secondary educational achievement is investigated.

7.4   Native speaker performance on an EAP reading test[3]

As mentioned above, some trialling of the IELTS reading sub-test was carried out as part of the development of the test, and more is planned.

TABLE 7.1   Results of Cambridge trials, IELTS reading sub-test (adapted from Clapham, 1996: 74)

Module	n	Raw score mean	Raw score SD
1 (Arts and Social Sciences)	29	27.52	3.42
2 (Life and Medical Sciences)	16	32.25	4.39
3 (Physical Science and Technology)	10	27.5	3.5

Clapham (1994, 1996) reports the results obtained in the earlier trials. The subjects were just completing the first year of a two-year course at a sixth form college in Cambridge, England, where they were preparing for the English A-level examinations. The three academic modules of the first live version of the reading sub-test were used. Subjects took the module that was most appropriate for their field of study. Results were as set out in Table 7.1.

In the studies reported below, the Arts and Social Sciences Module is used, so it is worth looking at the data from this module in a little more detail. Table 7.2 (adapted from Clapham, 1994: 327) reports frequency data for each raw score level. None of the native speakers taking this module could be classified as *Expert User* (Band 9, broadly corresponding to a raw score higher than the highest score here); the mean score (27.5, roughly equivalent to Band 6.5) was barely at the level at which foreign students are admitted to English-medium universities.

In order to investigate these matters further, two studies were carried out in Melbourne with groups of native speakers contrasting in their educational levels, as this had been found to be an important variable by Oller and Conrad (1971) on performance on the cloze test. In broad terms, Study 1 dealt with students studying at post-secondary level outside the University setting, while Study 2 examined the performance of graduates. These groups represent groups of native speakers with educational levels respectively lower (Study 1) and higher (Study 2) than the subjects used in the Cambridge trials.

TABLE 7.2   Cambridge trials, raw score frequency, Arts and Social Sciences Module (reading) (adapted from Clapham, 1994: 327)

Score	Frequency	Score	Frequency
21	1	27	1
22	1	28	3
23	3	29	4
24	1	30	3
25	3	31	3
26	3	33	3

7.4.1   Study 1

Hamilton (1991) investigated the performance of 84 native speakers of English on the exemplar version of the IELTS reading sub-test. The subjects were all enrolled in post-secondary courses in Colleges of Technical and Further Education (TAFE) in Melbourne. Such colleges offer a range of non-degree vocational training courses, usually requiring the successful completion of the final year of secondary education, and are the Australian equivalent of British Further Education (FE) Colleges and American Community Colleges. The groups tested were as follows:

    Group 1.1   Advanced Certificate of Marketing ($n=23$)
    Group 1.2   Traineeship Certificate in Clerical Skills ($n=20$)
    Group 1.3   Advanced Certificate of Secretarial Studies ($n=41$)

Entry to such vocational courses usually involves satisfactory completion of the final year of secondary education (Year 12), although students' scores would not in most cases guarantee them entry to a university place directly. Instead, TAFE courses articulate with university degree courses, with credit transfers after successful completion of part of the TAFE course. We can thus say that although these subjects are not in the first rank academically, they have satisfied entry requirements for post-secondary education. The relevance of educational background to performance on the tests is an issue that emerges in the study. The entrance requirements for the courses taken by the groups in this study differ: a higher Year 12 score is required for entry into the Marketing course (Group 1.1) than into the Secretarial Studies course (Group 1.3); admission to the Clerical Skills course (Group 1.2) does not require successful completion of Year 12, so the academic standard is likely to be lower again.

As explained earlier, the IELTS reading sub-test until recently came in four versions, depending on the type of course for which the candidate is applying. There were three academic modules in three broad subject areas, and a fourth general training module, designed particularly to cover the situation of shorter-term job-related training attachments in an English-speaking country (for example, firemen might come to the UK for updating on modern work methods). At one time there was considerable debate in Australia over which module was appropriate for the more academically oriented (as against technically oriented) TAFE courses, of which the above courses are examples. The problem was that the choices available were more suited to the British than to the Australian situation. In the latter, government policy is to increase retention in higher education and training substantially, and to blur the academic/non-academic

TABLE 7.3   Scores of three groups of native speakers on the IELTS exemplar reading test

Group	*n*	Mean	SD
1.1	23	22.0	5.74
1.2	20	18.5	5.33
1.3	41	17.88	6.28

divide, for example by allowing transfer with credits from TAFE courses to degree courses.[4] Ultimately, IELTS policy was clarified so that students in professionally oriented TAFE courses (of the kind involved here) were to take the relevant academic module, rather than the general training module, as previously. Inspection of the kinds of texts read by the students in the courses concerned here suggested that they were like those found in the academic module. The subjects thus took the exemplar version of Academic Module C, suitable for students in arts, law, business and the social sciences. This module was specifically recommended for (among others) candidates seeking entry into marketing/clerical studies programmes (British Council/UCLES/IDP, 1989: 1).

The means and standard deviations of scores for the three groups are reported in Table 7.3. The maximum possible score on the test was 37. The data reveal that the scores of the native speakers were neither homogeneous, nor high. The groups managed to score approximately half marks, the first group a little above that, with a fairly broad range of scores. Moreover, there was a significant overall difference between the group means, as revealed by an ANOVA: $F (2, 81) = 3.73$, $p < 0.05$. Inspection of the means suggested that the mean for Group 1.1 was contributing most to this difference; this was confirmed by a further *t*-test, which revealed that the means for Groups 1.2 and 1.3 were not significantly different.

7.4.2 Study 2

In view of the results of Study 1, and given that the native speakers concerned were of a lower academic level than many of the students taking the IELTS test, it was decided to replicate the study using a number of highly educated groups. Lopes (1992) investigated the performance of 73 native speakers on the same IELTS Academic Module C exemplar Reading sub-test. The subjects were all university graduates with a minimum of one degree. They comprised:

> Group 2.1   23 postgraduate students at a teacher training institute, Melbourne. Mean age 34.4 (SD 7.25) – M5, F18.

TABLE 7.4   Comparison of performance of native speaker groups in Studies 1 and 2

Study	n	Mean	SD
S1 (Groups 1.1, 1.2 and 1.3)	84	19.15	6.11
S2 (Groups 2.1, 2.2 and 2.3)	73	29.85	4.37

TABLE 7.5   Comparison of performance of Groups 2.1, 2.2 and 2.3

Group	n	Mean	SD
2.1 (postgraduates)	23	27.565	4.326
2.2 (lecturers)	30	29.6	4.328
2.3 (baby barristers)	20	32.85	2.477

Group 2.2   30 members of the academic staff at the same institute. Mean age 48.4 (SD 6.35) – M23, F7.

Group 2.3   20 junior barristers of the Victorian Bar ('baby barristers').[5] Mean age 33.4 (SD 6.06) – M15, F5.

The means and standard deviations of the total sample of this study were compared to the combined group of native speakers used in Study 1 (Table 7.4).

This comparison indicates clearly that native speakers with higher educational qualifications (i.e. Groups 2.1, 2.2 and 2.3) on average perform better on this test than native speakers with weaker educational qualifications (Groups 1.1, 1.2 and 1.3) and that their scores do not vary to the same extent. No statistical test was carried out as the difference in the means was very substantial and clearly statistically significant. The performances of the three highly educated groups were then compared (Table 7.5).

The data in Table 7.5 reveal that the means were progressively higher for each group. The variance of scores of the postgraduate student group (Group 2.1) and the lecturer group (Group 2.2) was almost identical even though the mean of the latter group was higher. The 'baby barristers' (Group 2.3) had a higher mean again and, differently, a narrower dispersion of scores. A one-way ANOVA was used to examine the differences between the means of Groups 2.1, 2.2 and 2.3 (Table 7.6). The results show that there was a significant difference between the three groups: $F (2, 70) = 9.864$, $p < 0.01$.

A variance ratio test between Group 2.1 and Group 2.3 was carried out and found to be significant: $F (22, 19) = 3.05$, $p < 0.01$, thus confirming the difference in the variances in the groups. It is acknowledged that ANOVA requires equal variances of the samples and we have shown that

TABLE 7.6 Analysis of Variance table for data from three highly educated groups

Source	df	Sum squares	Mean square	F-test	p
Between groups	2	301.94	150.97	9.864	0.0002
Within groups	70	1071.402	15.306		
Total	72	1373.342			

TABLE 7.7 Comparison between groups of highly educated native speakers

	Difference in means	Scheffé test
Groups 2.1 and 2.2	2.035	1.761
Groups 2.2 and 2.3	3.250	4.141*
Groups 2.1 and 2.3	5.285	9.76*

* $p < 0.05$

this assumption is violated in this instance; however, ANOVA is known to be robust to violations of this assumption (Hatch and Lazaraton, 1991: 352). A *post hoc* comparison of means (the Scheffé test) was used to indicate where the differences occurred (Table 7.7).

The Scheffé test revealed significant differences at the 5 per cent level between institute lecturers (Group 2.2) and 'baby barristers' (Group 2.3) as well as between postgraduate students (Group 2.1) and 'baby barristers' (Group 2.3), demonstrating a significant difference in these two populations, while confirming that the postgraduate student group (2.1) did not differ significantly from the lecturer group (2.2). Thus, significant differences were found between the performances of even very highly educated native speakers.

These findings clearly indicate that performance by native speakers on this test is far from uniform and is significantly related to educational level and work experience. We come closest to finding examples of the *Expert User* in the 'baby barrister' group, although by no means all of this group could be so classified; the *Expert User* is indeed an elusive creature. It is not surprising in view of the close reading and analysis of texts that is characteristic of the work of barristers that they had most success with the reading tasks on the test in question.

7.5 Native speaker performance on an EAP writing test[6]

Sheridan (1991), in a companion study to that reported in Study 1 above, administered the exemplar version of the IELTS writing sub-test, using Academic Module C, as before. The subjects were TAFE students undertaking similar courses to those reported in Study 1 above; that is, students enrolled in courses leading to the Advanced Certificate of Marketing and the Advanced Certificate of Secretarial Studies (cf. Groups 1.1 and 1.3 above; there was some, but not complete overlap between the subjects used in each study). Eighty-four students sat the test but only 62 completed it. Of these, 14 were found to be non-native speakers and 48 native speakers of English; of the native speakers, 32 came from a bilingual background (having exposure to one of eight immigrant languages in the home) and 16 from a monolingual background. All subjects classified as native speakers had completed at least the whole of their secondary education in Australia; most were Australian born; only four students had attended school overseas, usually for one or two years at lower primary level.

The writing sub-test of IELTS presents two tasks: Task 1 involves information transfer or reprocessing (15 minutes allowed) and Task 2 requires candidates to draw on information from the passages in the reading sub-test, together with their own experience, to present an argument or to suggest a solution to a problem. The scripts for both tasks were marked by trained and approved IELTS raters. Results are expressed on a 9-point scale in terms of defined band levels.

Before presenting the results, it is worth noting that because of the absence of surface grammatical errors the identity of the writers as native speakers (NS) would have been apparent to the raters, who may have applied different criteria or interpreted the set criteria differently as a result; it is possible that a kind of norm referencing may have been going on, despite the fact that raters were ostensibly using the level descriptions in the rating scales. Additionally, as in Study 1, the performance of the NS group may not have been optimal, because of factors relating to test familiarity and motivation. Usually, candidates have had some test preparation, and their performance on the test has relatively serious consequences for them; neither of these things was true for the NS group. It is indicative, for example, that 22 of the native speakers did not complete the writing test through fatigue or lack of motivation, and although their data have not been included, the performance of those who were included may have been affected by these factors.

TABLE 7.8 Performance of a group of NS on the IELTS exemplar writing test

Part of test	Native speaker group (n=48)	
	M	SD
Task 1	6.69	1.26
Task 2	6.56	1.37
Overall	6.65	1.36

The results are presented in Table 7.8. Mean band levels and standard deviations are given for each task, and for the test overall (there is a procedure for determining the final band score when the scores on the two sub-tests differ). The mean band score is around Band 6.5, a crucial point on the scale in terms of entry decisions for many courses.

7.6 Implications for the validity of EAP tests

(*The argument in this section represents the collective work of the authors of Hamilton et al. 1993*)

The results of the studies reported in sections 7.4 and 7.5 reveal that the performance of native speakers on two IELTS sub-tests was far from homogeneous.

On the *reading* sub-test, differences were found between two broad types of native speaker, those enrolled in non-university post-secondary courses (Study 1) and graduates (Study 2). Moreover, within these broad types, significant differences were found in each study between subgroups characterized in terms of educational background (Study 1) and educational and professional background (Study 2). For example, performance on the test was related to the entrance requirements for the courses taken by the groups in question: a higher year 12 score is required for entry into the Marketing course (Group 1.1) than into the Secretarial (Group 1.3) and Clerical Skills courses (Group 1.2). This is reflected in the scores of the three groups, as the mean score of Group 1.1 was significantly higher than that of the other two groups. It appears from Study 1 that educational achievement, as measured in terms of final year secondary school results, is related to performance on this test. In Study 2, differences were found between the performance of junior barristers, an academic élite whose reading skills are honed in their training and professional practice, and other graduates.

Looking at the native speaker groups in Study 1 as a whole (n=84), the mean score for the native speakers represented a mark of about 60 per cent. When this is converted into an approximate band score using the conversion table calculated for scores on the 'live' version of the test, this corresponds to Band 5. A person receiving this score is described as a *Modest User*, that is, slightly more than *Limited* (Band 4) and less than *Competent* (Band 6). A more detailed description of the band is given as follows:

Has partial command of the language, coping with overall meaning in most situations, though is likely to make mistakes. Should be able to handle basic communication in own field.

(British Council/UCLES/IDP, 1989: A1)

These results differ from the results of studies of native speaker performance on the TOEFL, where there is a relatively narrow spread of scores among native speakers, who perform significantly better than non-native speakers, and at the top of the scoring range. The reason for this is most likely to be that IELTS tests language skills in context, in performance situations, and TOEFL does not. (Alternative explanations in terms of test-wiseness and motivation for the poor performance of the native speakers should not of course be discounted.)

The Swedish study by Oscarson (1986) has been mentioned above. As stated earlier, despite a generally superior performance by native speakers overall, native and non-native speaker performance could not be distinguished on the reading proficiency sub-test. In his discussion of this point, Oscarson (1986: 104) suggested that certain 'non-language-specific variables' such as deductive ability, background knowledge related to the topic, associative memory and reasoning are more important in reading than in other language activities and therefore a smaller difference between native and non-native speaker performance on a reading task would be expected.

Lunzer *et al.* (1979) concluded that effective reading comprehension depends upon two conditions: comprehension and the application of appropriate study skills, which include such processes as skimming, scanning, and receptive and reflective reading. This distinction suggests that language proficiency is only one factor involved in reading comprehension and that other non-linguistic factors are involved. As long ago as 1917 Thorndike claimed that, in reading, the individual must 'select, repress, emphasize, correlate and organize, all under the influence of the right mental set or purpose or demand' (1917 [1971]: 431), such processes being similar to those required to solve a mathematical problem – in other words, 'reading is reasoning'.

Turning now to the *writing* sub-test: the native speakers performed neither homogeneously, nor homogeneously well. As with the reading sub-test, the band descriptors seem ill-matched to the performance of native speakers. The scale and sub-scales used in the actual assessment of the writing sub-test consider *communicative quality*, *arguments, ideas and evidence* and formal aspects (*word choice, form and spelling* and *sentence structure*). The second of these categories clearly introduces assessment of study skills rather than language proficiency conceived in some narrower sense; and there is no reason to suggest that native speakers may have any particular advantage in this area.

One way of understanding the results reported here is in terms of the distinction proposed in Chapter 2 between a *strong* and a *weak* sense of the term *performance test*. In the strong sense, knowledge of the second language is a necessary but not sufficient condition for success on the test tasks. Language is a means, but it is not (or not only) the means that is being investigated. Success is measured in terms of performance on the task, not only in terms of knowledge of language. The results suggest that the IELTS reading and writing sub-tests tend towards the strong end of the performance test continuum. In this, IELTS differs from TOEFL, which does not claim to be a performance test and measures mainly knowledge of language.

It is clear that reference to the native speaker as some kind of ideal or benchmark in scalar descriptions of performance on performance tests is not valid. IELTS does not strictly speaking do this, as we have seen, but clearly few of the native speakers in this study fell into its category of *Expert User*; and the relation of *Expert Users* to native speakers remains undefined.

Validity, as Bachman (1990: 243) reminds us, is currently understood in terms of the 'inferences that are made on the basis of test scores'; in the words of the American Psychological Association (1985: 9) validity is 'the appropriateness, meaningfulness, and usefulness of the specific infer-ences made from test scores'. In the case of communicatively oriented EAP tests such as IELTS, if a candidate performs poorly on the test, it is not clear what inference should be drawn. In what terms should such a performance be explained? Is it a problem of language proficiency, or other non-linguistic skills required in the performance task? If we are interested in whether or not the candidate can cope with the tasks expected of him or her in the study situation, it may not matter, except for diagnostic purposes. However, if the candidate is being denied access to training on the basis of a performance equivalent to that of a native speaker who has been accepted for training, then the differing bases for acceptance for the two groups needs to be investigated and perhaps, in the interest of equity and access, made equivalent.

In this first part of the chapter we have examined one aspect of criterion statements in rating scales, that is, the frequent reference to the presumed performance levels of native speakers. It is relevant to note that many of the important rating scales now in use ultimately derive from the FSI scale, developed originally in the 1950s at the height of the psychometric-structuralist period, in which a view of second language proficiency and its relation to first language proficiency gave the native speaker an impor-tant defining role as a kind of benchmark. The tradition of studying the performance of native speakers on non-performance based tests such as TOEFL, itself a product of the same period, was carried over into the newer communicative EAP tests such as TEEP, ELTS and IELTS with-out reflection on whether it was any longer appropriate. The Chomskyan 'ideal native speaker/hearer' remains the point of reference. In fact, an examination of the performance of native speakers reveals how elusive and untypical (of native speakers) this idealized performance is.

More generally, the fact that native speaker performance has not been consistently examined is a sign that rating scale descriptors themselves have not been sufficiently validated. Such examination has the potential to clarify what is being measured in communicatively oriented tests. The conclusion must be that more research effort must go into the validation of rating scales, which are central to the construct validity of the instruments with which they are associated.

7.7   Mapping skills and abilities: Rasch approaches

7.7.1   Introduction

In the second part of this chapter we will consider the way in which Rasch-based analysis of language test data can be used to generate criterion-referenced descriptions of the performance of candidates on assessment tasks. The discussion focuses on the way in which the analysis allows us to create visual *maps* of the relative degree of challenge provided by test tasks for test takers of different ability levels. Three different kinds of map are introduced. We will then look at the way in which description of the content of test tasks may be used to provide a verbal description of the continuum of difficulty and ability defined by the analysis. This technique is known as *content-referencing*. If a set of descriptions of gradually increasing levels of achievement and ability can be defined in this way, we have a potential improvement on the 'armchair expert' provenance of many rating scale descriptors. The empirically derived descriptions can be used for purposes of certification, for providing diagnostic information to teachers and learners, and for defining progress over time. It has been claimed (e.g. Henning, 1984) that Rasch approaches reconcile norm-referenced and criterion-referenced approaches to assessment, and the meaning of this claim will become clearer as we look at real examples from test development contexts. Developments in *language* assessment associated with these mapping and techniques have so far been the subject of controversy, and we will therefore consider research addressing the validity of this approach.

7.7.2   Item-ability maps

An example of the first and most basic kind of map, routinely produced as output from Rasch analysis of test data, is given in Figure 7.2.[7] The map illustrates the distribution of abilities of a group of Australian

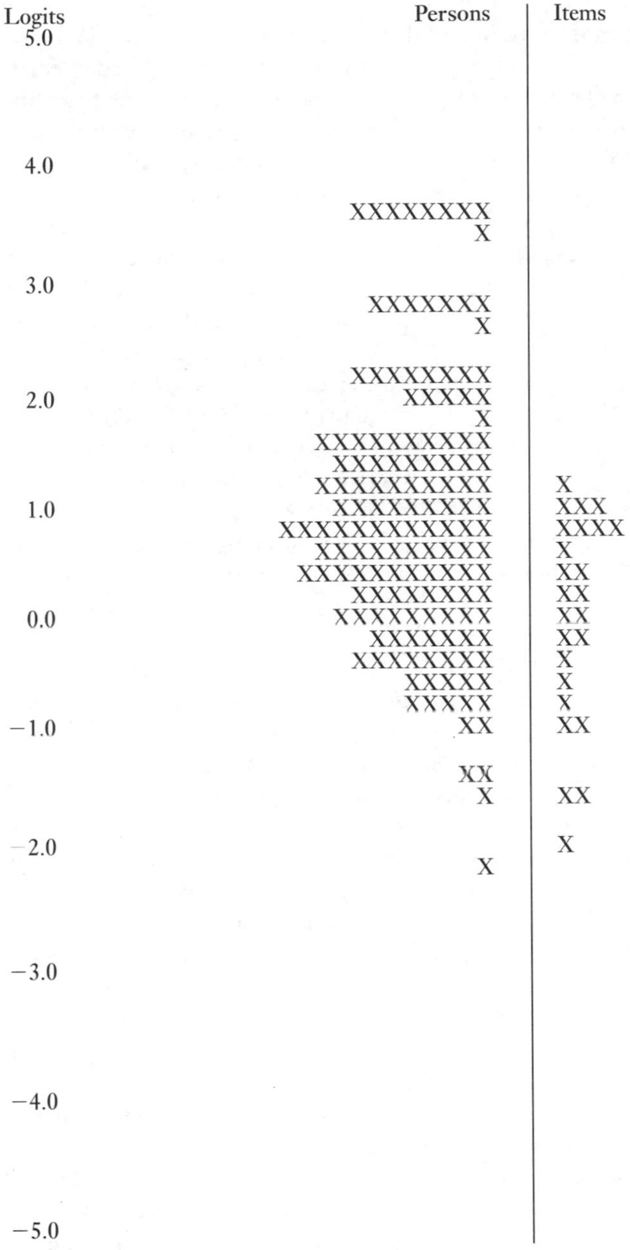

Logits	Persons	Items
5.0		
4.0		
	XXXXXXX	
	X	
3.0		
	XXXXXXX	
	X	
	XXXXXXXX	
2.0	XXXX	
	X	
	XXXXXXXXXX	
	XXXXXXXXX	
	XXXXXXXXX	X
1.0	XXXXXXXXX	XXX
	XXXXXXXXXXXX	XXXX
	XXXXXXXXX	X
	XXXXXXXXX	XX
	XXXXXXXX	XX
0.0	XXXXXXXX	XX
	XXXXXXX	XX
	XXXXXXXX	X
	XXXXX	X
	XXXX	X
−1.0	XX	XX
	XX	
	X	XX
−2.0		X
	X	
−3.0		
−4.0		
−5.0		

Each 'X' in the 'Persons' column represents 4 persons.

FIGURE 7.2   Item–ability map: performance of 13 year olds on a 25 item test of reading in Chinese (n=551)

schoolchildren in the second and third years of high school ($n=551$) on a 25-item test of reading in Chinese. (This test will be considered in detail below.) This first kind of map may be called an *item–ability* map to distinguish it from two further kinds of mapping to be presented below.[8]

In the example in Figure 7.2, estimates of *person ability* and *item difficulty* are expressed in terms of the relation between the ability of individual candidates and their relative chances of giving a correct response to items of given difficulty, these chances being expressed in logits (see Chapter 5).[9] Candidates in the test population are placed at relevant positions on one side of the scale and item difficulties on the other. This allows comparison of item difficulty and candidate ability on a given test. In the example given the map shows the candidature was more able than the general level of difficulty of the items. Whether or not this mismatch is a significant issue in a particular case depends on the purpose of the test. In this case, where the purpose of the test (as we shall see) was to certify achievement in a non-competitive context and to give the schoolchildren a sense of success in their studies, the relative easiness of the test for the candidates is actually quite appropriate.

7.7.3   Skill–ability maps

It is possible to use aspects of the information provided in such routinely produced maps as the basis for producing maps of a second, rather different type, which will be termed *skill–ability maps*. In these, an investigation is made of the content of items clustering at (and therefore in a sense defining) particular levels of difficulty/ability and this is then used as the basis for making statements describing the nature of the achievement at that level. This technique is known as *content-referencing*. It represents a *post hoc*, empirically based approach to defining achievement.

Following trialling of test materials, the usual item–ability map is available from the data analysis. Given a trial sample of representative ability and adequate size, the item difficulty estimates will be quite precise and can be safely generalized to the wider population of prospective test takers: that is, we can say that for the whole population of learners taking a particular test, each item will represent a given, precise level of challenge. If the knowledge or skills involved in the items found at a given level of achievement can be reliably identified, then we have a basis for characterizing descriptively that level of achievement. If successive achievement levels can be defined in this way, we have succeeded in describing a continuum of achievement in terms of which individual performances can be characterized. The resulting set of descriptive statements of the nature of achievement at successive levels can be called a *skill–ability* map.

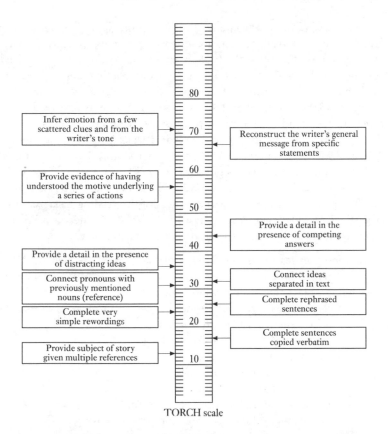

FIGURE 7.3   Skill–ability map: torch scale – reading tasks on a scale of increasing reading ability (from Mossenson *et al.*, 1987: 15)

Figure 7.3 shows the skill–ability map associated with the TORCH[10] tests of reading comprehension (Mossenson *et al.*, 1987).[11] Such a map represents an exploitation of the property of item invariance in Rasch analysis – that is, the independence of item estimates from the character-istics of the persons whose performance has been the basis for the item calibrations (cf. discussion in Chapter 6). In other words, the distribution of cases from the original item–ability map resulting from the analysis of test data has been ignored, and does not feature on the map. Further, the labelling of levels of achievement requires a content analysis of the test items: skills being tapped by items clustering at certain difficulty levels are identified and are used to describe the skills characteristic of ability at particular levels on the variable. In other words, generalized characteriza-tions of skill or task type replace item names or numbers.

The TORCH tests associated with the map in Figure 7.3 are 'a set of fourteen untimed reading tests for use with students in Years 3 to 10' (Mossenson *et al.*, 1987: 1) (ages 6 to 15, approximately), and have become widely used in Australia to measure reading development in English as a first or primary language. The reading passages, graded in difficulty, are between 200 and 900 words long. Students first read a passage, and then read a retelling of the passage in different words; it is in the latter text (the retelling) that the reading tasks (test items) are found. These items are gaps in the retelling text which the students are required to fill with one or more words of their choice. The advantage of using the retelling rather than the original text as the context for the test item is that it allows greater control over the focus of the reading tasks required at particular levels. Each reading tasks is believed to reflect a particular aspect of the reading skill (Mossenson *et al.*, 1987: 2):

> An important feature of TORCH is that all items have been analyzed to identify the types of reading tasks required by students to complete each item. Eleven distinct tasks were identified:
>
> Provide the subject of the story when given multiple references.
> Complete sentences copied verbatim from the text.
> Complete very simple rewordings.
> Complete rephrased sentences.
> Connect pronouns with previously mentioned nouns.
> Connect ideas separated in the text.
> Provide a detail in the presence of distracting ideas.
> Provide a detail in the presence of competing answers.
> Provide evidence of having understood the motive underlying a series of actions.
> Reconstruct the writer's general message from specific statements.
> Infer emotion from a few scattered clues and from the writer's tone.

The skill–ability map (Figure 7.3) appears to demonstrate a hierarchy of reading sub-skills development. In the case of the reading skills measured by TORCH tests, as children's reading skills develop over the course of years at school, their progress along the scale can be traced as they take successive tests involving passages and reading tasks of increasing complexity. The mapping of the development of the reading skill is central to the TORCH scheme, but it raises many questions of validity which will be discussed further below.

So far, then, we have considered two types of mapping, item–ability and skill–ability maps, each of which operates primarily at the level of the group. Information about individuals may of course be read off this group map, if we know the ability level of a particular individual.

However, it is desirable in many contexts to be able to provide detailed information on the performance of individual test takers, and in fact maps of *individual* ability (Figure 7.4) in relation to item difficulty are available in some programs.[12]

For each candidate, an individual analysis is available of his or her performance on items on the test. Items answered correctly are listed on the left of the ability/difficulty axis; those answered incorrectly appear on the right. The vertical dimension of the map gives information on three classes of items: those at or about the candidate's estimated ability; those clearly easier than the candidate's estimated ability, that is, items that he or she might have been expected to get correct; and items clearly above the candidate's estimated ability, that is, items that he or she might have been expected to get wrong.

It will be observed that the items fall into one of four quadrants. The upper right quadrant represents items that were too difficult for the candidate, who as expected, answered incorrectly. The lower left quadrant represents items that were estimated to be relatively easy for the candidate, who in fact (again as expected) answered correctly. So far, the candidate's actual performance has been accurately predicted on the basis of the behaviour of the others in the test cohort. Of more interest are items in the other two quadrants: in the upper left, items are listed that were answered correctly even though they had been seen as likely to be rather difficult for the candidate; and in the lower right quadrant are items which the candidate might have been expected to be able to answer correctly, but in fact had trouble with. This last quadrant is perhaps the most interesting, as the information contained within it can provide the teacher with a basis for remedial work; the output from the analysis can thus be used for diagnostic purposes. We can call these individual profiles *individual candidate maps* or (preferably) *learner maps*.[13]

In the case of these individual learner maps, the information they contain may be used in two ways, differing in terms of specificity and generality. That is, we may simply use them to report to candidates and teachers that particular items usually within the competence of candidates of such ability were not answered correctly by this particular candidate, and leave further interpretation of this fact to those concerned.

On the other hand, using the approach represented by the TORCH tests, we may prefer to present the diagnostic information in the map in terms of more general underlying abilities involved in the tasks represented by the items in question. The more general the characterization we can give of areas that learners need to work on, the more useful presumably this will be to learner and teacher alike.

UTESL TRIAL READING SUB-TEST

KIDMAP

Candidate:	87		ability:	0.26
group:	all		fit:	1.17
scale:	all		% score:	55.56

Harder Correct					Harder Incorrect		
					3		
					1		
					30		
			16.2		13		
					23	34	
			16.1		17		
					33	37	
					46		
			18.3				
					29		
					2	9	48
			15.3		8	50	
			38		40		
			18.2	XXX			
			26				
32	28	25	15.2		35	36	
			51		24		
			15.1				
					4		
			20				
			31		14		
		43	18.1				
		22	21				
			19				
			47		49		
			11				
			39				
	27	6	5				
			45				
			7				
			10				
			44		12		

| Easier Correct | | | | | Easier Incorrect | | |

FIGURE 7.4   Individual learner map: performance of a candidate on the University Test of ESL (UTESL) trial reading sub-test

7.8 The validity of content-referenced interpretations in skill–ability maps

The characterization of candidate ability on the basis of test content as in the development of skill–ability maps is the most powerful aspect of Rasch-based mapping. The skill–ability map is a central feature of the TORCH tests, and has been influential (cf. Griffin and Nix, 1991), but it is not clear how the descriptions of the content of items were arrived at, nor what independent confirmation of the hierarchy was attempted; Masters (personal communication) suggests that the content analysis was rather informal, and that it was incorporated into the manual for the tests without further validation. But while the practical usefulness of this mapping procedure is clear, is it valid? For example, much research literature has cast doubt on whether there is a hierarchy of reading skills; in fact there is debate over whether reading sub-skills exist at all, and if they do, how many and what kinds of sub-skills can be identified (cf. the discussion in Lumley, 1993; Alderson, 1990a, 1990b, 1995; Lumley, 1995; Weir *et al.*, 1990; Weir, 1994). In the remainder of this chapter we will consider an example of another large-scale language testing project, the Australian Language Certificates, in which skill–ability maps are used as the basis for making descriptive statements of student achievement. We will demonstrate the genesis of these descriptors, and research carried out into their validity.

7.8.1 The Australian Language Certificates test of reading ability in Chinese

The Australian Language Certificates (ALC) project (ACER, 1990; Elder and Zammit, 1992)[14] involved the development of nation-wide communicatively oriented tests of reading and listening in seven foreign languages[15] taught in the junior years of secondary school. The idea was to introduce the equivalent of 'swimming certificates' (a feature of the Australian educational scene) at early stages of foreign language learning as an incentive for children to continue studying the language in the face of pressure to choose other subjects in the crowded curriculum. Tests in each language are administered in Years 8 and 9, the second and third years of secondary school, when the students are approximately 13 or 14 years old. The tests take about 50 minutes altogether – 25 minutes for reading and 25 minutes for listening, in that order. Questions are in multiple-choice format. New versions are created for each administration. For each skill and for each language in each version, the complete data are subjected to Rasch-based analysis at the Australian Council for Educational Research (ACER). The resulting item–difficulty maps are sent to language testing specialists for interpretation, or, in our terms, conversion into skill–ability maps. A content analysis is done in conjunction with the test-writing teams for each of the seven languages involved, each team headed by a staff member from a relevant language-teaching section of the university. The point of the analysis is (1) to identify the language knowledge and language skills involved in each question on the item–ability map; (2) to look for groupings of knowledge areas and skills at three broad levels of ability as defined in the output; (3) to use these groupings as the basis for writing criterion-referenced statements of achievement at each of the three levels. The candidate receives a certificate with one of the three wordings for each of the two skills tested. An attempt is made to word even the lowest of the three achievement levels in terms of 'can do' or 'does know' statements, given the basic aim of the project (and sound educational practice, in any case). There is considerable pressure of time involved in the development of the descriptors, as the data on which they are based become available only after the performance of children on the test has been analysed, and before the certificates are issued; the printing of the certificates depends on the appropriate wording being determined.

As an illustration of the procedure, we will consider the results for the test of reading in Chinese from the test session of 1990 ($n=592$).[16] The item–ability map[17] is given in Figure 7.5.[18] It can be seen that the test was relatively easy for the candidature presenting, which is consonant with its purpose. Lines have been drawn on the map indicating the settings of the three levels. Level 1 (the lowest) contained 11 per cent of the candidates; Level 2, 35 per cent; and Level 3, 54 per cent. The resulting wording of the ability level descriptions which appeared on the certificates for this test is given in Figure 7.6. An example of the format of the certificate issued to the candidate can be seen in Figure 7.7, see page 211.

McQueen (1992)[19] analysed the reading sub-test of the Australian Language Certificates (ALC) test of Chinese administered in 1990 (cf. Figures 7.2 and 7.5). She examined two issues: (1) the validity of the approach to mapping and certification of skill levels used in the ALC project, and (2) in the case that the general approach is supported, the adequacy of the descriptors that were actually written for the test certificates. Her method was to attempt an independent validation of the scale of difficulty of items constructed by the analysis.

McQueen began with the assumption that word knowledge and the ability to decode the meaning of individual words is central to the reading tasks presented to these beginning readers in Chinese; that is, for the reading task in this test, candidates will be involved in basically a bottom-up process. Drawing initially on the framework proposed by Laufer (1989)

```
            Logits                Persons │ Items
            5.0



            4.0
                            XXXXXXXX
                                   X


            3.0
                             XXXXXXX
                                   X
LEVEL 3
(54%)                       XXXXXXXX
            2.0              XXXXX
                                 X
                        XXXXXXXXXX
                         XXXXXXXXX
                         XXXXXXXXX    │ 11
            1.0          XXXXXXXXX    │ 19, 15, 22
                       XXXXXXXXXXXX   │ 21, 16, 5, 9
                        ─────────────────────────
                        XXXXXXXXXX    │ 23
                       XXXXXXXXXXX    │ 8, 17
LEVEL 2                  XXXXXXX      │ 10, 6
(35%)       0.0        XXXXXXXXX      │ 7, 18
                         XXXXXXX      │ 12, 14
                        XXXXXXXX      │ 20
                        ─────────────────────────
                          XXXXX       │ 25
                          XXXXX       │ 13
            -1.0             XX        │ 2, 24
LEVEL 1                     XX
(11%)                        X        │ 1, 4


            -2.0
                               X      │ 3



            -3.0



            -4.0



            -5.0
```

Each 'X' in the 'Persons' column represents 4 persons.

FIGURE 7.5 Australian Language Certificates Chinese reading sub-test: item–ability map (cf. Figure 7.2) with groupings of items and ability levels

LEVEL 1

The questions in Level 1 (starting with the easiest) were 3, 1, 4, 2, 24, 13, 25. A typical student at this level can read Pinyin and understand some everyday words and phrases, such as names of family members, numbers and time, and pick out simple information from a short piece of writing or dialogue.

LEVEL 2

The questions in Level 2 were 20, 12, 14, 7, 18, 10, 6, 8, 17, 23.
A student at this level can read Pinyin and some Chinese characters covering everyday words and phrases such as time, dates and the location of people and objects, and pick out a piece of information from a dialogue or advertisement.

LEVEL 3 (highest level)

The questions in Level 3 were 21, 16, 5, 9, 19, 15, 22, 11.
A typical student at this level can understand a range of everyday words and expressions written in Pinyin or Chinese characters, pick out information from a piece of writing and make inferences from the information given.

FIGURE 7.6   Ability level descriptions, ALC reading (Chinese)

for examining the difficulty of vocabulary in a foreign language, and supplementing it with insights from other sources on readability and second language recognition, McQueen (1992: 14) drew up a list of possible influences on word difficulty in Chinese reading passages. This is presented in Table 7.9.

McQueen investigated correlations between each of these factors for items in the test and the difficulty of the items expressed on the logit scale constructed by the analysis. Table 7.10 indicates the results of the analysis.

TABLE 7.9   A list of possible influences on word difficulty in Chinese reading passages (McQueen, 1992)

Word form factors:	Length Pronounceability
Grammatical characteristics:	Derivational complexity Syntactic patterns
Semantic features:	Codability
Multiple meaning:	Polysemy and homonymy
Written form:	Script style: Pinyin vs characters Character complexity
Extralexical factors:	Order of presentation in text Presence of unknown lexical items in test passages Grouping of items for presentation in text

McQueen (1992: 29–30) concluded from this stage of the analysis that

a significant and positive relationship was found between item difficulty and the presence of unknown words, the candidate's relative
unfamiliarity with words in the test item (as measured by the Order of
Presentation [in the class text]), the use of characters rather than
Pinyin in the stimulus text, and the perceived difficulty of pronounc-
ing words included in the item.

A comparison of the mean difficulty of items associated with the six short
texts in the reading test generally supported these findings (McQueen,
1992: 31):

Texts associated with the highest level of item difficulty are the three
character texts, and the Pinyin text which contained the greatest number
of unknown words. It was not possible to quantify pronounceability in a
way which would allow meaningful comparison between stimulus texts.

McQueen then investigated the effect of test method facets (Bachman,
1990) on item difficulty. All of the items are multiple-choice items, so a
contrast between item types was not possible at that level. However, the
items represented different kinds of task. Each of the items in the test
required one or more of the following activities: locating information
within a text, translating, matching, combining information. The effects
of some of these tasks were not open to investigation in this context,
because there was a correspondence between task type and input

TABLE 7.10　Relationship between possible factors influencing difficulty of items
and logit estimates of item difficulty in a beginners' Chinese
reading test

Factor considered	Statistic	Value	*df*	Significance
Word length	*r*	0.319	23	ns†
Pronounceability (one-tailed)	*t*	2.778	23	$p<0.01$
Syntactic complexity	*t*	0.635	23	ns
Codability*	–	–	–	–
Multiple meaning	*t*	1.379	23	ns
Script (one-tailed)	*t*	2.329	19	$p<0.05$
Language of questions	*t*	0.118	23	ns
Character complexity	*r*	0.151	10	ns
Order of presentation (one-tailed)	*r*	0.524	23	$p<0.01$
Presence of unknown lexical items (one-tailed)	*t*	1.812	23	$p<0.05$
Grouping for presentation	*t*	0.464	23	ns

* Too few items to consider further.　† ns = Not significant at the 5% level.

210   *Measuring Second Language Performance*

material in some cases: this was the case for 'locate and combine' and 'diagram match'. 'Locating information' was the most frequently required activity. Following Bachman (1990: 128), it was hypothesized that items requiring candidates to locate information would be more difficult than those that did not: this was confirmed ($t = 1.821$, $df = 19$, $p < 0.05$, one-tailed).[20] The status of this method effect is not entirely clear, as the ability to manage this kind of reading task may be considered to be a function of reading ability in general, and certainly a relevant aspect of it; and in fact it appears in the level descriptors.

These descriptors (see Figure 7.6) were then examined and compared with the results of McQueen's analysis. Three major sub-skills were identified in addition to the rather broadly conceptualized abilities to read Pinyin and characters: recognizing vocabulary within semantic fields, picking out information and making inferences.

The first of these was found to coincide with the factor 'Order of presentation'; Levels 1 and 2 were distinguished on this basis, both in the descriptors and by examination of the presentation of the relevant semantic field in the textbook. 'Picking out information' clearly corresponds with 'locating information', and is used to distinguish Level 1 from the other two levels, as this task is not required in Level 1 items. McQueen comments that the term 'making inferences' suggests a higher order skill and is a somewhat inflated description of the processes required by items on the test.

McQueen (1992: 36–7) concludes that

> The study has examined the relationship of predictive variables to difficulty levels of foreign language reading test items. It has shown that certain of these predictors, in combination with aspects of the task itself, are related to the item–difficulty order established by the Rasch scaling procedure. This relationship gives support to the practice of using Rasch scaling as a basis for descriptions of candidates' performance on a test of the type described in this study. ... The dimension mapped out by the IRT scaling can be explained in terms of relative familiarity and orthographic characteristics of the stimulus text. ... The descriptors themselves were shown to have provided an adequate description of the foreign language reading skills demonstrated by candidates at various levels of performance.

In terms of her original research questions, McQueen's conclusions are as follows: the study provides some evidence for the validity of the mapping approach in general, or at least in the context of this test; as to the adequacy of the descriptors that were actually drawn up for this test, she suggests ways in which they might be improved.

FIGURE 7.7   An example of the Australian Language Certificate for Chinese

In both the TORCH test and the ALC tests, the content analysis of test items occurred *after* trialling, at the time of the creation of the content-referenced skill–ability map. *A priori* characterization of item content in the item specifications was apparently not available or not used if it was. A more powerful test of the validity of the skill–ability maps would be to consider items which, it was agreed *a priori*, were testing particular sub-skills, and then see how those items emerged in the Rasch analysis. In particular, we would expect items written to the same specifications to cluster together in terms of difficulty; any failure to observe this would suggest the presence of method effects in the item concerned, of the type noted by McQueen.

7.9 Summary

In this chapter we have examined issues concerning the way in which performance of learners on communicative tasks is reported. One common method is the use of descriptions of successive levels of performance on a single trait in rating scales. The rating scale tradition originated in the FSI test in the 1950s, and successive rating scales developed over the last four decades have been heavily influenced by the assumptions, and even the wording, of the original work, and little empirical validation of them has been attempted. A series of research studies looking at the performance of native speakers on a reading test where performance was reported in FSI-type bands reveals that the assumptions lying behind the descriptors in the scale cannot be supported by empirical evidence. More research effort must go into the validation of such rating scales, which are central to the construct validity of the instruments with which they are associated.

In the second part of the chapter, empirically based approaches to the definition of learner achievement have been considered. A number of different kinds of Rasch program output involving the mapping of ability estimates and item difficulty levels onto a single variable have been considered. *Item–ability* maps, *skill–ability* maps and *individual learner* maps have been distinguished, and their use illustrated from practical test development projects. Of these, the content-referenced interpretation of test achievement which leads to the development of skill–ability maps is the most powerful and the most controversial. Research on the use of content-referenced descriptors in the definition of learner achievement in a reading test of Chinese for young learners in the secondary school was presented and found to offer some support for this approach. Suggestions were made for more adequate and empirically verifiable procedures for the development of content-referenced descriptors.

It is clear that we are a long way from having validated rating scales or band level descriptors. Given their centrality to the construct validity of much performance testing, they deserve to be the subject of a much greater level of research. The debate on the nature of foreign language reading skills referred to above itself reveals that the wording of descriptors of successive levels of achievement in reading in the ASLPR and ACTFL and other scales is deeply problematic. Similarly, attempts to develop rating scales for the development of listening skills have been equally frustrating (Brindley and Nunan, 1992). The complacency evident in approaches such as the ASLPR and ACTFL should be replaced by a consistent research effort to validate the scales. In the following chapter, we will present Rasch-based research on a range of other aspects of language performance testing.

Notes

1. Alderson (1991) discussed the functions of rating scales, and distinguishes between the function of guiding the rating process and that of reporting to test users. He points out that different versions or formats of the scales may be required in order to reflect these different purposes.
2. Barnwell (1989) speaks of reference to the native speaker as 'hovering in the background' of the ACTFL Oral Proficiency Interview assessment scale. This is because of the origins of the ACTFL scale in the FSI scale, which as we saw above enshrines the native speaker at the top of the scale.
3. The material in this section is based on the work of Hamilton (1991) and Lopes (1992).
4. This will increasingly be the case in the UK also, given current UK government post-school education policy.
5. The Australian legal system, like its British source, has two broad categories of lawyers: barristers and solicitors. Barristers represent clients in court, and are briefed for their appearances by solicitors. Those beginning their careers as barristers are informally known as 'baby barristers'.
6. This section of the chapter is based on Sheridan (1991).
7. Item–ability maps are a feature of many Rasch-based programs, for example BIG-STEPS (Wright and Linacre, 1991) and Quest (Adams and Khoo, 1993). The output from one-parameter modelling in BILOG (Mislevy and Bock, 1990) does not include them as an option.
8. Wright and Stone (1979: 205–7) discuss a rather clumsy prototype of this kind of map, terming it a *map of the variable*. Wright and Masters (1982: 124, 126) discuss what they call *variable maps*, which are closer to the map in Figure 7.2. Adams and Khoo (1992: 21), following this terminology, refer to the equivalent part of the output of their program Titan (a fore-runner to Quest) as a *variable map* or an *item map*, stating that it shows 'the distribution of item difficulties and the distribution of case estimates over the variable'. Wright and Linacre (1991: 63) refer to such a map as a '(joint) distribution map'.
9. Frequently, these unfamiliar units are transformed into units on some more familiar scale, for example a 100-point scale, in the interest of ease of communication and interpretation.
10. TORCH is a partial acronym for 'Test of Reading Comprehension Skills'.
11. The same approach was used in a similar test, the TELS profiles, developed at the same time by Pollitt and Hutchinson (1987) in the United Kingdom.
12. For example, in Quest (Adams and Khoo, 1993).
13. Adams and Khoo (1992) refer to these individual profiles of test performance as 'kidmaps' (the idea originated in contexts involving schoolchildren).
14. The project was a joint venture between the NLLIA Language Testing Research Centre at the University of Melbourne and the Australian Council for Educational Research (ACER). It was funded by a semi-government agency, the Australian Bicentennial Multicultural Foundation.
15. Tests are currently available in the following languages: Chinese, Japanese, Indonesian, Italian, Modern Greek, German and French.

16. Ability estimates for only 551 candidates are reported in this map because as is typically the case in Rasch programs no ability estimates were computed for candidates with perfect or zero scores on the test.
17. Already reproduced above in slightly simpler format as Figure 7.2.
18. Candidates with person ability equivalent to any given point on the scale would have in this case a 70 per cent probability of supplying the correct response to items at the same level. Items are more usually located at the 50 per cent probability level, but where appropriate (as for this test), the level may be varied.
19. This work was done as a minor thesis for the MA in Applied Linguistics at the University of Melbourne.
20. Apart from this general effect, method effects peculiar to individual items were not investigated.

8 Using Rasch analysis in research on second language performance assessment

8.1 Introduction

This chapter reports on recent research involving the application of Rasch measurement within performance assessment contexts. It thus exemplifies one of the main arguments of this book, that research on performance assessment can be greatly helped by the new measurement approaches that are now available to us. The material in the chapter is drawn from research in test *development* contexts (including the Occupational English Test (OET): see Chapter 4), and from research into test validity in other contexts. It is by no means a comprehensive survey, but suggests the kind of research that may be carried out. Obviously, Rasch-based research on performance assessment is not the only kind of approach which is relevant, and studies using other methods, both quantitative and qualitative, are also important. This latter work, valuable as it is, is less central to the focus of this book.

Much of the research reported here is on aspects of rater behaviour, as one might expect, given the ease with which the facet 'rater' may be dealt with in a multi-faceted analysis. The following aspects have been investigated:

(1) how raters interpret rating scales and rating criteria in tests of speaking and writing;
(2) rater characteristics and their effect on the rating process;
(3) the conditions under which rating is carried out and their effect on rater behaviour.

Other research has involved studies of test *task*, and the relationship of task to performance level.

8.2 Research on rating scales and rating criteria

8.2.1 Overview

This section begins with a report of studies carried out by the author (McNamara, 1990a) on how trained raters in the Speaking and Writing sub-tests of the OET interpreted under operational conditions the rating scales they had been trained to use in training sessions. The analysis looked for underlying patterns beneath the surface of the set of scores from the test to see if there was any consistent (and probably unconscious) orientation in the raters to the criteria in the scales. In fact there was: contrary to the communicative spirit of the test, it turned out that the raters in each case were overwhelmingly influenced in their judgements of the candidates by their impressions of the grammatical accuracy of the candidates' output. This behaviour was totally unexpected, and unintended by the test constructor, and raises general questions about the validity of performance tests of speaking and writing. The studies illustrate again that much lies beneath the surface in performance testing, and that Rasch analysis is useful in revealing underlying patterns in ratings data which can be interpreted in ways that raise fundamental questions of test validity.

In the latter part of the section, three further studies using Rasch measurement in exploring the characteristics of rating scales and rating criteria are reported.

8.2.2   Rater interpretation of assessment categories in the OET Speaking sub-test

As explained in Chapter 4 above, the structure of the OET Speaking sub-test is as follows:

> Profession-specific content within a common format. 15 minutes. Role play-based interaction: candidate in own professional role, interlocutor in role of patient (client) or relative of patient (client). Two role plays, plus short (unassessed) interview. Assessment in six categories, using rating scale format scoring grid of the semantic differential type.[1]

Training of raters (qualified and experienced ESL teachers) and moderation of assessments were carried out around Australia by the researcher in November 1988. Inter-rater reliabilities based on earlier trials were satisfactory, averaging 0.87.

Data were available from 192 candidates who attempted the speaking sub-test in December 1988 and 198 candidates in April 1989. The data were in the form of marking sheets from raters. For each candidate, responses in six categories (*Overall communicative effectiveness, Intelligibility, Fluency, Comprehension, Appropriateness* and *Resources of grammar and expression*) on a 6-point scale were available for each of three assessments: *First provisional assessment* (made at the end of the first role play), *Second provisional assessment* (made at the end of the second role play) and *Final assessment* (made after the candidate had left the examination room).[2]

The data from each of these three assessments from each session of the test were analysed separately using the Rasch Rating Scale model (Andrich, 1978a; Wright and Masters, 1982; for further details, see discussion in Chapter 9). The data were analysed using a version of a Rating Scale program developed for the microcomputer by Geoff Masters. The program includes in its output the following:

- *Individual Results*: Estimates of person ability, errors of estimate and (person) fit *t*-statistics.
- *Analysis of Items* (the assessment categories): Estimates of item difficulty, errors of estimate and (item) fit *t*-statistics.
- Analysis of the *Response Categories* (the score points on the scale in each assessment category).

8.2.2.1 Assessment categories

The analysis treats the assessment categories in the scoring grid as test items. Item results for categories are reported in Table 8.1.[3] Measurement errors are low, and constitute further evidence of a high degree of measurement accuracy for this scoring grid. The difficulty estimates for categories are remarkably consistent across the two sessions of the test. In both test sessions, *Comprehension* was the most leniently

TABLE 8.1   Rasch analysis, items (assessment categories) (speaking sub-test)

December 1988 (n=192)

Item	Item difficulty	Error	Fit (*t*)
Overall effectiveness	0.17	0.13	−8.36
Intelligibility	0.10	0.13	0.86
Fluency	−0.18	0.14	−1.30
Comprehension	−1.42	0.15	−0.07
Appropriateness	0.32	0.13	−1.35
Resources of grammar	1.01	0.13	−5.10

April 1989 (n=198)

Item	Item difficulty	Error	Fit (*t*)
Overall effectiveness	0.25	0.13	−7.53
Intelligibility	−0.19	0.14	1.09
Fluency	0.15	0.13	−1.53
Comprehension	−1.47	0.15	0.43
Appropriateness	0.25	0.13	−2.24
Resources of grammar	1.02	0.13	−5.20

scored category, *Resources of grammar and expression* the most harshly scored.

8.2.2.2   *What is being measured in the Speaking sub-test?*

If we examine the fit statistics in Table 8.1, several points are worthy of comment. First, there are no items showing large positive misfit in either session (for an interpretation of fit values, see the discussion in Chapter 6). This suggests that in terms of the measurement dimension constructed by the analysis, it makes sense to add the scores from the different categories together. Scores in the categories *Intelligibility*, *Fluency*, *Comprehension* and *Appropriateness* are making independent contributions to the underlying measurement dimension constructed by the analysis;[4] in that sense the categories can be said to have been validated. Two categories, however, show large negative fit values in both sessions of the test: *Overall communicative effectiveness* and *Resources of grammar and expression*.[5]

The significance of negative fit statistics has been discussed in Chapter 6 above. They signal an 'unexpected interdependence' (Wright and Linacre, 1984: 4–15), who suggest (1984: 4–17) that with large negative fit *t*-values 'we should look for factors that tie the items together more tightly than expected'.

In the case of the overfitting of the category *Overall communicative effectiveness*, we may understand this in the following way: this item ranks the candidates more consistently with the 'average' ranking on the scale of ability constructed by the analysis than does any other item. This is hardly surprising. In other words, it is just doing what all the other items are doing in combination. The strength of the correlation between scores on this category and ability estimates for candidates resulting from the analysis is very strong, as indicated by the large negative fit value.

The same appears to be true of the category *Resources of grammar and expression*. This category is the best single way of getting at the dimension of speaking ability being measured by the scale as a whole and it is the strongest determinant of this variable. It seems, then, that a rater's perception of the grammatical and lexical accuracy of a candidate's performance is the most significant factor in the allocation of the candidate's total score.

In order to confirm this finding, a stepwise regression was carried out on data from each session of the test using scores in the category *Overall communicative effectiveness* as the dependent variable and scores in the other categories as the predictor variables. This statistical procedure allows us to see to what extent knowing scores in one of the other categories, or in a combination of categories, enables us to predict the pattern of scores, summarized as score variance, in the category *Overall communicative effectiveness*. The shared variance (R^2) between the two (or more) variables (categories) summarizes the extent to which the two patterns of scores overlap, i.e. the scores in one category are rendered predictable from a knowledge of scores in the other(s). The results of the analysis are reported in Table 8.2. In each session, *Resources of grammar* was the predictor variable entered on the first step (i.e. found to be the most economical single predictor), accounting for 68 per cent of the shared variance in December 1988 and 70 per cent in April 1989. (The column 'Change in R^2' in Table 8.2 tells you how much additional predictive power would be gained by knowing in addition the scores in each of the other categories in order, for example, a further 8.6 per cent in the case of *Fluency* in December 1988.)

These findings have significant implications for the construct validity of the OET Speaking sub-test. On the one hand, the analysis supports the inclusion in the scoring procedure of separate assessments of a number of aspects of speaking ability. On the other hand, perceptions of the candidate's resources of grammar are revealed as having a particular significance. This latter finding had not been anticipated at the test design stage, although, as we shall now see, this issue has been the focus of debate in the literature on the validity of assessments of speaking ability in oral proficiency interviews.

TABLE 8.2   Multiple regression analysis – speaking sub-test

December 1988 (n = 192)

Step	Variable entered	R^2	Change in R^2	*t*-ratio
1	Resources of grammar	0.678	0.678	20.02*
2	Fluency	0.764	0.086	8.29*
3	Intelligibility	0.802	0.038	5.97*
4	Appropriateness	0.835	0.033	6.11*
5	Comprehension	0.838	0.003	1.82†

April 1989 (n = 199)

Step	Variable entered	R^2	Change in R^2	*t*-ratio
1	Resources of grammar	0.695	0.695	21.20*
2	Fluency	0.757	0.062	7.09*
3	Appropriateness	0.771	0.014	3.47*
4	Intelligibility	0.780	0.009	2.77*
5	Comprehension	0.785	0.005	2.08*

* $p < 0.01$
† Not significant at the 5% level

8.2.2.3   Grammar in assessments of speaking

The place of grammar in assessments of oral production in a second language has been the subject of considerable debate, particularly in relation to the ACTFL/ETS Oral Proficiency Interview (OPI) (Clark and Clifford, 1988) and its forerunners. Studies have shown the centrality of raters' perceptions of structural accuracy in the assignment of proficiency ratings (Wilds, 1975; Raffaldini, 1988). Clark (1972) and Savignon (1985) have criticized the tension between criteria focusing on structural accuracy and other more communicative criteria in the level descriptions. Accuracy is one of three separate components of assessment in the OPI: *function, content* and *accuracy* (which Higgs and Clifford, 1982: 62 refer to as the 'functional trisection of speaking ability'). The descriptions of the different levels of proficiency make explicit reference to the criterion of structural accuracy. It therefore consciously and explicitly plays a crucial, even an 'overriding' role (Savignon, 1985: 131, quoting Lowe, 1982: 33).

The OET differs from the ACTFL/ETS OPI in that it adopts a different attitude to the role of grammatical accuracy in the assessment criteria. In the creation of the OET scoring grid, an attempt was made to define each of the assessment categories in exclusively communicative terms. Accuracy as such was not emphasized, only its perceived communicative effect: thus, *Pronunciation* as a category is replaced by *Intelligibility*, or the communicative effect of pronunciation features. Similarly, instead of separate categories for grammar and vocabulary, a single category was created which focused on grammar and vocabulary *as a communicative resource*, that is, as helping or hindering communication. In the training of raters, these points were spelled out and discussed in relation to the performances being rated. There was no resistance to the communicative orientation of the test among raters at training sessions, in fact quite the contrary. Raters were also aware that in determining the candidate's reported final score, the score in the category *Overall communicative effectiveness* is added to the average of scores in the other categories combined. This meant that the scores in the sub-category *Resources of grammar and expression* were relatively unimportant in themselves in determining the final score given to the candidate. In theory, a candidate could score poorly or well in this category and it would be unrelated to his or her final score.

At the conscious level, then, and in terms of the intention of the design of the test, grammatical accuracy was downplayed. Yet the Rasch analysis shows that in both sessions of the test perceptions of grammatical and lexical accuracy in fact played a crucial role in determining the candidate's total score.

TABLE 8.3   Rasch difficulty estimates and fit statistics for scoring categories at the completion of each role play, and at the final assessment

December 1988 (n=192)

Category	Grid #1		Grid #2		Final	
	Estimate	Fit	Estimate	Fit	Estimate	Fit
Overall	0.16	−5.48†	0.20	−8.07†	0.17	−8.36†
Intelligibility	0.01	−1.21	0.07	0.46	0.10	0.86
Fluency	−0.08	−3.24†	−0.15	−1.64	−0.18	−1.30
Comprehension	−1.28	0.89	−1.36	−0.20	−1.42	−0.07
Appropriateness	0.42	−1.21	0.23	−0.81	0.32	−1.35
Resources	0.77	−3.08†	1.02	−4.23†	1.01	−5.10†

April 1989 (n=198)

Category	Grid #1		Grid #2		Final	
	Estimate	Fit	Estimate	Fit	Estimate	Fit
Overall	0.44	−7.45†	0.31	−7.53†	0.25	−7.53†
Intelligibility	−0.14	1.77	−0.12	1.18	−0.19	1.09
Fluency	0.04	−2.33*	0.19	−1.54	0.15	−1.53
Comprehension	−1.33	0.79	−1.44	0.83	−1.47	0.43
Appropriateness	0.14	−2.66†	0.22	−2.58*	0.25	−2.24*
Resources	0.85	−4.59†	0.84	−4.71†	1.02	−5.20†

* $p < 0.05$ † $p < 0.01$

It might be thought that raters were consciously interpreting the *Resources* category simply as another overall category. That this category was being rated differently from the category *Overall communicative effectiveness* is revealed from the fact that in both sessions of the test the *Resources* category was scored considerably more harshly than any other category (cf. Table 8.1). Raters must therefore have been oriented to something different from the overall effectiveness of the communication when marking the *Resources* category if they consistently marked this category more harshly, by approximately 0.8 of a logit in each session (note that the errors of estimate for the logit difficulty of categories were small, 0.13 for the categories in question).

The imprecision of the category makes interpretation rather difficult. Was grammar or lexis the determining feature in allocation of scores in this category? (Note that linguists such as Halliday (1978) have proposed a continuum or cline between vocabulary and grammar, rather than a sharp categorical distinction, although it is not clear to what extent this position may be reflected in the responses of raters.) Were the raters indeed not interpreting this category in terms of accuracy, but truly only considering instances where command of grammatical structure and/or vocabulary assisted or hindered communicative effectiveness? Interviews with raters to determine their understanding of the category *Resources of grammar and expression* were not attempted, but would have been appropriate in view of the ambiguity of this category. However, given what Savignon (1985: 131) says about the pervasiveness of a structural orientation in the language-teaching profession, even among progressive and communicatively oriented teachers, it is likely that accuracy, including structural accuracy, is a strong determinant of scores given in this category.

The data from the successive completions of the grid (two provisional and one final) enable us to take 'snapshots' of the decision-making process (cf. Table 8.3). At Time 1 (Grid 1), at the completion of the first role play, the rater has been interacting with the candidate for approximately 8–10 minutes (including 4–5 minutes at the beginning in the interview component, which is not assessed). When the rater commits himself or herself to a preliminary judgement, two factors rank the candidates consistently with the 'average' ranking, taking the other categories into account: *Fluency* and *Resources*.[6] In other words, at this stage, raters are influenced in the score for *Overall effectiveness* as much by an impression of the candidate's overall fluency as they are by the candidate's formal resources. By Time 2, *Fluency* no longer bears such a relationship to the 'average' ranking; the rater is becoming more oriented to formal resources, and this is confirmed in the final assessment. Notice also that between Time 1 (Grid 1) and the final assessment, the difficulty estimate for the *Resources* category has increased by 0.24 in the December data and by 0.17 in the April data. As this increase represents between one and a half times and twice the error for these estimates, it is unlikely that this increase in the estimates represents random variability. Raters appear to be reflecting more critically on the formal resources of the candidate; that is, they appear to be evaluating the candidate's production more in purely lexico-grammatical terms. It is as if, as time passes and the candidate becomes more familiar, the rater adopts less of the role of communicative partner and more of the role of language analyst, becomes less impressed with what he or she is hearing because of the process of grammatical inspection of output, and marks the candidate down accordingly. In the final analysis, it is features of accuracy which count most heavily in the rater's mind. The above analysis is of course speculative, but consistent with the data.

8.2.3   Rater interpretation of assessment categories in the OET Writing sub-test

The structure of the OET Writing sub-test is as follows (see Chapter 4):

Profession-specific content within a common format. 40 minutes. Letter of referral (12–15 lines) based on case notes or extracts from medical records. Assessment in five categories, using rating scale format scoring grid of the semantic differential type.[7]

Data were collected from the second full session of the OET incorporating the new writing sub-test, held in April 1989. Training of raters in Canberra had been carried out by the researcher in November 1988. There were four raters, all of whom had been involved in marking the OET writing sub-test in its old format for a number of years.

Data from 214 candidates who took the test were used in the analysis. The data took the form of marking sheets from raters. For each candidate, responses in five categories (*Overall task fulfilment, Appropriateness of language, Comprehension of stimulus, Control of linguistic features (grammar and cohesion)* and *Control of linguistic features (spelling, punctuation)*) on a 6-point scale were available.[8]

Analysis was carried out using the same program as had been used for the Speaking sub-test data.

Grammar was revealed as the most difficult category, followed by *Presentation*. The most leniently scored category was *Comprehension*, followed by *Appropriateness*. This seems to confirm the findings of Pollitt and Hutchinson (1987: 86), who found that 'the four easiest "questions" on which to show competence were all assessments of appropriacy, while the five hardest were all assessments of expression'. Earlier (1987: 75), *expression* is defined as 'involving syntax, lexis and conventions of punctuation and spelling'. Pollitt and Hutchinson's category of *expression* thus covers the two sub-categories of *Grammar* and *Presentation* in the OET.

The fit statistics for items in Table 8.4 reveal that no items showed excessively large positive fit statistics. However, as with the speaking sub-test, there is significant overfit for three items: *Overall task fulfilment, Appropriateness* and *Grammar*. This will now be discussed.

TABLE 8.4   Rasch analysis of items (assessment categories), Writing sub-test, April 1989 (*n*=214)

Item	Item difficulty	Error	Fit (*t*)
Overall task fulfilment	0.05	0.12	−6.47
Appropriateness	−0.54	0.12	−3.68
Comprehension	−1.01	0.12	1.44
Grammar	0.94	0.12	−4.84
Presentation	0.56	0.12	−0.63

8.2.3.1   What is being measured in the Writing sub-test?

The interpretation of fit values in the Writing sub-test is essentially the same as in the Speaking sub-test. As before, it appears to make sense in terms of the measurement scale being constructed to combine scores from the sub-categories. Again, as expected, the strongest negative fit statistic is associated with the category *Overall task fulfilment*. We would expect this to be the case if the other rating categories reflect aspects of the overall task, as they are intended to do. This time two other categories show very significant ꓽoverfit: *Grammar* and *Appropriateness*, suggesting that they have a predominant influence on the allocation of the crucial *Overall* score, which is weighted in the same way as the equivalent category in the speaking sub-test.

In order to confirm this finding, a stepwise regression was carried out using scores in the category *Overall task fulfilment* as the dependent variable and scores in the other categories as the predictor variables. The results of the analysis are reported in Table 8.5. They confirm in particular the finding in relation to *Grammar*, which is the first variable entered in the regression equation and which accounts for 60 per cent of the shared variance.

A number of previous studies have investigated either directly or implicitly the role of grammar and other factors in the allocation of scores in writing tasks involving ESL learners. Many of these studies are summarized and discussed in Brown and Bailey (1984).

Mullen (1977) investigated the relationship of scores on four sub-scales (*Control over English structure*, *Organization of material*, *Appropriateness of vocabulary* and *Quantity of writing*) to scores in the category *Overall writing proficiency*. Regression analysis revealed significant (but unequal) contributions from each of the four sub-categories. *Appropriateness of vocabulary* accounted for 84 per cent of the variance; the addition of (in turn) *Quantity*, *Structure* and *Organization* increased the explained variance to 91, 93 and 94 per cent respectively.

It is difficult to compare these findings with those in the current study, where *Grammar* was found to account for 60 per cent of the variance,

TABLE 8.5   Multiple regression analysis – writing sub-test, April 1989 ($n = 214$)

Step	Variable entered	R^2	Change in R^2	t-ratio
1	Grammar	0.603	0.603	17.96*
2	Appropriateness	0.659	0.056	5.88*
3	Comprehension	0.680	0.021	3.69*
4	Presentation	0.685	0.005	1.87†

* $p < 0.01$ † Not significant at the 5% level

increasing to 66 per cent with the addition of *Appropriateness*. In the current study, *Grammar* seemed to play a more significant role than in Mullen's study. Despite the sharing of the term 'appropriateness', it is not clear that these categories refer to the same thing. In the OET, the category *Appropriateness* refers to the candidate's control of the genre of 'letter of referral' and the register (level of formality) required, which will include features of discourse organization and style that extend beyond the area of vocabulary. There is no separate assessment category for vocabulary, because of the nature of the task: much of the vocabulary required for the letter is provided in the case notes. This is unlike the University ESL students' compositions which formed the basis of Mullen's study, where there was presumably opportunity to display precision of vocabulary appropriate to the task.

Jacobs *et al.* (1981) reported on the use of a scoring procedure for ESL compositions which includes the following categories and weightings: *Content* (30 per cent), *Organization* (20 per cent), *Vocabulary* (20 per cent), *Language use* (25 per cent), and *Mechanics* (5 per cent). Although it is not clear how these weightings were derived (no empirical basis is provided), it is interesting to note that of the categories relevant to the OET Writing sub-test (where content was not being evaluated), *Language use* is weighted most heavily, *Mechanics* least. This corresponds in a general way to the findings of the current study.

Brown and Bailey (1984) also developed an analytical scoring procedure on the basis of the work of Mullen and Jacobs *et al.*, but did not investigate empirically the relationships between the sub-categories they used (*Organization*, *Logical development of ideas*, *Grammar*, *Mechanics* and *Style*). In their instrument there is no weighting of categories, and no overall impression category.

In studies of evaluations of native speaker compositions, Daiker *et al.* (1978) found that quality of sentence structure was the most significant influence on the evaluation. However, the relevance of studies on tests designed for native speakers is not entirely clear, as Perkins (1983: 665) points out. Perkins and Konneker (1981) found that performance on the *Test of Ability to Subordinate (TAS)* (Davidson, 1978) did not account for a significant amount of the variance in ESL compositions scored either analytically or holistically.

Homburg (1984) found that 84 per cent of the variance among holistic scores of ESL compositions could be accounted for by four measures of sentential grammatical competence (length, subordination/relativization, errors and sentential connecting devices). The latter two, possibly the latter three, are directly relevant to the OET category *Control of linguistic features (grammar and cohesion)*. However, Homburg argues that such measures may be relevant only at certain (lower) proficiency levels, and that discourse structures become more important as proficiency increases. The present findings seem to contradict this, as the candidates are at advanced levels of writing proficiency. On the other hand, it may be that the constraints of the OET writing task, involving a rather specific and formal genre and where the form and content are largely dictated by the task, mean that organizational issues are less central in this kind of task; they are not reflected in the scoring criteria. Composition tasks required in EAP contexts are typically more open-ended and may require different kinds of skills.[9]

Cohesion, an aspect of the category *Control of linguistic features (grammar and cohesion)*, has been investigated by Evola *et al.* (1980). They found weakly significant correlations between control of cohesive devices and holistic ratings of ESL students' essays. They concluded that while contributing to 'finer aspects' of communicative ability, cohesive devices were 'minimal indicators of overall language proficiency'. The fact that in the OET rating criteria cohesion is combined with the powerful category of grammar means that any separate effect of perceptions of cohesion on overall perceptions of the quality of the writing is obscured.

Research on the ability of objective measures of sentence-level syntactic features of ESL compositions to predict scores for the compositions deriving from more holistic measures has produced conflicting results (for summaries, cf. Brown and Bailey, 1984: 22–5 and Perkins, 1983: 661–2). Such studies have usually focused on measures of syntactic complexity, such as the T-unit, and/or measures of grammatical error. Some research has argued that it is the former, not the latter, which is significant; others the reverse; and others a combination of these two features.

Another relevant line of research has been the investigation of correlations between indirect measures of writing ability such as standardized tests focusing on discrete points of grammatical knowledge, e.g. the Michigan Test of English Language Proficiency (Upshur *et al.*, 1966). Much of this research has been limited to the discussion of the role of such tests for placement purposes in writing programs (cf. Perkins, 1983: 663–6), rather than on the light they might throw on the construct validity of writing tests. The objections to such tests (such as those of Perkins, 1983) are often based on *a priori* views of the construct validity of writing tests, in terms of which these indirect tests have low face validity. In the context of this discussion, however, such considerations are irrelevant, as the OET data reveal what raters are actually oriented towards, rather than what they think they are doing or what they should be doing.

Perkins (1983: 654) refers to the question of rater behaviour in a discussion of the problem of subjectivity and hence reliability in holistic scoring. He points out that one source of unreliability is that different raters 'may react to certain elements in the evaluation *or in the papers'* [emphasis added]. Later, in discussing analytical scoring schemes, Perkins (1983: 657) refers again to the danger of rater bias in the creation of scoring categories in such schemes:

> The choice of categories can be ... arbitrary because the categories themselves are determined by the graders. ... It has already been pointed out that different readers may value different aspects of a com-.position.

The issue raised by the OET data, on both the writing and speaking sub-tests, however, is different and more difficult to address, but nevertheless important. It is that high reliability may be achieved by raters agreeing, not necessarily consciously, on criteria for assessment which are only partially explicit in the scoring criteria: for example, by agreeing that the real basis for the candidate's final score should be the rater's perception of the candidate's control of linguistic features. Such agreement is likely to be a product of the training of the raters as language teachers, and survives the (by comparison) brief retraining they receive in how to interpret the scoring scheme. Raters' orientation to relevant features may be very deep-seated, and may involve substantial reinterpretation of criteria presented to them by test developers. This point is well stated by Carlson and Camp (1985: 10), who investigated the marking of pre-sessional academic essays by trained ESL teachers, teachers of English as a mother tongue, and university academic staff teaching in the subject areas the candidates were about to enter. They comment on inter-rater agreement as follows:

> When high interreader reliability coefficients are obtained, this may have two explanations: (1) the training sessions enabled readers, who may or may not have common views, to agree on common criteria for evaluation, and/or (2) despite the training, readers, especially those who are involved in the field of writing (English or ESL), tend to agree on criteria for evaluation.

Perkins is right to point out that certain features of the candidates' performance may be selectively focused on by such raters; but this is not a simple issue of reliability. The threat to the construct validity of the writing test then is generally not recognized and cannot be removed by *a priori* debate about what it is appropriate to measure. It is important, too, to distinguish construct from face validity; even (as in the OET) where the face validity of the test is good, *a posteriori* empirical analysis may show that all is not what it seems. The issues raised here are essentially similar to those raised in relation to the Speaking sub-test.

An implication of the line of argument put forward above is that raters who have not through their training been oriented to lexico-grammatical criteria for the evaluation of writing might rate scripts differently. Carlson and Camp (1985: 14), in the study mentioned above, concluded that

> Whatever differences in the perception of good writing may exist among regular English teachers, ESL teachers, social science teachers, and engineering teachers, these differences do not interfere with the ability of these diverse groups to rank students' writing samples in the same order. … This outcome … supports the assumption that *general agreement* exists, even when not formally identified and verbalized, concerning *standards for academic writing competence*. [Emphasis in original.]

It may be, then, that trained and untrained raters are oriented to the same features of the texts they are assessing.

8.2.3.2   Discussion

The analysis of the OET test data raises a number of issues in relation to the construct validity of communicative tests such as the OET and the potential of Rasch analysis for exploring such issues.

First, Weir (1988a: 16) distinguishes between *a priori* and *a posteriori* construct validation. In the former, test content at the design stage is based upon an explicit theory of language and language use. In the latter, the constructs posited at the design stage are validated empirically and statistically by data on performance on the test. In the case of the OET, *a posteriori* analysis appeared to validate the constructs in the design of the test, but also to suggest that one of the assessment criteria had a disproportionate role in the allocation of test scores in a way that calls into question the communicative orientation of the test. This may be overstating the issue as it was acknowledged earlier that it is not clear whether raters were oriented to grammar simply as form, or as carrier/vehicle of functional value. However, for the reasons given earlier it is plausible that an orientation to formal accuracy was central to the raters' stance. To the extent that this interpretation is correct, it illustrates the difficulty of communicative language testing in general. It shows that despite advances such as the work of Bachman (1990) in the understanding of notions such as communicative competence, and attempts to measure aspects of communicative competence as defined in current models, it may be difficult to fully apply such models in the actual implementation of tests. *A priori* construct validation by itself is insufficient to reveal the nature of the test.

Secondly, the measurements that were made were a result of an interaction between the behaviour of candidates and the behaviour of raters. We saw in Chapter 2 (Figure 2.1) that this is an integral part of performance assessment, but the behaviour of *raters* has not always been recognized as an appropriate subject for analysis. Candidates were to some extent measured not on the communicative ability which they may or may not have displayed, but on features which were important to the raters, independently of the design of the test.

Thirdly, unlike in the OPI, where the debate about whether or not grammar is central to the assessment makes the issues explicit and disagreement (where it exists) is overt, an important issue of construct validity in the OET is covert and presumably unconscious as far as the raters are concerned. It remains to be seen whether further rater training can alter this situation (such training might, for example, make the raters conscious of the findings of this study).

Fourthly, to the extent that overall ratings in the speaking sub-test were grammatically based, such ratings themselves may lack validity considered from the perspective of findings in Second Language Acquisition. The point has been made in relation to the OPI by Savignon (1985: 133) and in relation to the ASLPR by Pienemann and Johnston (1987) and by Pienemann *et al.* (1988: 219) that the view of grammatical development implicit in the rating scale descriptors has little support from the findings of SLA research.

In conclusion, the study shows the potential of Rasch analysis in the exploration of issues of construct validity, and suggests that it will be a valuable tool in *a posteriori* validation of tests which appear to have validity in an *a priori* sense. The results of the particular analysis reported here show how difficult it may be to achieve fully communicative language tests.

8.2.4   Other studies of rating scales and rating criteria

Two studies by Henning and Davidson were among the earliest to apply Rasch analysis to the investigation of the properties of rating scales. Henning and Davidson (1987) used Rasch analysis to investigate a rating scale for evaluating performance on an ESL writing test. The scale had five assessment categories (*Expression, Structure, Content, Organization* and *Mechanics*), each of which was rated on a scale from 1 to 5. The authors used Rasch analysis to estimate the difficulty of each of the categories and the errors associated with these estimates, and to derive fit statistics for these difficulty estimates. They also established difficulty estimates for each of the score points in each category, and derived fit statistics for these estimates. That is to say, the authors investigated:

(1) the extent to which the assessment categories (*Expression, Structure,* etc.) worked consistently to define a continuum of ability/difficulty in relation to the construct 'ESL writing ability';

(2) the extent to which the score points in each assessment category worked consistently to define a continuum of ability/difficulty in relation to the same construct.

The analysis established that the assessment categories did appear to work together, lending support to the view that it was reasonable to add scores across these categories to arrive at a measure of 'ESL writing ability'. (This is not a self-evident result; a contrasting finding is reported in O'Loughlin, 1992 – discussed in Chapter 9 – in relation to another measure of writing.)

On the second question, the score points within the assessment categories were more instrumental in defining levels of difficulty and ability than differences in difficulty among the categories themselves. (We saw in Chapter 7 that matching of item difficulty and level of ability is important for achieving a precise definition of ability levels.) This became clear when the difficulty estimates of the categories and the score points were compared. The difficulty estimates for the categories represented quite a narrow range in relation to the ability of the group. This was not surprising. On the one hand, one might have expected to find that the difficulty of various categories was not uniform. This was indeed the case: the categories were found to be ranked in order of difficulty from easiest to hardest, as follows: *Mechanics; Expression; Structure; Organization; Content.* In other words, it was considerably more difficult to score high marks for *Content* than it was for *Mechanics.* On the other hand, the range of ability of the students was better reflected in the range of difficulty of the score points *within* each category than in the range of difficulty *across* categories. We are not provided with data on the range of subject abilities, but the range of difficulty across categories was −0.87 to 0.57 logits (a range of 1.44 logits), whereas the range of difficulty across score points within categories was 4.87 logits (values ranged from −2.01 to 2.86 logits). Henning and Davidson (1987: 33) stressed that as the burden in discriminating between subjects thus fell on differences between score points *within* categories: ' ... a great deal of training and norming effort should go into a clear understanding and interpretation of each scale value increment; for example, what is the difference between a 4 and a 5 in Content?'

The analysis of responses at each score point showed a major problem in rater behaviour in this regard: there was an unacceptably high level of misfit in the difficulty estimates at the crucial midrange score points of 3 and 4. In other words (Henning and Davidson, 1987: 34), 'raters were not sufficiently uniform in their interpretation and application of the rating scale'.

Davidson and Henning (1985) encountered a similar weakness in a self-rating scale of difficulty with aspects of English as a second language. A group of subjects (ESL learners) rated perceived degree of difficulty on a 7-point scale for each of 11 aspects of ESL proficiency. Aspects of aural/oral proficiency were analysed separately from aspects of reading and writing ability, on the basis of a two-factor solution from a factor analysis of data from the scale. Response categories for self-rating of diffi-culty with each aspect were as follows: *none, very little, some, average, more than average, much, extreme*. The analysis revealed weakness in the way in which the response categories were working, particularly in rela-tion to aural/oral skills. There were very large positive misfit values for the first four of these response categories, indicating that they were not working satisfactorily to define a continuum of ability/difficulty. Also, inspection of the responses showed a tendency for students, particularly in relation to aural/oral skills, to inflate the estimate of their ability. Davidson and Henning (1985: 176) concluded that 'little confidence should be placed in these particular student self-ratings'.

By comparison, a classical test theory analysis of the data had been reassuring, with reliabilities for the two factors (aural/oral and read-ing/writing) at a respectable 0.83 and 0.80, respectively. The study demonstrates the analytical power that Rasch analysis can bring, this time in terms of what Henning (1987a: 96) refers to as 'response validity':

> If examinees respond in a haphazard or nonreflective manner, their obtained scores may not represent their actual ability. Also, if instruc-tions are unclear and the test format is unfamiliar to the students, their responses may not reflect their true ability, and in this way the test may be said to lack response validity.

Davidson and Henning discuss aspects of the procedure and the format for self-rating that may have led to the lack of response validity revealed by the analysis.

Milanovic *et al.* (1992) report on the use of Rasch analysis in the development of rating scales for the Cambridge Assessment of Spoken English (CASE). The authors comment (1992: 18) that 'It has not been the tradition in language testing to devote much time to the empirical validation of rating scales prior to tests being widely used', and note that their own project is committed to validation prior to use. (This unsatis-factory state of affairs, already discussed in Chapter 7, is in contrast to the effort that routinely goes into the empirical validation of fixed response test formats, and suggests that performance assessment has some way to go before acceptable standards of practice are achieved.) Their own research provides evidence on the overall workability of their scales in terms of model-data fit, the quality of measurement as expressed in person misfit, and the sensitivity of the raters to particular sub-scales. The latter analysis provided several specific points for scale revision and for rater training.

8.3 Research on characteristics of individual raters

Much of the research reported in Section 8.2 was carried out before multi-faceted Rasch measurement had become available, and so could not examine differences between individual raters.[10] In this section, we will consider some examples of research on rater characteristics using multi-faceted Rasch measurement[11] (see Chapter 5 for an introduction). The following issues will be considered:

- What is the effect of rater training?
- Do differences in rater harshness survive training?
- Do rater characteristics persist over time?
- What is the effect of background in raters?

8.3.1 What is the effect of rater training?

It was argued in Chapter 5 that the traditional aim of rater training – to eliminate as far as possible differences between raters – is unachievable and possibly undesirable. What, then, is the function of rater training? Is it a waste of time? This issue has been investigated using Rasch techniques by Weigle (1994), who found that rater training was crucial in getting novice raters to concentrate on what they were doing, and to become self-consistent, the necessary quality in a rater for calibration of rater qualities to be achieved. Rater qualities must be relatively *consistent* if they are to be modelled and estimated.

8.3.2 Do differences in rater harshness survive training?

It was argued in Chapter 5 that training cannot hope to, even should not, eliminate differences between raters. To what extent then do such differences survive training? How seriously must we take such differences, what is their effect on the rating process and what can be done to compensate for them if they are found to be having a significant effect? As multi-faceted measurement routinely reports the extent of such differences between raters, evidence on these questions is rapidly accumulating. All the evidence points to substantial differences which materially affect the chances of individual candidates being deemed to meet (or not to meet) levels of performance required for access to further educational and employment opportunities. Real issues of fairness are revealed in such studies.

What empirical evidence is there then for this view? McNamara and Adams (1991/1994), in the first study to apply multi-faceted measurement in the context of second language performance assessment, revealed extensive variability in the characteristics of trained raters of the IELTS writing test. The variability was at a number of levels. Let us begin with overall severity.

In the study, four trained and experienced IELTS raters were each asked to rate 50 IELTS scripts. Differences between raters are reported in Table 8.6. The severity span between the most lenient rater (No. 2) and the most severe (No. 3) is about 2 logits. Table 6.7 in Chapter 6 helps us to interpret this difference. If a candidate had a 50 per cent chance of getting a required score (say, the score on the writing sub-test required for admission to the course of the candidate's choice) from the most lenient rater, then the chance of getting that same score from the harshest rater would only be 12 per cent.

Differences in overall severity constitute a broad, generalized level of difference between raters. In actuality, consistent differences will be found in more complex ways. These differences may be modelled in multi-faceted analysis with differing degrees of delicacy or specificity. For example, on the IELTS writing sub-test, one of the writing tasks is assessed in terms of three criteria: *task fulfilment; coherence and cohesion;* and *sentence structure.* We saw in Chapter 5 that raters consistently interpret the steps on the rating scale differently, in terms of their propensity when faced with a binary choice ('Is this candidate a level 5 or a level 6?') to allocate cases on the borderline between the two levels to one or other of the available score categories. Raters may vary in the patterns of behaviour they display across the rating scale categories, depending on the criterion

TABLE 8.6   Differences in severity between trained raters, IELTS writing sub-test (from McNamara and Adams, 1991/1994: 8)

Rater ID	Severity (logits)	Error
1	−0.04	0.11
2	−1.01	0.14
3	1.03	0.14
2	0.01	0.13

being assessed. (You may get a certain pattern for Rater 1 on the criterion *coherence and cohesion* that distinguishes her from other raters on this criterion, or from her own behaviour when judging on other criteria.) That is, there may be a three-way interaction between particular judges, particular criteria and particular steps (thresholds) on the rating scale.

This level of complexity can be modelled, and the resulting analysis in the study in question revealed considerable differences between raters at this level. It may be that for certain research purposes we are interested in a more global picture, for example of the interpretation of the step thresholds by the raters *in general* on a particular item such as *coherence and cohesion*; or by one particular rater across the items (criteria) in general. In other words, we can choose to generalize across raters, or across criteria; at the most abstract level, we can generalize across the thresholds and across criteria – thus giving us the overall severity measures we started with, as reported in Table 8.6. It is as if our research tool is a microscope with differing settings, which allow increased or decreased magnification; we can choose to observe at the greatest level of detail, or we can choose a level of generalization which allows us to see the 'bigger picture'. McNamara and Adams (1991/1994) demonstrate what information on the IELTS raters the differing types of analysis provide, and identify tentative 'rater types'. A variety of modelling capabilities is available in Rasch analysis, which has been developed to the point where it constitutes a family of models. This point is explained in detail in Chapter 9.[12]

In case the picture in Table 8.6 of differences in overall rater severity should be considered atypical, or the result of poor rater training, numerous examples can be produced to show that such differences are the rule. For example, Lumley and McNamara (1995), in a study to be considered in detail below, provide incidental data on rater differences, this time 13 trained and experienced raters for the OET. The range from the harshest to the most lenient rater was 2.43 logits; as the error of estimate for individual raters was relatively low (approximately 0.20 logit), the observed differences between raters could not be accounted for by error. Lumley and McNamara (1995: 69) comment: 'One point that emerges consistently and very strongly from all of these analyses is the substantial variation in rater harshness, which training has by no means eliminated, nor even reduced to a level which would permit reporting of raw scores for candidate performance.'

As further examples, Wigglesworth (1993: 312) provides a rater measurement report for raters of oral interaction participating in a trial of an Australian government test of ESL for intending immigrants, the **access:** test. An extract from the report for four raters who rated large

TABLE 8.7   Differences in severity between trained raters, **access**: test (from Wigglesworth, 1993: 312)

Rater ID	Severity (logits)	Error
3	0.80	0.03
1	'0.45	0.03
4	−0.69	0.03
2	−1.52	0.03

numbers of tapes of oral interactions, and whose calibration is very reliable, is provided in Table 8.7. The span of severity is 2.32 logits. Tyndall and Kenyon (1995) found a range of approximately 5 logits in the severity of raters in the composition component of the George Washington University English as a Foreign Language Placement Test.[13]

Such results are replicated in study after study, and must be seen as a stable finding. The conclusion must be that assessment procedures in performance tests which rely on single ratings by trained and qualified raters are hard to defend. This has implications for the cost of performance assessment, as it means that, in the case of high-stakes assessment, two raters at least are required; the ratings should be averaged, or, where facilities exist, the matrix of ratings should be analysed and adjusted measures reported instead of raw scores. (Multi-faceted measurement allows designs where only part of the performances require double marking; cf. Chapter 5.) The argument in favour of multiple ratings is far from new; it is orthodoxy in the classical tradition. Multi-faceted measurement has simply made possible routine exposure of the extent of disagreement among judges, and has the potential to offer a new way out where the technology is available. It is important to stress again that we should not conclude that rater training is a waste of time; as we have said elsewhere, it helps raters achieve *self*-consistency, the *sine qua non* of acceptable rater behaviour.

8.3.3   Do rater characteristics persist over time?[14]

The question of the stability of rater characteristics even over relatively short periods has been little considered in published research. Using traditional methods, Coffman and Kurfman (1968) and Wood and Wilson (1974) produced evidence of instability in marking behaviour in the course of an extended marking period when a large number of scripts are involved. Using multi-faceted measurement, Lunz and Stahl (1990) showed, in the context of an essay examination, a clinical examination and an oral examination, inconsistencies in judges' level of severity across half-day grading periods, within grading sessions of between one and a half and four days.

The question of the stability of rater characteristics over time is of both theoretical and practical interest. Practically, it has to do with the amount of retraining and monitoring of raters that may be required under operational conditions. The issue is in fact made more pressing by the existence of the new technical possibilities of multi-faceted measurement. The question arises as to whether it is reasonable to build what is known of a rater's characteristics at the time of rater training into the estimation of candidates' abilities at the time of the analysis of data from actual test administrations. Or do such characteristics need to be recalibrated in relation to the new data set – a procedure that will involve relatively complex design of the analysis? An additional feature of multi-faceted measurement which has the potential to be of use in the investigation of such issues is its capacity to investigate interactions between elements of facets, that is, interactions between particular raters and particular conditions of each facet of interest. It is possible, for example, that only certain raters may vary their characteristics across occasions, but not others, and that no overall or general pattern emerges across raters. In this case, an appropriate strategy may be to give feedback to individual raters on these interactions, in the hope that this feedback will remove the unwanted interaction effect. But even here, further questions arise. If a rater's characteristics are successfully modified by training, are these changes stable over time, or does the rater revert to old habits? How often do raters need to be retrained?

Lumley and McNamara (1995) investigated some of the questions in the context of rater training for the Speaking sub-test of the Occupational English Test. Assessment is carried out by raters who have participated in a training session followed by rating of a series of audiotaped recordings of speaking test interactions to establish their reliability. The assessment is either carried out live, during the test, by a trained rater acting as interlocutor, or later, by a trained rater using an audiotape of the interaction. In either case the interaction is recorded. The study examined the stability of ratings by a group of raters on three occasions over a period of 20 months.

The specific substantive issues considered were:

(1) whether or not trained raters of spoken performance demonstrated consistency in the level of severity of their assessments over time, and
(2) what implications the findings might have for rater training.

The methodological issue of interest were:

(1) the extent to which multi-faceted Rasch measurement assists in investigating the issue of the stability of rater characteristics over time, and

(2) specifically, the relative usefulness of the technique of *bias analysis* in the investigation of this question.

Data from two rater training sessions (Times 1 and 2, 18 months apart), and a subsequent operational test administration (Time 3, approximately 2 months after the second training session), were used. Thirteen raters (Group A) gave ratings at Times 1 and 2 only; of these, four raters (Group B) gave ratings on all three occasions. The tapes rated were identical at Times 1 and 2, and different at Time 3. The data for these two groups of raters formed part of a much larger (and therefore richer) data matrix which was used in the calibration of the characteristics of these particular groups of raters (cf. Table 8.8).

Two different kinds of analysis were attempted. First, rater harshness was calibrated on each of the three occasions, and compared. Table 8.9 shows a comparison between harshness of these 13 raters in terms of logits, on the two occasions.

It will be seen that the error associated with each logit measure of rater harshness accounts for all or almost all of the change in harshness for all of the raters, with the exception of the first two raters shown here, Rater

TABLE 8.8 Aspects of study design in Lumley and McNamara (1995)

Times	No. of raters studied	No. of tapes rated	Total number of raters in matrix
1&2	13 (Group A)	10	Time 1 = 55 Time 2 = 32
3	4 (Group B)	73	6

TABLE 8.9 Stability of rater characteristics, Times 1 and 2 (Group A)

Rater ID	Time 1	Error	Time 2*	Error	Change
6	−1.78	0.19	−0.02	0.18	1.76
20	0.24	0.18	−0.80	0.19	−1.04
30	0.04	0.20	−0.42	0.18	−0.46
1	−0.80	0.19	−1.25	0.20	−0.45
8	−0.80	0.19	−0.40	0.21	0.40
32	0.12	0.21	−0.22	0.20	−0.34
24	−0.29	0.21	−0.62	0.18	−0.33
2	−0.41	0.19	−0.11	0.19	0.30
9	−0.64	0.19	−0.89	0.20	−0.25
14	−0.96	0.18	−0.76	0.16	0.20
3	−1.14	0.19	−0.98	0.18	0.16
7	0.65	0.19	0.53	0.20	−0.12
10	−0.94	0.19	−1.02	0.21	−0.08

* Values have been adjusted to make them comparable with those of Time 1.[15]

TABLE 8.10   Changes in rater severity over the three occasions (Group B)

Rater ID	Change Times 1–2	Change Times 1–3	Change Times 2–3
2	0.30	−0.14	−0.44
6	1.76	0.18	−1.58
8	0.40	1.36	0.96
10	−0.08	−0.70	−0.62

6, who has become harsher by 1.76 logits, and Rater 20, who has become more lenient by 1.04 logits. There has otherwise been relatively little shift in rater harshness. It appears, then, that there is non-uniform variation in severity amongst the 13 raters over the two occasions (18 months apart). However, the significant variations appear to be restricted to a relatively small number of raters (2 out of 13).

A similar comparison was carried out for the sub-group of four raters (Group B) who participated on all three rating occasions. Table 8.10 summarizes the extent of change for each rater across each pairing of times.

This table partially confirms the picture obtained from the earlier analyses, suggesting non-uniform change in levels of rater severity over the three occasions. However, it also appears that there may be wider variation in raters' consistency across rating times than suggested by the earlier analysis.

In order to confirm these findings, and in order to compare methodologies for investigating these questions, bias analysis was carried out on the data from Times 1 and 2. 'Occasion' was treated as a facet in the analysis, and 'Rater by Occasion' interactions ('bias') were examined. The conclusion reached earlier, using the overall estimates of rater harshness, was confirmed, that Raters 6 and 20 showed significant changes in their severity between Times 1 and 2 (cf. Table 8.9); in addition, the analysis identified Rater 7 as changing in severity, although there was some inconsistency in this pattern.

Since the rating occasion in this study was shown to influence different raters in different ways, it would be appropriate to supply rater performance reports (cf. Chapter 5) for each rating time to individual raters identified as rating harshly or leniently on particular occasions. A follow-up study could then be carried out to determine whether rater characteristics stabilize as a result of such feedback. Such reports could be complemented by protocol or interview analysis, prior to the FACETS analysis, to see if it were possible to identify beforehand the likelihood of personal circumstances influencing a rater's severity or leniency on a particular occasion.

The variability that was discovered in the study, particularly between the rater training session and the actual test administration, means that we should call into question the practice sometimes adopted, e.g. by IELTS and the ASLPR, of certifying raters and then basing judgements of candidates on single ratings by such certified raters. Just as the analyses confirm yet again that rater differences survive training, so intra-rater differences are likely to be an issue for at least some raters over different rating occasions. It seems that, at every administration, new calibrations of rater characteristics are required; failing that, the traditional technique of double and if necessary multiple ratings seems amply justified.

8.3.4 What is the effect of background on raters?

As we saw in Chapter 2, some writers on performance assessment (e.g. Wiggins, 1989) require that the test replicate the *standards* by which performance would be assessed in the real world. This point was the basis for the distinction presented in that chapter between a *strong* and a *weak* sense of the term *second language performance assessment*. As performance testing in occupational settings becomes more common, the issue arises as to who should be responsible for the rating process: should it be language teachers who have been trained as raters (the normal practice), or those responsible for the employment or the professional work of the candidates? Can trained language teachers replicate the judgements made by non-teachers in the workplace setting?

There has been surprisingly little research on this important subject. Two recent studies have addressed the question using multi-faceted Rasch measurement.

Brown (1995) investigated rater background factors in assessment on the Japanese Language Test for Tour Guides, an advanced level occupation-specific oral test designed to measure the Japanese language skills of Australian Japanese-speaking tour guides and intending tour guides. The test has five assessable phases, each involving the simulation of a typical tour-guiding task; assessment criteria differ from task to task, as appropriate. The context of test development meant that assessors were preferably from within the tourist industry (experienced tour guides, tour coordinators and tour guide trainers); however, in order to provide the number of raters needed, experienced teachers of Japanese as a foreign language were also used.

Data from ratings by 33 trained and accredited raters on the performances of 51 candidates were used in the analysis. Brown's results show that the occupational background of raters (with and without industry experience) had no bearing on the degree of consistency (fit) or the overall harshness of raters. Greater variability in levels of severity was found among the non-teacher group. Differences between the groups did emerge at the level of individual criteria: teachers were harsher on three of the language-related criteria (*grammar and expression, vocabulary* and *fluency*) than industry raters, whereas industry raters were harsher on the criterion *pronunciation*. Perhaps teachers have become inured to bad pronunciation. In terms of test tasks, industry raters were harsher than teachers on the task 'Dealing with an upset or worried client'; it seemed that they viewed the ability to handle this sort of situation as crucial, whereas teachers tended to be sympathetic to candidates' attempts at what they perceived to be a difficult task. There were some differences between the two groups in their interpretation of the rating scale scoring categories, with teachers being less prepared to award very high or very low scores, particularly in relation to the criterion *task fulfilment*. This, according to Brown (1995: 12), may suggest some uncertainty in teacher raters as to what constitutes 'good' occupational performance; or it may simply be a tendency in teachers to avoid extreme judgements of language proficiency. Bias analysis failed to reveal any potential tendency in industry-based raters to favour those candidates with industry experience.

In general, from a practical point of view, the observed differences were not such as to suggest that the two groups differ in their suitability as raters. From a research point of view, there are differences; these were obscured in practice in this study partly because both sides jointly negotiated a common framework for assessment under the supervision of the test designer. Left to themselves, Brown (1995: 13) argues, they might have produced 'schemes which lead to quite different evaluations of candidates' ability'. This raises the issue of the relative validity of the two viewpoints: whose view should be reflected in the assessment procedures?

Similar issues arise in a study by Lumley *et al.* (1994) which elicited ESL teachers' and doctors' perceptions of acceptable pass levels on the Speaking sub-test of the Occupational English Test. The body administering the test had received complaints from Australian doctors responsible for the clinical examinations in medicine required of overseas-trained medical practitioners that English standards of those presenting for the test were low; these complaints were echoed by the views of clinical supervisors in hospital settings responsible for the examination preparation of the candidates. It was therefore decided to elicit judgements from these doctors of the relative acceptability of performances on the OET; these would then be compared with standards being applied by OET examiners, who were repeatedly criticized for being too lenient.

Audiotaped performances of 20 candidates were thus assessed by two groups of raters, doctors (*n*=9) and trained OET raters (*n*=10). The assessment procedure resembled that used in the OET: ratings were made using the grid in Appendix 4A, Chapter 4, except that in the case of the doctors, because of time constraints and of their likely unfamiliarity with the technical language used in some of the rating categories, only the category *Overall communicative effectiveness* was used. As reported earlier in this chapter (cf. Table 8.1) this criterion is an effective summary of scores given in other categories.

The results were contrary to expectation. There was no difference between the two groups in terms of leniency; if anything, the doctors were slightly more lenient. The doctors generally interpreted the scale consistently with the ESL raters. One of the doctors was found to be misfitting as a rater; there was no greater misfit when the data from the two groups were combined, nor were any candidates mismeasured. There was a slightly greater tendency for doctors to show biased ratings, but these ratings were in the main associated with the ratings of the one misfitting doctor.

This result appears reassuring, in that trained ESL raters and doctors in the clinical setting appear to be applying similar standards when judging the speaking skills of non-native speakers of English in simulated clinical communication tasks. However, the result, looked at in another way, may have disconcerting implications for the validity of the test: whatever the doctors were complaining about was *not* being captured by the OET. Some evidence in favour of this interpretation came from comments made by the doctors in the study, several of whom remarked that they were not certain that the test task to which the candidates responded was sufficiently representative of the clinical situation in which they would ultimately be judged. The inevitable simplification and dilution of the real-world task when simulated in performance test conditions may result in substantial loss of validity (cf. discussion of this issue in Chapters 2 and 4). Whether this can be improved by altering the design of the test task, or is a fundamental weakness of this kind of test, is not clear. Clearly, a cycle of test development/post-test validation studies/test revision is called for.

8.4   How do assessment conditions affect rater behaviour?

In this section we will consider some recent research on the issue of what facets of the assessment context, other than the characteristics of raters, will have a bearing on candidates' scores, and how great the effect may be.

The discussion of the factors affecting performance on tests in Chapters 2 and 3 suggests that a myriad of factors, barely yet conceptualized in our field, may account for variance in test scores. Furthermore, as we saw in Chapter 5, and as we have discussed above, the set of variables surrounding the behaviour of *raters* will have an effect; the score awarded is the result of a complex interaction between characteristics of the test takers, characteristics of the assessment setting, and the way each of these is mediated by the reactions of raters, who will themselves differ. There is a rich agenda for research here to unpack the possible variables and their influence on patterns of scores.

An example of this issue is to be found in cases where performances of speaking are rated from tape, as they are in many tests around the world. Cases where the factors involved are beginning to be studied include the **access:** test (see Chapter 5) and the Occupational English Test. In each case, the tests are administered world wide, and ratings are done centrally in Australia. In the case of the OET, the training received by the interlocutors varies, but it minimally consists of watching a videotape of a typical speaking test interaction, to allow interlocutors to familiarize themselves with appropriate procedures for conducting the test, and familiarization with the test administration kit. Interlocutors engage the candidates in oral interaction, and the performances are audio-recorded and rated subsequently in Australia by trained raters.

Two features of the audio-recordings – (1) the audibility of the interaction due to misuse of or poor equipment, and (2) the competence of the interlocutor – were raised in anecdotal complaints by raters. McNamara and Lumley (1993) investigated the extent and the consequences of these aspects of the test context using multi-faceted Rasch measurement. With regard to the competence of the interlocutor, three factors were identified as possibly playing a role. The first of these was the general competence of the interlocutor: his or her ability to conduct, seriously and in an appropriate manner, the various procedures required by the test. The second was the competence of the interlocutor in adopting realistically the role of patient or client during the simulated consultations. The third was the emotional climate established between the participants, or *rapport*.

Data were gathered using material collected during 1992 overseas test administrations. Seventy audio-recordings of speaking test interactions were each rated twice. Seven raters were involved. The raters each completed a questionnaire for each tape, in which they were asked to evaluate the audibility of the tape, and the three aspects of the interlocutor's performance listed above. Each of the four variables was then treated as a facet in the analysis. The results of the study are given in Table 8.11.

8.4.1   Audibility

The analysis revealed a significant effect of audibility: tapes perceived by raters as being imperfectly audible were rated more harshly than tapes

TABLE 8.11   Summary of findings, McNamara and Lumley (1993)

Facet	Level	Ratings given	Effect size (maximum)
Audibility of tape	↑	↑	0.5 logit
Interlocutor competence (General)	↑	↓	0.7 logit
Interlocutor competence (as Patient)	↑	↓	0.9 logit
Rapport established	↑	↓	1.0 logit

perceived as perfectly audible; this finding is reliable (index of reliability of difference = 0.89). The effect, while significant, is not very large in practical terms (from Table 6.7 in Chapter 6, it means that at worst the chances of a candidate who would have a 50 per cent chance of reaching a required score under favourable audibility conditions would have this reduced to 40 per cent if rated by a rater who perceived the tape quality as poor). It is not clear how many borderline decisions would be changed if this issue were taken into account.

However, given that audibility problems cannot be entirely eliminated, then action needs to be taken to sensitize judges to this issue. Ideally, analyses resulting in candidate measures should include raters' perceptions of audibility as a facet, so that the effect can be neutralized in the resulting measures. Alternatively, candidates at borderline decision points should be monitored so that the possible effect of harshness resulting from audibility could be taken into account in making pass/fail decisions.

8.4.2   Competence

The analysis showed a significant and consistent effect for competence, but in a somewhat surprising direction: candidates interacting with interlocutors perceived to be less competent appear to be favoured by raters. Raters, that is, appear to compensate for what they perceive to be the relative incompetence of interlocutors. Bias analysis suggested that the effect was general, and not restricted to any single rater. The effect was relatively large, about 0.7 of a score point in raw score terms; put another way, in the most extreme case a candidate who would have a 50 per cent chance of reaching a required score where the interlocutor was perceived as being very competent would see this chance increased to about 65 per cent if rated by a rater who perceived the interlocutor as being less than perfectly competent. A similar but stronger effect was found if the interlocutor was perceived to have established good rapport: candidates were favoured by raters if they were interacting with an interlocutor who failed to achieve good rapport, by almost a full score point in raw score terms (alternatively, in the most extreme case, a candidate who would have a 50

244 Measuring Second Language Performance

per cent chance of reaching a required score where the interlocutor was perceived as having established good rapport, would have this chance increased to about 73 per cent if rated by a rater who perceived the interlocutor as having failed to achieve this).

In general, an effect was found for competence across the three aspects of interlocutor competence studied. The effect was larger than for audibility, and thus a real issue, as it would alter the likely outcome in borderline pass/fail cases. Large numbers of interactions were also involved. On the one hand, more rigorous interlocutor selection, training and monitoring would seem to be called for; but the proportion of interlocutors rated as less than *adequately* competent is in fact very small, so that simply training interlocutors may not necessarily provide a solution.

Curiously, the effect was in the reverse direction than for audibility: perceptions of problems with interlocutor competence led to higher ratings. There are at least two possible explanations for this finding. First, a perception of lack of competence on the part of the interlocutor may have been interpreted as raising an issue of fairness in the mind of the rater, who may then have made a sympathetic compensation to the candidate. Secondly, the effect of the lack of competence may have been that the interlocutor 'hogged' the interaction, giving the candidate too little time to speak, so that the evidence available to the rater may have been restricted, with the result that the rater gave the candidate the 'benefit of the doubt'. It is regularly the case that when 'comprehension' on the part of the candidate is rated in oral interviews, as in the OET, it is rated more leniently than any other aspect of the candidate's performance (cf. Table 8.1, above). This is probably because the evidence for the level of comprehension is hard to interpret in the absence of very obvious difficulty, and the presumption is in favour of the candidate.

8.5 Investigations of test task

The potential for the use of Rasch analysis in the exploration of test task has been under-explored to date. We can expect further research on this in future. Two kinds of research will be mentioned here to indicate what has been done.[16]

In a series of studies, Stansfield and Kenyon have explored the extent to which empirical data on task difficulty bear out the assumptions about task difficulty found in the ACTFL Proficiency Guidelines (ACTFL, 1986). Stansfield and Kenyon (1992) and Kenyon and Stansfield (1992) used Rasch analysis to compare language teachers' estimates of the difficulty of speaking tasks in the (Simulated) Oral Proficiency Interview

(SOPI) with the assumptions about the difficulty of the tasks implicit in the ACTFL guidelines. Kenyon (1995) extended this study to the investigation of students' perceptions of the difficulty of the tasks in the SOPI. The conclusion of this research is that the perceptions of both groups of the relative difficulty of specific tasks accord in large part with the position taken in the ACTFL guidelines. What is less clear is that the research supports the grouping together of tasks into the separate proficiency levels defined in the ACTFL procedure; in fact a gradual continuum of task difficulty is defined by the Rasch analysis, which does not entirely concur with the categorical grouping imposed by the reduction to a few levels of proficiency. As always in rater judgements, there will be disagreement between judges about where one category ends and the next begins (cf. discussion in Chapter 5; such differences between individual teacher and student judges were not explored in the papers cited).

In another line of research, Clapham (1994) used Rasch bias analysis as one among several lines of investigation in a thorough analysis of the effect of background knowledge on performance on the subject-specific modules of the IELTS reading test. The bias analysis confirmed the results of other analyses that there was only limited interaction between background knowledge and performance on the texts chosen for the reading test under investigation.

None of the studies reported so far used multi-faceted Rasch analysis in the investigation of task effects. Other studies have done so. Bachman *et al.* (1993) and Lynch and McNamara (1994) report on the interaction of raters and task using the bias analysis function of multi-faceted analysis. The former study using data from a performance test of Spanish as a foreign language found few such interactions to be significant. The latter study, using data from the **access:** test (see above), found that no fewer than 48 per cent of all possible rater–task interactions showed significant bias, although the results of an accompanying G-theory study suggested that the overall impact of these interactions on candidates' total scores was fairly negligible. Nevertheless from a research point of view at least such interactions are of interest, and potentially important in practical terms.

8.6 Conclusion

The scope for the application of multi-faceted Rasch measurement to research on the validity of performance tests is great, because of the complexity of factors to do with the interaction of candidate, rater and test setting introduced by the performance requirement. The studies reported here only scratch the surface of what it is possible (and profitable) to study. For example, Brown (1995), in the study reported above, also investigated potential differences between native- and non-native speaker raters, an issue which is also taken up by Elder (1994) in her study of an occupationally based performance test for teachers of Italian in primary school settings. But the studies reported here demonstrate the potential for illuminating some of the factors posing threats to the validity of inferences about candidates made in the context of performance tests. Naïve views of the advantages of the 'directness' of tests with a performance requirement are clearly inappropriate. We must remain sceptical about the meaning of our test scores, and do everything we can to improve our understanding of what they mean, in the interests primarily of fairness to the test candidates, but also of the informativeness of our reports on candidates to test users.

Of course, the use of multi-faceted measurement is only one of many possible approaches to research on these questions; extremely useful work is being done in other research traditions. For example, the question of the orientation to assessment criteria on the part of ESL teachers and teachers of mathematics is addressed using different methods in Elder (1993), which reports on the development of an observational schedule for assessing the classroom second language proficiency of teachers of science and mathematics. As mentioned in Chapter 3, the tradition of the study of interaction in language tests initiated by Lazaraton (1991) is very active (cf., for example, Young, 1994; He, 1994; Ross, 1992, 1994); more broadly, studies of language use in tests of oral interaction have addressed fundamental questions of validity (cf. Shohamy, 1994; O'Loughlin, 1995; Wigglesworth, 1994). A study by Morton and Wigglesworth (1994) similarly investigates patterns of language use in order to address the question of the effect of variability in interlocutor behaviour in oral tests where the interlocutor is not the assessor – for example, in tests of oral interaction rated from audiotape or videotape.

While Rasch measurement, particularly multi-faceted measurement, is thus only one of many possible research tools, it has a particularly powerful role to play, as the research reported in this chapter shows. In order for a research agenda in this area to be articulated, we need complex views of the range of factors involved in performance assessment, that is, the construct of language test performance needs to be theorized, as we attempted to do in earlier chapters. Better theory and new research tools in combination offer us the chance to make important advances in our understanding and practice in second language performance assessment.

Notes

1. An example of materials used in the Speaking sub-test is shown in Figure 4.1 in Chapter 4.
2. The scoring grid for the Speaking sub-test is presented in Appendix 4A of Chapter 4.
3. As Davidson and Henning (1985: 170) and Henning and Davidson (1987: 33) point out (cf. Section 8.2.4), the operationalization of difficulty rests on the score points (0 to 4) within a scale category as much as on the categories themselves, a finding confirmed in the present data, where the score points define a much broader range of difficulty than do the categories themselves, and much closer to the ability range of candidates. Further details of step difficulty and person ability are available in McNamara (1990a). The *tau* estimates of the step difficulty between score points within categories in both sets of data are approximately equivalent, confirming the appropriateness of using the Rating Scale model (as against the Partial Credit model) for the analysis (cf. Chapter 9 and the discussion of this issue in Pollitt and Hutchinson, 1987: 78–9, 84).
4. The nature of measurement dimensions in Rasch analysis is discussed in detail in Chapter 9.
5. In April, although not in December, the category *Appropriateness* is also slightly overfitting. The significance of this appears to be that some raters may have experienced trouble in interpreting this category. The difficulty estimate for this category is close to the difficulty of the category *Overall communicative effectiveness* in each case, and suggests that where raters have had difficulty in determining an independent score for the category, they have simply recorded as the score in this category something approximating their overall impression of the candidate.
6. An interpretation of the significance of the relatively slight overfit of the category *Appropriateness* in the April 1989 session has been given above (note 5).
7. An example of materials used in the Writing sub-test is shown in Figure 4.2 in Chapter 4.
8. The scoring grid for the Writing sub-test is presented in Appendix 4B of Chapter 4.
9. In fact, some raters report that organization is an issue in the candidate scripts and would prefer to see it included in the scoring criteria.
10. Although multi faceted Rasch analysis was available to Milanovic *et al.* (1992), it was not used in their study.
11. Implemented through the FACETS program (Linacre and Wright, 1992).
12. Information is also provided in Chapter 9 on how to request the differing kinds of analysis in the computer program FACETS.
13. This range is very large: again referring to Table 6.7 in Chapter 6, this would mean that a candidate who would have a 50 per cent chance of getting a given rating from the most lenient rater would have a negligible chance (about 1 per cent) of getting this rating from the harshest rater.
14. This section is based on Lumley and McNamara (1995).
15. The mean rater harshness for the groups of raters contained in the calibration differed on each occasion (Time 1: -0.27 logit; Time 2: -0.17 logit). The logit values for Time 2 therefore need to be adjusted to make them comparable with Time 1 values. By adding -0.10 to individual rater harshness values from this second analysis the two sets of data were then made comparable, and logit values of the 13 individual raters common to both rating periods could be compared.
16. We can add here the studies by Pollitt and Hutchinson (1987) and McNamara (1991) already mentioned elsewhere in this text.

9 Data, models and dimensions

9.1 Introduction

Despite the great practical benefits of Rasch measurement for helping us understand and control the complexity of language performance testing, its introduction into the field has not been entirely smooth. The validity of Rasch measurement for the analysis of language test data has been challenged on a number of grounds. In this last chapter of the book, we take up this debate. Researchers obviously need to feel confident that the analysis they propose to carry out on test data, or that they are presented with in research papers or test manuals, is appropriate.

The appropriateness of Rasch analysis for language test data has been questioned by some researchers on one of two grounds.

1. For test data where responses from candidates can simply be marked 'right' or 'wrong', some researchers have questioned whether the Rasch model provides an adequate basis for analysing the data, or whether mathematically more complex analyses are required. This issue involves a debate over the merits of the Rasch model (the so-called *one-parameter*[1] model) versus other Item Response Theory (IRT)[2] models (so-called *two-* and *three-parameter* models).

2. For all language tests, particularly those involving language performance in occupational or academic contexts, some researchers have asked whether the simple but powerful assumptions of Rasch analysis can adequately reflect the complexity of the skills involved. The issue here is a claim made by critics of Rasch analysis that the nature of the skills and abilities underlying performance on language tests is at variance with the *unidimensionality assumption* of Rasch (and other IRT) models, that is, the way the analysis tries to look within the variability of candidate responses to different test items for evidence of an underlying relationship between the difficulty of the items and the ability of the candidates which will make the pattern of responses coherent and interpretable.

In this chapter we consider each of these criticisms in some depth. It is important to do so, as they have not been well understood in the language-testing literature to date. Some basic understanding of the points dealt with here is necessary for the meaningful analysis of performance test data and for participation in ongoing debates about the nature of performance assessment as revealed in research. In relation to (1), the particular advantages of the Rasch model over other IRT models will be considered; in relation to (2), it will be argued that much of the concern about uni-dimensionality derives from a failure to distinguish *measurement* models from *psychological* models of the various skills and abilities involved in language performance.

Before we begin this discussion, however, we need to clear a little more terminological ground. Rasch analysis has developed rapidly over the past decade and a half, and the basic model proposed by Rasch has been extended and developed in important ways to handle different kinds of test data and newer approaches to assessment, most importantly perfor-mance testing, where judgements and ratings of performance are made on *rating scales*. As Rasch measurement thus now comprises a family of related models, we need to be in a position to understand the basis for an appropriate choice among them. This choice, then, is not so much one of principle (as between Rasch and non-Rasch models) but more of tech-nique, namely the choice of the right *kind* of Rasch analysis to answer the questions we have about the data. Briefly, four types of model are available:

(1) the *Basic Rasch model*, for dichotomous (right/wrong) data;
(2) the *Andrich* or *Rating Scale* model, for handling data from rating scales;
(3) the *Masters* or *Partial Credit* model, also for rating scale data;
(4) Linacre's extended or *multi-faceted* model.[d]

We begin the chapter with a brief look at the family of models, and then deal with the debates about the appropriateness of using any of these models at all. As previously in this book, the approach will be relatively non-technical and will assume no greater knowledge on the reader's part than that set out in the previous chapters, particularly the discussions of the principles of Rasch measurement in Chapters 5 and 6. The argument is sequential and cumulative, so the reader who is dipping into this book would be advised to read the material in those chapters before embarking on this one.

9.2 The Rasch family of models

In this section an outline of different models developed within the Rasch tradition of analysis will be outlined. We will begin with a brief explana-tion of different types of data, and the implications of these for model choice at the data analysis stage.

9.2.1   Types of response formats and scoring procedures

First, it is necessary to match the kind of analysis to the scoring procedure. Were answers scored simply right/wrong? Could part marks be given? Alternatively, did judges make an overall assessment of the quality of an extended response, using particular criteria? We need some terminology concerning response formats and scoring procedures. These will determine the form of response data to be analysed, and will thus affect our choice of Rasch model.

9.2.1.1   *Response formats yielding dichotomous data*

The simplest scoring scheme is automatic right/wrong scoring, which results in *dichotomous* data. The data from the OET reading sub-test trials presented in Chapter 6 are an example. This kind of data can be handled by the *basic* Rasch model, which was presented in that chapter. Test formats eliciting dichotomous data are frequently of the *fixed response* type, where the candidate responds to a test item by choosing one of a number of presented alternatives; only one is correct. The candidate's response can be marked as 'right' or 'wrong'; this is often done by machine in the interests of efficiency and cost. There is a simple coding of responses: either no marks (0) for an incorrect answer or one mark (1) for a correct answer. If the candidate does not answer the question, this can either be coded as 0 (incorrect) or treated as missing data by using some other code (frequently * or 9) to represent it.[4] Data from multiple-choice questions (MCQ) (as in the above example) represent the most frequently occurring type of dichotomous data. Fixed response formats have many practical advantages: the problem of interpreting the candidate's answer (i.e. making clear what the candidate intended) is reduced; and scoring is simple and fast. For performance-based tests of receptive skills (reading and listening) such response formats may be acceptable. But even in this context the candidate's score may be affected by how good he or she is at handling multiple-choice questions, a skill which can be developed by training. Moreover, these formats are unsuitable for eliciting from candidates instances of actual language use in the productive skills of speaking and writing, or for eliciting an extended response which may be more revealing of the candidate's understanding of texts which have been read or heard.

As a result, alternative response formats and scoring procedures are being used, particularly in performance-based language assessment. Three of these will now be considered.

9.2.1.2   Test formats yielding responses scored with a range of marks

First, in comprehension tasks (either listening or reading), increasing use is being made of *constructed response* formats. Items in short answer question (SAQ) format involve the candidate in providing a brief answer (a few words) to questions on the passage. In this case, *partial credit* may be allowed for partially satisfactory answers; responses may thus be scored 0, 1 or 2, or perhaps 0, 1, 2 or 3, depending on the quality of the response.

The second and third types of scoring involve a more *extended response* on the part of the candidate, for example in a speaking or writing task. In this case, more complex judgements of the quality of the response may be required of raters, and the coding of the rater responses will lead to a type of data loosely referred to as rating scale data.[5] Typically, in the assessment of speaking and writing, the performance of candidates may be rated either on a rating scale with a number of levels, or using Likert or semantic differential procedures. Figure 9.1 illustrates a *rating scale*, in this case the self-assessment version (Wylie and Ingram, 1991) for the speaking sub-skill of the Australian Second Language Proficiency Rating Scale (Ingram, 1984), a widely used Australian general proficiency rating scale based on American models originally developed by the Foreign Service Institute (Clark and Clifford, 1988). In the case of such rating scales, scores for a particular performance (or aspect of a single performance) can typically have values between 1 and 5, let us say, or between 1 and 9. Such scales can be holistic, as here, where the skill is assessed once and as a whole, or analytic,[6] where the performance is judged repeatedly, each time on a separate criterion (such as *Fluency*, *Appropriateness* or *Intelligibility* (as in the assessment of speaking) or *Organization* (as in the assessment of writing)).

Alternatively, *Likert* and *Semantic differential* scales may be used to judge the whole performance, or different aspects of it. A *Likert scale* (Figure 9.2) is one in which a person is asked to indicate which of a range of named categories, arranged in increasing order of intensity of a trait (for example, liking for something, or approval), best represents their point of view.

The numbering of the categories in square brackets in Figure 9.2 does not usually appear on the rater response sheet, but responses are coded using such numerical equivalents for subsequent analysis. Commonly, Likert scales are used (Henning, 1987a: 23) 'to elicit extent of agreement with some statement of opinion or attitude', with typical categories being 'Strongly agree', 'Agree', 'Undecided', 'Disagree' and 'Strongly disagree'. *Semantic differential scales* (Figure 9.3) similarly offer raters a range of categories in which to respond, for example in judging a performance on

SPEAKING

0   I can't communicate anything at all in the spoken language.

0+   I can communicate by using a limited range of simple stock phrases I have learned.

1−   I communicate mainly with simple stock phrases. I can be 'creative' (i.e. say new things I have *not* learned as stock phrases) but any creative language consists of no more than (for example) a subject and verb with perhaps also an object or adverb, and I make so many mistakes that most people have great trouble understanding what I say unless the context makes it very predictable.

1   I can communicate my basic needs and basic factual information in situations or on topics which are very familiar (e.g. I can conduct basic shopping transactions and outline how long and where I have learned the language). I can maintain a very simple conversation (satisfying minimum courtesy requirements) with a simple series of exchanges, using complete, though very simple, sentences (generally consisting of a single clause). I make a lot of mistakes and I may have to repeat myself often to be understood.

1+   I can speak well enough to take part in simple conversations in face-to-face situations. My language is 'creative' enough (see above) to allow me to interact as an individual, and complex enough to convey my simple opinions about familiar matters. I make a lot of mistakes, and I often have great trouble coming up with the vocabulary and structures I need.

2   I can speak well enough to take part in face-to-face or telephone conversations, describing familiar things and relating familiar events, and conveying my opinions about them fairly precisely 'off the cuff'. I use a range of complex sentences (e.g. with 'if' and 'because'). I make a lot of mistakes, and I often have trouble coming up with the vocabulary or structures I need. Beyond basic courtesy forms such as greetings, I have limited ability to tailor my language as outlined below.

2+   I am midway between the description above and the one below.

3   I can speak well enough to substantiate my own and discuss other people's opinions effectively in conversations or unprepared monologues, though I can't pursue my 'argument' to great depth. I make mistakes, though these rarely confuse or amuse the listener. In familiar situations I can generally tailor what I say and how I say it to considerations such as the formality of the occasion and whether the person I am talking to is older or younger than me, though I can't always come up with the appropriate vocabulary or structure.

3+   I am midway between the description above and the one below.

4   I can operate effectively in complex, in-depth discussions or monologues in social and academic or work situations. My language is mostly accurate, fluent and appropriate to the situation. Someone might think I was a native speaker for a few moments, but they wouldn't be fooled for long.

4+   I am midway between the description above and the one below.

5   I speak the language just as well as similarly educated native speakers do. There is nothing about the way I speak that suggests that I am not a native speaker.

FIGURE 9.1   Proficiency Rating Scale (Wylie and Ingram, 1991)

How adequate was this performance?

|_____| |_____| |_____| |_____| |_____|

Very inadequate	Inadequate	Adequate	More than adequate	Outstanding
[0	1	2	3	4]

FIGURE 9.2   Likert scale

OVERALL COMMUNICATIVE EFFECTIVENESS

Near-native flexibility
and range   ___ ___ ___ ___ ___ ___   Limited

FLUENCY

Even   ___ ___ ___ ___ ___ ___   Uneven

FIGURE 9.3   Criteria defined using a semantic differential scale – Occupational
English Test

TABLE 9.1   Data type, response formats/scoring procedures and appropriate
analyses

Data type	Response format/ scoring procedure	Possible analysis	Simplest available program
Dichotomous	Multiple choice question True–false question Short Answer Question (SAQ) (no partial credit scoring)	Basic Rasch model	Quest
Polytomous (without or ignoring judge mediation)	Short Answer Question (SAQ) (with partial credit scoring) Rating scale Likert scale Semantic differential scale	Rating Scale model (Andrich) Partial Credit model (Masters)	Quest
Polytomous (taking judge mediation into account)	Rating scale Likert scale Semantic differential scale	Extended (multi- faceted) model (Linacre) using *either* Rating Scale model (Andrich) *or* Partial Credit model (Masters)	FACETS

successive criteria, each criterion being defined in terms of a pair of anton-
ymous anchor terms (words which define the extremes of the attribute
being assessed). For example, in the Occupational English Test, judges are
asked to performance on a role play-based speaking task in terms of six
criteria. Two of the criteria, with their anchor terms, are illustrated in
Figure 9.3.

Responses of judges may thus be coded numerically (from 0 to 5) for
the analysis. In general, item types in which responses may be scored
with a range of marks are called *polytomous* items.

The different data types, their relation to scoring formats/scoring procedures and the implications for choice of analysis are summarized in
Table 9.1.

9.2.2   Rasch models

It will be noted in Table 9.1 that different kinds of data (dichotomous vs
polytomous, ratings mediated by judges vs ratings where judge mediation
is not an issue) require different kinds of Rasch analyses. In this section,
the Rasch family of models will be introduced, quite non-technically. (In
Appendix 9A at the end of the chapter, the reader is introduced to some
simplified formal statements of the models; manuals often make reference
to these formal statements, and it is helpful to be able to recognize them.)
We can distinguish three main branches in this family:

(1) the *Basic model* for the analysis of dichotomous data,
(2) models which can handle data from *rating scales* and the like, and
(3) *many-faceted* models which allow exploration of rater characteristics,
     test tasks, test conditions and the like.

The three branches correspond to three stages in the evolution of the
family.

9.2.2.1   The Basic Rasch model

The *Basic model*, that originally developed by Rasch (1960 [1980]),
handles data from dichotomous items. This model is explained in detail
in Wright and Stone (1979). The characteristics and assumptions of this
model, the most fundamental of the Rasch models, were presented in
Chapter 6.

9.2.2.2   Rating Scale model (Andrich)

The extension of the basic Rasch model to handle *polytomous data*
occurred in two stages. The first is represented by the work of the

Australian David Andrich, to enable it to handle scores derived from rat-ing scales in general, including Likert and semantic differential scales. One of the advantages of a Rasch analysis of such data from rating scales is that it enables us to convert the raw scores and plot the ratings on a new, constructed measurement scale which is a true interval scale. This enables us to compare how judges are interpreting the rating scale with which they are working.[7] As we saw from Figure 5.2 in Chapter 5, the movement along the continuum of the rating scale, from the point of view of the candidate, can be equated to climbing up stairs. How much ability (or proficiency, or whatever is being measured by the scale) is required to take the first step (that is, to be awarded a score in the next from lowest rating category rather than in the lowest category)? How much more ability is required to take the next step (that is, to score in the next higher category)? (We cannot assume that such steps are equivalent in height: the next step may be a relatively low or easy one, and the fol-lowing step may be a very high or demanding one.) The analysis made possible by Andrich's work enables us to calculate the exact *step difficulty* for each step (movement from one numbered rating category to the next higher one) on the scale. This kind of analysis is referred to as *Rating Scale analysis* (Andrich, 1978a, 1978b). From a practical point of view, Rating Scale analysis enables us to establish how the judges are interpret-ing each raw score point (each step) on the rating scale they are working with in general, that is, averaged across all items, and how consistent this interpretation is at each step.

Note that the term *Rating Scale model* is a technical label; it is not the only or even the most appropriate form of analysis for data from rating scales in general. The Partial Credit model (below) represents a refine-ment in that it allows analysis of step structure for *individual* items. Andrich's model by itself allows for interpretation of step structure aver-aged across judges as well as across items; combined with *multifaceted* analysis using Linacre's Extended model (below), it permits us to see how to look at average step structure for each judge individually.

9.2.2.3 *Partial Credit model (Masters)*

The second extension of the basic model to enable it to handle data from rating scales and items scored using partial credit scoring, was achieved in the work of another Australian, Geoff Masters, working with Ben Wright at the University of Chicago. Masters saw that the step structure of the rating scale, or the step structure of partial credit items, might vary from item to item or from one aspect of performance to the next. For example, in a language-testing context, judges may be asked to rate a number of aspects of a performance; consider the example from the OET above, in which ratings of *Overall communicative effectiveness* and *Fluency* are given, among others. Obviously, the step difficulty of ratings on one of these aspects of the performance may be independent of the step difficulty of ratings on the other aspect. For example, it may be that judges are unwilling to give marks readily in the top-scoring category for *Overall communicative effectiveness*; they may require a lot for a candidate to be considered in this category, whereas they may be more generous in scoring *Fluency*. Or consider the possibility that judges may be behaving inconsistently in their interpretation of relative step difficulty when judging *Fluency*, but being consistent in their interpretation of the equivalent steps in the scoring of *Overall communicative effectiveness*. Essentially, Masters's contribution was to enable the separate estimation of step difficulties for each item in a test, or each aspect of a performance, without averaging over items or generalizing over aspects. Master's model is called the *Partial Credit model* (Wright and Masters, 1982); the name is unfortunate as the use of this model is not restricted to partial credit items in the sense described above. It simply allows item-by-item analysis of step structure with items involving rating scale steps of any kind. In addition to making it possible to understand more finely the structure of rating scales in judgement tasks, a Partial Credit analysis enables us to examine the scoring structure of any individual items which have partial credit scoring in, let us say, a listening test. Such items can, as a result of the analysis, also be placed on the same scale of difficulty as other items in the test which are scored dichotomously; for example, we can see how difficult it is to score two points on a particular question relative to the difficulty of scoring a correct answer on a particular dichotomous item.

The Partial Credit model is the most general of the three models we have examined so far; the Basic model and the Rating Scale model may be seen as sub-sets of the Partial Credit model.[8]

Quest (Adams and Khoo, 1993) is a recent and quite user-friendly program for handling Partial Credit and Rating Scale analyses; it has the valuable mapping capacities which were discussed in Chapter 7. (It can also analyse data from dichotomously scored items.) The more cumbersome BIGSTEPS program (Wright and Linacre, 1991) is available to carry out Partial Credit analysis on IBM compatible microcomputers; it can also carry out Rating Scale analysis or analysis of dichotomously scored items if required.

9.2.2.4   *Extended (multi-faceted) model (Linacre)*

The most recent stage in the development of the family of Rasch models, known as many-faceted Rasch measurement (Linacre, 1989b), was introduced in Chapter 5. As we saw there, in this model, aspects (or *facets*) of the rating situation can be modelled and their effect on scores estimated. For example, characteristics of judges (the severity of particular judges, their consistency, the way they interpret the scoring scheme) are crucial in determining the pattern of scores allocated to candidates in a performance task, and these characteristics can be modelled in many-faceted measurement; this is only one example of a facet that might be modelled. FACETS (Linacre and Wright, 1992) is available to carry out the analysis on IBM compatible microcomputers. The multifaceted model is in fact now the most general Rasch model, and all other models can be derived from it.

9.3 Alternatives to Rasch models: the debate over 'parameters'

While Rasch models constitute a family of models, as we have seen, they are themselves only one development within the broader field of Item Response Theory (IRT) in general. As might be expected, debates have raged over the relative advantages of these models and alternative ones. This debate has been joined in general measurement,[9] and it has also surfaced in the language-testing literature (cf., for example, Choi and Bachman, 1992). In this section we will consider the nature of the debate, and the merits of the various positions. Participation in these debates as a reader, and the ability to make informed choices about models as a test developer and researcher, require an understanding at some level of the issues involved. We may note that the debate in fact seems to be abating in language testing now as the potential of multi-faceted measurement (only available within the Rasch tradition) for the analysis of data from language performance tests is increasingly recognized and exploited in research papers and the development of performance-testing procedures.

9.3.1 Item Response Theory

Item Response Theory (IRT) is a powerful general measurement theory which was developed in the 1950s and 1960s independently, it seems, in two different locations: by Alan Birnbaum in the United States and by the Danish mathematician Georg Rasch in Denmark. Rasch's work was promoted and extended by an American, Ben Wright, who attended a series of invitational lectures given by Rasch in Chicago in 1960 and became his pupil and the advocate of his ideas in North America (cf. Wright's account of the history of this relationship in Wright, 1988). Two main branches of Item Response Theory (or Latent Trait Theory as it is

sometimes still known), stemming from these two developmental traditions, are recognized. (Thorndike, 1982 gives a summary of the field.)
They differ theoretically and practically. The essential feature of both is
that they attempt to model statistically patterns in data from performances by candidates on test items, in order to draw conclusions about
the underlying difficulty of items and the underlying ability of candidates. They differ mainly in the number of item parameters (characteristics of the interaction between a test taker and a test item) being
estimated in the analysis: Rasch analysis considers one item parameter
(item difficulty), while other models consider one or more further
parameters (item discrimination, and a guessing factor). They also differ
theoretically in relation to the question of 'specific objectivity'. Each of
these points will now be considered in brief outline.

9.3.2   Parameters

Before discussing the difference between one-, two- and three-parameter
IRT models, it is important to realize that the debate over the appropriateness of the use of these models applies only where dichotomous data
are involved, such as the OET reading test data explored in Chapter 6.
Where test scores are the result of a subjective judging process involving
partial credit and rating scale data, as is typically the case in performance
testing (cf. Chapter 5), the issue does not arise as only the one-parameter
model can operationally deal with judge-mediated data at this time.

The *Rasch one-parameter model*, deriving from the work of Rasch
(Rasch, 1960 [1980]), is concerned with defining a single variable or
dimension on which to measure two variables: candidate ability and item
difficulty. The 'one-parameter' label is thus misleading, as *two* aspects of
the interaction between test taker and test item are estimated simultaneously in the analysis: *person* ability and *item* difficulty. However, by convention, IRT models are distinguished from each other by the number of
item characteristics that are being estimated. In traditional ('classical')
analysis of item characteristics, the discrimination of items (the extent to
which the item discriminates between higher and lower scoring candidates) is also calculated; this is (deliberately) not done directly in a Rasch
analysis. It is a requirement of the Rasch model that items are equally discriminating; this is unlikely to be the case in most tests, and has caused
some understandable consternation, even confusion, among language test
developers and researchers, to the point where some have questioned the
value of the Rasch model for the analysis of dichotomous data. In fact, as
we saw in the discussion of 'fit' in Chapter 6, the Rasch model is considerably more sophisticated in its treatment of item discrimination than

is often supposed,[10] and can in fact handle in a perfectly satisfactory manner data from items which do not conform to this assumption (as most will not). Information on how well the data being analysed conform (or otherwise) to the expectations of the model, and the consequences of such 'misfit', are routinely available as output from the analysis; in other words, there are built-in checks of the model's assumptions, the extent to which they are being violated, and the consequences of any such violation, in relation to any data set. The Rasch assumption should not be regarded as just a blindness to the facts, but should be seen as a deliberate simplifying working assumption. We will consider this issue further below.

The *two-parameter IRT model* (Birnbaum, 1968; Lord and Novick, 1968; Hambleton *et al.*, 1991) includes an additional item parameter of *discrimination*. The *three-parameter model* (Lord and Novick, 1968; Lord, 1980; Hambleton *et al.*, 1991) incorporates a further parameter, this time for *guessing*. As we have stated, the two- and three-parameter models are practically speaking restricted at this time to the analysis of data from dichotomous items (computer packages exist for the handling of polytomous items but they are extremely unwieldy and not widely used as yet).

Another practical advantage of the one-parameter Rasch model is that Rasch analysis can be done with smaller data sets than those required for the two- and three-parameter models. For example, Hulin, Lissak and Drasgow (1982) recommend a minimum of 30 items and 500 subjects for analysis with the two-parameter model, and 60 items and 1000 subjects with the three-parameter model; data sets smaller than these will prevent the successful execution of the program. Rasch analyses on dichotomous items can be carried out with a recommended minimum of 20 such items (Wright and Stone, 1979) and approximately 100 subjects, although larger data sets will enable more precise estimates. De Jong and Stoyanova (1994) have raised the issue of the data requirements for multi-faceted measurement, and have criticized some studies for their small data sets. Rasch programs can be successfully executed even with smaller data sets; the output from analyses with small data sets will indicate the resulting degree of imprecision of estimates, so that one is not left entirely in the dark about the consequences of data sets that do not meet the normal requirements. The relative imprecision of estimates of person ability and item difficulty may not matter for a range of practical and research purposes.

The fact that the one-parameter model does not estimate item discrimination and guessing parameters (in the case of dichotomously scored items) may not, in practice, be as significant as it may seem at first sight. As has been pointed out above, although the one-parameter model does not estimate item discrimination directly, information on discrimination is available indirectly from the results of the analysis in information on item 'fit', as was shown in Chapter 6. Additionally, although the three-parameter model is specifically designed to deal with guessing in multiple-choice format tests, the one-parameter model has been shown not to result in a high level of error even when guessing is a significant factor in the performance of candidates; in other words, the Rasch model is 'robust' (Izard, 1981; Choppin, 1982). On the other hand, Choi and Bachman (1992) have demonstrated that for a particular set of dichotomous data, the two- and three-parameter models showed consistently greater model–data fit than the one-parameter model, and argue against the use of the Rasch model with such data on these grounds; they also strongly recommend that the issue of model–data fit should be addressed in any study in which a choice of models is possible (that is, in which dichotomous data are involved). It is not clear nevertheless what the practical consequences of this lack of fit might be, for example, on ability estimates; this was not done in the Choi and Bachman (1992) study, and also needs to be investigated.

9.3.3 Rasch models and objective measurement: the property of 'specific objectivity'

There are also theoretical arguments in favour of using Rasch models over other IRT models: these relate to the property, unique to the Rasch model, of *specific objectivity* (Rasch, 1966). This is a technical term which is explained by Wilson (1991: 4) as follows:

> It should not matter who else is measured when you are measured, nor should it matter which particular measuring instruments are used to measure you, so long as they all belong to the relevant class. Rasch named this quality 'specific objectivity'.

Rasch (1961: 330–1) himself defines the features of 'objective measurement' (Wilson, 1991) in the following way:

> The comparison of two stimuli should be independent of which particular individuals were instrumental for the comparison; and it should also be independent of which other stimuli within the considered class were or might also have been compared. Symmetrically, a comparison between two individuals should be independent of which particular stimuli within the class considered were instrumental for the comparison; and it should also be independent of which other individuals were also compared, on the same or on some other occasion.

Put more technically, 'specific objectivity' refers to the model's assumption of the separability of the parameters of person ability and item difficulty (Griffin, 1985: 151; Wright and Masters, 1982: 6–8; Douglas, 1982: 130–1). This means that the probability of a candidate achieving a correct response (in the case of dichotomously scored items) or a certain level of score (in the case of polytomous items) is purely a question of the difference between the candidate's ability and the difficulty of the item or the difficulty of achieving a particular score level on an item.[11] In other words, to take the simplest case – that is, one involving dichotomous items – the Rasch model proposes that it is only the difference between candidate ability and item difficulty which determines the chances of a correct score.

We are now in a position to understand a little more clearly why a 'discrimination parameter' is deliberately absent in the Rasch model. The inclusion of discrimination would mean that the property of specific objectivity would be lost. Thus, the apparently rather perverse position the Rasch model adopts on the question of item discrimination has the great advantage that the *relative* difficulty of items (that is, the difficulty of items relative to each other for any pair of candidates) as estimated by the analysis remains invariant for all pairings of ability levels, and the *relative* abilities of individual candidates (that is, the abilities of candidates relative to each other for any pair of items) does not depend on which items we are considering. This means that for all candidates, we can map the order of difficulty of items, and a single order will result. Similarly, we can map the ability of candidates onto this single order. As we saw in Chapter 7, this mapping facility, which is characteristic of Rasch analysis, has many practical benefits.

It is worth explaining a little more about the connection between the lack of a discrimination parameter in the Rasch model and the kind of mapping that is available as a result of Rasch analysis, itself an outcome of the Rasch model's property of 'specific objectivity'. We saw that the basic, simplest model is the one that can handle data from dichotomous (right–wrong) items. In this model, the probability that a person will get a score of 1 (as against a score of 0) on a given item is the difference between the ability of the person taking the item and the difficulty of that item. When the person's ability is at least as great as the item difficulty, he or she has a 50 per cent chance or greater of getting the item correct (this is so by definition: the difficulty of an item is conventionally located at the point on the ability–difficulty continuum constructed by the analysis at which a person of a given ability has a 50 per cent chance of getting the item right). The chance will increase as the person's ability outstrips the item difficulty. Similarly, if an item's difficulty exceeds the person's ability, he or she will have a less than 50 per cent chance of getting the item correct, and their chances will diminish progressively as his or her ability falls short of the difficulty of the item. Table 6.7 in Chapter 6 gave some idea of the way in which a person's chance of success on an item is affected by that person's 'distance' from the difficulty of the item.

Figure 9.4 (adapted from Wright and Stone, 1979) demonstrates this relationship between person ability, item difficulty and the probability of a correct score. On the vertical axis (the y-axis) is mapped the probability of a person giving a correct response.[12] The horizontal axis (the x-axis) represents the difference between a person's ability and the difficulty of an item.[13] The rising line traces the increasing probability of a correct response as the difference between the person's ability and the difficulty of the item changes.

The probability of a person producing a particular kind of response to an item is a function, then, of the difficulty of that item relative to the person's ability. Figure 9.5 shows an Item Characteristic Curve (ICC) for one dichotomous item. The probability of a correct response on the item, represented on the y-axis, is a function of the ability of the individual taking the item, represented on the x-axis. The discrimination of the item may be represented by the slope of the curve. This means that the steeper the slope of the ICC for an item, the higher the discrimination of that item. Let us consider two items which differ in their discrimination to see how this works (Figures 9.6 and 9.7).

The item in Figure 9.6 has a moderate level of discrimination – that is, as we move along the ability continuum represented on the x-axis, the chances of answering the item correctly increase only gradually; in other words, there is not a great deal of difference in the probability of a correct response from relatively more able and relatively less able candidates. In

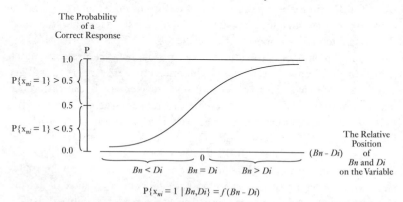

FIGURE 9.4   Relationship of probability of success on an item to the difference between person ability and item difficulty (adapted from Wright and Stone, 1979: 14)

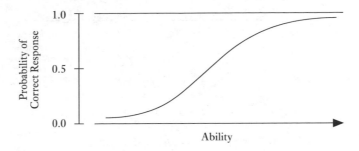

FIGURE 9.5   Item characteristic curve (ICC) for a single dichotomous item

the item in Figure 9.7, on the other hand, a relatively modest increase in ability more dramatically increases the chances of answering the item correctly; in other words, the item distinguishes more sharply between relatively more able and less able candidates.

Now let us take the case of two items (A and B) of equal discrimination, whose ICCs are plotted in Figure 9.8. Let us take two individuals of differing ability, b_1 and b_2. For each of the two items, the chances are greater for the more able candidate (b_2) of getting the item right. In other words, the relative difficulty of the items for pairs of candidates at any two levels of ability does not depend on which candidate is answering them; the items represent a continuum of difficulty which is consistent regardless of who is attempting the items. Relative item difficulty is independent of the ability of candidates

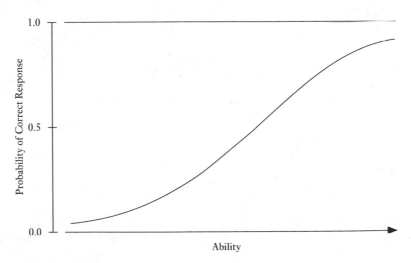

FIGURE 9.6   ICC for a moderately discriminating dichotomous item

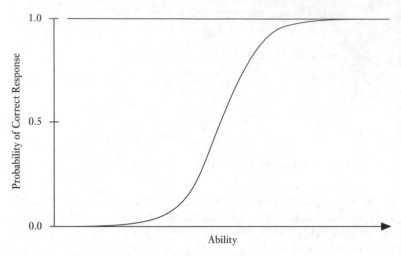

FIGURE 9.7   ICC for sharply discriminating dichotomous items

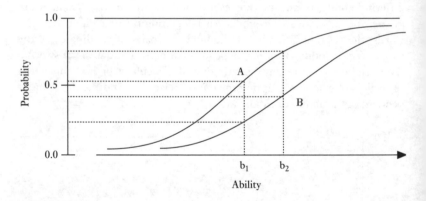

FIGURE 9.8   ICCs for two dichotomous items of equal discrimination

Consider, however, the case in which items differ in their discrimination. As the slopes of the ICCs reflect this discrimination, there will be a point at which the ICCs, as they are no longer parallel, cross over. Figure 9.9 represents items (C and D) in which this is the case.

Now let us consider again the relative ability of two candidates. We find that the situation is now more complicated. If we consider the chances of a candidate (b_3) whose ability lies to the left of the cross-over point, we can say that Item C is more difficult than Item D; the chances of an individual of that ability level scoring a correct response are lower for Item C than for Item D. However, if we consider the case of a person (b_4) whose ability

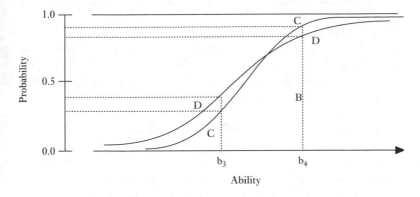

FIGURE 9.9   ICCs for two dichotomous items of differing discrimination

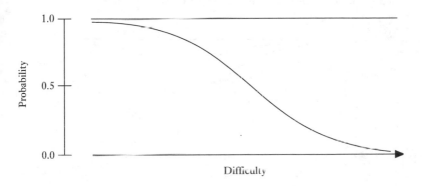

FIGURE 9.10   Person characteristic curve (PCC)

level lies to the right of the cross-over point, we find that the order of difficulty of the items is reversed. This candidate has a higher chance of scoring a correct response on Item C than on Item D; that is, Item C is easier that Item D. In other words, the relative difficulty of items is dependent on the ability of the individual we happen to be considering.

The same thing is true for estimates of ability. Consider the plot of the probability of a correct response on items of increasing difficulty by a person of a given ability: this plot is called a Person Characteristic Curve (PCC) (Figure 9.10).

Now let us consider PCCs for a pair of individuals (J and K) in the case where item discrimination is invariant; the curves will be parallel (Figure 9.11). This means that the relative abilities of individuals do not depend on the items chosen. At any point on the item difficulty scale, Person K will have a greater chance of giving a correct response than Person J; the estimates of their abilities are independent of which items are being considered.

However, in the case where item discrimination varies, we have the situation illustrated in Figure 9.12. In this case, the relative abilities of the two individuals (L and M) being measured depends on which items we are considering. For example, in the case of an item (d_1) to the left of the cross-over point, we find that Person L is more able than Person M, because Person L has a higher chance of giving a correct response than Person M does. However if we choose an item (d_2) to the right of the cross-over point, then the relative abilities of the two individuals are reversed: M has a higher probability of getting such an item correct. We cannot answer the question, 'Who is the more able individual?' Or rather, we have to answer 'It depends on the items on which you test them'. Similarly above, we cannot say 'Which item is more difficult?' Again, the answer will be, 'It depends on the people on whom you test them'.

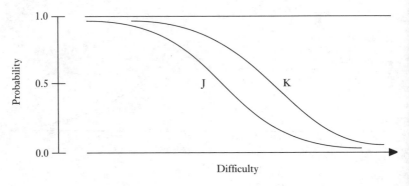

FIGURE 9.11   Pair of PCCs with equal slopes

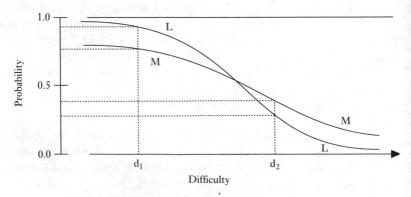

FIGURE 9.12   Pair of PCCs with unequal slopes

In the case where item discriminations are allowed to vary, it is not possible to provide a general mapping of ability and difficulty in the way we would prefer, because the maps will vary according to individuals. For example, in Figure 9.13, we have item difficulty maps for two individuals in such a case; the relative ordering of items in terms of difficulty differs in each case.

Similarly, in Figure 9.14, we have two person ability maps, one for each of two items with differing discriminations, in which the persons are ranked in different orders.

So in order to make use of the mapping facility discussed in Chapter 7, we have to assume consistency of item discrimination. This is obviously a simplification of reality; but it is a convenient one, for the reasons just outlined. All models are simplifications of reality; they are to be judged in terms of their usefulness for our purpose. This point will be developed further below. The Rasch analysis represents a convenient simplification and averaging over individuals in order to secure certain practical advantages, in this case in terms of mapping.

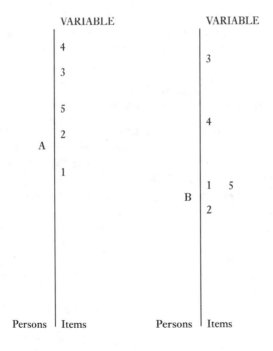

FIGURE 9.13   Possible item difficulty maps for two individuals on the same set of items

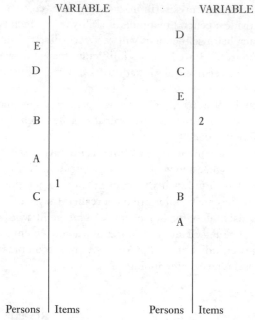

FIGURE 9.14   Possible person ability maps for the same set of persons on two items

9.4 Rasch models and language test data: the debate over 'constructs' and 'dimensionality'

A more broadly based objection to Rasch models, and by implication to all IRT models, is that their assumptions, in particular the so-called 'uni-dimensionality' assumption, are inappropriate to the analysis of language test data (Hamp-Lyons, 1989; Buck, 1992, 1994).[14] Skehan (1989: 4) expresses reservations about the appropriateness of Rasch analysis in the context of ESP testing, given what we know about the complexity of the 'enabling skills' involved in, for example, comprehension tasks in EAP contexts. This problem is not, of course, restricted to ESP contexts: as Skehan (1984: 216) remarks in the context of a discussion of criterion-referencing: 'The problem is, fundamentally, that any language performance that is worthy of interest will be complex and multidimensional.'

The issue of unidimensionality will be discussed in detail below. More broadly, applied linguists have been anxious to warn against what they see as the danger that narrowly based measurement approaches will lead researchers and test developers to ignore fundamental questions of validity. For example, writers such as Nunan (1987b, 1989) have been concerned at what they see as the danger that the impressive power and sophistication of the technical analysis of Rasch measurement will distract from a recognition of fundamental misconceptions about the validity of test constructs, or the undesirable pedagogical implications of the introduction of tests of a certain type.

This latter, more general, issue is raised by a study by de Jong and Glas (1987), which illustrates both the potential of Rasch analysis for the examination of test constructs, and the possible pitfalls in the interpretation of the results of such an analysis. The researchers examined the construct validity of tests of foreign language listening comprehension by comparing the performance of native and non-native speakers on the tests. It was hypothesized in this work that native speakers would have a greater chance of scoring correct answers on items: this was largely borne out by the data. Moreover, an interpretation of item misfit was offered in terms of this distinction between the performance of native and non-native speakers: on 'misfitting' items native speaker performance would show greater overlap with the performance of non-native speakers than was the case on items with acceptable fit values. This hypothesis was also supported by the results.

The researchers concluded (de Jong and Glas, 1987: 191):

> The ability to evaluate a given fragment of discourse in order to understand what someone is meaning to say cannot be measured along the same dimension as the ability to understand aurally perceived text at the literal level. Items requiring literal understanding discriminate better between native speakers and non-native learners of a language and are therefore better measures of foreign language listening comprehension.

This finding is provocative, as it seems to go against current views on the role of inferencing processes and reader/listener schemata in comprehension (cf. Carrell *et al.*, 1988; Widdowson, 1983; Nunan, 1987a). Looking at the issue another way, one might argue that the analysis has simply confirmed the erroneous assumption that the essential dimension of measurement is whatever distinguishes the listening abilities of native- and non-native speakers. As the data in Chapter 7 showed, there is in fact likely to be considerable overlap between the abilities of native and non-native speakers in higher-level cognitive tasks involved in discourse comprehension. If the analysis of listening test data reveals that all test items fail to lie on a single measurement dimension of listening ability, then this may be a reflection of the multi-dimensional nature of listening comprehension in a foreign language and should be acknowledged. The point is that interpretation of the results of Rasch analysis must be informed by an in-principle understanding of the relevant constructs.[15]

9.4.1 Rasch analysis and the 'unidimensionality assumption'

In this section, we will consider the debate about the 'unidimensionality assumption' in Rasch models. What is unidimensionality? Let us consider the performance of children on a mathematics test, which consists of items of two basic types: items where figures only are used ('naked number' problems) and items where the problem is presented in a real-world context, thus involving language ('worded' problems). Imagine that students taking the test come from two linguistic backgrounds: in the first group (Group A), children are native speakers of the language of the test (e.g. English) and have few problems in understanding the language in which the worded problems are presented; in the second group (group B), the children are recently arrived immigrants who have studied mathematics in their country of origin but who have varying degrees of difficulty with the language of the test. Performance on the test will be inconsistent for the latter group compared with the former. For example, assume that the ranking of four students from each group on the basis of the 'naked number' problems only is as shown in Table 9.2. It looks as if the students from Group B are more able. However, Table 9.3 shows the way in which the rankings emerge when we include performance on the 'worded' problems as well as on the 'naked number' problems.

TABLE 9.2

Rank	Student No.	Group
1	5	B
2	8	B
3	1	A
4	6	B
5	7	B
6	4	A
7	3	A
8	2	A

TABLE 9.3

Rank	Student No.	Group
1	1	A
2	4	A
3	3	A
4	5	B
5	2	A
6	6	B
7	7	B
8	8	B

The picture is now different: it looks as if the native speaker group (Group A) is the more able. Within that group, the relative positions of its four members have remained constant across the two types of problem; that is, students who are better on one type tend also to be better on the other type. This is not so true for the non-native speaker group (Group B); their relative rankings across the two types of problem have changed.

Clearly, no single thing is being measured in this test as a whole: it is a test of language as much as it is a test of mathematical knowledge. Moreover, *within* the native speaker student group, the two types of item seem to be measuring the same kind of ability – the rankings of the candidate across the two types of item remain constant. This is not so within the non-native speaker group, where differing degrees of proficiency in the language result in different outcomes on the worded problem items in the test compared with the other type of item. To the extent that this was unintended by the test constructors, then the test is invalid as a test of mathematics; language skill is obscuring our picture of the ability of individual students to handle mathematical problems. Across the whole test-taking population (Groups A and B combined), and for the non-native speaker group, the test is not unidimensional in a construct sense, nor is it unidimensional in a measurement sense (no single consistent pattern of item difficulty or person ability is emerging from the matrix of student responses to the test items). For the native speaker group considered separately, however, the test *is* unidimensional in terms of measurement, despite the existence of the two item types: a single pattern of ability emerges for this group across all the items in the test.

The term 'unidimensionality' thus has two separate meanings (McNamara, 1991; Henning, 1992). It is used in *psychology* to refer to a single underlying (psychological) construct or trait and in *measurement* to refer to a single underlying measurement dimension; loosely, a single underlying pattern of scores in the data matrix. (We saw such an emergent overriding single pattern in the data matrix in Table 6.4 in Chapter 6; the pattern was sufficiently strong that it could be identified by a visual inspection of the matrix once it had been organized in a·particular way.) Rasch analysis assumes (or rather, looks for) unidimensionality in this latter measurement sense only; but there is nothing unusual about this. *All analyses which involve the summing of scores across different items or different test parts make the same assumption.* It should be pointed out, for example, that classical item analysis makes the 'assumption' of unidimensionality, but, unlike Rasch analysis, lacks tests of this 'assumption' to signal violations of it (through 'fit' statistics; see Chapter 6, and below). It will be argued here that this distinction between the two senses of unidimensionality is critical in understanding the question of the validity of Rasch models for the analysis of language test data.

We can consider the role of each of these meanings in relation to the example just given. At the test design and construction stage, the test developers must have formulated an idea of what the test was measuring (the test *construct*). It was presumably something like 'mathematical ability' or 'mathematical ability in relation to a particular domain of mathematical knowledge and skill'. They may not have been aware at the time of the fact that they had also designed a language test. The analysis of the data attempted to find *psychometric* (measurement) unidimensionality in the data – a single clear emergent pattern of scores on the items – but failed to find it; instead, multi-dimensionality was discovered in the data. This search for unidimensionality and the failure to find it is then fed back to the test designers, who can then interpret the failure to establish statistical unidimensionality in the light of their understanding of what is involved in answering the test items; they would presumably then become aware of the fact that the items causing the problem were ones in which a certain level of language proficiency was required. They are then faced with a difficult decision – which again can only be made in the light of the theory and principles of the teaching of mathematics – about whether the ability to handle worded problems in the language of the local educational system is a necessary part of the mathematical skill being developed in that system. If so, they will decide to retain the worded problems, but it would be necessary to report the scores on the two item types separately, as they do not go together, at least for the whole group of test takers: the two types of item are apples and oranges, so to speak, and scores on the items cannot simply be added together from the measurement point of view, at least for the non-native speakers, and therefore for the test takers as a whole.[16]

We have then a kind of interplay between two sources of insight into what the test is measuring:

(1) the professional and theoretical knowledge and skill of the test developers, who will have (*a priori*) theories of the construct(s) underlying their tests at the test design stage and who will interpret the output of the data analysis in the light of their understanding of these constructs; and

(2) the empirical evidence from data analysis (*a posteriori* evidence) which may confirm or disconfirm the claims for the construct validity of the test made by the test constructors.

There should be no real danger that the former will somehow 'swamp' the latter; criticisms of studies using Rasch measurement are most profitably directed not at the measurement model, but at the applied linguistics of the study, if that is the problem, as it so often will be. There is more, rather than less, need for applied linguistics expertise in such studies. The problem is sometimes that applied linguists, untrained in measurement, lack confidence in tackling the issues raised in these studies; it is hoped that this book will contribute to changing this state of affairs.

A further issue arises when the data analysis establishes a single *measurement* dimension where it is proposed that multiple psychological constructs are involved. This is likely to happen where performances of test takers on the separate constructs are correlated. In this case we cannot of course argue that the test developers or theorists are wrong about the multiplicity of constructs involved, but that the multiplicity of constructs has not prevented a single, orderly measurement process being achieved. After all, every human activity is bound to be made up of countless different sub-skills, not all of which it is desirable to measure separately (indeed, it may not be possible even to conceptualize them). Given then that psychometric and psychological unidimensionality do not map onto one another in any simple one-to-one fashion, the question arises as to how sensitive the Rasch measurement model is to departures from unidimensionality in the data, which may perhaps be open to interpretation in terms of test constructs. This is both a theoretical and an empirical question: it has to do with the 'robustness' of the measurement model, and can be addressed empirically: In what circumstances is multi-dimensionality in the data signalled in practice? We will consider these issues below.

Let us now consider the debate about Rasch measurement and unidimensionality in the language-testing literature. It will be considered first in relation to an example, the Interview Test of English as a Second Language (ITESL) (Adams, Griffin and Martin, 1987), which used Rasch analysis in its development and was the focus of such debate when it first appeared. The test is an oral placement procedure for elementary and intermediate level adult learners of ESL, in which mastery of particular points of grammar is tested in the context of very controlled, short spoken tasks. Griffin *et al.* (1988: 12) argue that their research confirms the existence of a hypothesized 'developmental dimension of grammatical competence ... in English S[econd] L[anguage] A[cquisition]'. Spolsky (1988: 123), in a generally highly favourable review of the test, urges some caution in relation to the claims for its construct validity:

> The authors use their results to argue for the existence of a grammatical proficiency dimension, but some of the items are somewhat more general. The nouns, verbs and adjectives items for instance are more usually classified as vocabulary. One would have liked to see different kinds of items added until the procedure showed that the limit of the unidimensionality criterion had now been reached.

Although on the face of it this comment about the test content may seem reasonable, it is worth noting that many grammarians do not make such a sharp distinction between 'grammar' and 'vocabulary' (cf. Halliday's lexico-grammar: Halliday, 1978).

In contrast to Spolsky, Nunan (1988: 56) is sweepingly dismissive of the test: 'The major problem that I have with the test ... [is] that it fails adequately to reflect the realities and complexities of language development.' It is not clear what would constitute an 'adequate' reflection of these 'realities and complexities', or how it could be incorporated into test design. The comment reflects a failure to recognize the tension between the two types of model referred to above (in this case, the measurement model and models of second language acquisition), and the implications of this for test development.

Hamp-Lyons (1989: 117) is equally trenchant, and perhaps equally unfair: 'This study ... is a backward step for both language testing and language teaching.' A number of grounds are put forward for this view. First, Hamp-Lyons takes the writers to task for failing to characterize properly the dimension of 'grammatical competence' which the study claims to have validated, and shares Nunan's and Spolsky's anxieties about the homogeneity of items included in the test. But this is perhaps simply a question of revision of the test content. Secondly, she argues against the logic of the design of the research project (1989: 115):

> Their assumption that if the data fit the psychometric model they de facto validate the model of separable grammatical competence is questionable. If you construct a test to test a single dimension and then find that it does indeed test a single dimension, how can you conclude that this dimension exists independently of other language variables? The unidimensionality, if that is really what it is, is an artifact of the test development.

It seems that here, too, rather different senses of the term 'dimension' are being confused: as was argued above, it is crucial to distinguish between dimensions in *psychological* models and dimensions in *measurement*. Also, it is not clear from Adams *et al.* (1987) that claims about separability and independence are in fact being made.

Hamp-Lyons (1989: 114) warns the developers of the ITESL test that they have a responsibility to acknowledge

> the limitations of the partial credit model, especially the question of the unidimensionality assumption of the partial credit model, the conditions under which that assumption can be said to be violated, and the significance of this for the psycholinguistic questions they are

investigating. ... They need to note that the model is very robust to violations of unidimensionality.

It seems that Hamp-Lyons may have misinterpreted the claims of the model. The 'assumption' of unidimensionality underlying Rasch model applications is not an *a priori* requirement to perform the analysis. Rather, the model hypothesizes (but does not assume in the sense of 'take for granted' or 'require') a single *measurement* dimension of ability and difficulty. Its analysis of test data represents a test of this hypothesis in relation to the data. As we saw in Chapter 6, the function of the fit statistics (mean square or t), a feature of Rasch analysis, is to indicate the probability of a particular pattern of responses (to an item or on the part of an individual) in the case that this hypothesis is true. Extreme mean square or t values are an indication that the hypothesis is unlikely to be true for the item or the individual concerned. If items or individuals are found in this way to be disconfirming the hypothesis, this fact may be interpreted in a number of ways. In relation to items, it may indicate (1) that the item is poorly constructed; or (2) that if the item is well constructed, it does not form part of the same dimension as defined by other items in the test, and is therefore measuring a different construct or trait. In relation to persons, it may indicate (1) that the performance on a particular item was not indicative of the candidate's ability in general, and may have been the result of irrelevant factors such as fatigue, inattention, failure to take the test item seriously, factors which Henning (1987a: 96) groups under the heading of response validity; (2) that the ability of the candidates involved cannot be measured appropriately by the test instrument, that the pattern of responses cannot be explained in the same terms as applied to other candidates, that is, there is a heterogeneous test population in terms of the hypothesis under consideration; (3) that there may be surprising gaps in the candidate's knowledge of the areas covered by the test; this information can then be used for diagnostic and remedial purposes.

Further, and crucially, the dimension defined in Rasch analysis is a measurement dimension which is constructed by the analysis, and must be distinguished from dimensions of underlying knowledge or ability which may be hypothesized on other, theoretical grounds. Rasch analyses do not 'discover' or 'reveal' existing underlying dimensions, but rather construct dimensions for the purposes of measurement on the basis of test performance.[17] The relationship between these two conceptions of dimensionality has been discussed in general terms above, and will be discussed further below.

Hamp-Lyons is in effect arguing, then, that Rasch analysis is insufficiently sensitive in its ability to detect in the data departures from its hypothesis about an underlying ability–difficulty measurement continuum. The evidence for this claim, she argues, is in a paper by Henning *et al.* (1985), in which the appropriateness of Rasch analysis with its attempt to construct a single dimension is investigated in the light of the fact that in language test data (Henning *et al.*, 1985: 142)

> examinee performance is confounded with many cognitive and affective test factors such as test wiseness, cognitive style, test-taking strategy, fatigue, motivation and anxiety. Thus, no test can strictly be said to measure one and only one trait.

In fact, it should be noted that the role of these factors, usefully grouped together elsewhere by Henning (1987a) under the heading of *response validity*, is not the only or even the most important basis for objection to the supposedly unidimensional nature of performance on language tests. The more usual argument is that the linguistic and general reasoning skills underlying performance on language tests cannot be conceptualized as being of one type (cf. Skehan, 1989: 4).

Henning *et al.* examined performance of some 300 candidates on the UCLA English as a Second Language Placement Examination (ESLPE). There were 150 multiple-choice items, 30 in each of five sub-tests: listening comprehension, reading comprehension, grammar accuracy, vocabulary recognition and writing error detection. Relatively few details of each sub-test are provided, although we may conclude that the first two sub-tests focus on language use and the other three on language usage. This assumes that inferencing is required to answer questions in the first two sub-tests; it is of course quite possible that the questions mostly involve processing of literal meaning only, and in that sense these sub-tests are rather more like the other sub-tests (cf. the discussion of this point in relation to de Jong and Glas (1987) above). The data were analysed using the Rasch one-parameter model (Rasch, 1960 [1980]), and although this is not reported in detail, it is clear from Table 2 on p. 153 of the paper that 11 misfitting items were found, with the distribution over the sub-tests as follows: listening, 4; reading, 4; grammar, 1; vocabulary, 3; writing error detection, 3. (Interestingly, the highest numbers of misfitting items were in the listening and reading sub-tests.) One might reasonably conclude that the majority of test items may be used to construct a single continuum of ability and difficulty. We must say 'the majority' because in fact the Rasch analysis does identify a number of items as not contributing to the definition of a single measurement dimension; unfortunately, no analysis is offered of these items, so we are unable to conclude whether they fall into the category of poorly written items or into the category of sound items which define some different kind of ability. On the other hand, the ESLPE items were developed and reviewed by committee prior to administration (Henning, personal communication), so the latter explanation is perhaps more likely. It is not clear what the dimension so defined should be called; as stated above, investigation of what is required to answer the items, particularly in the reading and listening comprehension sub-tests, is needed. In order to gain independent evidence for the successful construction in the Rasch analysis of a single dimension for measuring performance on the majority of items in the test, Henning *et al.* report two other findings. First, factor analytic studies on previous versions of the test showed that the test as a whole demonstrated a single factor solution. Secondly, the application of a technique known as the Bejar technique for exploring the dimensionality of the test battery appeared to confirm the Rasch analysis findings.[18] Henning *et al.* conclude that the fact that a single dimension of ability and difficulty was defined by the Rasch analysis of their data, despite the apparent diversity of the language sub-skills included in the tests, shows that Rasch analysis is (Henning *et al.*, 1985: 152) 'sufficiently robust with regard to the assumption of unidimensionality to permit applications to the development and analysis of language tests'. Note that the robustness has no longer to do with response validity factors, as had been proposed earlier, but with the fact that a single measurement dimension can be constructed from performance on a battery of language tests designed to sample a range of arguably rather diverse language skills; we are here closer to the usual grounds for objection to the appropriateness of Rasch models for use with language test data.

The problem here, as Hamp-Lyons is right to point out, is that what Henning *et al.* call 'robustness' and take to be a virtue, leads to conclusions which, looked at from another point of view, seem worrying. That is, the unidimensional construct defined by the test analysis seems in some sense to be at odds with the *a priori* construct validity, or at least the face validity, of the test being analysed. Whether there is in fact disagreement between the two sources of validation – *a priori* and empirical – is unclear; as has been shown above, it is somewhat difficult to decide what the results of the Rasch analysis in the Henning *et al.* study should lead us to conclude in term of test dimensionality. More information is needed on the nature of tests items, particularly those identified as misfitting; the test's *a priori* construct validity in terms of a single dimension is plausible on one reading of the sub-tests' content. Clearly, as the results of the study by de Jong and Glas (1987) discussed above show (and whether or not we agree with their interpretation of those results), Rasch analysis is capable of defining different dimensions of ability within a test of a single language sub-skill, and is not necessarily 'robust' in that sense – that is, the sense that troubles Hamp-Lyons.

Further evidence of this is provided in a study by O'Loughlin (1992),[19] who designed a comprehension-based writing task and scored the following as separate items: (1) *comprehension of the stimulus texts*, (2) *evaluation of argument*, (3) *overall task fulfilment*, (4) *arguments and evidence*, (5) *organization*, (6) *grammar and cohesion*, (7) *appropriateness* and (8) *spelling and punctuation*. When the items were analysed together, responses to the item *comprehension of the stimulus texts* were found not to fit the dimension of ability which could be constructed from responses to the other items. Productive writing skills and comprehension skills, in other words, appeared to represent different dimensions in the analysis; *psychometric* multi-dimensionality was found in the *data*, and this could readily be interpreted in terms of multi-dimensionality of *construct*. O'Loughlin therefore decided to report comprehension scores separately from writing ability scores. (When the first two items were analysed separately they showed good fit.) When the items focusing on productive skills in writing were analysed without the inclusion of the responses on the comprehension items, responses on the item *spelling and punctuation* were found to be mildly misfitting – that is, another level of multi-dimensionality was revealed in the data; again, it was easy to interpret this in the light of our understanding of the components of the writing skill, as this item focuses on mechanical aspects involved in the surface editing of text, rather than in the expressive aspects of writing. It may be wondered why this item was not misfitting in the original analysis. The answer is that this more subtle degree of multi-dimensionality was masked by the grosser level of multi-dimensionality apparent in the first analysis. In other words, scores on the item *spelling and punctuation* were more closely correlated with performance on the other items involving productive writing skills than on the comprehension items; so scores on *spelling and punctuation* clustered more with the other writing skill scores rather than with the comprehension scores. When the comprehension scores were removed, the diversity within the 'writing' cluster became clearer.

Multi-dimensionality in data sets is therefore a relative matter. The more that disparate things are thrown together in the analysis, the more the analysis will try to fit all the elements together, and the more difficult it will be to get any clear view of detail. It is like trying to take a photograph to include a family group in the left middle ground and a church in the right background. You can only fit them both in by standing well back, in which case it may be difficult to recognize detail on the faces of the family members. But if we abandon the attempt to include the church, and focus just on the family group, a lot more detail can be revealed. A further example of the point is to be found in the results of a recent survey of social attitudes among the majority community to minority ethnic groups (both Aboriginal and immigrant) in Australia. When the data on the majority attitudes to the Aboriginal minority (a heavily stigmatized group) were included, no differences could be seen in attitudes to the immigrant groups; these differences were, by comparison, too fine-grained to count. When the data on attitudes to Aborigines were not included, then an elaborate 'pecking order' of majority attitudes to different immigrant groups was revealed. It is, in other words, a matter of perspective.

It seems, then, that the Rasch model, for all its robustness, is capable of detecting psychometric multi-dimensionality in the data, which can then be interpreted in the light of views on the nature of the skills and abilities involved which would account for the observed multi-dimensionality. Henning (1988: 95), using an artificially constructed multi-dimensional data set, showed that Rasch analysis was as sensitive to the multi-dimensionality in the data as factor analysis, principal components analysis and other non-Rasch-based techniques.

To sum up the argument being made in this section: it is crucial to the discussion of unidimensionality to distinguish consistently between two types of model: a measurement model and a model of the various skills and abilities potentially underlying test performance. The measurement model posited and tested by Rasch analysis deals with the question, 'Does it make sense in measurement terms to sum scores on different parts of the test? Can all items be summed meaningfully? Are all candidates being measured in the same terms?' This is the 'unidimensionality' assumption (made also within traditional ('classical') analysis); the alternative position requires us to say that separate, qualitative statements about performance on each test item, and of each candidate, are the only valid basis for reporting test performance. As for the interpretation of test scores, this must be done in the light of our best understanding of the nature of language abilities, that is, in the light of current models of the constructs underlying test performance. *A priori* models of this latter type are in a kind of critical tension with the findings of empirical analysis based on measurement models such as the Rasch model, and both kinds of analysis have the potential to illuminate the nature of what is being measured in a particular language test.

One can go further and say that even when it is clear that the assumptions of the measurement model are at variance with what is known independently of the nature of the abilities being measured, a useful measurement instrument may still be constructed. Choppin (1982: 46) has pointed out that modelling of abilities in this way may be compared to the creation of two-dimensional maps to represent distances and areas on the earth's surface. Even when it is known that the assumption of flatness is incorrect, that is, the model is at variance with what is known of the reality being modelled, such maps are useful and adequate for most purposes. It is not a question either of it being necessary to know to what extent our measurement model involves a simplification or distortion; all scientific models are approximate representations of reality, wittingly or unwittingly.

Henning (1992) presents data in support of the view taken here. As we have done, he distinguishes *psychological* from *psychometric unidimensionality*. The former he defines in the following way (Henning, 1992: 2):

> Psychological unidimensionality in a test implies that the test scores are intended to be interpreted as reflective of the extent of the presence of some known unitary psychological construct or trait. ... Inferences may be drawn about the extent of the presence of the intended construct from item performance.

Psychometric unidimensionality, on the other hand (Henning, 1992: 3),

> can be present when the test measures a variety of correlated underlying psychological dimensions ... even when there is no explicit interpretation possible of the primary dimension said to be measured, apart from the operational definition of the items themselves.

Henning produces artificially constructed data sets in which he shows that psychological unidimensionality may be present in the context of psychometric multi-dimensionality, and, more importantly for the present discussion, that psychometric unidimensionality may be present in the context of psychological multi-dimensionality. Henning (1992: 9) concludes that

> since test modelling procedures involving item response theory assume psychometric unidimensionality rather than psychological unidimensionality, it is apparent that such procedures need not be restricted from application to most language testing data that may be psychologically multidimensional in character.

Henning (1992: 10) presents a strong case for the independence of psychometric and psychological dimensionality:

> Psychometric unidimensionality may be present without any theoretically satisfying definition of the single dimension said to be measured, other than the operational definition provided by the items themselves. It is also possible that items and persons could be chosen so as to satisfy the psychometric demands of unidimensionality even though the items may be highly diverse in content focus (i.e., may lack psychological unidimensionality) and the persons may be highly varied in age, intelligence, native language and educational background.

It seems, then, that criticisms of Rasch analysis on the score of uni-dimensionality by Hamp-Lyons, Buck and others are unwarranted, although, as stated above, results always need to be interpreted in ,the light of independent theoretical perspectives. In fact, independent evid-ence (for·example, via factor analysis) may be sought for the conclusions of a Rasch analysis when there are grounds for doubting them, for example when they appear to overturn long- or dearly-held beliefs about the nature of aspects of language proficiency. Also, without wishing to enter into what Hamp-Lyons (1989: 114) calls 'the hoary issue of whether language competence is unitary or divisible', it is clear that there is likely to be a degree of commonality or shared variance on tests of language proficiency of various types, particularly at advanced levels (cf. the dis-cussions in Henning (1989: 98) and de Jong and Henning (1990) of evid-ence in relation to this point.)

9.5 Test dimensionality and ESP tests

As ESP tests are a particularly important type of performance test, it is necessary for the argument of this book to respond to the view expressed by Skehan (1989) that ESP tests in particular represent an inappropriate context for analyses which require an assumption of unidimensionality, given what we know of 'the dimensions of proficiency or enabling skills in ESP' (Skehan, 1989: 4). This issue can, as we have argued, be investi-gated empirically. In this final part of the chapter, we will report on such a study, in the context of the 50-minute Listening sub-test of the Occupational English Test.

This sub-test has two parts, each intended to test a different aspect of the listening skill in the occupational settings of health professionals. Part A involves listening to a talk on a professionally relevant subject. There are approximately 12 short answer questions, some with several parts; the maximum attainable score on this part of the test is usually about 25. Part B involves listening to a consultation between a general practitioner and a patient. There are approximately 20 short answer questions (again, some have several parts); the maximum score here is usually 25, giving a total maximum attainable score of approximately 50 on 32 items.

One hundred and ninety-six candidates took the listening sub-test in August 1987, using materials which had been trialled and revised prior to the test administration.[20] Part A of the test consisted of short answer ques-tions on a talk about communication between different groups of health professionals in hospital settings. Part B of the test involved a guided his-tory taking in note form, based on a recording of a consultation between a doctor and a patient suffering from headaches subsequent to a serious car accident two years previously. Part A thus required candidates to follow an abstract monologic discourse, and items on this part of the test were found to be relatively difficult, whereas Part B involved understanding details of concrete events and personal circumstances in the case history, within the context of a dialogue. The two types of listening task can be viewed in terms of the continua of more or less cognitively demanding and more or less context embedded tasks proposed by Cummins (1984).

Data from performances of the candidates were analysed using the Rasch Partial Credit model, and the results were considered in the light of the following questions:

> Given that different kinds of listening task are represented in the two parts of the sub-test, that is, the test is multi-dimensional from a *construct* point of view, is it possible to construct a single *measurement* dimension of 'listening ability within professional contexts' from the data from the sub-test as a whole? Does it make sense to add the scores from the two parts of the listening sub-test? That is, is the listening sub-test psychometrically unidimensional?

Two sorts of evidence were available in relation to these questions. Candidates' responses were analysed twice.

In the first analysis, data from Parts A and B were combined, and estimates of item difficulty and person ability were calculated (that is, the test was assumed to be unidimensional from a psychometric point of view). Information about departures from unidimensionality were available in the usual form of information about item and person misfit (see Chapter 6 for an explanation of these concepts). Two items (both on Part A) out of a total of 50 items were found to be 'misfitting'; and two candidates showed unacceptable fit (well within the expected extent of such misfit: cf. Pollitt and Hutchinson, 1987: 82). When the test data are treated as a single test, then, all the items except two combine to form a single measurement dimension, and the overwhelming majority of candidates can be measured meaningfully in terms of the dimension of ability so constructed. On the basis of this standard analysis, our questions have been answered in the affirmative.

In order to confirm this result, a second analysis was carried out, in which Part A and Part B were treated as separate tests, and estimates of item difficulty and person ability were made on the basis of each test separately. Following Wright and Masters (1982: 114–17), if the test as a whole is unidimensional, then it should be possible to produce estimates of person ability using items from different parts of the test, and the estimates should be identical (allowing for the inevitable measurement error in each case). Two different types of statistical test were carried out on the two sets of person ability estimates, and were found to provide further strong support for the assumption of psychometric unidimensionality in the test as a whole. Details of the study and of the statistical tests used are provided in McNamara (1991). It seems, then, that the misgivings expressed by Skehan (1989) are unfounded in terms of the empirical evidence of the psychometric properties of the analysis. It is appropriate, in other words, to use Rasch procedures to analyse data from performance tests of this type.

9.6 Summary

In this chapter, a number of issues have been raised about the use of Rasch methods in the analysis of performance test data. First, different types of response format were considered, and the terminology to describe the corresponding data types was introduced. These were related to kinds of data analysis within the Rasch family of models. Then some debates about the appropriateness of Rasch analysis of performance test data were considered. First, a case was made for using the Rasch model against other IRT models, both in terms of its practical advantages, and on theoretical grounds. Secondly, theoretical and empirical arguments were advanced for the suitability of Rasch analysis of performance test data, including its use in occupational and academic contexts, as this has been much disputed in the past on the grounds of the 'unidimensionality assumption' of the Rasch model. A distinction was drawn between the properties and requirements of *measurement* models and the characteristics of models of test constructs proposed on *a priori theoretical* grounds.

This chapter has been somewhat technical, and was left until last for that reason, but an understanding of its material is crucial for participation in debate and research on the qualities of performance tests. This book has argued that we need the new tools available within Rasch measurement to tease out the complexities that the contextual richness of performance assessment introduces, in order to get beyond mere face validity in performance assessment.

Appendix 9A   Formal statements of Rasch models

9A.1   Formal statements of Rasch models

In this appendix, we will give a brief introduction to some formal statements of Rasch models. The reader who is not involved in actually using programs such as Quest and FACETS may wish to skip this section, which is intended for those needing to make sense of the accompanying computer manuals.

9A.2   Basic Rasch model

We saw that the basic, simplest model is the one that can handle data from dichotomous (right–wrong) items. In this model, the probability that a person will get a score of 1 (as against a score of 0) on a given item is the difference between the ability of the person taking the item and the difficulty of that item.

In very simple terms we may express this formally as follows:

$$P = B_n - D_i$$

where $P =$ a mathematical expression of the probability of a correct response,

$B_n =$ the ability (B) of a particular person (n) and

$D_i =$ the difficulty (D) of a particular item (i).

9A.3   Rating Scale model (Andrich)

The next two members of the Rasch family of models involve data either from rating scales, or items where partial credit is given for answers; for example, the scores available for a particular question are a range of scores, say 3, 2, 1 or 0, depending on the quality of the answer. (In a comprehension question where the candidate is asked to express his or her understanding freely, points may be allocated according to the amount and relevance of the information provided in the answer.) In this case, a new term is introduced into the model statement: the model statement expresses not only the overall difficulty of any particular item (D_i), but the difficulty of gaining a score in each of the available scoring categories for any item, that is, the *step difficulty* (cf. Chapter 5 for an explanation of this concept).

We can express this as

$$P = B_n - D_i - F_k$$

where $P =$ a mathematical expression of the probability of achieving a score within a particular score category on a particular item,

$B_n =$ the ability (B) of a particular person (n) and

$D_i =$ the overall difficulty (D) of a particular item (i), and

$F_k =$ the difficulty (F) of achieving a score within a particular score category (k) on any item.

This is known as Andrich's Rating Scale model.

An important feature of this model is that the step difficulty of an item is assumed to be the same for all items containing a given number of steps; the step difficulty is an average across all items. The possibility of differences in step difficulty between individual items is not considered, or is ignored.

9A.4   Partial Credit model (Masters)

A refinement of the previous model, an expression of a more general case, is Masters's Partial Credit model. In this model, the step difficulty of the available scoring categories in each item is calculated independently of the step difficulty of each other item; there is no averaging out. We can express this symbolically as follows:

$$P = B_n - D_i - F_{ik}$$

where $P =$ a mathematical expression of the probability of achieving a score within a particular score category on a particular item,

$B_n =$ the ability (B) of a particular person (n)

$D_i =$ the difficulty (D) of a particular item (i) and

$F_{ik} =$ the difficulty of scoring within a particular score category (k) on a particular item (i).

Further and rather more technical aspects of the differences between the approaches of Andrich and Masters, which are helpful in interpreting manuals or output for the programs listed above, are explained in Appendix 9B, below.

9A.5   Multi-faceted or extended Rasch model (Linacre)

Linacre's contribution was to show that it was possible to extend the model to add a further term (or terms) to this sequence, as required. For example, it was possible to add a term for judges; another for task difficulty; and it was also possible to add terms for the interaction between particular judges, particular items and particular rating categories. Each of the aspects of the rating situation – item, ability, task, judge, etc. – is termed a *facet*.

There is no limit in principle to the number of facets that may be specified – the number of aspects of the rating situation considered relevant to the chances of a candidate achieving a particular score on a particular item – but we will restrict ourselves to the common three-facet situation, where the facets are *candidate*, *item* and *judge*. Analyses at varying levels of delicacy are possible, depending on how complexly we wish to model the way judges are interpreting step difficulty: for each item separately, or averaged across all items; or for each judge separately, or averaged across all judges? McNamara and Adams (1991/1994) demonstrate the different kinds of information that can be obtained in practice by specifying each of these levels in an analysis of data from the scores of four judges for performances on the writing sub-test of IELTS, a British/Australian test of English for Academic Purposes.

What follows may appear a little dauntingly abstract and complex, but the possibilities for specification are in fact limited, and represent simple combinations of types of analysis already discussed. It is important to have some understanding of these possibilities in order to carry out a multi-faceted analysis as it is necessary to specify the level of delicacy you require. Four commonly used model statements are given below. It is not important to try to be able to reproduce these statements from memory, but simply to appreciate that choices of analysis are possible and in fact practically necessary.

1. Assuming a common step structure across all items and for all judges (i.e. the rating scale is assumed to have the same structure for each observation, regardless of the examinee, item or judge concerned – Andrich's model), we have the *common step* model:
   $$P = B_n - D_i - C_j - F_k$$
   where P = a mathematical expression of the probability of achieving a score within a particular score category on a particular item from a particular judge
   B_n = the ability of examinee n
   D_i = the difficulty of item i
   C_j = the severity of judge j
   F_k = the difficulty (F) of achieving a score within a particular score category (k) averaged across all judges and all items.[21]

2. We may wish to continue to ignore differences among *judges* in the way they are interpreting the internal structure (the step difficulties) of the rating scale, but incorporate the refinement of considering the scale structure separately for each *item*. In this case, we get the *item–step* model:
   $$P = B_n - D_i - C_j - F_{ik}$$
   where F_{ik} = the difficulty (F) of achieving a score within a particular score category (k) averaged across all judges but for each item separately.

   That is, in this case, each *item* is acknowledged to have its own separate step structure, but differences between *judges* are ignored; in other words, we will use the Partial Credit model for items, but the Rating Scale model for judges.[22]

3. In the *judge–step* model, on the other hand, the situation is reversed. Differences in step difficulty among items are ignored, but we model how each individual judge is interpreting these step difficulties:

$$P = B_n - D_i - C_j - F_{jk}$$

where F_{jk} = the difficulty (F) of achieving a score within a particular score category (k) averaged across all items but for each judge separately.

In this case, we specify the Partial Credit model for *judges*, but the Rating Scale model for *items*.[23]

4. The most delicate level of analysis involves modelling the way each individual judge interprets the scoring categories for each item separately. This is the *judge–item–step* model:

$$P = B_n - D_i - C_j - F_{ijk}$$

where F_{ijk} = the difficulty (F) of achieving a score within a particular score category (k) modelled separately for each item/judge combination.

In this case we are specifying the Partial Credit model for both judges and items.[24]

Table 9A.1 summarizes the possible model specifications in a multi-faceted analysis involving the facets candidate, item and judge, and the relevant coding for the FACETS program (the Rating Scale model is currently coded as '?', the Partial Credit model as '#').

TABLE 9A.1   Model specifications in multi-faceted measurement (example using three facets: person, item, judge)

Model name	Item	Judge	Model statement	FACETS code (person, item, judge)
Common step	Rating Scale (Andrich)	Rating Scale (Andrich)	$P = B_n - D_i - C_j - F_k$	?,?,?
Item–step	Partial Credit (Masters)	Rating Scale (Andrich)	$P = B_n - D_i - C_j - F_{ik}$	?,#,?
Judge–step	Rating Scale (Andrich)	Partial Credit (Masters)	$P = B_n - D_i - C_j - F_{jk}$	?,?,#
Judge–item–step	Partial Credit (Masters)	Partial Credit (Masters)	$P = B_n - D_i - C_j - F_{ijk}$	?,#,#

Appendix 9B   Ways of talking about item and step difficulty in Rasch rating scale and partial credit analyses

9B.1   Imagine that responses to an item on an attitude questionnaire are given on a rating scale as follows:

Strongly disagree	Disagree	Agree	Strongly agree
1	2	3	4

We have decided to allocate scores to the scale as shown by the number under the wording. Each subject will get a score for the item; these are the item raw scores.

The score points are referred to as 'rating categories'. This is a little counter-intuitive, particularly in the case where data are derived from judges' ratings of different aspects of a performance, as for example in scoring written scripts, where scores may be given for 'Organization', 'Content', 'Control of language', etc. It seems natural to refer to these *aspects* as 'categories'; but in the analysis we should refer to these as separate *items*, and reserve 'categories' for the score points within the item. Moving up to the next scoring category is called a *step*. A dichotomous item has two scoring categories (0 and 1) and a single step. An item with three scoring categories (0, 1 and 2) has two steps; it is a two-step item, and so on.

We then use a Rating Scale or Partial Credit analysis to reveal the structure of the scoring scheme for the item – how difficult the item is overall, and the difficulty of each step. There are various ways in which the results of such an analysis may be expressed. It is worth sorting out the possible confusion over terminology here.

By convention, Rasch analyses will recode the raw scores to make the lowest score point (rating category) zero, as follows:

Strongly disagree	Disagree	Agree	Strongly agree
0	1	2	3

Let us say that the analysis reveals that the structure of the scale is approximately as follows:

0	1	2	3

i.e. that moving from category 0 to category 1 is a big step, moving from category 2 to 3 is an even bigger step, and that the step from 1 to 2 is relatively smaller.

9B.2   For *Masters* (1982, and in *Rating Scale Analysis* (Wright and Masters, 1982: 40–4)) the difficulty of a step is the answer to the question: How much ability is required to achieve a score in the *next* rating category? (He uses the symbol delta (δ) to express this.) The difficulty of moving to the next step, *assuming you have successfully completed the previous step*, is expressed *independently* of the difficulty of the previous step.

Consider Figure 9B.1 (adapted from *Rating Scale Analysis*, p. 44), which shows the category probability curves for a two-step item, i.e. one with three scoring categories, 0, 1 and 2. The step difficulty is the point on the ability scale (along the x-axis) at which the probability curves (P_{ni0}: the probability of a person n scoring a 0 on item i; P_{ni1}: ditto for a score of 1; P_{ni2}: ditto for a score of 2) for the adjacent categories intersect. In this case, the difficulty of the step between 0 and 1 on the item is shown as δ_{i1}, which corresponds to the point of intersection between the probability curve for the category 0 and the category 1. The difficulty of the step between 1 and 2 is shown as δ_{i2}, and corresponds to the point of intersection between the probability curves for the categories 1 and 2.

Note that the step difficulty in this formulation is *not* necessarily the point at which the chance of scoring in the next category is 50 per cent. This may appear to be in contrast to the dichotomous case, where the curves will be found to intersect at the point at which there is a 50 per cent probability of scoring a correct answer (a score in the rating category '1'). Nor will the deltas in one sense even necessarily be ordered. Consider Figure 9B.2. In this case, the point of intersection of the curves for categories 0 and 1, which defines δ_{i1}, is further along the ability scale than the point of intersection of the probability curves for categories 1 and 2, which defines δ_{i2}. However, it must be remembered that δ_{i2} is only expressing how much *more* ability is required to take step 2, assuming you've already made it through step 1; as Wright and Masters (1982) put

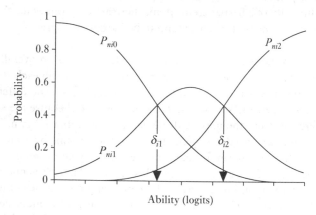

FIGURE 9B.1   Category probability curves for two–step item *i*

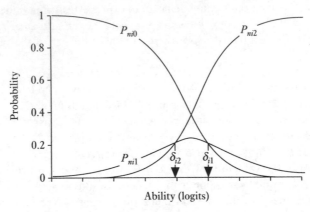

FIGURE 9B.2   Category probability curves for the case $\delta_{i2} < \delta_{i1}$

it, 'Even though the second step is easier than the first, the defined order of the response categories requires that this easier second step be undertaken only after the harder first step has been successfully completed.'

The deltas will express the relative distances between the score points, so that in our attitude questionnaire example above, the delta to move from 0 to 1 (step 1) will be relatively large, the delta to move from 1 to 2 (step 2) relatively smaller, and the delta to move from 2 to 3 (step 3) the largest of all. That is, the size of each delta is independent of the size of any other one, including the previous one. The deltas will not necessarily be ordered in *size*. But this does not mean that it's easier to 'agree' (step 2) than to 'disagree' (step 1) in our example! The delta for each new step assumes that you have already made it through the preceding ones.

Another point here is that in this approach, there is no statement of the overall difficulty of a partial credit item; there are only values for the step difficulties. In general, the deltas tend to be hard to interpret.

9B.3 *Andrich* takes a different approach. He estimates an overall difficulty for the *item*, and then considers the amount by which each *step* differs from that average: some will be lower, some higher; the differences he calls *tau* values; the sum of the *tau* values is zero (because the sum of the differences from the mean will be zero, by definition) Again, in this approach, the *tau*s need not be ordered, as the amount by which each step differs from the mean difficulty of the item may be any amount.

Note that this difference between Masters and Andrich is one of terminology, deriving ultimately from their differing approaches to modelling and estimating. These other, more important, differences between Andrich's Rating Scale model and Masters's Partial Credit model are to do with assumptions about the structure of the rating scale across different items; these differences have resulted in the problem of terminology being discussed here.

9B.4   We obviously need some way of referring to the cumulative difficulty of a particular step, and various ways have been found of doing this. Masters (1982) has introduced a simpler and more intuitively appealing way of expressing step difficulty. He uses the term *item step threshold*, which is defined as the ability level that is required for an individual to have a 50 per cent chance of passing that step. Obviously, such ability levels must increase as we move across the structure of the rating scale; each step requires progressively more ability (or an increasingly positive attitude measure, in our example). These item thresholds are thus necessarily ordered. BIGSTEPS refers to these as 'Thurstone thresholds' in its output. Quest produces such item thresholds as its default option, but you have the option of selecting *delta*s or *tau*s as well or alternatively, if you prefer.

9B.5   The Rasch model can only be estimated using *tau* or *delta*, not the threshold. So the issue really is one of communication, between measurement expert and test user. As this communication problem has been realized, the notion of thresholds has been introduced as a means of reporting the results of the analysis, which were previously reported only in the terms in which the analysis was carried out. More of this negotiation between measurement experts and innocent test users needs to be done.

Notes

1. In the analysis of test data, a parameter is a characteristic of a set of responses to test items. Such characteristics can be summarized statistically; for example, for a test *item*, parameters will typically include the difficulty of the item, how well it discriminates between stronger and weaker students, and how easy it is to guess.
2. See Section 9.3, below.
3. Implemented by the computer program FACETS (Linacre and Wright, 1992).
4. Choosing whether to score a missing response 'incorrect' or 'missing' is an important decision with significant consequences for the analysis. The appropriate thing to do in most cases is to treat the responses as missing, that is, as providing no information relevant to the determination of item difficulty and candidate ability. Treating the missing responses as incorrect may artificially boost the desirable properties of test items in terms of their discrimination, and give a misleading picture of the test.
5. This term has several senses: (1) the overall sense expressed here; (2) data from a rating scale as distinct from a Likert or semantic differential scale (see below); (3) data analysed using Andrich's Rating Scale model as compared with Masters's Partial Credit model (see below).

6. Hamp-Lyons (1991) prefers the term *multiple-trait marking*, which she sees as a holistic approach; she reserves the term *analytic* for older approaches focusing on discrete, atomistic features of texts such as grammar, vocabulary, etc.

7. The question sometimes arises in discussions of the analysis of data from rating scales using conventional techniques such as correlation (for example, in calculating the degree of agreement between judges, or inter-rater reliability) as to whether the data meet the requirements of interval level data or should be treated as rank-order (ordinal) data. This distinction is a fundamental one in statistics (for a discussion, cf. Hatch and Lazaraton, 1991). With interval scales, we assume that the distance or interval between each pair of adjoining 'marks' on the measurement instrument is equal, i.e. represents a constant interval, a consistent amount of the thing being measured. For example, on a ruler, we know that the interval between any two marks indicating centimetres is going to be the same: the distance between 9 and 10 centimetres is the same as the distance between 3 and 4 centimetres, and so on. Ordinal data allow us to rank the measures but not to say by how much any adjacent pair of rankings differ in any sense other than that they occupy different, sequential ranks. For example, we might say that Bettina is more proficient than Carlos, who in turn is more proficient than Eric, but we don't know by exactly how much more. It is as if in estimating height we could see who was tallest, next tallest, and so on, but without any information on the exact height of the individuals involved, and thus by how much they differed from each other. Data from rating scales, Likert scales or semantic differential scales may have the appearance of being interval-level data, but are in fact ordinal data. For example, in a language assessment context, consider the intervals between the levels on language proficiency rating scale such as the FSI and the ASLPR. Such levels may be labelled with numbers, giving the appearance of an interval scale, but it is clear that the 'distance' between adjacent levels does not remain uniform across the scale. For example, if the intervals are conceptualized in terms of the amount of language training required to move from one level to the next, then intervals between adjacent lower levels would represent smaller amounts of time or learning than the distance between adjacent levels near the top of the scale. Levels at the top of the scale often make reference to features of 'native-like performance', and the amount of learning required for a learner to move from one of these higher levels to the next may be very extensive indeed. The intervals on the scale do not therefore represent equal amounts of the thing measured on the scale ('proficiency'), and are properly not true interval scales. The fact that numbers are generated in such ratings should not lead us to conclude that an interval scale is available from the raw scores alone (cf. the discussion of this point in Bachman, 1990: 44–5). One of the attractions of Rasch measurement is that it enables us to convert raw scores on a rating scale or similar instrument into measures which have the properties of data from an interval scale. This may have important advantages in certain research contexts, and also for drawing policy/curricular conclusions.

8. It is possible to simplify the Partial Credit model so that it is reduced to the Rating Scale model, by setting the analysis so that all items with responses scored on a rating scale will have the same step structure. The dichotomously scored basic model can be seen as the case where the number of possible score points is set at two, that is 0 or 1. In this way, the Basic model and the Partial Credit model bear a relationship to each other similar to that between two commonly used formulae for establishing internal reliability in classical approaches to test analysis. Cronbach's alpha, capable of handling items on which a range of marks may be awarded, is the more general formula and reduces to the Kuder–Richardson formulae (KR 20 and KR 21, cf. Henning, 1987a: 84), which are used for dichotomously scored items, when the possible responses are 0 and 1.

9. See, for example, the debate between Hambleton and Wright entitled 'IRT in the 1990s: which models work best?' at the 1992 National Council on Measurement in Education Annual Meeting in San Francisco. Wright's contribution is available in Wright (1992).

10. For example, through the item fit statistics, which are sensitive to departures from the mean discriminating power of items in the test. In addition, the model is robust with regard to violations of the assumption of equal discrimination of items.

11. We shall ignore, for the sake of simplicity, the question of the effect of the characteristics of raters in rating tasks.
12. This is expressed in mathematical symbols as $P\{x_{ni} = 1\}$ (the probability of a person n getting score of 1 on an item i).The range of possibilities goes from 0 to 1; that is, from no chance at all (zero chance) to a perfect chance (100 per cent chance). Halfway up this axis is the 50 per cent chance of a person responding correctly: here P is 0.5. The lower half of the axis is bracketed together as indicating that the probability of a correct response is less than half: $P\{x_{ni} = 1\} < 0.5$. The upper half of the axis is bracketed together and indicates that here there is a better than even (greater than 50 per cent) chance of the person getting the item correct: $P\{x_{ni} = 1\} > 0.5$.
13. Ability is represented by the mathematical symbol B; the subscript next to B tells us the identity of the individual whose ability we are considering; n refers in general terms to any particular individual, so that B_n represents the ability of any particular individual. Item difficulty is represented by D, and the identity of an item in general by i, so that D_i means the difficulty of item i. Thus the x-axis represents $B_n - D_i$, the difference between person ability and item difficulty. Halfway along the x-axis is the point where the ability of the individual (B_n) is equivalent to the difficulty of the item (D_i), that is, the difference between person ability and item difficulty $(B_n - D_i)$ is zero, and at this point the probability of the individual getting the item correct is 0.5. To the right of this point the person's ability exceeds the item's difficulty $(B_n > D_i)$ and the person's chances of responding correctly exceed 50 per cent; to the left of this point the person's ability is lower than the difficulty of the item $(B_n < D_i)$, and the chances of a correct response are correspondingly below 50 per cent. The legend at the bottom of the figure may be read as follows: the probability of a person n whose ability is B_n scoring a correct response on item i whose difficulty is D_i is a function (f) of the difference between the ability of the person and the difficulty of the item $(B_n - D_i)$.
14. This reflects a questioning of the appropriateness of the use of Rasch IRT at all in the wider field of educational measurement in general (Goldstein, 1979; Traub, 1983).
15. It is not clear whether the misfit identified in this study represents 'overfit' or 'misfit' in the senses set out in Chapter 6. If it is the former, a possible explanation would be that the two aspects of performance on the listening comprehension material (ability to interpret literally and ability to draw inferences) were positively correlated. If this were so, it would not be unusual to find a higher discrimination for those items that required both skills; this would be reflected as strong negative fit in the Rasch analysis.
16. For native speakers, of course, the two item types do go together from a *measurement* point of view, and so scores on both could be added together for this sub-group of test takers.
17. Adams *et al.* unfortunately blur this issue by their choice of the wording 'confirm [the] *existence*' of 'a dimension of grammatical competence' (1987: 13; emphasis added). Adams (personal communication) acknowledges this as an 'error', adding: 'I should have said that we successfully "constructed" a useful dimension and we confirmed its utility. We did not confirm the "existence" of a dimension. Dimensions do not exist, they are invented.'
18. The use of the Bejar method with item parameter estimates in this study has been the subject of some debate (Spurling, 1987a, 1987b; Henning, 1987b, 1988). The Bejar method as applied in Henning (1988) is a general method of comparison of item and ability estimates derived from sub-tests and the whole test; in this way it resembles the procedures for assessing dimensionality suggested by Wright and Masters (1982: 114–17). It differs somewhat in that the Bejar method involves part-whole comparisons, which are likely to be less sensitive than estimates from entirely separate sets of items from within a test as recommended by Wright and Masters. McNamara (1991) (cf. Section 9.5) takes up the issue of appropriate further tests for unidimensionality in relation to data from the Listening sub-test of the Occupational English Test; two such statistical tests are described and found to confirm unidimensionality in the data.
19. Already discussed in the context of 'misfit' in Chapter 6.

20. Full details of the materials and the trialling of the test can be found in McNamara (1990b).
21. In the program FACETS, this model corresponds to the selection of the code '?' for each facet in the 'model statement' (a line of commands required in the control file). Thus, where the facets are in the order candidate, item, judge, the model statement would contain the string '?,?,?'. For further information, consult the manual to the FACETS program.
22. The relevant string in the model statement is '?,#,?'.
23. The relevant string in the model statement is '?, ?, #'.
24. The relevant string in the model statement is '?, #, #'.

References

Adams R J and Khoo S T 1992 *Titan: The Interactive Test Analysis System [computer program]*. Australian Council for Educational Research, Hawthorne, Victoria

Adams R J and Khoo S T 1993 *Quest: The Interaction Test Analysis System [computer program]*. Australian Council for Educational Research, Hawthorne, Victoria

Adams R J, Griffin P E and Martin L 1987 A latent trait method for measuring a dimension in second language proficiency. *Language Testing* 4(1): 9–27

Alderson J C 1980 Native and non-native speaker performance on cloze tests. *Language Learning* 30(1): 59–76

Alderson J C 1988 New Procedures for validating proficiency tests of ESP? Theory and Practice. *Language Testing* 5(2): 220–32

Alderson J C 1990a Testing reading comprehension skills (Part 1). *Reading in a Foreign Language* 6: 425–38

Alderson J C 1990b Testing reading comprehension skills (Part 2). *Reading in a Foreign Language* 7: 465–503

Alderson J C 1991 Bands and scores. In Alderson C J and North B (eds) *Language Testing in the 1990s*. Modern English Publications and the British Council, London

Alderson J C 1995 Response to Lumley. *Language Testing* 12(1): 122–5

Alderson J C, Candlin C N, Clapham C M, Martin D J and Weir C J 1986 *Language proficiency testing for migrant professionals: new directions for the Occupational English Test. A report submitted to the Council on Overseas Professional Qualifications*. Institute for English Language Education University of Lancaster, Lancaster

Alderson J C and Hamp-Lyons L (in preparation) *Washback and the TOEFL preparation classroom*. (Working title)

Alderson J C and Hughes A 1981 *Issues in language testing. ELT Documents III*. British Council, London

Alderson J C, Krahnke K J and Stansfield C W (eds) 1987 *Reviews of English language proficiency tests*. Teachers of English to Speakers of Other Languages, Washington DC

Alderson J C and Lukmani Y 1989 Cognition and reading: cognitive levels as embodied in test questions. *Reading in a Foreign Language* 5(2): 253–70

Alderson J C and Wall D 1993 Does washback exist? *Applied Linguistics* 14(2): 115–29

Allen P, Cummins J, Mougeon R and Swain M 1983 *Development of bilingual proficiency: second year report*. Ontario Institute for Studies in Education, Toronto

American Council on the Teaching of Foreign Languages 1986 *ACTFL proficiency guidelines*. American Council on the Teaching of Foreign Languages, Hastings-on-Hudson, NY

295

American Psychological Association 1985 *Standards for educational and psychological testing*, American Psychological Association, Washington DC

Andrich D 1978a A rating formulation for ordered response categories. *Psychometrika* 43: 561–73

Andrich D 1978b Scaling attitude items constructed and scored in the Likert tradition. *Educational and Psychological Measurement* 38: 665–80

Angoff W H and Sharon A T 1971 A comparison of scores earned on the Test of English as a Foreign Language by native American college students and foreign applicants to US colleges. *TESOL Quarterly* 5(2): 129–36

Anstey E 1966 *Psychological tests*. Nelson, London

Australian Council for Educational Research (ACER) 1990 *Report on the Australian Language Certificates to the Australian Bicentennial Multicultural Foundation, 1989–1990*. ACER, Hawthorne, Victoria

Bachman L F 1988 Problems in examining the validity of the ACTFL Oral Proficiency Interview. *Studies in Second Language Acquisition* 10(2): 149–64

Bachman L F 1990 *Fundamental considerations in language testing*. Oxford University Press, Oxford

Bachman L F and Clark J L D 1987 The measurement of foreign/second language proficiency. *Annals of the American Academy of Political and Social Science* 490: 20–33

Bachman L F, Lynch B K and Mason M 1995 Investigating variability in tasks and rater judgements in a performance test of foreign language speaking. *Language Testing* 12(2): 238–57

Bachman L F and Palmer A S 1982 The construct validation of some components of communicative language proficiency. *TESOL Quarterly* 16(4): 449–65

Bachman L F and Palmer A S 1984 Some comments on the terminology of language testing. In Rivera C (ed.) *Communicative competence approaches to language proficiency assessment: research and application*, Multilingual Matters, Clevedon Avon pp 34–43

Bachman L F and Palmer A S (in press) *Language testing in practice: designing and developing useful language tests*. Oxford University Press, Oxford

Bachman L F and Savignon S J 1986 The evaluation of communicative language proficiency: a critique of the ACTFL Oral Interview. *The Modern Language Journal* 70(4): 380–90

Baker E 1995 *Validity and equity issues in educational assessment*. Paper presented at 17th annual Language Testing Research Colloquium, Long Beach CA, March

Barnwell D 1989 'Naive' native speakers and judgements of oral proficiency in Spanish. *Language Testing* 6(2): 152–63

Berk R A (ed.) 1986 *Performance assessment. Methods and applications*. The Johns Hopkins University Press, Baltimore MD

Bernstein J 1994 *Language testing with speech recognition: methods and validation*. Paper presented at the 16th annual Language Testing Research Colloquium, Washington DC, March

Bialystok E and Sharwood-Smith M 1985 Interlanguage is not a state of mind: an evaluation of the construct for second language acquisition. *Applied Linguistics* 6(2); 101–17

Birnbaum A 1968 Some latent trait models and their use in inferring an examinee's ability. In Lord F and Novick M *Statistical theories of mental test scores*. Addison-Wesley, Reading MA pp 397–472

Borow H 1980 Performance testing and social responsibility: an issues analysis. In Spirer J E (ed.) *Performance testing: issues facing vocational education.* National Center For Research in Vocational Education, Columbus OH pp 21–32

Bray D W, Campbell R J and Grant D L 1974 *Formative years in business: a long-term study of managerial lives.* Wiley and Sons, New York

Bray D W and Grant D L 1966 The Assessment Center in the measurement of potential for business management. *Psychological Monographs* 80(17)

Brennan R L 1983 *Elements of Generalizability Theory*, The American College Testing Program, Iowa City IO

Brière E J 1971 Are we really measuring proficiency with our foreign language tests? *Foreign Language Annals* 4: 385–91

Brindley G 1986 *The assessment of second language proficiency: issues and approaches.* National Curriculum Resource Centre Adult Migrant Education Program Australia, Adelaide SA

Brindley G 1989 *Assessing achievement in the learner-centred curriculum.* National Centre for English Language Teaching and Research, Macquarie University, Sydney

Brindley G and Nunan D 1992 *IELTS Research Projects Project 1. Draft Bandscales for Listening.* National Centre for English Language Teaching and Research, Macquarie University, Sydney

British Council/UCLES 1989 *IELTS specifications.* British Council/UCLES, Cambridge

British Council/UCLES 1990 *IELTS specimen materials handbook.* British Council/UCLES, Cambridge

British Council/UCLES/IDP 1989 *IELTS users' handbook.* British Council/UCLES, Cambridge

Brown A 1993 The role of test-taker feedback in the test development process: test-takers' reactions to a tape-mediated test of proficiency in spoken Japanese. *Language Testing* 10(3): 277–303

Brown A 1995 The effect of rater variables in the development of an occupation-specific language performance test. *Language Testing* 12(1): 1–15

Brown A and Lumley T 1991a *The University of Melbourne ESL Test: final report.* Language Testing Centre, University of Melbourne

Brown A and Lumley T 1991b *Some practical applications of Item Response Theory in language programmes.* Paper presented at 4th ELICOS Association Conference, Monash University, August

Brown J D and Bailey K M 1984 A categorical instrument for scoring second language writing skills. *Language Learning* 34(4): 21–42

Buck G 1992 *The construction of multidimensional data sets.* Paper presented at the 14th annual Language Testing Research Colloquium, Vancouver, February 27th–March 1st

Buck G 1994 The appropriacy of psychometric measurement models for testing second language listening comprehension. *Language Testing* 11(2): 145–70

Byrne P S and Long B E L 1976 *Doctors talking to patients.* Her Majesty's Stationery Office, London

Canale M 1983a From communicative competence to communicative language pedagogy. In Richards J C and Schmidt R W (eds) *Language and communication.* Longman, London pp 2–27

Canale M 1983b On some dimensions of language proficiency. In Oller J W (ed.) *Issues in language testing research.* Newbury House, Rowley MA pp 333–42

Canale M and Swain M 1980 Theoretical bases of communicative approaches to second language teaching and testing. *Applied Linguistics* 1(1): 1–47

Candlin C N 1986 Explaining communicative competence: limits of testability? In Stansfield C W (ed.) *Toward communicative competence testing: proceedings of the Second TOEFL Invitational Conference. TOEFL Research Report* 21. Educational Testing Service, Princeton NJ pp 38–57

Candlin C N, Burton J and Coleman H 1980a *Dentist–patient communication. A report to the General Dental Council.* Department of Linguistics and Modern English Language/Institute for English Language Education, University of Lancaster, Lancaster

Candlin C N, Burton J and Coleman H 1980b *Evaluating the communicative proficiency of overseas dentists. Annex to General Dental Council Report.* Department of Linguistics and Modern English Language/Institute for English Language Education, University of Lancaster, Lancaster

Candlin C N, Coleman H and Burton J 1983 Dentist–patient communication: communicating complaint. In Wolfson N and Judd E (eds) *Sociolinguistics and language acquisition.* Newbury House, Rowley MA pp 56–81

Candlin C N, Leather J H and Bruton C J 1974 *English language skills for overseas doctors and medical staff. Work in progress, Reports I–IV.* University of Lancaster, Department of Linguistics and Modern English Language, Lancaster

Carlson S B and Camp R 1985 *Relationships between direct and indirect measures of writing ability.* Paper presented at the annual meeting of the National Council on Measurement in Education, Chicago IL, March 31–April 4 (ERIC document ED 255 543)

Carrell P L, Devine J and Eskey D E (eds) 1988 *Interactive approaches to second language reading.* Cambridge University Press, Cambridge

Carroll B J 1977 *Specifications for a new English language examination.* Mimeo Royal Society of Arts, London

Carroll B J 1978 *An English Language Testing Service: specifications.* Mimeo British Council, London

Carroll B J 1980 *Testing communicative performance.* Pergamon, Oxford

Carroll B J 1985 *Make your own language tests: a principal guide to writing language performance tests.* Oxford Pergamon Press, Oxford

Carroll J B 1954 *Notes on the measurement of achievement in foreign languages.* Mimeo

Carroll J B 1961 [1972] Fundamental considerations in testing for English language proficiency in foreign students. In Allen H B and Campbell R N (eds) 1972 *Teaching English as a second language: a book of readings. Second edition.* McGraw-Hill, New York pp 313–21

Carroll J B 1968 The psychology of language testing. In Davies A (ed.) *Language testing symposium: a psycholinguistic approach.* Oxford University Press, London pp 46–69

Carroll J B 1986 LT +25, and beyond? Comments. *Language Testing* 3(2): 123–9

Choi I C and Bachman L F 1992 An investigation into the adequacy of three IRT models for data from two EFL reading tests. *Language Testing* 9(1): 51–78

Chomsky N 1965 *Aspects of the theory of syntax.* MIT Press, Cambridge MA

Chomsky N 1975 *Reflections on language.* Temple Smith, London

Chomsky N 1980 *Rules and representations.* Blackwell, Oxford

Choppin B 1982 The use of latent trait models in the measurement of cognitive abilities and skills. In Spearritt D (ed.) *The improvement of measurement in education and psychology: contributions of latent trait theories.* Australian Council for Educational Research, Hawthorn Victoria pp 41–63

Clapham C M 1994 *The effect of background knowledge on EAP reading test performance.* Unpublished PhD thesis, Lancaster University

Clapham C M 1966 *The development of IELTS: a study of the effect of background knowledge on reading comprehension.* Cambridge University Press, Cambridge

Clark J L D 1972 *Foreign language testing: theory and practice.* Center for Curriculum Development, Philadelpha PA

Clark J L D 1975 Theoretical and technical considerations in oral proficiency testing. In Jones R L and Spolsky B (eds) *Testing language proficiency.* Center for Applied Linguistics, Arlington VA pp 10–28

Clark J L D 1977 *The performance of native speakers of English on the Test of English as a Foreign Language.* Educational Testing Service, Princeton NJ

Clark J L D and Clifford R T 1988 The FSI/ILR/ACTFL proficiency scales and testing techniques: development, current status and needed research. *Studies in Second Language Acquisition* 10(2): 129–47

Coffman W E and Kurfman D 1968 A comparison of two methods of reading essay examinations. *American Educational Research Journal* 5: 101–20

Cohen A D 1984 On taking language tests: what the students report. *Language Testing* 1(1): 70–81

Coleman H 1980 Evaluating the communicative proficiency of overseas dentists. In Candlin C, Burton J and Coleman H *Evaluting the communicative proficiency of overseas dentists. Annex to General Dental Council Report.* University of Lancaster Department of Linguistics and Modern English Language/Institute for English Language Education, Lancaster pp 4–43

Constable E and Andrich A 1984 *Inter-judge reliability: is complete agreement among judges the ideal?* Paper presented at the annual meeting of the National Council on Measurement in Education, New Orleans LA

Cooper R L 1968 An elaborated language testing model. *Language Learning*, Special Issue No 3: 57–72

Coulthard M and Ashby M 1975 Talking with the doctor, 1. *Journal of Communication* 25(3): 140–7

Criper C and Davies A 1988 *ELTS Validation Project Report.* The British Council/Cambridge: University of Cambridge Local Examinations Syndicate, London

Cronbach L J 1971 Test validation. In Thorndike R L (ed.) *Educational measurement. 2nd edition.* American Council on Education, Washington DC

Cummins J 1984 Wanted: a theoretical framework for relating language proficiency to academic achievement among bilingual students. In Rivera C (ed.) *Language proficiency and academic achievement.* Multilingual Matters, Clevedon Avon pp 2–19

Cziko G A 1983 Psychometric and edumetric approaches to language testing. In Oller J W (ed.) *Issues in language testing research.* Newbury House, Rowley MA pp 289–307

Daiker D, Kerek A and Morenberg M 1978 Sentence combining and syntactic maturity in freshman English. *College Composition and Communication* 19(1): 36–41

Davidson D M 1978 *Test of ability to subordinate.* Language Innovations Inc, New York

Davidson F and Henning G 1985 A self-rating scale of English difficulty: Rasch scalar analysis of items and rating categories. *Language Testing* 2(2): 164–79

Davidson F G and Lynch B K 1993 Criterion-referenced language test development: a prolegomenon. In Huhta A, Sajavaara K and Takala S (eds) *Language testing: new openings.* University of Jyväskylä Institute for Educational Research, Jyväskylä Finland pp 73–89

Davies A 1968 Introduction. In Davies A (ed.) *Language testing symposium: a psycholinguistic approach.* Oxford University Press, London pp 1–18

Davies A 1977 The construction of language tests. In Allen J P B and Davies A (eds) *Testing and experimental methods. The Edinburgh Course in Applied Lingusitics* vol 4 Oxford University Press, Oxford p 38–104

Davies A 1981 Review of J Munby, Communicative syllabus design. *TESOL Quarterly* 15(3): 332–6

Davies A 1984a Validating three tests of English language proficiency. *Language Testing* 1(1): 50–69

Davies A 1984b ESL expectations in examining: the problem of English as a Foreign Language and English as a Mother Tongue. *Language Testing* 1(1): 82–95

Davies A 1989 Communicative competence as language use. *Applied Linguistics* 10(2): 157–70

Davies A 1991 *The native speaker in applied linguistics.* Edinburgh University Press, Edinburgh

Davies A 1992 Is language proficiency always achievement? *Melbourne Papers in Language Testing* 1(1): 1–17

de Jong J H A L and Glas C A W 1987 Validation of listening comprehension tests using item response theory. *Language Testing* 4(2): 170–94

de Jong J H A L and Henning G 1990 *Test dimensionality in relation to student proficiency.* Paper presented at the 12th annual Language Testing Research Colloquium, San Francisco, March

de Jong J H A L and Stoyanova 1994 *Theory building: sample size and data-model fit.* Paper presented at the 16th annual Language Testing Research Colloquium, Washington DC, March

Diederich P B, French J W and Carlton S T 1961 Factors in judgments of writing ability. *Research Bulletin* 61(15) Educational Testing Service, Princeton NJ (ERIC Document Reproduction Service ED 002 172)

Douglas D and Selinker L 1985 Principles for language tests within the 'discourse domains' theory of interlanguage: research, test construction and interpretation. *Language Testing* 2(2): 205–26

Douglas G A 1982 Conditional inference in a generic Rasch model. In Spearritt D (ed.) *The improvement of measurement in education and psychology: contributions of latent trait theories.* Australian Council of Educational Measurement, Hawthorn Victoria pp 129–57

Duranti A 1988 The ethnography of speaking: toward a linguistics of the praxis. In Newmeyer T (ed.) *Linguistics: the Cambridge survey. Vol. IV: Language, the socio-cultural context.* Cambridge University Press, Cambridge pp 210–28

Duranti A and Goodwin C (eds) 1992 *Rethinking context: language as an interactive phenomenon.* Cambridge University Press, Cambridge

Elder C 1993a Language proficiency as a predictor of performance in teacher education. *Melbourne Papers in Language Testing* 2(1): 68–89

Elder C 1993b How do subject specialists construe classroom language proficiency? *Language Testing* 10(3): 235–54

Elder C 1994 Performance testing as benchmark for LOTE teacher education. *Melbourne Papers in Language Testing* 3(1): 1–25

Elder C, McQueen J and Zammit S 1992 *Rewarding second language learning achievement: the Australian Language·Certificates scheme.* Paper presented at the 7th Annual International Conference of the Hawaii Association of Language Teachers, March

Elder C and Zammit S 1992 Assessing performance in languages other than English: the contribution of the Australian Language Certificates. *Vox: The Journal of the Australian Advisory Council on Language and Multicultural Education* 6: 14–21

Emmett A 1985 The Associated Examining Board's Test in English for Educational Purposes (TEEP). In Hauptman P C, LeBlanc R and Wesche M B (eds) *Second language performance testing.* Ottawa University Press, Ottawa pp 131–51

Evans R 1990 *The IELTS: Is it suitable for adult immigrant students who apply for tertiary entrance?* Unpublished MA thesis, University of Melbourne

Evola J, Mamer E and Lentz B 1980 Discrete point versus global scoring for cohesive devices. In Oller J W and Perkins K (eds) *Research in language testing.* Newbury House, Rowley MA pp 177–81

Filipi A 1994 Interaction in an Italian oral test: the role of some expansion sequences. *Australian Review of Applied Linguistics* Series S Number 11: 119–36

Fisher W P 1992 Stochastic resonance and Rasch measurement. *Rasch Measurement* 5(4): 186–7

Fitzpatrick R and Morrison E J 1971 Performance and product evaluation. In Thorndike R L (ed.) *Educational measurement. Second edition.* American Council on Education, Washington DC pp 237–70. Reprinted in Finch F L (ed.) 1991 *Educational performance assessment.* The Riverside Publishing Company, Chicago pp 89–138

Frederiksen J R and Collins A 1989 A systems approach to educational testing. *Educational Researcher* 18(9): 27–32

Fries C C 1945 *Teaching and learning English as a foreign language.* University of Michigan Press, Ann Arbor MI

Garfinkel H 1967 *Studies in ethnomethodology.* Prentice Hall, Englewood Cliffs NJ

Glaser R 1963 Instructional technology and the measurement of learning outcomes: some questions. *American Psychologist* 18: 519–21

Goffman E 1967 *Interaction ritual.* Doubleday, New York

Goldstein H 1979 Consequences of using the Rasch Model for educational assessment. *British Educational Research Journal* 5: 211–20

Graham J G 1987 English language proficiency and the prediction of academic success. *TESOL Quarterly* 21(3): 505–21

Griffin P 1989 *Characteristics of the test components of the IELTS battery: Australian trial data.* Paper presented at the annual conference of the Applied Linguistics Association of Australia, Monash University, September

Griffin P E 1985 The use of latent trait models in the calibration of tests of spoken language in large-scale selection-placement programs. In Lee Y P, Fok A C Y Y, Lord R and Low G (eds) *New directions in language testing.* Pergamon, Oxford pp 149–61

Griffin P E, Adams R J, Martin L and Tomlinson B 1988 An algorithmic approach to prescriptive assessment in English as a Second Language. *Language Testing* 5(1): 1–18

Griffin P and Nix P 1991 *Educational Assessment and Reporting: a new approach.* Harcourt Brace Jovanovich, Sydney

Haertel E 1992 Performance measurement. In Alkin M C (ed.) *Encyclopedia of educational research*, 6th edition pp 984–9

Halliday M A K 1978 *Language as social semiotic. The social interpretation of language and meaning.* Edward Arnold, London

Halliday M A K and Hasan R 1976 *Cohesion in English*, Longman, London

Hambleton R K, Swaminathan H and Rogers H J 1991 *Fundamentals of Item Response Theory.* Sage, Newbury Park CA

Hamilton J 1991 *Native and non-native speaker performance on the IELTS reading test.* Unpublished MA thesis, University of Melbourne

Hamilton J, Lopes M, McNamara T F and Sheridan E 1993 Rating scales and native speaker performance on a communicatively oriented EAP test. *Language Testing* 10(3): 337–53

Hamp-Lyons L 1989 Applying the partial credit model of Rasch analysis: language testing and accountability. *Language Testing* 6(1): 109–18

Hamp-Lyons L 1991 *Holistic scoring of LEP student writing.* Center for Research in Applied Language, University of Colorado Denver (Text of paper presented to National Conference on Bilingual Education, 1991, Office of Bilingual Education Management, US Government)

Hatch E and Lazaraton A 1991 *The research manual: design and statistics for applied linguistics.* Newbury House, New York

He A W 1994 *Elicited vs. volunteered elaboration: Talk and task in language proficiency interviews.* Paper presented at the annual conference of the American Association for Applied Linguistics, Baltimore MD, March

Henning G 1984 Advantages of latent trait measurement in language testing. *Language Testing* 1(2): 123–33

Henning G 1987a *A guide to language testing: development, evaluation, research.* Newbury House, Cambridge MA

Henning G 1987b Is the Bejar test of unidimensionality appropriate? A response to Spurling. *Language Testing* 4(1): 96–8

Henning G 1988 The influence of test and sample dimensionality on latent trait person ability and item difficulty calibrations. *Language Testing* 5(1): 83–99

Henning G 1992 Dimensionality and construct validity of language tests. *Language Testing* 9(1): 1–11

Henning G and Davidson F 1987 Scalar analysis of composition ratings. In Bailey K M, Dale T L and Clifford R T (eds) *Language testing research. Selected papers from the 1986 colloquium.* Defense Language Institute, Monterey CA pp 24–38

Henning G, Hudson T and Turner J 1985 Item response theory and the assumption of unidimensionality for language tests. *Language Testing* 2(2): 141–54

Heritage J 1984 *Garfinkel and ethnomethodology.* Polity Press, New York NY

Higgs T V and Clifford R 1982 The push toward communication. In Higgs T V (ed.) *Curriculum, competence and the foreign language teacher.* National Textbook Company, Skokie IL pp 57–79

Hill K 1995 *The use of questionnaire feedback in the development and validation of an oral interaction test in two formats*. Paper presented at 17th annual Language Testing Research Colloquium, Long Beach CA, March

Homburg T J 1984 Holistic evaluation of ESL compositions: can it be validated objectively? *TESOL Quarterly* 18(1): 87–107

Hornberger N H 1989 *Trámites* and *Transportes*: the acquisition of second language communicative competence for one speech event in Puno, Peru. *Applied Linguistics* 10(2): 214–30

Hughes A (ed.) 1988 *Testing English for university study*. Modern English Publications/British Council, London

Hughes A 1989 *Testing for language teachers*. Cambridge University Press, Cambridge

Hughes A, Porter D and Weir C (eds) 1988 *ELTS Validation Project: Proceedings of a conference held to consider the ELTS Validation Project Report. English Language Testing Service Research Report 1 (ii)*. British Council/University of Cambridge Local Examinations Syndicate, London

Hulin C L, Lissak R I and Drasgow F 1982 Recovery of two- and three-parameter logistic item characteristic curves: a Monte Carlo study. *Applied Psychological Measurement* 6: 249–60

Huot B 1990 The literature of direct writing assessment: major concerns and prevailing trends. *Review of Educational Research* 60(2): 237–63

Hymes D H 1967 Models of the interaction of language and social setting. *Journal of Social Issues* 23(2): 8–38

Hymes D H 1972 On communicative competence. In Pride J B and Holmes J (eds) *Sociolinguistics: selected readings*. Penguin, Harmondsworth, Middlesex pp 269–93

Hymes D H 1973 Toward linguistic competence. *Texas Working Papers in Sociolinguistics*, 16

Hymes D H 1984 *Vers la compétence de communication*. Hatier-Crédif, Paris

Hymes D H 1989 Postscript. *Applied Linguistics* 10(2): 244–50

Ingram D E 1981 The Australian Second Language Proficiency Ratings: their nature, development and trialling. In Read J A S (ed.) *Directions in language testing*. Singapore University Press/SEAMEO Regional Language Centre, Singapore pp 108–36

Ingram D E 1984 *Report on the formal trialling of the Australian Second Language Proficiency Ratings (ASLPR)*. Australian Government Publishing Service, Canberra

Ingram D and Wylie E 1984 *Australian second language proficiency ratings*. Australian Department of Immigration and Ethnic Affairs, Canberra

Iwashita N 1993 *Comprehensible output in NNS-NNS interaction in Japanese as a foreign language*. Unpublished MA thesis, University of Melbourne

Izard J 1981 *The robustness of Rasch analysis procedures*. Mimeo Australian Council for Educational Research, Hawthorn Victoria

Jacobs H L, Zinkgraf S A, Wormuth D R, Hartfiel V F and Hughey J B 1981 *Testing ESL composition: a practical approach*. Newbury House, Rowley MA

Jacoby S 1995 *The interactional complexity of face-to-face evaluation*. Paper presented at the annual TESOL Convention, Long Beach CA, March

Jacoby S and Ochs E 1995 Co-construction: an introduction. In Jacoby S and Ochs E (eds) *Special issue on Co-construction. Research on Language and Social Interaction* 28(3): 171–83

Jakobovits L 1969 A functional approach to the assessment of language skills. *Journal of English as a Second Language* 4: 63–76

Jakobson R 1960 Closing statement: linguistics and poetics. In Sebeok T A (ed.) *Style in Language*. The MIT Press, Massachusetts Institute of Technology, Cambridge MA pp 350–77

Johnson D C 1977 The TOEFL and domestic students: conclusively inappropriate. *TESOL Quarterly* 11(1): 79–86

Jones R L 1977 Testing: a vital connection. In Phillips J (ed.) *The language connection: from the classroom to the world. The ACTFL Review of Foreign Language Education*, vol. 9 National Textbook Co, Skokie IL pp 237–65

Jones R L 1979 Performance testing of second language proficiency. In Brière E J and Hinofotis F B (eds) *Concepts in language testing: some recent studies*, TESOL, Washington DC pp 50–7

Jones R L 1985 Second language performance testing: an overview. In Hauptman P C, LeBlanc R and Wesche M B (eds) *Second language performance testing*. University of Ottawa Press, Ottawa pp 15–24

Kelly R 1978 *On the construct validation of comprehension tests: an exercise in applied linguistics*. Unpublished PhD thesis, University of Queensland

Kenyon D 1992 Introductory remarks at symposium on *Development and use of rating scales in language testing*, 14th Language Testing Research Colloquium, Vancouver, February 27th–March 1st

Kenyon D M 1995 *An investigation of the validity of the demands of tasks on performance-based tests of oral proficiency*. Paper presented at the 16th annual Language Testing Research Colloquium, Long Beach CA, March

Kenyon D M and Stansfield C W 1992 *Extending a scale of language proficiency using concurrent calibration and the Rasch model*. Paper presented at the annual meeting of the American Educational Research Association, San Francisco CA, April

Krashen S D 1982 *Principles and practice in second language acquisition*. Pergamon, Oxford

Krzanowski W J and Woods A J 1984 Statistical aspects of reliability in language testing. *Language Testing* 1(1): 1–20

Labov W 1970 The study of language in its social context. *Studium Generale* 23: 30–87

Lado R 1961 *Language testing: the construction and use of foreign language tests*. Longman, Green and Co Ltd, London

Lantolf J P and Frawley W 1985 Oral proficiency testing: a critical analysis. *The Modern Language Journal* 69: 337–45

Lantolf J P and Frawley W 1988 Proficiency: understanding the construct. *Studies in Second Language Acquisition* 10(2): 181–95

Laufer B 1989 A factor of difficulty in vocabulary learning: deceptive transparency. In Nation P and Carter R (eds) *Vocabulary Acquisition. AILA Review* 6: 10–20. AILA: Amsterdam

Lazaraton A L 1991 *A conversation analysis of structure and interaction in the language interview*. Unpublished PhD dissertation. University of California, Los Angeles CA

Lazaraton A 1994 *Question turn modification in language proficiency interviews*. Paper presented at annual conference of the American Association for Applied Lingusitics, Baltimore MD, March

Light R L, Ming X and Mossop J 1987 English proficiency and academic performance of international students. *TESOL Quarterly* 21(2): 251–61

Linacre J M 1989a *Objectivity for judge-mediated certification examinations.* Paper presented at annual meeting of the American Educational Research Association, San Francisco CA, March

Linacre J M 1989b *Many-faceted Rasch measurement.* MESA Press, Chicago IL

Linacre J M 1993 *Many-facet Rasch measurement and the challenges to measurement.* Paper presented at the annual meeting of the American Educational Research Association, Atlanta GA, April

Linacre J M and Wright B 1992 *Facets: Rasch Measurement Computer Program, version 2.6.* Chicago: MESA Press

Lindquist E F 1951 Preliminary considerations in objective test construction. In Lindquist E F (ed.) *Educational Measurement.* American Council on Education, Washington DC pp 119–84

Linn R L, Baker E L and Dunbar S B 1991 Complex, performance-based assessment: expectations and validation criteria. *Educational Researcher* 20(8): 15–21

Lopes M 1992 *Native speaker performance on the IELTS reading test.* Unpublished MA thesis, University of Melbourne

Lord F M 1980 *Applications of Item Response Theory to practical testing problems.* Lawrence Erlbaum Associates, Hillsdale NJ

Lord F M and Novick M R 1968 *Statistical theories of mental test scores.* Addison-Wesley, Reading MA

Lowe P 1982 *ILR handbook on oral interview testing.* Defense Language Institute/CIA Language School, Washington DC

Lowe P 1988 The unassimilated history. In Lowe P and Stansfield C W (eds) *Second language proficiency assessment: current issues.* Prentice Hall Regents, Englewood Cliffs NJ pp 11–51

Lumley T 1992 *Reading comprehension sub-skills in an EAP test: teachers' perceptions of what is tested.* Unpublished MA thesis, University of Melbourne

Lumley T 1993 The notion of subskills in reading comprehension tests: an EAP example. *Language Testing* 10(3): 211–34

Lumley T 1995 Response to Alderson. *Language Testing* 12(1): 125–30

Lumley T and Brown A 1991 *The development of a diagnostic EAP test: the application of Item Response Theory.* Paper presented at the 16th Applied Linguistics Association of Australia Conference, James Cook University, Townsville, September 30–October 2

Lumley T, Lynch B K and McNamara T F 1994 *A new approach to standard setting in language assessment. Melbourne Papers in Language Testing* 3(2): 19–40

Lumley T and McNamara T F 1995 Rater characteristics and rater bias: implications for training. *Language Testing* 12(1): 54–71

Lunt H, Morton J and Wigglesworth G 1994 *Rater behaviour in performance testing: evaluating the effect of bias feedback.* Paper presented at 19th annual congress of Applied Linguistics Association of Australia, University of Melbourne, July

Lunz M E and Stahl J 1990 Judge consistency and severity across grading periods. *Evaluation and the Health Professions* 13: 425–44

Lunzer E, Waite M and Dolan T 1979 Comprehension and comprehension tests. In Lunzer E and Gardner K (eds) *The effective use of reading.* Heinemann Educational Books, London pp 37–71

Lynch B K and Davidson F G 1994 Criterion-referenced language test development: linking curricula, teachers and tests. *TESOL Quarterly* 28(4): 727–43

Lynch B K and McNamara T F 1994 *Using G–theory and multi-faceted Rasch measurement in the development of performance assessments of the ESL speaking skills of immigrants.* Paper presented at the 16th Annual Language Testing Research Colloquium, Washington DC, March

Maatsch J and Gordon M 1978 Assessment through simulation. In Morgan M and Irby D (eds) *Evaluating clinical competence in the health professions.* C V Mosby, St Louis MO pp 123–38

Macken M and Slade D 1993 Assessment: a foundation for effective teaching in the school context. In Cope B and Kalantzis M (eds) *The powers of literacy: a genre approach to teaching writing.* Falmer Press, London pp 203–30

Maclean J 1985 Descriptions of doctor–patient communication. *International Journal of the Sociology of Language* 51: 131–4

Martin J R 1984 Language, register and genre. In *ECT418 Language Studies: Children Writing.* Deakin University Press, Geelong, Victoria pp 21–30

Masters G 1982 A Rasch Model for partial credit scoring. *Psychometrika* 47: 149–74

Masters G N 1990 Psychometric aspects of individual assessment. In de Jong J H A L and Stevenson D K (eds) *Individualizing the assessment of language abilities.* Multilingual Matters, Clevedon Avon and Philadelphia PA pp 56–70

Matthiessen C M I M, Slade D and Macken M 1992 Language in context: a new model for evaluating student writing. *Linguistics in Education* 4(2): 173–95

Mawer G 1991 *Language audits and industry restructuring.* National Centre for English Language Teaching and Research, Macquarie University, Sydney

McIntyre P N 1993 *The importance and effectiveness of moderation training on the reliability of teacher assessments of ESL writing samples.* Unpublished MA thesis, University of Melbourne

McNamara T F 1987 *Assessing the language proficiency of health professionals. Recommendations for reform of the Occupational English Test. A Report submitted to the Council on Overseas Professional Qualifications.* University of Melbourne Department of Russian and Language Studies, Parkville Victoria

McNamara T F 1988a *The development of an English as a Second Language speaking test for health professionals. Part One of a Report to the Council on Overseas Professional Qualifications on a consultancy to develop the Occupational English Test.* University of Melbourne Department of Russian and Language Studies, Parkville Victoria

McNamara T F (ed.) 1988b *Language testing colloquium.* Selected papers from a Colloquium at the Horwood Language Centre, University of Melbourne, 24–25 August, 1987. *Australian Review of Applied Linguistics* 11(2)

McNamara T F 1989a *The development of an English as a Second Language writing test for health professionals. Part Two of a Report to the Council on Overseas Professional Qualifications on a consultancy to develop the Occupational English Test.* University of Melbourne Department of Russian and Language Studies, Parkville Victoria

McNamara T F 1989b ESP testing: general and particular. In Candlin C N and McNamara T F (eds) *Language, learning and community.* National Centre for English Language Teaching and Research, Macquarie University, Sydney pp 125–42

McNamara T F 1990a Item Response Theory and the validation of an ESP test for health professionals. *Language Testing* 7(1): 52–75

McNamara T F 1990b *Assessing the second language proficiency of health professionals.* Unpublished PhD thesis, University of Melbourne

McNamara T F 1991 Test dimensionality: IRT analysis of an ESP listening test. *Language Testing* 8(2): 45–65

McNamara T F and Adams R J 1991/1994 Exploring rater characteristics with Rasch techniques. In *Selected papers of the 13th Language Testing Research Colloquium (LTRC).* Educational Testing Service, Princeton NJ (ERIC Document Reproduction Service ED 345 498)

McNamara T F and Hamilton J 1991 *EAP tests as performance tests.* Paper presented at the 4th ELICOS Association Educational Conference, Monash University, August

McNamara T F, Hamilton J and Sheridan E 1992 *Rating scales and native speaker performance on a communicatively oriented EAP test.* Paper presented at the 14th annual Language Testing Research Colloquium, Vancouver, February 27th–March 1st

McNamara T F and Lumley T 1993 *The effects of interlocutor and assessment mode variables in offshore assessment of speaking skills in occupational settings.* Paper presented at the 15th annual Language Testing Research Colloquium, Cambridge, August (ERIC Document Reproduction Service ED 364 066)

McNamara T F and Lynch B K (in press) A Generalizability Theory study of ratings and test design in the writing and speaking modules of the **access:** test. In Wigglesworth G and Brindley G (eds) (in press) *access: Issues in English language test design and delivery.* National Centre for English Language Teaching and Research, Macquarie University, Sydney

McNamara T F, O'Loughlin K and Wigglesworth G 1993 *Bias analysis in Rasch programs: analyzing interactions between judges, items and persons in performance assessment settings.* Paper presented at the annual conference of the American Association for Applied Linguistics, Atlanta GA, April

McQueen M J 1992 *Item difficulty and Rasch scaling in a test of foreign language reading.* Unpublished MA thesis, University of Melbourne

Mead R 1982 Review of J Munby, Communicative syllabus design. *Applied Linguistics* 3(1): 70–8

Messick S 1989 Validity. In Linn R L (ed.) *Educational measurement. Third edition.* Macmillan, New York pp 13–104

Messick S 1994 The interplay of evidence and consequences in the validation of performance assessments. *Educational Researcher* 23(2): 13–23

Milanovic M, Saville N, Pollitt A and Cook A 1992 *Developing rating scales for CASE: theoretical concerns and analyses.* Paper presented at the 14th annual Language Testing Research Colloquium, Vancouver, February 27th–March 1st

Mislevy R J and Bock R D 1990 *BILOG 3. Item analysis and test scoring with binary logistic models. 2nd edition.* Scientific Software, Mooresville IN

Moller A D 1982 *A study in the validation of proficiency tests of English as a Foreign Language.* Unpublished PhD thesis, University of Edinburgh

Morgan J 1994 *Literacy and Productivity.* Paper presented at Seminar on 'Language and cultural diversity at work: the changing shape of competency standards and competency assessment', Language Expo Australia, Sydney, July

Morrow K 1977 *Techniques of evaluation for a notional syllabus.* Royal Society of Arts, London

Morrow K 1979 Communicative language testing: revolution or evolution? In Brumfit C J and Johnson K (eds) *The communicative approach to language teaching.* Oxford University Press, Oxford pp 143–57

Morrow K 1983 The Royal Society of Arts Examinations in the Communicative Use of English as a Foreign Language. In Jordan R R (ed.) *Case studies in ELT.* Collins ELT, London and Glasgow pp 102–7

Morton J and Wigglesworth G 1994 *Evaluating interviewer input in oral interaction tests.* Paper presented at the Second Language Research Forum, Montreal, October

Mossenson L, Hill P and Masters G 1987 *TORCH: tests of reading comprehension. Manual.* Australian Council for Educational Research, Hawthorn Victoria

Mullen K 1977 Using rater judgments in the evaluation of writing proficiency for non-native speakers of English. In Brown H D, Yorio C A and Crymes R H (eds) *Teaching and learning English as a second language: trends in research and practice.* TESOL, Washington DC pp 309–20

Munby J 1978 *Communicative syllabus design.* Cambridge University Press, Cambridge

Nunan D 1987a *Developing discourse comprehension: theory and practice.* SEAMEO Regional Language Centre, Singapore (Occasional Papers No. 43)

Nunan D 1987b Methodological issues in research. In Nunan D (ed.) *Applying second language acquisition research.* National Curriculum Resource Centre, Adelaide SA pp 143–71

Nunan D 1988 Commentary on the Griffin paper. In McNamara T F (ed.) *Language testing colloquium.* Selected papers from a Colloquium held at the Horwood Language Centre, University of Melbourne, 24–25 August, 1987. *Australian Review of Applied Linguistics* 11(2): 54–65

Nunan D 1989 Item Response Theory and second language proficiency assessment. *Prospect* 4(3): 81–93

Ochs E 1988 *Culture and language development: language acquisition and language socialization in a Samoan village.* Cambridge University Press, Cambridge

Oller J W 1979 *Language tests at school.* Longman, London

Oller J W Jr and Conrad C 1971 The cloze technique and ESL proficiency. *Language Learning* 21(2): 183–95

O'Loughlin K 1992 *Final report of the University of Melbourne Trial English Selection Test.* NLLIA Language Testing Research Centre, University of Melbourne

O'Loughlin K 1995 Lexical density in candidate output on direct and semi-direct versions of an oral proficiency test. *Language Testing* 12(2): 217–37

Omaggio A 1983 Methodology in transition: the new focus on proficiency. *The Modern Language Journal* 67(4): 330–41

Oscarson M 1986 *Native and non-native speaker performance on a national test of English for Swedish students. A validation study.* Goethenberg University Department of Educational Research, Goethenberg

Paltridge B 1994 Genre analysis and the identification of textual boundaries. *Applied Linguistics* 15(3): 288–99

Pendleton D 1983 Doctor–patient communication: a review. In Pendleton D and Hasler J (eds) *Doctor–patient communication.* Academic Press, London pp 5–53

Pennycook A 1990 Towards a critical applied linguistics for the 1990s. *Issues in Applied Linguistics* 1(1): 8–28

Perkins K 1983 On the use of composition scoring techniques, objective measures and objective tests to evaluate ESL writing ability. *TESOL Quarterly* 17(4): 651–71

Perkins K and Konneker B H 1981 *Testing the effectiveness of sentence-combining in ESL composition*. Paper presented at the annual TESOL Convention, Detroit Michigan, March

Perrett G 1990 The language testing interview: a reappraisal. In de Jong J H A L and Stevenson D K (eds) *Individualizing the assessment of language abilities*. Multilingual Matters, Clevedon Avon pp 225–38

Pienemann M and Johnston M 1987 Factors influencing the development of language proficiency. In Nunan D (ed.) *Applying second language acquisition research*. National Curriculum Resource Centre, Adelaide SA pp 45–141

Pienemann M, Johnston M and Brindley G 1988 Constructing an acquisition-based procedure for second language assessment. *Studies in Second Language Acquisition* 10(2): 217–43

Pollitt A and Hutchinson C 1987 Calibrated graded assessments: Rasch partial credit analysis of performance in writing. *Language Testing* 4(1): 72–92

Porter D 1991 Affective factors in language testing. In Alderson C J and North B (eds) *Language testing in the 1990s*. Modern English Publications and The British Council, London pp 32–40

Powers D 1986 Academic demands related to listening skills. *Language Testing* 3(1): 1–38

Quinn T J 1993 The competency movement, applied linguistics and language testing: some reflections and suggestions for a possible research agenda. *Melbourne Papers in Language Testing* 2(2): 55–87

Quinn T J and McNamara T F 1987 Issues in second language learning. Monograph. Deakin University Victoria

Raffaldini T 1988 The use of situation tests as measures of communicative ability. *Studies in Second Language Acquisition* 10(2): 197–216

Rasch G 1960 [1980] *Probabilistic models for some intelligence and attainment tests*. Danmarks Paedogogiske Institut, Copenhagen [University of Chicago Press, Chicago]

Rasch G 1961 On general laws and the meaning of measurement in psychology. In *Proceedings of the Fourth Berkeley Symposium on Mathematical Statistics and Probability*. University of California Press, Berkeley CA 4: 321–33

Rasch G 1966 An individualistic approach to item analysis. In Lazarsfeld P F and Henry N (eds) *Readings in mathematical social science*. Science Research Associates, Chicago, IL pp 89–107

Richards J C 1985 Planning for proficiency. *Prospect* 1(2): 1–17

Ross S 1992 Accommodative questions in oral proficiency interviews. *Language Testing* 9(2): 173–86

Ross S 1994 *Formulaic speech in language proficiency interviews*. Paper presented at the annual conference of the American Association for Applied Linguistics, Baltimore MD, March

Ryans D G and Frederiksen N 1951 Performance tests of educational achievement. In Lindquist E F (ed.) *Educational measurement*. American Council on Education, Washington DC pp 455–91

Ryle G 1949 *The concept of mind*. Hutchinson, London

Sacks H, Schegloff E A and Jefferson G 1974 A simplest systematics for the organisation of turn-taking for conversation. *Language* 50(4): 696–735

Savignon S J 1972 *Communicative competence: an experiment in foreign language teaching.* The Center for Curriculum Development, Philadelphia PA

Savignon S J 1983 *Communicative competence: theory and classroom practice.* Addison-Wesley, Reading MA

Savignon S J 1985 Evaluation of communicative competence: the ACTFL Provisional Proficiency Guidelines. *The Modern Language Journal* 69(2): 129–34

Schegloff E A, Jefferson G and Sacks H 1977 The preference for self-correction in the organization of repair in conversation. *Language* 53: 361–82

Schieffelin B and Ochs E (eds) 1986 *Language socialization across cultures.* Cambridge University Press, New York

Sheridan E 1991 *A comparison of native/non-native speaker performance on a communicative test of writing ability (IELTS).* Unpublished MA thesis, University of Melbourne

Shohamy E 1983 The stability of oral proficiency assessment on the oral interview testing procedures. *Language Learning* 33(4): 527–40

Shohamy E 1988 A proposed framework for testing the oral language of second/foreign language learners. *Studies in Second Language Acquisition* 10(2): 165–79

Shohamy E 1990 Language testing priorities: a different perspective. *Foreign Language Annals* 23(5): 385–94

Shohamy E 1993 The exercise of power and control in the rhetorics of testing. In Huhta A, Sajavaara K and Takala S (eds) *Language testing: new openings.* University of Jyväskylä Institute for Educational Research, Jyväskylä Finland pp 23–38

Shohamy E 1994 The validity of direct versus semi-direct oral tests. *Language Testing* 11(2): 99–123

Shohamy E, Gordon C M and Kraemer R 1992 The effect of raters' background and training on the reliability of direct writing tests. *The Modern Language Journal*, Spring

Siegel A I 1986 Performance tests. In Berk R A (ed.) *Performance assessment. Methods and applications.* The Johns Hopkins University Press, Baltimore MD pp 121–42

Skehan P 1984 Issues in the testing of English for specific purposes. *Language Testing* 1(2): 202–20

Skehan P 1988 Language testing. Part I. *Language Teaching* 21(4): 211–21

Skehan P 1989 Language testing. Part II. *Language Teaching* 22(1): 1–13

Skopek L 1979 Doctor–patient conversation: a way of analyzing its linguistic problems. *Semiotica* 28(3/4): 301–11

Slater S J 1980 Introduction to performance testing. In Spirer J E (ed.) *Performance testing: issues facing vocational education.* National Center for Research in Vocational Education, Columbus OH pp 3–17

Sollenberger H E 1978 Development and current use of the FSI Oral Interview Test. in Clark J L D (ed.) *Direct testing of speaking proficiency: theory and application.* Educational Testing Service, Princeton NJ pp 1–12

Spolsky B 1968 Language testing: the problem of validation. *TESOL Quarterly* 2(2): 88–94

Spolsky B 1973 What does it mean to know a language, or how do you get someone to perform his competence? In Oller J W (ed.) *Focus on the learner.* Newbury House, Rowley MA pp 164–76

Spolsky B 1978 Introduction: linguists and language testers. In Spolsky B (ed.) *Approaches to language testing. Advances in languages testing series:* 2. Center for Applied Linguistics, Arlington VA pp v–x

Spolsky B 1985 The limits of authenticity in language testing. *Language Testing* 2(1): 31–40

Spolsky B 1988 Test review: P E Griffin *et al*. 1986 Proficiency in English as a second language. (1) The development of an interview test for adult migrants. (2) The administration and creation of a test. (3) An interview test of English as a second language. *Language Testing* 5(1): 120–4

Spolsky B 1989a Competence, proficiency and beyond. *Applied Linguistics* 10(2): 138–56

Spolsky B 1989b *Conditions for second language learning.* Oxford University Press, Oxford

Spolsky B 1995 *Measured words.* Oxford University Press, Oxford

Spolsky B, Sigurd B, Sato M, Walker E and Aterburn C 1968 Preliminary studies in the development of techniques for testing overall second language proficiency. In Upshur J (ed.) Problems in foreign language testing. *Language Learning,* Special Issue No. 3: 79–98

Spurling S 1987a Questioning the use of the Bejar method to determine uni dimensionality. *Language Testing* 4(1): 93–5

Spurling S 1987b The Bejar Method with an example: a comment on Henning's 'Response to Spurling'. *Language Testing* 4(2): 221–3

Stahl A and Lunz M E 1992 *Judge performance reports.* Paper presented at the annual meeting of the American Educational Research Association, San Francisco CA, April

Stahl A and Lunz M E 1993 *A comparison of Generalizability Theory and multifaceted Rasch measurement.* Paper presented at the annual meeting of the American Educational Research Association, Atlanta GA, April

Stansfield C W (ed.) 1986 *Toward communicative competence testing: Proceedings of the Second TOEFL Invitational Conference.* Educational Testing Service, Princeton NJ

Stansfield C W 1991 A comparative analysis of simulated and direct oral proficiency interviews. In Anivan S (ed.) *Current developments in language testing.* SEAMEO Regional Language Centre, Singapore pp 199–209

Stansfield C W and Kenyon D M 1992 Research on the comparability of the oral proficiency interview and the simulated oral proficiency interview. *System* 20(3): 347–64

Stern H H 1983 *Fundamental concepts of language teaching.* Oxford University Press, Oxford

Stevenson D K 1985 Authenticity, validity and a tea-party. *Language Testing* 2(1): 41–7

Stiggins R 1981 *Strategies for optimizing and documenting the quality of oral and practical examinations in medical education.* Northwest Regional Educational Laboratory, Clearinghouse for Applied Performance Testing, Portland, OR (ERIC Document Reproduction Services: ED 206 634)

Stiggins R J 1987 Design and development of performance assessments. *Education Measurement: Issues and Practice* 6(3): 33–42

Swain M 1984 Large-scale communicative testing: a case study. In Savignon S J and Berns M S (eds) *Initiatives in communicative language teaching.* Addison-Wesley, Reading MA pp 185–201

Swales J 1990 *Genre analysis*. Cambridge University Press, Cambridge

Taylor D S 1988 The meaning and use of the term 'competence' in linguistics and applied linguistics. *Applied Linguistics* 9(2): 148–68

Thorndike E L 1917 [1971] Reading as reasoning: a study of mistakes in paragraph reading. *Journal of Educational Psychology* 8: 323–32. Reprinted in *Reading Research Quarterly* 6(4): 425–34

Thorndike R L 1982 Educational measurement–theory and practice. In Spearritt D (ed.) *The improvement of measurement in education and psychology: contributions of latent trait theories*. Australian Council for Educational Research, Hawthorn Victoria pp 3–13

Traub R E 1983 *A priori* considerations in choosing an item response model. In Hambleton R K (ed.) *Applications of item response theory*. Educational Research Institute of British Columbia, Vancouver BC pp 57–70

Tyndall B and Kenyon D M 1995 Validation of a new holistic rating scale using Rasch multifaceted analysis. In Cumming A and Berwick R (eds) *Validation in language testing*. Multilingual Matters, Clevedon, Avon

Upshur J A 1979 Functional proficiency theory and a research role for language tests. In Brière E J and Hinofotis F B (eds) *Concepts in language testing: some recent studies*. Teachers of English to Speakers of Other Languages, Washington DC pp 75–100

Upshur J A et al. 1966 *Michigan test of English language proficiency (Forms A–E)*. University of Michigan Testing and Certification Division English Language Institute, Ann Arbor MI

van Lier L 1989 Reeling, writhing, drawling, stretching and fainting in coils: oral proficiency in interviews as conversation. *TESOL Quarterly* 23(3): 489–508

van Naerssen M M 1978 ESL in medicine: a matter of life and death. *TESOL Quarterly* 12(2): 193–203

Wall D and Alderson J C 1993 Examining washback: the Sri Lankan impact study. *Language Testing* 10(1): 41–69

Weigle S C 1994 *Using FACETS to model rater training effects*. Paper presented at the 16th annual Language Testing Research Colloquium, Washington DC, March

Weir C J 1983a *Identifying the language problems of overseas students in tertiary education in the United Kingdom*. Unpublished PhD thesis, University of London

Weir C J 1983b The Associated Examining Board's Test in English for Academic Purposes: an exercise in content validation. In Hughes A and Porter D (eds) *Current developments in language testing*. Academic Press, London pp 147–53

Weir C J 1988a Construct validity. In Hughes A, Porter D and Weir C (eds) *ELTS Validation Project: Proceedings of a conference held to consider the ELTS Validation Project Report*. English Language Testing Service Research Report 1 (ii). British Council/University of Cambridge Local Examinations Syndicate, London pp 15–25

Weir C J 1988b The specification, realization and validation of an English language proficiency test. In Hughes A (ed.) *Testing English for university study*. Modern English Publications/British Council, London pp 45–110

Weir C J 1994 *Reading as multidivisible or unitary: between Scylla and Charybdis*. Paper presented at RELC Seminar, SEAMEO Regional Language Centre, Singapore, April

Weir C J, Hughes A and Porter D 1990 Reading skills: hierarchies, implicational relationships and identifiability. *Reading in a Foreign Language* 7: 505–10

Wesche M B 1985 Introduction. In Hauptman P C, LeBlanc R and Wesche M B (eds) *Second language performance testing.* University of Ottawa Press, Ottawa

Wesche M B 1987 Second language performance testing: the Ontario Test of ESL as an example. *Language Testing* 4(1): 28–47

Wesche M B 1992 Performance testing for work-related second language assessment. In Shohamy E and Walton R (eds) *Language Assessment for feedback: testing and other strategies.* National Foreign Language Center Publications, Washington DC pp 103–22

Widdowson H G 1979 *Explorations in applied linguistics.* Oxford University Press, Oxford

Widdowson H G 1983 *Learning purpose and language use.* Oxford University Press, Oxford

Widdowson H G 1984 *Explorations in applied lingusitics 2.* Oxford University Press, Oxford

Widdowson H G 1989 Knowledge of language and ability for use. *Applied Linguistics* 10(2): 128–37

Wiggins G 1989 A true test: toward more authentic and equitable assessment. *Phi Delta Kappan* 70(9): 703–13

Wigglesworth G 1993 Exploring bias analysis as a tool for improving rater consistency in assessing oral interaction. *Language Testing* 10(3): 305–35

Wigglesworth G 1994 *The effect of information gap on elicited discourse of candidates in an oral test of English.* Paper presented at the 16th annual Language Testing Research Colloquium, Washington DC, March

Wilds C P 1975 The oral interview test. In Jones R L and Spolsky B (eds) *Testing language proficiency.* Center for Applied Linguistics, Arlington VA pp 29–44

Wilkins D A 1973 An investigation into the Linguistic and Situational Common Core in a Unit/Credit System. In *Systems Development in Adult Language Learning.* Council of Europe, Strasbourg

Williams R and Swales J (eds) 1984 *Common ground: shared interests in RSP and Communication Studies. ELT Documents 117.* British Council/Pergamon, Oxford

Wilson M 1991 (ed.) *Objective measurement: theory into practice.* Ablex, Norwood NJ

Wood R and Wilson D 1974 Evidence for differential marking discrimination among examiners of English. *The Irish Journal of Education* 8: 37 *et seq.*

Woods A, Fletcher P and Hughes A 1986 *Statistics in language studies.* Cambridge University Press, Cambridge

Wright B D 1988 *Georg Rasch and measurement.* Informal Remarks at the Inaugural Meeting of the American Educational Research Association Rasch Measurement SIG, New Orleans April 8

Wright B D 1992 IRT in the 1990s: which models work best? *Rasch Measurement* 6(1): 196–200

Wright B D, Congdon R T and Rossner M 1987 *MSCALE Version 2.4.* MESA Press, Chicago IL.

Wright B D and Linacre J M 1984 *Microscale manual for Microscale version 1.2.* Mediax Interactive Technologies, Westport CT

Wright B D and Linacre J M 1991 *A user's guide to BIGSTEPS Rasch-model computer program. Version 2.2.* MESA Press, Chicago IL

Wright B D and Masters G N 1982 *Rating scale analysis.* MESA Press, Chicago IL

Wright B D and Stone M H 1979 *Best test design.* MESA Press, Chicago IL

Wylie E and Ingram D E 1991 *Self-assessment version of Australian Second Language Proficiency Ratings (ASLPR).* NLIA Language Testing and Curriculum Centre, Griffith University, Queensland

Young R 1994 Conversational styles in language proficiency interviews. *Language Learning* **45**(1): 3–42

Zeidner M and Bensoussan M 1988 College students' attitudes towards written versus oral tests of English as a foreign language. *Language Testing* **5**(1): 100–14

Index